# READING
# PATRISTIC TEXTS ON
# SOCIAL ETHICS

# CUA STUDIES IN EARLY CHRISTIANITY

# READING

## PATRISTIC TEXTS ON SOCIAL ETHICS

ISSUES AND CHALLENGES FOR
TWENTY-FIRST-CENTURY CHRISTIAN
SOCIAL THOUGHT

EDITED BY

*Johan Leemans*

*Brian J. Matz*

*Johan Verstraeten*

*The Catholic University of America Press*
*Washington, D.C.*

Library of Congress Cataloging-in-Publication Data
Reading patristic texts on social ethics : issues and challenges for
twenty-first-century Christian social thought / edited by Johan Leemans,
Brian J. Matz, Johan Verstraeten.
p. cm. — (Cua studies in early Christianity)
Includes bibliographical references and index.
ISBN 978-0-8132-1859-5 (cloth : alk. paper)
1. Christian literature, Early—History and criticism.
2. Fathers of the Church—Influence. 3. Christian sociology—
Catholic Church. I. Leemans, Johan, 1965–
II. Matz, Brian J. III. Verstraeten, J. (Johan)
BR60.A65R43 2011
261—dc22
2010040746

# CONTENTS

Acknowledgments vii

Abbreviations ix

Introduction xi

### PART I. APPROACHING PATRISTIC SOCIO-ETHICAL TEXTS

1. Texts That Create a Future: The Function of Ancient Texts   3
for Theology Today
*Reimund Bieringer*

2. Challenges in Approaching Patristic Texts from the   30
Perspective of Contemporary Catholic Social Teaching
*Pauline Allen*

### PART II. CONTEXTS FOR PATRISTIC SOCIO-ETHICAL TEXTS

3. Social Ethics and Moral Discourse in Late Antiquity   45
*Peter Van Nuffelen*

4. Wealth, Poverty, and Eschatology: Pre-Constantine Christian   64
Social Thought and the Hope for the World to Come
*Helen Rhee*

5. The Audience(s) for Patristic Social Teaching: A Case Study   85
*Wendy Mayer*

## PART III. ISSUES IN PATRISTIC AND CATHOLIC SOCIAL THOUGHT

6. Out of the Fitting Room: Rethinking Patristic Social Texts on "The Common Good"    103
   *Susan R. Holman*

7. "That which has been wrung from tears": Usury, the Greek Fathers, and Catholic Social Teaching    124
   *Brenda Llewellyn Ihssen*

8. The Principle of Detachment from Private Property in Basil of Caesarea's *Homily 6* and Its Context    161
   *Brian Matz*

9. Social Justice in Lactantius's *Divine Institutes*: An Exploration    185
   *Thomas Hughson, S.J.*

## PART IV. REFLECTIONS ON THE THEME

10. The Church Fathers and Catholic Social Thought: Reflections on the Symposium    209
    *Richard Schenk, O.P.*

11. The (Im)possible Dialogue between Patristics and Catholic Social Thought: Limits, Possibilities, and a Way Forward    222
    *Johan Leemans and Johan Verstraeten*

Contributors    233
Bibliography    235
Index    265

# ACKNOWLEDGMENTS

This is the second of four publications to emerge from a research project carried out by the Centre for Catholic Social Thought of the Faculty of Theology at the Catholic University of Leuven during the years 2005 to 2009. The research project investigated the potential for a dialogue between the Church Fathers and Catholic social thought, and this volume reflects an important stage in that research. Specifically, the contributions for this volume emerged out of an expert seminar on the theme of the Church Fathers and Catholic social thought held in Leuven in 2007. Our aim was to tease out the contours of a dialogue between scholars both of patristics and of Catholic social thought.

At the seminar's conclusion we expressed to those who attended our deep thanks not only for their contributions, but also—and perhaps more importantly—for their time. Time is a precious resource in our day. For nearly twenty scholars to give of their time to travel to Leuven and to discuss this admittedly strange confluence of subjects, we are immensely grateful. Those who contributed papers for this volume deserve further thanks, for this required of each one the setting aside of additional time to prepare new drafts of papers or to revise earlier remarks. Together, their papers represent such a wide array of expertise that this volume opens many more doors of inquiry than anything we could have written by ourselves.

Naturally, the expert seminar itself could not have taken place without the financial support of others. Principally, we wish to thank the Flemish government's Fund for Scientific Research, which funded the entirety of the research project spanning the academic years 2005 to 2009. In addition, we thank the Porticus Foundation for their funding of the expert seminar.

The seminar was held in the recently renovated buildings and grounds of the Irish College in Leuven. We wish to thank Orla Kelly and her staff at the college for her tremendous help from the earliest planning stages of the seminar through to the seminar itself. Finally, we reserve for the end the extension of our deepest thanks to Lucrèce de Becker. She was the administrative engine behind the entire expert seminar. There were literally hundreds of details and financial arrangements, but Lucrèce knew exactly what to do in every situation, knew whom to contact to fix problems, and was extremely well-organized. Not only this book, but also we would be the poorer were it not for her contributions.

# ABBREVIATIONS

| | |
|---|---|
| ACW | Ancient Christian Writers |
| *ANF* | *Ante-Nicene Fathers* |
| ANL | Annua Nuntia Lovaniensia |
| BETL | Bibliotheca ephemeridum theologicarum Lovaniensium |
| CathST | Catholic Social Thought (as opposed to CST) |
| *CBQ* | *Catholic Biblical Quarterly* |
| CCSG | Corpus Christianorum: Series graeca |
| CCSL | Corpus Christianorum: Series latina |
| *CPG* | *Clavis patrum graecorum.* 5 vols. and supplement. |
| CSEL | Corpus scriptorum ecclesiasticorum latinorum |
| CSLP | Corpus scriptorum latinorum Paravianum |
| CST | Catholic Social Teaching (as opposed to CathST) |
| CWS | Classics of Western Spirituality |
| FOTC | Fathers of the Church (CUA Press) |
| FP | Florilegium patristicum |
| GCS | Die griechische christliche Schriftsteller der ersten Jahrhunderte |
| GNO | Gregorii Nysseni opera |
| *JECS* | *Journal of Early Christian Studies* |
| *JSNT* | *Journal for the Study of the New Testament* |
| JSOT | *Journal for the Study of the Old Testament* |
| LCL | Loeb Classical Library |
| MGH | Monumenta Germaniae Historicae |
| *NIDNTT* | *New International Dictionary of New Testament Theology* |
| *NPNF* | *Nicene and Post-Nicene Fathers*, Series 1 and 2 |

| | |
|---|---|
| PG | Patrologia graeca. Edited by J.-P. Migne. |
| PL | Patrologia latina. Edited by J.-P. Migne. |
| PTS | Patristische Texte und Studien |
| NRSV | New Revised Standard Version of the Bible[1] |
| SC | Sources chrétiennes |
| Tanner I/II | Decrees of the Ecumenical Councils, 2 vols. |
| *TDNT* | *Theological Dictionary of the New Testament* |
| *VC* | *Vigiliae christianae* |
| WSA | The Works of Saint Augustine: A Translation for the 21st Century |
| WUNT | Wissenschaftliche Untersuchungen zum Neuen Testament |
| *ZNW* | *Zeitschrift für die neutestamentliche Wissenschaft* |
| *ZTK* | *Zeitschrift für Theologie und Kirche* |

---

1. Unless otherwise noted, all quotations from the Bible used in this volume are from the NRSV.

# INTRODUCTION

This volume investigates the potential for a dialogue between the social teachings of the Fathers and the living theology of Catholic social thought today. Although creating a dialogue between worlds of ideas separated by fifteen centuries would seem to pose some difficulties, the contributors to this volume express such wide-ranging concerns that one wonders if success is even likely. At the same time, this volume explores several important features of any attempt at a dialogue.

This dialogue was constructed with Catholic social thought in mind, but this and other phrases deserve clarification before proceeding further with an introduction to the volume's contents. "Catholic social thought" (CathST) is the extension of the official teachings of the Catholic Church into the day-to-day lives of Catholic men and women who work on behalf of social justice. Catholic social thought concerns the unofficial activities of priests and laity who engage in the work of alleviating injustice and caring for the marginalized and continually exhort the hierarchy to rethink its commitment to those concerns. A second, related phrase is "Catholic social teaching" (CST) that refers to the official teaching of the Vatican or regional bishops' conferences on socio-ethical topics. It is a body of literature that is generally accepted as beginning with the promulgation of *Rerum novarum* (1891) and continues to this day, most recently including the encyclical *Deus caritas est* (2005).[1] Not

---

1. For a list of documents on Catholic social teaching, the reader is invited to consider David J. O'Brien and Thomas A. Shannon, *Catholic Social Thought: The Documentary Heritage* (Maryknoll, N.Y.: Orbis Books, 1992); Kenneth Himes, ed., *Modern Catholic Social Teaching: Commentaries and Interpretations* (Washington D.C.: Georgetown University Press, 2005). Of course, social teaching existed prior to the late nineteenth century and interested readers are directed to Michael Schuck, *That They Be One: The Social Teaching of the Papal Encyclicals, 1740–1989* (Washington, D.C.: Georgetown University

unfairly, one may think of Catholic social teaching as a subset of Catholic social thought. A third and final important phrase is "Christian social thought,"
which is not abbreviated in this volume. This phrase widens the scope of unofficial ideas and work on behalf of social justice to include Protestant and Orthodox voices.

Although this volume focuses on the potential for a dialogue between the
worlds of patristic social thought and Catholic social thought, our aim was
to enrich Christian social thought. The task of reading patristic texts in light
of contemporary concerns is not only the work of Catholics. Indeed, the patristic heritage is common to all Christians, and so the fruit of this volume
should assist all Christians that wish to incorporate into their socio-ethical reflections the ideas of the Fathers.

The impetus for the volume emerged from the results of an earlier diag-
nostic study of the uses of patristic sources in Catholic social teaching. The
study catalogued 110 patristic citations or allusions in twenty-one Catholic social teaching documents.[2] It concluded the documents treated patristic sources as second-class citizens in their consideration of proper historical authorities for the presentation of their socio-ethical ideas. Important socio-ethical
homilies and treatises from the patristic world are almost entirely absent from
the patristic sources cited in Catholic social teaching; instead, one encoun-
ters, for example, eight different citations of Augustine's *Confessions* I.1.: "Our
hearts are restless until they rest in Thee." This may be a good quotation for
many reasons, but it is not a socio-ethical comment per se.

Based upon this study, it was clear further work needed to be done on
how best to read and to appropriate patristic socio-ethical texts in a contemporary framework. This volume not only initiates such a dialogue, but it alerts
readers to the potential benefits and pitfalls of the task. First, there are hermeneutical questions: What is an early Christian homily? What are we doing

---

Press, 1991). The present study is limited to so-called modern CST documents because they are the particular focus of study for many scholars of CST. A similar study might also be possible using premodern
CST documents.

    2. Brian Matz, *Patristic Sources and Catholic Social Teaching: A Forgotten Dimension. A Textual,
Historical, and Rhetorical Analysis of Patristic Source Citations in the Church's Social Documents*, Annua
Nuntia Lovaniensia 59 (Leuven: Peeters Press, 2008). The conclusions of the study were also published as
a separate article: Brian Matz, "Problematic Uses of Patristic Sources in the Documents of Catholic Social Thought," *Journal of Catholic Social Thought* 4 (2007): 459–85.

when we read them? What questions are we allowed to ask of the text? What questions does the text ask of us? At the same time, there are historical and contextual questions, including some related to particular issues. For example, slavery in late antiquity was perceived differently than today and the same is true for usury. Also, any dialogue must ask basic methodological questions: How does one select early Christian texts? How does one go about incorporating them in a twenty-first century document? For example, how is it helpful to a Christian today to know that Gregory Nazianzen believed Christians are obliged to meet the needs of lepers? In Matthew 25 Jesus gave his disciples the fundamental principles for social ethics. Are the Fathers redundant?

Our own research has suggested that the Fathers are not superfluous to the debate. For one, the Fathers do not simply repeat what may be found in pithier form in the New Testament. On the subject of private property, for example, the Fathers say things that seem out of step with the New Testament texts. For another, even when the Fathers do repeat the New Testament arguments, they do so in different ways than we are used to hearing in modern sermons. Reading early Christian homilies causes us to rethink our understanding of the biblical text. The homily is an interpretive aid that assists in the formation of our moral imagination. Still another point is that the Fathers add to the biblical stories and commands some stories and commands of their own that extend the implications of the biblical teaching into additional areas of our lives. For example, the Bible says surprisingly little about usury except that it is not allowed for loans between fellow believers in God (see Deut 23:19–20). The Fathers extend the commands against usury to include all persons, and they situate this broad injunction in the context of their own labor-driven economy. This volume sorts out some of these issues.

## Structure

The work is organized into four parts, and these four parts roughly follow the outline summarized above with respect to the dialogue between early Christian homilies and Christian social thought. In part I there are two essays on how to approach early Christian texts. Reimund Bieringer, a New Testament scholar, for a number of years has been advancing a new hermeneutical theory in collaboration with Mary Elsbernd. In his essay he articulates this theory, which he calls "normativity of the future." Bieringer explains that ancient texts contain lines of evil that we may take steps to correct in our construction of a better future. Although he works almost exclusively in the field of New Testament studies, here Bieringer suggests some ways in which this theory might be of use in reading early Christian texts. Specifically, he considers a passage from Theodoret of Cyrus' *On Providence* 6.

The second article in this first part of the volume is from Pauline Allen, a scholar of early Christian studies, who, at the time of the seminar, was also running a research project at Australian Catholic University on the theme of poverty in early Christianity. From her long acquaintance with early Christian homilies and, more specifically, homilies concerned with social ethics, Allen has offered a thoughtful and provocative challenge to contemporary readers of early Christian texts. She is not very hopeful that early Christian texts will be helpful, for their teachings are buried under layers of editing, time-bound rhetoric, and theological debates. Her essay is a warning against a too-casual approach to patristic sources in Catholic social teaching, a point she makes clear towards the end of her essay.

From the perspective of this volume's aim to foster a dialogue between patristic teachings on social ethics and Catholic social teaching, the first essay is a match capable of starting a warming fire, while the second is a bucket of the cold water of historical reality capable of quickly dousing the flames. Far from being disappointing, however, this balance is precisely what is needed for any fruitful conversation to take place between the two worlds of texts and traditions. Christians today need tools that both open their imagination to the ideas of ancient texts and that warn them of the difficulties inherent in doing so.

Turning to part II, the work considers some contextual matters related to early Christian texts. To any scholar of early Christianity, it will be clear that the essays here only scratch the surface of a wider field of inquiry. For scholars of Catholic social teaching, who are perhaps unaware of some of the wider contexts for early Christian teaching, these essays serve mainly as an introduction to these concerns. In any case, the papers included here represent the special concerns of the contributors themselves and are an important place from which to start additional conversations. Having said that, the first paper in this section is from Peter Van Nuffelen, professor of classical languages and culture, who argues that in late antiquity a variety of moral *topoi* were reconfigured by individual authors to suit their own purposes. He provides as an example the coexistent lives of the two concepts, *liberalitas* and *caritas*. He argues it was not the case that the latter took over the former as the empire was increasingly Christianized. Both maintained a life of their own in public discourse well into the sixth century. Christians were pleased to use *liberalitas* as a foil to their idea of *caritas* even as they recognized the poor were themselves becoming more and more an object of episcopal patronage.

Helen Rhee's essay introduces us to the eschatological framework from which early Christians wrote and which informed their concern for social justice. Catholic social teaching is almost entirely bereft of this eschatological orientation to social ethics, so it is an important, contextual concern for scholars of Catholic social teaching and Catholic social thought. Drawing on Christian texts from the first through third centuries CE and Jewish texts that preceded them, Rhee argues early Christian and, indeed, Jewish eschatology was built around a deep respect for an ultimate divine judgment that would, in the eschatological age, reverse the fortunes of the rich and the poor that exist in the present age. Also, Rhee explores the dualistic language of Christian eschatology in those early centuries. Christians recognized a dualism both between their earthly and heavenly homes and between their earthly and heavenly riches. These dualisms supplemented the warnings of coming divine judgment in their appeal for behavior modification.

Wendy Mayer introduces us to a third contextual matter—the audiences of patristic homilies, including especially those homilies concerned with socioethical themes. Her article examines John Chrysostom's homily against Eutropius and explores its multiple audiences, including not only those in mind by the homilist himself, but also unintended audiences, among whom we may count ourselves. In the course of her investigation, Mayer reminds us of the need to consider that preachers in large cities conducted their work amidst only a part of the city's Christian community. Moreover, preaching in Constantinople meant that audiences could have comprised non-native Greek speakers, and so Chrysostom's preaching, for example, including both his words and his exempla, may have gone over the heads of many in the audience. Indeed, Mayer warns of too quickly appropriating preaching delivered to ancient audiences for teaching to contemporary audiences.

Whereas in part I it was suggested that scholars of the Christian social tradition needed first either to begin or to renew an interest in the texts from Christian antiquity, part II commends to Christian social thought a nuanced approach to the these texts. Moral discourse in late antiquity, early Christian eschatology and the audiences for patristic teaching are three of many contextual issues that ought to inform the reading of patristic texts in Christian social thought circles. Some examples of an interchange between these communities are modeled in part III of the volume.

We have placed as bookends to the papers in part III those of Susan Holman and Thomas Hughson. These two papers most nearly approach the interest of the Leuven seminar to construct a dialogue between patristic social thought and the Christian social tradition, but their approaches are quite different and so readers of this volume are invited to consider the merits of each approach.

Susan Holman's paper opens part III with an examination of "common good" in patristic teaching. Holman's paper is groundbreaking, for it is, to our knowledge, the first to have ever explored the meaning of this term in the Greek patristic literature. This is surprising since most scholars today operate from the assumption (and correctly so) that language of common good first developed in the Greek philosophical milieu of the fifth century BCE. Those who trace the history of the phrase too quickly jump from Aristotle to Aquinas without pausing long with Augustine. For her part, Holman explores how language about the common good in the Greek Fathers referred both to theological unity among Christians and to social unity among citizens. Holman then goes on to connect her construction of common good in the Greek Fathers with David Hollenbach's now-standard construction of common good for contemporary Christian social ethicists.

Brenda Ihssen's paper on patristic understandings of usury continues part III's aim to foster a dialogue between the patristic and modern worlds. Ihssen catalogues the long history of patristic denunciations of the practice of loaning any amount of money at interest, despite the fact that Roman law consistently allowed 12 percent per annum. The Fathers were upset with usury for the myriad of social problems it created, which, Ihssen suggests, usury still creates today. The paper asks to what extent Christian social thought today is comfortable with the Fathers' unequivocal condemnations of all forms of interest. To reinforce the point, Ihssen blurs the line between interest and usury, using the terms almost interchangeably. She does this in order to reinforce the point that Christians today, like most everyone else, unfortunately have come to accept a distinction between the two terms. Yet, Ihssen argues the Fathers would have seen this as a slippery slope, for the line separating appropriate interest from usury is not fixed.

Brian Matz's paper explores the development of a detachment view of private property in Graeco-Roman and, eventually, early Christian thought, with special consideration of Basil of Caesarea's use of this principle in his *Homily* 6. The paper argues the theological principles operating behind a detachment view in Basil's homily are better able than Basil's particular teachings to foster a conversation between contemporary Christian social thought and patristic texts.

The final paper in this third part of the volume is Thomas Hughson's on justice in the writings of Lactantius. As noted above, Hughson's paper, like Holman's, most nearly approaches the task of the Leuven seminar to construct a dialogue between patristic social thought and Christian social thought, in particular, CathST. Unlike Holman's, which is that from one trained in patristics, Hughson's paper is that of a systematic theologian engaged with contemporary issues. This paper does not incorporate the historical digressions quite standard in discourse within early Christian studies. Hughson takes a very direct approach to his subject, Lactantius: Does he say the same thing about justice that CST and CathST say today? Hughson concludes that Lactantius does, and wonders whether the Catholic Church has neglected a rapprochement with patristic sources to its own detriment.

The reader of the first through third parts of the volume may be wondering at that point to what extent shall there be a real synthesis of the question of a dialogue between patristic and contemporary Christian social thought. Moving beyond some of the skepticism about the value of such a dialogue at all as expressed by Allen, the two papers in part IV of this volume contend there may be some room for development of a constructive dialogue. Richard Schenk considers Ricoeur's ideas about memory and constructive forgetting in suggesting that a healthy dialogue between the past and present social teachings should begin by acknowledging what is worth remembering and forgetting. Schenk offers several criteria for the type of patristic texts that are worth remembering today, to include those that articulate common principles, that elucidate marginal voices and that fail adequately to bury radical expressions of discipleship under layers of institutionalization.

The concluding paper by Johan Verstraeten and Johan Leemans reviews the overall contribution of this collection of papers to the work of the research program outlined at the beginning of the introduction. In hindsight, the Leuven seminar, from which the papers in this volume emerged, did not adequately address the questions our research team had hoped it would. Verstraeten and Leemans suggest that one major reason for this may be the structure of the seminar itself, geared as it was around themes rather than particular texts. The paper suggests some future directions for scholarship on the question of how best to proceed with a study of the contribution of patristic texts to contemporary Christian social thought.

# PART I

# APPROACHING PATRISTIC SOCIO-ETHICAL TEXTS

*Reimund Bieringer*

---

# 1. Texts That Create a Future

## *The Function of Ancient Texts for Theology Today*

The way in which we anticipate the future defines the meaning the
past can have for us, just as the way in which we have understood the past
and the way in which our ancestors have projected the future
determines our own range of possibilities.[1]

The relationship of the present to the past is constitutive for Christianity and many other religions. In the religious context of the earthly Jesus, texts of the past that have come to us as Old Testament play a decisive role. They are consulted to explain the present and to anticipate the future. The authors of the texts that have been handed down to us as the New Testament made ample use of their Bible to make sense of the Jesus event. They saw continuity between what the texts of the past had been saying and what they understood to be the significance of Jesus. Many texts of early Christianity were preserved, copied, and handed down. They were read and reread, commented on, and discussed. They had a central place in the life of Christian communities in their liturgy and prayer and in their preaching and teaching. In a gradual process certain texts gained a special status and eventually a canon of sa-

---

1. Georgia Warnke, *Gadamer: Hermeneutics, Tradition and Reason* (Stanford: Stanford University Press, 1987), 39.

cred books was formed. In addition to the canon, the oral traditions handed down since the time of the apostles continued to play a role. Throughout the centuries Christian communities also developed their own oral and written tradition. In the Christian tradition, the works of the generation of theologians and preachers who followed the New Testament era were held in high esteem.[2] Their writings were considered to be authoritative interpretation of the Scriptures. For the greater part of the history of Christianity, the importance of Scripture and tradition and their binding authority and normativity for contemporary life was never an issue. The assumption was that texts of the past had significance and even authority for the present. In fact, the very topic of this paper would have been unthinkable. For people of the twenty-first century, and especially for theologians trained in the post-Enlightenment period, however, the question of the role of the past for the present is one of the more unsettling questions. We shall approach this topic in three steps. First, we try to understand the shifts in western societies and especially in theology that caused the link between the present and the past to become problematic. Second, we analyze a representative selection of attempts to bridge the perceived gulf between the present and the past. Finally, we develop our own hermeneutical approach called "Normativity of the Future" as our way of understanding the impact of the past on the present.

## The Gulf between the Present and the Past

The very topic of this paper presupposes a profound change in the attitude of western culture toward the past. While it is impossible to give a specialized account of these changes, we need to review the broad lines in order to

2. See, for example, Pope Leo XIII who says in his encyclical *Providentissimus Deus* of 1893: "The Holy Fathers 'to whom, after the Apostles, the Church owes its growth—who have planted, watered, built, governed, and cherished it,'(39) the Holy Fathers, We say, are of supreme authority, whenever they all interpret in one and the same manner any text of the Bible, as pertaining to the doctrine of faith or morals; for their unanimity clearly evinces that such interpretation has come down from the Apostles as a matter of Catholic faith. The opinion of the Fathers is also of very great weight when they treat of these matters in their capacity of doctors, unofficially; not only because they excel in their knowledge of revealed doctrine and in their acquaintance with many things which are useful in understanding the apostolic Books, but because they are men of eminent sanctity and of ardent zeal for the truth, on whom God has bestowed a more ample measure of His light. Wherefore the expositor should make it his duty to follow their footsteps with all reverence, and to use their labours with intelligent appreciation" (14).

gain the necessary background for what follows. Before this change our topic was not an issue, because the texts of Scripture and tradition were not primarily perceived as texts of the past but rather as containers of eternal truths ("perennialism"). In an approach where the authoritative texts are understood to contain eternal truths, a potential gulf between the present and the past is of no relevance, since the focus is on a deposit of propositional truth revealed once and for all.[3] Insofar as there was an awareness of the past, the relationship between the present and that past was facilitated by a lack of historical consciousness and by an unquestioned respect for tradition. One implication of the lack of historical consciousness is the absence of historical investigation and consequently a lack of historical knowledge. As a result people were inclined to project their own world into the world of the past. Such an anachronistic procedure was also supported by the fact that since change happened only gradually there was more continuity. Also, the uncritical respect and esteem people used to have for tradition implied a strong sense of oneness with the past.

This harmonious relationship with the past decisively changed as a result of the Enlightenment and the concomitant shifts in thought and practice. Hans-Georg Gadamer has the following to say about the Enlightenment's attitude toward the past and texts of the past:

In general, the Enlightenment tends to accept no authority and to decide everything before the judgment seat of reason. Thus the written tradition of Scripture, like any other historical document, can claim no absolute validity; the possible truth of the tradition depends on the credibility that reason accords it. It is not tradition but reason that constitutes the ultimate source of all authority. What is written down is not necessarily true. We can know better: this is the maxim with which the modern Enlightenment approaches tradition and which ultimately leads it to undertake historical research. It takes tradition as an object of critique, just as the natural sciences do with the evidence of the senses.[4]

By prioritizing reason, the Enlightenment caused a distanciation from authoritative texts of the past and from tradition in general. Critique and suspicion replaced blind obedience to the authority of tradition. The emancipation from traditions, called into question by reason, resulted in the claim of the au-

---

3. See, for example, Avery Dulles, *Models of Revelation* (Garden City, N.Y.: Image Books, 1985), 36–52.
4. Hans-Georg Gadamer, *Truth and Method*, 2nd ed., trans. Joel Weinsheimer and Donald G. Marshall (New York: Continuum, 1989), 272.

tonomy of human thinking. The critique of tradition led to an intensification of historical research. The study of history fostered the development of the historical situatedness of the objects of research and the growth of historical consciousness of the subjects of research. Comparative historical studies relativized the absolute claims of tradition by bringing to light how traditions had changed over time. The Enlightenment was not opposed to tradition on principle, rather it insisted that the traditions that could not withstand the test of human reason needed to be abandoned for the sake of human liberation.

The changed attitude toward tradition implies that people do not so easily move back and forth between the past and the present. Coupled with the Enlightenment belief in progress, the critique of tradition led to a sense of superiority with regard to the past. Traditions are abandoned for the sake of development and progress. Before the Enlightenment, Scripture and tradition were seen as containers of eternal truth, therefore, transcending their historical situation. Historical research of the post-Enlightenment period discovered the historical situatedness of the text, but at the same time (ironically) assigned to the interpreting subject an objective observer position. As a result of these shifts a deep gulf developed between past and present, which was perceived as impossible to cross without a bridge.

The implications for theology were far-reaching. Gradually the historical-critical method was introduced in all its subdisciplines. History became the central category of theology. From now on, everyone who asked a theological question was first subjected to a more or less complete historical overview of the answers. While the Enlightenment approach had intended emancipation from oppressive traditions, the historical research that it fostered in many regards favored a normativity of the past, albeit a past which had been vindicated before the tribunal of reason. The conviction of an unbridgeable gulf between the present and the past resulted in a division of labor in the discipline of theology. The historical subdisciplines of exegesis and Church history were assigned the task to concentrate exclusively on the past of the Christian community, to focus on the written sources and to study the texts of the past as texts of the past. The systematic and pastoral disciplines were expected to provide theological theory for the present building on the results of the historical disciplines. In the day-to-day practice of theology this ideal expectation met with serious obstacles. As the historical-critical researchers inescapably brought their own past and present to the so-called objective practice of their discipline, they rarely arrived at unanimous results that could be the basis for their colleagues of the systematic and pastoral disciplines to build on. Moreover, under the guise of historical-critical methodology and claiming that they were exclusively concentrating on the past, exegetes and church historians implicitly and unconsciously did some of the work assigned to their colleagues of the systematic and pastoral disciplines. On the other hand, systematic and pastoral theologians often were disillusioned with the work of historical criticism and turned to other human sciences for support. The gulf between the present and the past was mirrored in the gulf between the historical and systematic subdisciplines in theology.

## Bridging the Gulf

After the Enlightenment, the link between the past and the present could no longer be taken for granted. A deep gulf was seen as separating the one from the other. But this does not imply that the two were seen as totally unrelated. It means, however, that deliberate efforts are needed to build bridges between the present and the past. A great variety of bridges have been built and will be surveyed briefly here.

Before looking at the various types of bridges, we first need to turn to the positions that oppose the idea of a bridge. Strict historical critics often claim that they study the documents of the past purely for their own sake. They study the past exclusively to come to know more about the ancient world. This almost ascetical restriction is meant to ascertain the scientific objectivity.[5] Any link with the present is feared to mar the scientific value of their work with subjectivity and to compromise the disinterested nature of their endeavour. If at all, a link with the present could be made in a second phase of study called application. Moreover, there are positions that deliberately reject bridging the gulf between the present and the past based on the conviction that past texts carry a predominantly and irredeemably harmful message to which contemporary readers should not be exposed. We are thinking here, for example, of

5. Ibid., "This was . . . the naive assumption of historicism, namely, that we must transpose ourselves into the spirit of the age, think with its ideas and its thoughts, not with our own, and thus advance toward historical objectivity" (297).

radical feminist rejectionism (Mary Daly). Its proponents consider the biblical tradition to be irredeemably patriarchal and blow up all the bridges that might connect them with it.[6] At the other end of the spectrum we encounter positions that oppose the idea of a bridge, but from the perspective of the present or perhaps even more accurately from a perspective of timelessness. Here we refer to various kinds of synchronic approaches (e.g., Biblicism, structuralism, and some types of narrative criticism), which do not consider the historical situatedness of a text either temporarily bracketing it or completely denying its relevance.[7] While for the previous positions a bridge between the present and the past was not possible since present and past were seen as different planets, here a bridge is not needed as the distance between the past and the present is collapsed into an artificial construct of a decontextualized now.

In the post-Enlightenment hermeneutical discussion these extreme positions are exceptional. The larger part of scholarship continued attempts to determine how the past could have a role for the present. In the spirit of the Enlightenment the focus was on the authority of tradition and on the rational discernment between acceptable and unacceptable traditions. We shall first turn to those positions that implicitly continued to accept the virtually unquestioned authority of those traditions, which they considered acceptable based on their respective hermeneutical approaches. The first such approach is revisionism. It holds that in the tradition we need to distinguish between a theological kernel and a historical shell. While the time- and situation-bound wrappings are seen as irretrievably past and potentially marred by sin, the theological core of the tradition is accepted as timeless eternal truth.[8] Therefore they see the task of interpretation as separating the kernel from the shell and presenting the decontextualized kernel for recontextualization in the present. A similar hermeneutical strategy is used by positions that identify a kind of "canon within the canon." They identify a central theme within a tradition, for exam-

6. See Carolyn Osiek, "The Feminist and the Bible: Hermeneutical Alternatives," in *Feminist Perspectives on Biblical Scholarship*, SBL Biblical Scholarship in North America, ed. Adela Yarbro Collins (Atlanta: Scholars Press, 1985), 93–105, esp. 97–99.

7. We avoid here the term "fundamentalism" because of manifold uses and abuses in recent usages of the word.

8. Strictly speaking, revisionism does not need a bridge between the present and the past. For concerning the irretrievable part of the past their position is similar to rejectionism, and with regard to the theological kernel they return to the pre-Enlightenment position of perennialism (see above, 2).

ple, liberation from oppression in liberation theologies, and reject everything in the tradition that is not in keeping with it. The second approach is reconstructionism, which accepts unquestioning authority only for "the great deeds of God in history," especially Jesus' life, ministry, death, and resurrection.[9] The biblical tradition relates these events by means of grace and sin. To Ricoeur, it is the task of the interpreter to reconstruct the salvation-historical events on the basis of our fragmentary evidence and imagination.[10] Reconstructionism has in common with revisionism that there is no real attempt to bridge the present and the past, since it is assumed that the reconstructed salvation-historical events have more or less the status of unchanging eternal truth, which is not part of the past and therefore needs no mediation to the present.[11]

The real challenge to hermeneutics is the question of whether historically situated texts can be understood beyond their original context and how they can have meaning and significance in the present.[12] These issues were of primary concern to romantic hermeneutics whose proponents, according to Gadamer, understand "homogenous human nature as the unhistorical substratum," that is, as the bridge between the present and the past.[13] This enables people to transpose themselves into the mental life of others.[14] Ricoeur aptly characterizes the romantic hermeneutics of Schleiermacher and Dilthey as "a hermeneutic that subsumes the understanding of texts to the laws of understanding another person who expresses himself therein." This hermeneutic enterprise is therefore "fundamentally psychological" because its ultimate aim is "not *what* a text says, but *who* says it."[15] This is also evident from the oft-quoted

9. Dulles, *Models of Revelation*, 60.

10. A prime example is found in Elisabeth Schüssler Fiorenza, *In Memory of Her: A Feminist Theological Reconstruction of Christian Origins* (New York: Crossroad, 1983).

11. See Didier Pollefeyt and Reimund Bieringer, "The Role of the Bible in Religious Education Reconsidered: Risks and Challenges in Teaching the Bible," *International Journal of Practical Theology* 9 (2005): 117–39, esp. 121–24.

12. Similarly, the approach we call perennialism needs to face questions like, How can so-called eternal truths be understood by, be meaningful for, and mean the same thing to people of different periods in history? These issues, however, have not occupied the hermeneutical discussion.

13. Gadamer, *Truth and Method*, 290.

14. See Paul Ricoeur, *From Text to Action: Essays in Hermeneutics II*, trans. Kathleen Blamey and John B. Thompson (Evanston, Ill.: Northeastern University Press, 1991), 59: "Every *human science*—and by that Dilthey means every modality of the knowledge of man which implies a historical relation—presupposes a primordial capacity to transpose oneself into the mental life of others."

15. Ibid., 62.

programme of romantic hermeneutics "to understand an author as well as and even better than he understands himself."[16]

Heidegger's *Being and Time* marks a notable shift away from romantic hermeneutics. In his essay, "The Task of Hermeneutics," Ricoeur compares Heidegger's position to that of romantic hermeneutics.

> It is therefore not astonishing that it is by a reflection on *being-in*, rather than *being-with*, that the ontology of understanding may begin; not *being-with* another who would duplicate our subjectivity, but *being-in-the-world*. . . .The question of the *world* takes the place of the question of the *other*. In thereby making understanding *worldly*, Heidegger *depsychologizes* it.[17]

For Heidegger the element of continuity between the past and the present that makes understanding across the centuries possible is not the human psyche, but our being-in-the-world. This being-in-the-world is a being-thrown (Geworfensein) that precedes everything else, is shared by every human being without exception and is the condition of possibility for situation, understanding, and interpretation. Understanding a text is for Heidegger neither finding a sense that would be contained in it nor transposing ourselves into the mind of its author, but unfolding "the possibility of being indicated by the text."[18] It is our own being-in-the-world as projected being that enables us to recognize and unfold the new possibilities that the text projects for us.

In *Truth and Method* Gadamer intends to rehabilitate authority and tradition.[19] He calls into question the basic presuppositions of Enlightenment and romantic hermeneutics, namely, the claim that there is a gulf between the present and the past.

> Time is no longer primarily a gulf to be bridged because it separates; it is actually the supportive ground of the course of events in which the present is rooted. Hence temporal distance is not something that must be overcome. . . . In fact the important thing is to recognize temporal distance as a positive and productive condition enabling understanding. It is not a yawning abyss but is filled with the continuity of custom and tradition, in the light of which everything handed down presents itself to us.[20]

No bridge is needed, according to Gadamer, since present and past are solidly connected by the process of tradition and by historically effected consciousness (wirkungsgeschichtliches Bewußtsein). The ongoing process of tradition

---

16. Friedrich Schleiermacher, *Hermeneutik*, ed. H. Kimmerle (Heidelberg: Carl Winter, 1959), 56.
17. Ricoeur, *From Text to Action*, 65–66.         18. Ibid., 66.
19. See Gadamer, *Truth and Method*, 277–85.      20. Ibid., 297.

mediates constantly between past and present.[21] Texts do not exclusively belong to their authors and the situations into which they speak originally, rather they transcend their original situations and potentially belong to everyone independent of time and space.

Every age has to understand a transmitted text in its own way, for the text belongs to the whole tradition whose content interests the age and in which it seeks to understand itself. The real meaning of a text, as it speaks to the interpreter, does not depend on the contingencies of the author and his original audience. It certainly is not identical with them, for it is always co-determined also by the historical situation of the interpreter and hence by the totality of the objective course of history.[22]

The concept of historically effected consciousness describes another way in which the past and the present are closely linked. Contemporary readers of ancient texts are linked to those texts before they ever come in contact with them if their own traditions and communities are part of the history of effect of that text, if their own traditions were at least partially shaped by that text. "Understanding is to be thought of less as a subjective act than as participating in an event of tradition, a process of transmission in which past and present are constantly mediated."[23]

Gadamer also identifies a specific category of texts in which the distance between past and present is transcended and which he calls "the classical."[24] "What we call 'classical' does not first require the overcoming of historical

21. According to Gadamer, the ongoing process of tradition comes about by a continuous fusion of horizons. "In a tradition this process of fusion is continually going on, for there old and new are always combining into something of living value"(*Truth and Method*, 306). Ricoeur's comments on the "fusion of horizons" helps to clarify its significance: "Another index of the dialectic of participation and distanciation is provided by the concept of the *fusion of horizons*. . . . For according to Gadamer, if the finite condition of historical knowledge excludes any overview, any final synthesis in the Hegelian manner, nevertheless this finitude does not enclose me in one point of view. Wherever there is a situation, there is a horizon that can be contracted or enlarged. We owe to Gadamer this very fruitful idea that communication at a distance between two differently situated consciousnesses occurs by means of the fusion of horizons, that is, the intersection of their views on the distant and the open. . . .This concept signifies that we live neither within closed horizons nor within one unique horizon. Insofar as the fusion of horizons excludes the idea of a total and unique knowledge, this concept implies a tension between what is one's own and what is alien, between the near and the far; and hence the play of difference is included in the process of convergence" (Ricoeur, *From Text to Action*, 73).

22. Gadamer, *Truth and Method*, 296; see esp. 290: "Not just occasionally but always, the meaning of a text goes beyond its author."

23. Ibid., 290.

24. Ibid., 285–90. "This is just what the word 'classical' means: that the duration of a work's power to speak directly is fundamentally unlimited" (290).

distance, for in its own constant mediation it overcomes this distance by itself. The classical, then, is certainly 'timeless,' but this timelessness is a mode of historical being."[25] The classical cannot be fully grasped in a diachronic or in a synchronic approach. Rather it needs an approach which we could call "metachronic," one that respects the fact that the classical, while fully rooted in a historical situation, transcends it and is able to be recontextualized in new times and places. The classic itself becomes a bridge between its original world and the many worlds of the readers.[26]

Ricoeur continues in the line of the new insights of Heidegger and Gadamer, in many regards relying on their insights and joining them in critiquing romantic hermeneutics. Like Gadamer, Ricoeur acknowledges that without distanciation there is no text and that distanciation is not an obstacle to understanding, but rather constitutive for any interpretation.[27] Ricoeur carefully analyzes the differences between (oral) discourse and (written) text. He arrives at conclusions that are very similar to what Gadamer calls "the classical."

An essential characteristic of a literary work, and of a work of art in general, is that it transcends its own psychosociological conditions of production and thereby opens itself to an unlimited series of readings, themselves situated in different sociocultural conditions. In short, the text must be able, from the sociological as well as the psychological point of view, to "decontextualize" itself in such a way that it can be "recontextualized."[28]

In earlier publications Ricoeur called this phenomenon that is a consequence of the fixation of texts in written form "the surplus of meaning."[29] Another

25. Ibid., 290.

26. Ibid.: The classical is "a historical phenomenon that can be understood solely in terms of its own time. But understanding it will always involve *more* than merely historically reconstructing the past 'world' to which the work belongs. Our understanding will always retain the consciousness that we too belong to that world, and correlatively, that the work too belongs to our world."

27. Ricoeur, *From Text to Action*, 84: Distanciation "is constitutive of the phenomenon of the text as writing . . . it is the condition of interpretation." Ibid., 76: "The dominant problematic is that of the text, which reintroduces a positive and, if I may say so, productive notion of distanciation. In my view, the text . . . is the paradigm of distanciation in communication. As such it displays a fundamental characteristic of the very historicity of human experience, namely, that it is communication in and through distance." See also Paul Ricoeur, *Interpretation Theory: Discourse and the Surplus of Meaning* (Forth Worth: Texas Christian University Press, 1976), 44: "Interpretation, philosophically understood, is nothing else than an attempt to make estrangement and distanciation productive."

28. Ricoeur, *From Text to Action*, 83; see also 83–84: "In contrast to the dialogical situation, where the vis-à-vis is determined by the very situation of discourse, written discourse creates an audience that extends in principle to anyone who can read."

29. See Ricoeur, *Interpretation Theory*, 45–46.

important change in written texts is "the abolition of the ostensive character of reference."[30] In its place comes a second-order reference that Ricoeur calls "a proposed world." Relying heavily on Heidegger, Ricoeur describes the task of interpretation as

> to explicitate the type of being-in-the-world unfolded in front of the text . . . what must be interpreted in a text is a *proposed world* that I could inhabit and wherein I could project one of my ownmost possibilities. That is what I call the world of the text, the world proper to this unique text.[31]

For Ricoeur the ultimate goal of the interpretation of texts is self-understanding. At the same time he sees the need of a distanciation of the self to itself, a need to critique the illusions of the subject. "The critique of ideology is the necessary detour that self-understanding must take if the latter is to be formed by the matter of the text and not by the prejudices of the reader."[32] Ricoeur borrows the expression "the matter of the text" from Gadamer and uses it synonymously with "the world of the text" or "the proposed world." Critique of ideology is needed according to Ricoeur to help readers overcome their own illusions to allow them to be formed by the alternative world which the text projects and offers to the readers as a new possibility. In this final point, Ricoeur differs from his predecessors who did not integrate critique of ideology into their hermeneutics.[33]

This second section analyzes major post-Enlightenment attempts to bridge the gap between the past and the present. In the course of our discussion it became clear that some approaches do not really bridge the gulf, but rather try to work out ways that would allow them to dismiss the historical

30. Ricoeur, *From Text to Action*, 85.

31. Ibid., 86; see also Paul Ricoeur, *Hermeneutics and the Human Sciences: Essays on Language, Action and Interpretation*, ed. and trans. John B. Thompson (Cambridge: Cambridge University Press, 1981, repr. 1990), 176–81, here 177: "The nature of reference in the context of literary works has an important consequence for the concept of interpretation. It implies that the meaning of a text lies not behind the text but in front of it. The meaning is not something hidden but something disclosed. What gives rise to understanding is that which points toward a possible world, by means of the non-ostensive references of the text. Texts speak of possible worlds and of possible ways of orienting oneself in these worlds. In this way, disclosure plays the equivalent role for written texts as ostensive reference plays in spoken language. Interpretation thus becomes the apprehension of the proposed worlds which are opened up by the non-ostensive references of the text."

32. Ricoeur, *From Text to Action*, 88.

33. Werner G. Jeanrond, *Theological Hermeneutics: Developments and Significance* (New York: Crossroad, 1991), 74: "Ricoeur's hermeneutics represents the first effort in hermeneutics to integrate critical concerns into interpretation theory proper."

aspects and to accept the eternal truths. Those who truly face the problem take different directions to solve it. Romantic hermeneutics proposed a psychological solution placing the continuity in the encounter between two subjects, namely, the ability of the readers to transpose themselves into the psyche of the author. Heidegger saw continuity in ontological terms, namely, in the shared condition of being-in-the-world as being-thrown. For Gadamer it was rather the ongoing participation in the process of tradition that assured the continuity between past and present. Finally Ricoeur considered the "world of the text," the proposed world that the text projects to be the bridge between present and past. While Ricoeur is critical of those approaches that understand interpretation as trying to grasp the soul of the author of a work, his own position can be called psychological insofar as he conceives hermeneutics as self-understanding.[34] This brings us to our third step in which we present our own approach developed in continuation of the trajectory presented so far.

## The Future as the Bridge

In the discussion of the role of the past for the present, the future has been conspicuously absent. In our own approach we shall take a careful look at the future in order to see how the present and the past are connected. Texts can be seen as functioning in relation to three worlds, the world *behind* the text, the world *of* the text and the world *before* the text.[35] We develop our own approach in dialogue with how texts are related to each of these worlds.[36]

34. This is evident in a number of quotations from Ricoeur, *From Text to Action*, 87: "the text is the medium through which we understand ourselves"; "we understand ourselves only by the long detour of the signs of humanity deposited in cultural works"; and 88: "to understand is to understand oneself in front of the text"; "the *self* is constituted by the 'matter' of the text."

35. See Gadamer, *Truth and Method*, 438–53; Paul Ricoeur, *Time and Narrative I* (Chicago: University of Chicago Press, 1984), 52–82; Sandra M. Schneiders, *The Revelatory Text: Interpreting the New Testament as Sacred Scripture* (San Francisco: Harper, 1991), which uses these three worlds as the titles of three chapters of her book (chs. 4–6), but she never seems to discuss these concepts as such or indicate their origin in scholarly discussion. The expression "the world of the text" plays an important role in Ricoeur's hermeneutics, as we have seen previously.

36. For earlier articulations of this approach see Reimund Bieringer, "The Normativity of the Future: The Authority of the Bible for Theology," *ET Bulletin: Zeitschrift für Theologie in Europa* 8 (1997): 52–67; Reimund Bieringer, Didier Pollefeyt, and Frederique Vandecasteele-Vanneuville, "Wrestling with Johannine Anti-Judaism: A Hermeneutical Framework for the Analysis of the Current Debate," in *Anti-*

A text comes about in a particular world. This is the world in which the (real) author and the original text intended readers live. The historical-critical method essentially means studying ancient texts as part of their original historical context. This method focuses on the authors of the texts. In order to understand the authors of texts, we need to study the world in which they live, by which they are formed, informed, and transformed. From the perspective of the text, the world in which the authors live is the "world behind the text." Texts belong to a historical context, a situation. Each text has its own horizon. Texts always say what they say from a certain historical (social, personal) perspective. They do not tell us "what happened" but someone's perspective on "what happened." In as much as texts are windows to the past, the glass in the window is always colored or slightly convex, changing to a degree what you see through it. The historical dimension includes all spheres of human life. In this approach the emphasis is on "information."

Many academic approaches to texts in the fields of theology are exclusively interested in the world behind the text. As we saw in the previous discussion, the historical-critical approaches content themselves with studying a past text as a past reality and to leave it at that. Recent hermeneutic discussions, however, point out that interpreters cannot abstract from their own situation and their own horizon that which is not contemporary with an ancient text.[37] Thus any reading of an ancient text is in and of itself a bridging of the distance between the present and the past. But how does such a bridging work? What makes it possible?

Do we assume that the historical context is only a shell that hides a core of timeless truth that speaks to people independently of their contexts or horizons? When we ask "what contribution, if any, patristic sources can make to

---

*Judaism and the Fourth Gospel*, ed. Reimund Bieringer, Didier Pollefeyt, and Frederique Vandecasteele-Vanneuville (Louisville, Ky.: Westminster John Knox, 2001), 3–37; Reimund Bieringer, "'Come, and You Will See' (John 1:39): Dialogical Authority and Normativity of the Future in the Fourth Gospel and in Religious Education," in *Hermeneutics and Religious Education*, BETL 180, ed. Herman Lombaerts and Didier Pollefeyt (Leuven: Leuven University Press–Peeters, 2005), 179–201; Didier Pollefeyt and Reimund Bieringer, "The Role of the Bible in Religious Education Reconsidered: Risks and Challenges in Teaching the Bible," *International Journal of Practical Theology* 9 (2005): 117–39; Mary Elsbernd and Reimund Bieringer, "Interpreting the Signs of the Times in the Light of the Gospel: Vision and Normativity of the Future," in *Scrutinizing the Signs of the Times in Light of the Gospel*, BETL 208, ed. Johan Verstraeten (Leuven: Leuven University Press–Peeters, 2007), 41–97.

37. See Richard S. Briggs, "What Does Hermeneutics Have to Do with Biblical Interpretation," *Heythrop Journal* 47 (2006): 55–74, here 69: "the self stubbornly refuses to keep out of the way."

contemporary ethical discussions," as post-Enlightenment theologians we have been taught by our historical-critical formation to "explore the specific contexts in which the patristic authors wrote, and it is important to ask to what extent those contexts are able to be translated into the contexts into which Catholic social thought speaks."[38] For such translation work we are inclined to look at the parallels and differences between the two contexts. The question is, however, What do we actually expect to translate? Do we assume that the text of the past contains something like a timeless truth that, disembodied from its original context, can be reincarnated in a contemporary context? Such a dualistic way of conceiving the relationship between the context and the meaning of a text or between the time-immanent and the time-transcending aspects of texts seems problematic since it does not take the historicity of the human condition seriously. History is reduced to being the clothing of the actors on the stage of life. We need to look for alternatives.

According to romantic hermeneutics, this bridging implies the capacity of contemporary persons to transpose themselves into the psyche of the ancient author and thus presupposes a psychological continuity of human subjectivity throughout the centuries. Gadamer, on the other hand, sees our connection with the past as the result of an ongoing fusion of horizons at the heart of the process of transmitting tradition. Understanding is participation in this ongoing process of tradition. These two positions offer important building blocks for our approach but they do not suffice.

For texts are not only part of the historical context of their genesis, they also transcend this world. One dimension that enables them to transcend their place- and time-bound context, and to have a function in new contexts, is their literary dimension. Insofar as they are literary they create their own world, the world of the text, with its own time, space, plot, actors, language, etc. Historical approaches have been called diachronic, since they study a text as it was composed, intended, or interpreted "through time." Literary approaches are synchronic, that is, they are studied independently of historical issues.

Texts follow certain conventions in the way they are written depending on their literary genre. Literary-critical approaches study texts as literature.

---

38. Brian Matz with Johan Verstraeten, and Johan Leemans, "The Church Fathers and Catholic Social Thought with a Case Study of Private Property," position paper prepared for the 2007 seminar, 1 and 3.

The focus is no longer on the author but on the text itself. Any text whether it is a historical study or a novel is to some degree "fiction." Any writer needs to make a selection of the material (also story time and story place) that is presented, put it into a certain sequence and suggest a certain causality between the events. Texts have a perspective (e.g., I-narratives, third person narratives), a plot, laws and rules, as well as actors and characters (heroes and villains). There is also narrative time and place. In and through the way the texts express their message, they are holding up a mirror to their readers in which they can have a deeper insight into the fundamental realities of their life and life in general. Even literary genres of texts that have no direct historical basis (like a parable) can convey a deep wisdom. In this approach the emphasis is on "confrontation," that is, confronting us with ourselves and our existential questions.

Gadamer points to a category of literature called "the classical" that is "significant in itself and interprets itself" and therefore speaks to its readers directly, independent of temporal or spatial distance.[39] Gadamer does not explain which qualities of "the classical" enable it to have such universal appeal. Ricoeur is convinced that written texts in general have a "surplus of meaning" in comparison with the spoken word, that is, that written texts have meanings that transcend their author's intention and the limitations of their original context.[40] More specifically, as we have seen, Ricoeur is convinced that in texts of fiction and poetry we encounter a second-order reference, namely, the world of the text or a projected world which enables these texts to transcend time and space.[41] This decisive insight of Ricoeur will be the starting point of our own approach, which we develop primarily in view of the world before the text.

Religious texts (understood in the broadest sense) are neither only part of the historical context of their composition nor restricted to their literary dimensions. They transcend both their original historical settings and their character as literature. They not only originate in a certain world (which enters the text through the author), they not only create their own internal worlds (through their literary qualities), but they also transform the world before them into a new world. Texts project future worlds as alternatives to the existing worlds in which we live. Thus they are not only directed toward the

39. Ibid., 7, nn 23 and 25; see also Gadamer, *Truth and Method*, 285–290, esp. 289.
40. See above, 8, including n. 28.
41. See above, 8.

past and the present, texts also have a future dimension.[42] It is this future, utopian dimension that makes literary texts attractive and potentially subversive, inspiring people to change the existing world according to the new world the text projects. We can call this future dimension the dream or the vision that the text proposes explicitly or implicitly. It is not impossible that the future dimension of a text is in contradiction with aspects of its past and present dimensions.

The historical approach is mainly concerned with the authors and their worlds, while the literary approach mainly focuses on the text. The future approach pays special attention to the readers, the communities of readers and traditions formed by the text and the world that is envisioned. It is also concerned with the effect the text intends to have or in fact has on them. In this approach the emphasis is thus on the transformative qualities of the text. Interpretations that focus on the world before the text are neither diachronic nor synchronic, but rather "metachronic." We mean by this term that they are rooted in the past and formed by the present, but transcend ("meta") both of them into the future. While the historical approach sees texts as sources and the literary approach considers them as resources, the future approach sees (religious) texts as symbols, even sacraments. Such texts are not only witnesses to an absent reality of the past, or simply resources to draw on for our individual growth, they are also and primarily an encounter of the reading community with unspeakable mystery.[43] The religious text is neither a dead fossil of past life nor a self-help book to enhance present life but an invitation, even a summons, to participate in building a better world for the full life of all creatures. The text is thus not just a window that provides access to information about the world behind the text. The religious text is also more than a mirror in which, by looking at the world of the text, we are confronted with ourselves. Religious texts are icons, windows into the mysterious reality of the future which God has in store for all of creation.

Christians spontaneously connect the revelatory dimension of religious texts with the past or with a timeless dimension of the text. Religious texts have

---

42. While we assume that all classic texts have past, present, and future dimensions to some degree, we acknowledge that the emphasis varies greatly depending on the literary genre of a text.

43. Here we differ from Schneiders, *The Revelatory Text*, 167, when she says: "The ultimate objective of reading is enhanced subjectivity" or "the existential augmentation of the reader." A similar individualist position was already espoused by Ricoeur.

often been seen as revelation of God insofar as they are faithful accounts by reliable eyewitnesses of God's action in the world in a past event (e.g., the Exodus or the raising of Lazarus). Historical and literary criticisms have, however, seriously challenged this view. They have called into question that biblical books were written by the person (eyewitness) who is claimed by the book itself (e.g., the Deutero- and the Trito-Pauline letters) or by tradition (e.g., John, son of Zebedee, as the author of the gospel of John) to be the author. Moreover, in some cases it has proved impossible to establish the historicity of certain key events of the Bible (e.g., the Exodus, the raising of Lazarus). Consequently, theologians have looked for revelatory dimensions in the literary character of the texts. Even though a story (like the raising of Lazarus) may not be historical, it can still contain a theological message that can be accepted as revelatory. Revelation not only happens through the eyewitnesses or through exact historical accounts, but also through the plot of a narrative that was constructed by a later writer, through the stylistic beauty of a second-generation text, or through the faith witness of a later Christian community.

But revelation happens not only in the past and present dimensions of the text. Perhaps primarily the revelation of God happens in the future dimension. From a Christian perspective we call this future dimension eschatological. Religious texts are revelatory foremost because of the working of the Holy Spirit, thus they have the ability to propose God's dream for the world.[44] This eschatological perspective implies that Jesus' first coming set in motion the realization of God's dream for the world. In the time before his second coming, Christians are called to continue this work and, under the guidance of the Holy Spirit, to participate in bringing about God's dream for the world. The most important roles of the Bible are to put before us the vision of this alter-

---

44. See Ricoeur, *From Text to Action*, 96–97: "In this way . . . is placed the proposal of a world, which in the language of the Bible, is called a new world, a new covenant, the Kingdom of God, a new birth. These are realities that unfold before the text, unfolding to be sure for us, but based upon the text. This is what can be called the 'objectivity' of the new being projected by the text. . . . If the Bible can be said to be revealed, this is to be said of the 'thing' it says, of the new being it unfolds. I would then venture to say that the Bible is revealed to the extent that the new being that is in question is itself *revealing* with respect to the world, to all of reality, including my existence and my history. In other words, revelation, if the expression is to have a meaning, is a feature of the biblical *world* . . . we stated that the world of the literary text is a projected world, one that is poetically distanced from everyday reality. Is this not the case par excellence of the new being projected and proposed by the Bible? Does not this new being make its way through the world of ordinary experience, despite the closedness of this experience? Is not the power of projection belonging to this [projected] world the power to make a break and a new beginning?"

native world and to provide the motivation and inspiration for people to get involved in it.

In the future-oriented hermeneutics which we propose, texts of the past have meaning in the present and the future because they are always already, at least partially, involved in creating the world they propose. The inherent future dimensions of the text are a "living" bridge between the past and the present, one that is constantly made, unmade, and remade. Texts are constitutive for forming the communities that read them and live by them. Understanding texts means understanding oneself before the texts, as Ricoeur and Schneiders have pointed out. However, we need to complement the spheres of psychology and individualism with a communitarian and praxis-oriented perspective. Understanding also means that a community understands its identity in the process of its participation in realizing the vision of its foundational texts.

Speaking about the reference of literary works, Ricoeur uses the Heideggerian expression "being-in-the-world," but also "world of the text," "proposed world," and "world in front of the text." This apparently deliberate ambiguity calls for some clarifications. The ability of texts to offer their readers new possibilities of being-in-the-world is rooted in their literary capacity of creating their own text-immanent worlds. This can be meant by "the world of the text," which some prefer to call "the world *inside* the text." We would, however, seriously misunderstand Ricoeur, if we were to think that this is all there is to it. The reference of literary works is not purely text-immanent to an imaginary idealistic or utopian world, but also a text-transcendent world, which is a real possibility and which the text has already begun to assist in becoming real.[45] Here again we need to avoid the pitfalls of individualism. For the world of the text to become world before the text, we need the participation of the reading community and its creational and cultural context.

From a theological point of view the proposed future world is an eschatological reality. Text-immanent and text-transcendent dimensions, therefore, need to be complemented by a reality that breaks into our world from outside.

---

45. See Schneiders, *The Revelatory Text*, 167: "It is important to realize that the 'world the text projects' is not the imaginative, fictional world of the work, for example, the land of Oz or the inn to which the Good Samaritan took the victim of the robbers. The fiction is the vehicle that carries the reader into a possible alternative *reality*. This is precisely the dynamic of the parable"; and 168: "To really enter the world before the text . . . is to be changed, to 'come back different,' which is a way of saying that one does not come 'back' at all but moves forward into a newness of being. From the genuine encounter with the true in the beautiful one cannot go home again."

For Christian believers the proposed world is not just a new possibility but a gift from God, not primarily a projection, but the in-breaking of God into the world.[46] The alternative world is not of our own making, but a new creation. It is God's vision or dream for the world. In our eschatological hermeneutics the Holy Spirit has a central place in the process of interpretation.[47] Through the working of the Holy Spirit the in-breaking of God's future, the realization of God's dream for the world is realized. The Holy Spirit enables persons and communities to participate in the realization of this dream. This requires openness and receptiveness.[48] The Holy Spirit thus assures the continuity between the revelatory potential of the ancient text, which as Gadamer's notion of effective historical consciousness has taught us, is never completely past and the in-breaking of God's future.[49]

As previously noted, Ricoeur acknowledges the need for a critique of ide-

46. Elsbernd and Bieringer, *Interpreting the Signs of the Times*, 80: "We see 'signs of the times' as places where the in-breaking of God's future into the world can occur. As such they are constitutively eschatological. The new epochal developments in our world are not just that, but they are at least potentially the tangible representations of how God enters into this world and moves it toward its final destination." See also Hans-Joachim Sander, "Die Zeichen der Zeit erkennen und Gott benennen. Der semiotische Charakter von Theologie," *Theological Quarterly* 182 (2002): 27–40.

47. See Elsbernd and Bieringer, *Interpreting the Signs of the Times*, 55–56. See also the question of Briggs, *Hermeneutics*, 65: "has Ricoeur secularized biblical imagination by turning the power of appropriation of biblical narrative over from the Holy Spirit to the creative imagination?" While this question is to the point, we may not overlook that there was a nascent awareness of the need for the "spirit" in the hermeneutic process in Ricoeur's work, albeit a spirit with a small "s." See Ricoeur, *From Text to Action*, 63, where he says in relation to Dilthey: "But the claim that this hermeneutics of life is history remains incomprehensible. For the passage from psychological to historical understanding assumes that the interconnection of works of life is no longer lived or experienced by anyone. Precisely therein lies its objectivity. Hence we may ask if, in order to grasp the objectifications of life and to treat them as givens, it is not necessary to place speculative idealism at the very roots of life, that is, ultimately to think of life itself as spirit *(Geist)*. Otherwise, how can we understand the fact that it is in art, religion, and philosophy that life expresses itself most completely by objectifying itself most entirely? Is it not because spirit is most at home here?"

48. See Elsbernd and Bieringer, *Interpreting the Signs of the Times*, 82: "Authoritative texts which explicitly deal with the future are threaded through with visions, longings, desires, hope, Spirit and imagination. Raising consciousness to the Spirit's activity, keeping alive longings, invigorating hope, investigating how norms flow from visions and studying their impact on people's lives are constitutive tasks of the normativity of the future approach. Fostering such openness to the in-breaking future is a significant contribution of normativity of the future to social transformation."

49. See the Dogmatic Constitution on Divine Revelation: "But, since Holy Scripture must be read and interpreted according to the same Spirit by whom it was written *(eodem Spiritu quo scripta est)*, no less serious attention must be given to the content and unity of the whole of Scripture if the meaning of the sacred texts is to be correctly worked out" *(DV 12)*. The translation is taken from Walter M. Abbott, *The Documents of Vatican II: All Sixteen Official Texts Promulgated by the Ecumenical Council 1963–1965* (Chicago: Follett, 1966), 120.

ology to be part of interpretation.[50] According to him, critique of ideology is to counteract the prejudices and illusions of the interpreter. From a theological point of view we not only see the need of debunking prejudice and illusions, we also have to take into account the effects of human sinfulness on the endeavour of hermeneutics.[51] Since Scripture is word of God in word of humans, it is to be expected that human sinfulness has left its traces in Scripture.[52] Many pages of Scripture have as their main concern to show how "God writes straight with crooked lines," how despite human sin God succeeds in realizing God's dream for humanity.[53] "In determining what in a text is sin-filled and what is grace-filled we propose the following criterion: inclusivity that makes possible a future for all."[54] This criterion of inclusivity is the content of God's dream for the world. Insofar as this criterion points to a norm and inasmuch as inclusivity is still to be realized, we speak of "normativity of the future."

> By bringing the two seemingly contradictory terms "normativity" and "future" together, we deliberately create a dialectic tension which invites us to reassess the meanings of both terms. In the expression "normativity of the future" both "normativity" and "future" no longer simply carry their usual meaning, but "normativity" gains a dynamic dimension from "future" and the future is reined in by the concreteness of normativity.[55]

In this hermeneutical approach texts that are obviously marred by human sinfulness are not to be banned from the books in which they appear, but the interpreters are challenged to find in these very texts the inclusive vision of the future that is its explicit or implicit horizon.[56]

In this eschatological hermeneutic the task of the reading community with regard to the ancient text is neither to repeat it, to reenact it as if it was a script for their lives, nor is their task to find its timeless core in order to recontextualize it. In a very real sense the past text has passed and cannot be resuscitated. Perhaps one could say that the text does not have intrinsic, but

---

50. Ibid., 8.

51. See Elsbernd and Bieringer, *Interpreting the Signs of the Times*, 45–46.

52. See *Dei Verbum*, 11–12.

53. See, for example, Gn 45:5: "And now do not be distressed or angry with yourselves, because you sold me here; for God sent me before you to preserve life."

54. See Elsbernd and Bieringer, *Interpreting the Signs of the Times*, 60.

55. Ibid., 53–54.

56. For an attempt to apply this approach to John 8:31–59, see Bieringer, Pollefeyt, and Vandecasteele-Vanneuville, "Wrestling with Johannine Anti-Judaism," 28–37.

paradigmatic value. This means that the reading community has the task of reading and internalizing the ancient text as the first chapters of a chain novel of which they have to write the next chapter.

Suppose a novel were being written through the efforts of many authors working serially rather than in collaboration. One received the first three chapters of the novel and had been asked to write the fourth chapter. In order to help create a good novel, it would be necessary to pay careful attention to the plot and to the established characterizations, among other things. . . . In short, when deciding how to continue the novel, one's choice would depend on how well it "fit" with the preceding chapters as a whole *and* on how well it articulated substantial insights, from one's own lights, about human experience.[57]

## Wealth and Poverty in Light of Divine Providence: Reading a Sermon of Theodoret of Cyrus in a Future Perspective

In the last part of this study we shall give an example of our future-oriented hermeneutical approach. We shall use it to interpret the sixth of Theodoret's ten discourses or sermons on divine providence.[58] Born around 386 in Antioch, Theodoret became bishop of Cyrus in Syria in 423.[59] He was a leading theologian of his time and a prolific writer. He was a prominent figure in the Nestorian and Eutychian controversies. His work consists of exegetical, apologetic, and dogmatic writings. His book *De providentia* is an apologetic work written during the so-called cold war years between the councils of Ephesus (431) and Chalcedon (451) and consisting of ten sermons or discourses "probably delivered before a well-educated audience in Antioch."[60] To situate these sermons historically Thomas Halton says:

The great extremes of wealth and poverty that prevailed in Antioch in the time of St. John Chrysostom and Theodoret, the extent of slavery, and manifest wickedness of many of the

57. See Linell E. Cady, "Hermeneutics and Tradition: The Role of the Past in Jurisprudence and Theology," *Harvard Theological Review* 79 (1986): 439–63, esp. 445. See also St. Gregory of Nazianzus, *Select Orations*, FOTC 107, trans. Martha Vinson, (Washington, D.C.: The Catholic University of America Press, 2003), *Oration* 6.9, on 9: "a new chapter has been added to the stories of old."
58. Theodoret of Cyrus, *On Divine Providence*, ACW 49, trans. Thomas Halton (New York: Newman Press, 1988), 73–87: *Discourse* 6 ("That Wealth and Poverty Both Have Their Uses in Life").
59. See ibid., 1, for references to the discussion concerning the date of his birth.
60. István Pásztori-Kupán, *Theodoret of Cyrus*, The Early Church Fathers (London: Routledge, 2006), 18. For a discussion of the date and place, see Theodoret of Cyrus, *On Divine Providence*, 2–3.

prosperous, gave the question of divine providence a special topicality and urgency. The skeptical had a ready breeding ground for arguments denying the existence of providence and the good-living poor were hard put to see how God could be provident and yet allow such anomalies to continue.[61]

This apologetic-homiletic context needs to be kept in mind when interpreting De providentia. Theodoret intends "to convince primarily by arguments from reason and concrete experience."[62] After trying to prove divine providence from the physical order in the first sermons, beginning with the sixth sermon, Theodoret focuses on the moral and social order.

The sixth sermon is entitled "That wealth and poverty both have their uses in life" and tries to convince those who are "complaining about the inequalities of life."[63] Theodoret tries to answer three objections which are formulated as questions: first, "Why are sinners wealthy and the virtuous poor?" (§§ 4–16); second, "Why are riches not distributed among all men equally?" (§§ 17–35); and third, "Why do the majority of the wealthy live immoral lives?" (§§ 36–41).

For our topic it is important to know that by the age of twenty-three Theodoret had given his entire heritage to the poor and become a monk. In Letter 81 to the consul Nomus, Theodoret describes his attitude toward possessions as a bishop:

In so many years I never took an obol or a garment from anyone. Not one belonging to my household ever received a loaf or an egg. I could not endure the thought of possessing anything save the rags I wore. From the revenues of my see I erected public porticoes; I built two large bridges.[64]

We now turn to the first objection which points to the riches and abundant blessings of the sinners and to the poverty of the virtuous as a proof against divine providence. Theodoret answers this objection by focusing on virtue as "the supreme blessing" (§ 6). According to him wealth is "the enemy rather than the friend of virtue" (§ 9). On the other hand, Theodoret claims that "poverty is a help to the good life, and the only sure road to perfect virtue" (§ 11). Nevertheless, Theodoret does not call wealth as intrinsically evil, rather he maintains

61. Halton, *Discourse 6*
62. Ibid., 7.
63. Discourse 6, § 3. We follow the translation and paragraph division of Thomas Halton (see n. 58).
64. SC 98, 196; *NPNF* 3: 277.

"that wealth and poverty, like raw materials or instruments, are given to men by the Creator and that with these, men, like sculptors, either fashion the statue of virtue or strike the figure of evil" (§ 15). However, Theodoret is convinced that virtuous rich people are the exception whereas the virtuous poor are many.

Theodoret's apologetic reflections are driven by the conviction that every person is called to happiness, good fortune, and supreme blessing. This is the inclusive horizon of this text. No one is *a priori* excluded from this blessing, neither poor nor rich persons. Through the acquisition of virtue, it is open to everyone. Theodoret invites his audience neither to scoff at poverty, nor to slander wealth (§ 15). The major problem with Theodoret's answer is that he downplays the seriousness of the problem of poverty that his opponents address. They speak about people who "are short of the necessities of life; . . . live in squalor and dirt; . . . are hounded down to earth, treated with violence, trampled in the mire, and forced to put up with countless hardships of a similar nature" (§ 4). It is not acceptable to romanticize such abject poverty which in the described, extreme forms leaves little room to acquire or practice virtue. Theodoret oversimplifies by opposing poverty and wealth as if there were only one type of poverty and one type of wealth. There are, however, many types of poverty and wealth, and what Theodoret says about "poverty" and "wealth" as such only applies to a few forms of them, namely, extreme wealth and moderate poverty. With his moral Romanization Theodoret runs the risk of legitimizing the social status quo and the excessive wealth of some as well as the abject poverty of others. This tendency reaches its climax in the statement, "What we maintain is that wealth and poverty . . . are given to men by the Creator" (§ 15), thus giving all forms of poverty and wealth divine legitimation. Thus he covers up that some forms of wealth and poverty are the result of injustice, of stealing and robbing in all its overt and covert forms, and thus not God's doing, but the doing of sinful human beings who turn against God and God's desire for all. In this way Theodoret's words are ideological, serving the selfish interests of the powerful. They ignore or deny that true happiness, even if it stems from a virtuous life, needs a certain amount of "wealth" to meet the necessities of life.

Theodoret's answer to the second objection ("Why are riches not distributed among all men equally?") is equally beset with ideologies that defend the rich against the poor. Theodoret's most basic ideological assumption is again that God is the one who allots wealth and poverty. Then the text compares God's allotting wealth and poverty to the body and its many members (see 1 Cor 12:12–30): "I would like to ask a man such as they why has the Creator not given the same faculty to all the members of the body?" The way Theodoret uses the body-members metaphor is highly problematic. While Paul's text is about giving one type of gift to one and another type of gift to another, Theodoret applies the text to God giving gifts (wealth) to some and little or nothing (poverty) to others. The ideological abuse of the metaphor is obvious. In so doing, Theodoret actualizes a dangerous potential of the body-members metaphor. In extra-biblical texts this metaphor was often used to legitimize the status quo of social inequality.[65] Exegetes are, however, convinced that in 1 Cor 12:12–30 Paul avoids this danger.[66] While Paul uses the metaphor to stress the equality of the members, Theodoret uses it to legitimate the inequality.

Theodoret even stretches his argument to the point of claiming that life would be impossible if wealth were distributed equally. To prove his point, Theodoret points to everyday experience as self-evident proof of his position.

> Who would lead the oxen under the yoke to plow, renew the land, sow the seeds, reap the grain when it sprouts in full bloom, deliver it to the thresher and separate the chaff, if poverty did not spur him on to toil? . . . If all were equally well off, nobody would ever be another person's servant. One of two things would happen. Either everybody would eagerly take to every kind of work through necessity, or we would all perish simultaneously through lack of the necessities of life (§§ 22–23).

In this way of reasoning we encounter an author who is totally caught up in the social order of his own time and cannot think beyond it. All his line of reasoning or rather his self-evident experiential wisdom proves that the type of social order Theodoret knows would collapse if there were no poor. But even here it is not abject poverty that is needed but rather unequally distributed wealth where some have more than others, but where no one is suffering from extreme poverty. Indirectly Theodoret admits this by his rhetorical strategy in

---

65. Andreas Lindemann, "Die Kirche als Leib. Beobachtungen zur 'demokratischen' Ekklesiologie bei Paulus," *ZTK* 92 (1995): 140–65, esp. 143: "In den genannten Textbeispielen dient das Bild vom Leib und den Gliedern jedenfalls primär der Bestätigung und Verfestigung einer bestehenden gesellschaftlichen und politischen Ordnung und deren Verteidigung gegen Kritik."

66. See, for example, ibid., 164: "In der paulinischen Rezeption und Explikation des Bildes befinden sich die Glieder des Leibes in einer vollständigen wechselseitigen Abhängigkeit und Gleichheit."

§ 21: "You are very indignant, however, because all men are not swimming in riches, do not live in grand houses." In fact, as we pointed out before, his opponents had not postulated extreme wealth for all, but had castigated the extreme poverty of many. Theodoret continues his line of argument by arguing that God "has given the earth as a foundation common to all" (§ 25). With regard to the basic realities of birth (§§ 26–28) and death (§§ 29–30) all are created equal. While these observations are basically correct, they cover up the inequalities that nevertheless exist between rich and poor in these basic areas of life, and by covering up, they give the impression that after all it is not all that bad that the poor are poor. We only mention one example: infant mortality is much higher and life expectancy is lower among the poor than among the rich.

Despite these ideological distortions, we do not consider Theodoret's sermon hopelessly locked up in its own time and dangerous for the cause of justice. In what follows we shall analyze the world this text projects. Implicitly the text frequently assumes a world in which everyone is well. Even when the text is stating, "If there were equal provision of wealth, the result would be that all would face annihilation" (§ 23), the basic assumption is that no one should be annihilated. The text takes great pains to show that, after all, the poor are well off and in some ways better off than the rich. Even if this runs the risk of romanticizing poverty and of covering up that the poor are getting a bad deal, it nevertheless reinforces that they should all be well.

Another strategy of Theodoret is, as we have seen above, to emphasize that despite the differences in poverty and wealth, everyone is equal when seen from the perspective of creation (§§ 25–30). It will not take much to discover in this basic equality the dream of God for all and to use it against the unequal distribution of poverty and wealth. This will be supported by the realization that the equality with regard to creation is God's doing whereas the unequal wealth distribution is human doing. Here one dimension of the text, namely, the stress on the basic equality, needs to be used to debunk the other, namely, the legitimation of social injustice.[67]

At the end of his sermon, Theodoret briefly answers a third objection,

---

67. See, for example, how "All men are created equal," in the American Declaration of Independence is read, "All are created equal." See Schneiders, *The Revelatory Text*, 175–76.

namely, "Why do the majority of the wealthy live immoral lives?" Here he stresses the free will God has given to all. Here he reiterates that the "Creator . . . placed at man's disposal poverty and riches like raw materials" (§ 37). Here for the first time he shows evidence of his awareness that riches are not simply gifts from God, but can also be the result of increasing them "at the expense of other people's misfortunes" (§ 37). This awareness is in strange tension with all the other places in the sermon where wealth and poverty are "given to men by the Creator" (§ 15) and "everything that happens" is to be regarded "as coming from the providence of God" (§ 42). On the other hand, Theodoret moves away for a moment from romanticizing poverty and admits that some "have learned evil doing while living in poverty" (§ 37). However, immediately after this he adds an extended section in which he tries to illustrate that God "gave health to the poor as their special portion" (§ 38). In a fairy tale-like idealization Theodoret claims that what doctors, medicine, and good living conditions cannot achieve for the rich, divine providence achieves directly for the poor. "Nature satisfies his needs and takes the place of doctors when he is ill" (§ 41). In this way he covers up the fact that many poor people die because of the lack of healthy living conditions and adequate medical care. Once again Theodoret's text transcends its own exclusionary tendencies that belittle the suffering of the poor and make it look as if their plight was not all that bad after all. The self-transcendence of the text is found in the implicit horizon, which unmistakably means that God wants the poor to be blessed with good health and happiness.

The significance of Theodoret's sermon for us today is neither to satisfy our curiosity about the past, nor to provide eternal truths that survive the time-bound dimensions of the text; rather it is in dialoguing with the ancient text of Theodoret that we respect the irreducible otherness we encounter in it, both in terms of its witness of the past and its projection of the future. At the same time, in the dialogue we go beyond reconstructing the past by engaging the future dimension of the text in writing the next chapter of the chain novel. While trying to be very respectful of Theodoret's past text, we as persons from a different age cannot help but bring his text into our own time by interacting with its potential of creating a future in which the dichotomy of abject poor and excessively rich is overcome in a community of love.

## Conclusion

In this paper we wrestled with one of the decisive questions of Christianity today, namely, the role of the past, specifically past texts for the present. We tried to show that the question itself and the way we formulate the question implies important hermeneutic assumptions. We are primarily concerned with the fact that the way the question is formulated excludes the future. It has proved to be rather naïve to think that one can rid the world of evil by severing it from its roots in the past. It is, however, equally naïve to think that one can protect the world from evil to come by fearfully repeating the past. Some hermeneutic approaches seem to think of texts of the past in the same way dualistic anthropology conceives the human person. They assume that at the death of a text, the immortal soul (that is, its eternal truth) survives while the mortal body, the time-bound aspect, is buried and in later centuries the same eternal truth can be reincarnated in new historical contexts. The hermeneutics of Gadamer and Ricoeur have taught us that it is not a matter of reincarnating ancient texts. Interpreting ancient texts is rather more like conceiving new life, that is, composing new texts in which the interpreter plays the role of an author. Interpretation is part of the movement from generation to generation, part of the process of transmitting tradition from age to age. The element of continuity in this movement is the dream of God for an inclusive community mediated by the Holy Spirit. The struggle to understand texts of the past is a commitment to the realization of the promise, hope, and continuing discovery of what it means to be human.

*Pauline Allen*

---

# 2. Challenges in Approaching Patristic Texts from the Perspective of Contemporary Catholic Social Teaching

## Reading Patristic Socio-Ethical Texts

From a twenty-first century perspective, whether one reads patristic socio-ethical texts in the original or in translation, there are difficulties, pitfalls, and caveats. One of the most important facets to take into consideration when reading these texts is their genre. A homily delivered live in the ancient Church, for example, would be a public event, often taking account of audience reaction and of the circumstances behind its delivery (the presence of catechumens, newly baptized, imperial family; commemoration of local saints; recent natural disasters, and so on). Typically homilies on socio-ethical themes were delivered during the periods of fasting and in Easter week to the newly baptized. On the other hand, the "desk-homily" was akin to an academic document and was intended to be read either individually or in a group, which may well have been a kind of preaching to the converted. One immediately recognizable difficulty here is that of distinguishing between the two types of homilies and thus between the two types of audiences or readers.[1]

If we may continue with homiletic texts, a further complication is the

---

1. In general, on preacher and audience from the Greek side, see Mary B. Cunningham and Pauline Allen, eds., *Preacher and Audience: Studies in Early Christian and Byzantine Homiletics*, A New History of the Sermon 1 (Leiden: Brill, 1998), with lit.

large number of homilies that are anonymous or wrongly attributed or pastiches of works of more than one homilist, customized to suit later liturgical developments. A different kind of trap to be guarded against is the reworking of homilies into treatises, such as the homilies of Ambrose on the prophets, originally delivered to well-to-do adult converts from paganism then recycled into tractates on the social ethics of the common man.[2] Once removed from their original liturgical context—the Lenten sermon—these works no longer have the immediacy of live delivery and become subject to the needs of a different, perhaps wider and more reflective audience. This is an example of what Wendy Mayer, in her contribution to this volume, denotes as a secondary audience. Of course we can continue with third-level audiences, who are reached by translation, and fourth-level audiences, among whom we could classify ourselves today.

In a similar way to the live homily, a letter could also be regarded as a public document, being read aloud to the recipient and the recipient's friends on its arrival. Although according to the rules of ancient epistolography, the letter was theoretically limited in length,[3] in practice the crossover from letter to treatise was a relatively easy one, such that Augustine, for example, was sometimes unsure of which was which.[4] Among the letter collections that survive to us we have a huge variation in length, some communications from Innocent I, Basil, Gregory Nazianzen, and Theodoret of Cyrrhus, for example, containing only a few lines, whereas others, among which the famous or infamous Letter to Flavian or *Tome* of Leo I, are the length of a tractate. Also to be included in this latter group is the striking collection of letters which are really treatises emanating from the Pelagians.[5] Exceptional in length is the writing of Salvian of Marseille bearing the title *To the Church or Against Avarice*, pur-

---

2. Marcia L. Colish, *Ambrose's Patriarchs: Ethics for the Common Man* (Notre Dame: University of Notre Dame Press, 2005), 149.

3. On epistolary brevity, see Michaela Zelzer, "Die Briefliteratur. Kommunikation durch Briefe: Ein Gespräch mit Abwesenden," in *Neues Handbuch der Literaturwissenschaft* 4, *Spätantike mit einem Panorama der Byzantinischen Literatur,* ed. Lodewijk J. Engels and Heinz Hofmann (Wiesbaden: AULA Verlag, 1997), 322 and 347. On epistolary theory, see the texts assembled and translated by Abraham J. Malherbe, *Ancient Epistolary Theorists*, Society of Biblical Literature, Sources for Biblical Study 19 (Atlanta: Scholars Press, 1988); additionally, Carol Poster and Linda C. Mitchell, eds., *Letter-Writing Manuals and Instruction from Antiquity: Historical and Bibliographic Studies.* Studies in Rhetoric/Communication (Columbia, N.C.: University of South Carolina Press, 2007).

4. This was the case with Letter 140, which in his *Retractationes* 2.6 he described as a book.

5. See B. R. Rees, *Pelagius: Life and Letters* (Woodbridge, N.Y.: Boydell Press, repr. 1998).

portedly a letter, which runs to about one hundred pages. Both letter and tractate are intended for public consumption, but they have different audiences in
mind, and therefore, theoretically at least, they should employ different styles,
as Gregory Nazianzen explains:

> The measure for letters is what is needed, and the writing should not be too long where there
> is not a great deal of subject-matter, nor too short where there is a great deal. . . . In terms of
> clarity, you need to know this: one should avoid as much as possible what looks like a dis-
> course, and incline rather towards the conversational.[6]

How far Gregory heeded his own advice with regard to letter-writing, however, remains dubious.

Because of the high mortality rate of ancient letters, what has come down
to us is sometimes not representative of a particular author. Thus in the surviving correspondence of Basil of Caesarea, an author well known for his engagement with socio-ethical issues, there are no letters which concentrate on
almsgiving, a constant theme in his other writings.[7] Another problem is that
in a letter-collection spanning the lifetime of the writer we can encounter,
quite naturally, opposing ideas. An example of this is Basil's attitude to almsgiving, discussed by Susan Holman in this volume, where as a young man the
Cappadocian maintains that donors should give directly to the poor (*Ep.* 42),
while later in his episcopal role he declares that almsgiving should be effected
through the intermediary of the bishop (*Ep.* 150).[8] A different problematic in
approaching the epistolary genre is sometimes presented by the rationale of
the compiler of letter-collections. A notable instance of this is the nature of
the letters of Severus, patriarch of Antioch from 512 to 518, almost all of which
are devoted to matters of ecclesiastical discipline or canon law. The pieces are
fewer than 300, whereas we know that the total number of the patriarch's let-

---

6. *Ep.* 51. 2, 4; *Saint Grégoire de Nazianze. Correspondance*, Tome I, Lettres I-C, 2nd ed., ed. and
trans. Paul Gallay (Paris: Les Belles Lettres, 2003), 66–67.

7. See Benoît Gain, *L'église de Cappadoce au IVᵉ siècle d'après la correspondance de Basile de Césarée*
(330–79), Orientalia Christiana Analecta 225 (Rome: Pontificium Institutum Orientale, 1985), 273. Peter
R. L. Brown, *Poverty and Leadership in the Later Roman Empire*, The Menahem Stern Jerusalem Lectures
(Hanover, N.H.: University Press of New England, 2002), 132, n. 56, points out that Basil concentrates in
his letters on widows, a "privileged and influential group among the 'poor.'"

8. On the case of Bishop John Chrysostom's assumption of the supervision of Constantinople's
charitable institutions, see Daniel Caner, *Wandering, Begging Monks: Spiritual Authority and the Promotion of Monasticism in Late Antiquity* (Berkeley: University of California Press, 2002), 197.

ters must have exceeded 3,759. The compiler had an obvious agenda that was not necessarily that of Severus himself.[9]

These socio-ethical patristic texts must also be read with the bias of their authors in mind. The bias might depend on such factors as the genre of the document, the audience, or the extent to which the authors are rigorist (like Jerome, the Pelagians, or Salvian),[10] or liberal (like Clement of Alexandria or Ambrosiaster).[11] The author's philosophical bent also comes into play, the influence of Stoicism on Clement of Alexandria and John Chrysostom, for example, who on occasions put forward the view that all material things in themselves are indifferent (ἀδιάφορα): it is the use to which they are put that determines vice or virtue.[12] Different modes of discourse and their associated forms of rhetoric result in varying socio-ethical exhortations: Basil's concerns when talking about social issues are clearly different from his agenda when discussing monastic ideals. Augustine's handling of poverty in *Ep.* 158, where he disputes the claims of the Pelagians that the wealthy must renounce all their riches if they are to enter the kingdom of heaven, stands in contrast to his emphasis in the *Enarrationes in Psalmos* on the seeming prosperity of the wealthy and evil over against the enduring hardships of the innocent and the just—an emphasis born of the theme of the "suffering of the righteous under the onslaught of the godless, developed in so many psalms."[13]

The background of the audience, too, affected the pitch of the authors' injunctions on socio-ethical themes. Those who had come to Christianity from paganism had a suspicious attitude to almsgiving and a quite different under-

---

9. See further Pauline Allen, "Severus of Antioch and Pastoral Care," in *Prayer and Spirituality in the Early Church* 2, ed. Pauline Allen, Wendy Mayer, and Lawrence Cross (Brisbane: Centre for Early Christian Studies, 1999), 387–400 at 388–89.

10. On the rigorism of Jerome and Salvian, see Eberhard Friedrich Bruck, *Die Kirchenväter und soziales Erbrecht. Wanderungen religiöser Ideen durch die Rechte der östlichen und westlichen Welt* (Berlin: Springer-Verlag, 1956), 77–84 and 105–17, respectively; on the Pelagians, see Rees, *Pelagius. Life and Letters*, passim.

11. On Clement's stance see, for example, L. William Countryman, *The Rich Christian in the Church of the Early Empire: Contradictions and Accommodations*, Texts and Studies in Religion (New York: Edward Mellen Press, 1980), 51–69; on Ambrosiaster, see Sophie Lunn-Rockliffe, "A Pragmatic Approach to Poverty and Riches: Ambrosiaster's *quaestio* 124," in *Poverty in the Roman World*, ed. Margaret Atkins and Robin Osborne (Cambridge: Cambridge University Press, 2006), 115–29 at 129.

12. For the case of Chrysostom, see Wendy Mayer's contribution to this volume.

13. Michael Fiedrowicz, General Introduction to *Expositions of the Psalms 1–32*, WSA III/15, trans. Maria Boulding (Hyde Park, N.Y.: New City Press, 2000), 62.

standing of *philanthropia* from their fellow Christians who had converted from Judaism.[14] Again, geographical differences must be taken into account in our reading. Augustine's representation of poverty, for instance, involving what Richard Finn calls Augustine's foreshortening of the distance between rich and poor,[15] stands in stark contrast to the distancing, vivid pictures of poverty and the lives of the poor in the Cappadocians and John Chrysostom.[16] But further to the east we find yet another approach to poor and sick relief in the very hands-on welfare provided by Rabbula, bishop of Edessa. With regard to the inmates of the leprosarium he had built outside the city, his biographer writes:

> Through the action of his charismatic gifts, he healed the suffering of their diseases; through the word of God he comforted their mind, that it not be choked by distress. How many times, as a comfort to their souls, did he place the peace of a holy kiss upon the rotting lips of men whose bodies were putrefying, and strengthen them so that their mind not lose hope because of the chastisement of God towards them?[17]

Clearly we run the risk of oversimplifying patristic socio-ethical teaching and practice if we do not take such cultural and geographical differences into account.

If we remain with the topic of poverty for a moment, we will realize that there has been a considerable amount of recent scholarly debate on the defi-

---

14. On pagan *philanthropia*, see Arthur Robinson Hands, *Charities and Social Aid in Greece and Rome* (London: Thames and Hudson, 1968); Anneliese R. Parkin, "Poverty in the Early Roman Empire: Ancient and Modern Conceptions and Constructs," (Ph.D. diss., Cambridge, 2001), 114–49; Parkin, "'You do him no service': An Exploration of Pagan Almsgiving," in *Poverty in the Roman World,* ed. Atkins and Osborne, 60–82.

15. "Portraying the Poor: Description of Poverty in Christian Texts from the Late Roman Empire," in *Poverty in the Roman World*, ed. Atkins and Osborne, 130–44.

16. See Michael J. De Vinne, "The Advocacy of Empty Bellies: Episcopal Representations of the Poor in the Late Empire," (Ph.D. diss., Stanford University, 1995); Susan R. Holman, *The Hungry Are Dying: Beggars and Bishops in Roman Cappadocia* (Oxford: Oxford University Press, 2001).

17. On Syriac models of poor relief, see Susan Ashbrook Harvey, "The Holy and the Poor: Models from Early Syriac Christianity," in *Through the Eye of a Needle: Judeo-Christian Roots of Social Welfare,* ed. Emily Albu Hanawalt and Carter Lindberg (Kirksville, Mich.: Thomas Jefferson University Press, 1994), 43–66; Harvey, "Praying Bodies, Bodies at Prayer: Ritual Relations in Early Syriac Christianity," in *Prayer and Spirituality in the Early Church* 4, The Spiritual Life, ed. Wendy Mayer, Pauline Allen, and Lawrence Cross (Strathfield: St. Paul's Publications, 2006), 149–67. The passage quoted is from *Stewards of the Poor: The Man of God, Rabbula, and Hiba in Fifth-Century Edessa,* trans. and intro. Robert Doran (Kalamazoo, Mich: Cistercian Publications, 2006), 101. It cannot be ruled out that kissing the leprous is a topos as it is also said about Basil of Caesarea: see Brown, *Poverty and Leadership,* 40.

nition of the poor in the pagan Roman world as well as in the New Testament and patristic periods. In particular, Steven Friesen's seven-step classification of the scale between very rich and very poor has provoked thought and reaction in Pauline scholarship.[18] According to this classification, in the areas where Paul worked the mega-rich made up 2.8 percent of the population, and most others lived at or below subsistence level. Even using this as a rough guide and transplanting it from the first century, we arrive at the probable conclusion that the majority of the audiences who heard patristic homilies on socio-ethical themes relating to poverty were themselves poor. Terminological descriptions of the poor have been investigated by Evelyne Patlagean on the Greek side and by Denise Grodzynski for Latin authors (limited to the *Codex Theodosianus*).[19] However, Carrié has warned us that a taxonomy of poverty in our period is impossible.[20]

From the modern point of view there are certain limitations in using patristic socio-ethical texts: for example, these people thought within the parameters of the Christian οἰκουμένη, often bound together by mutual almsgiving, rather than thinking globally—indeed it would be anachronistic on our part to expect otherwise—and the Fathers, themselves more often than not from the upper echelon, had no intention of changing the status quo.[21] For example, what we now call human rights were not an issue for them.[22] Only some monastics and a few rigorists upheld the dominical command to sell all and give to the poor, and we must not lose sight of the fact that some at least

18. Steven J. Friesen, "Poverty in Pauline Studies: Beyond the So-Called New Consensus," *Journal for the Study of the New Testament* 26.3 (2004): 323–61. Rejoinders by John Barclay, "Poverty in Pauline Studies: A Response to Steven Friesen," ibid., 363–66; Peter Oakes, "Constructing Poverty Scales for Graeco-Roman Society: A Response to Steven Friesen's 'Poverty in Pauline Studies,'" ibid., 367–71.

19. Evelyne Patlagean, *Pauvreté économique et pauvreté sociale à Byzance 4ᵉ–7ᵉ siècles* (Paris: Mouton, 1977); Denise Grodzynski, "Pauvres et indigents, vils et plebeiens. (Une étude terminologique sur le vocabulaire des petites gens dans le Code Théodosien)," *Studia et documenta historiae et iuris* (Rome: Apollinaris, 1987), 140–218.

20. Jean-Michel Carrié, "*Nil habens praeter quod ipso die vestiebatur.* Comment définir le seuil de pauvreté à Rome?" in Consuetudinis amor: *fragments d'histoire romaine (IIᵉ–VIᵉ siècles) offerts à Jean-Pierre Callu*, ed. François Chausson and Étienne Wolff (Rome: L'Erma di Bretschneider, 2003), 71–102 at 75.

21. On this point see, for example, Bruck, *Kirchenväter und soziales Erbrecht*, 2; Jean Gribomont, "Un aristocrate révolutionnaire, évêque et moine: s. Basile," *Augustinianum* 17 (1977): 79–191 at 191: "malgré sa conversion révolutionnaire, Basile était resté de bon sang aristocratique et ecclésial"; Holman, *The Hungry Are Dying*, 32.

22. See Susan R. Holman, "The Entitled Poor: Human Rights Language in the Cappadocians," *Pro Ecclesia* 9.4 (2000): 476–88.

of those conjunctural poor who embraced voluntary poverty in a monastic setting—in a haven of stabilized poverty—ended up better off than they were formerly.[23] For our patristic authors and their audiences the poor were mostly an instrument for the salvation of the rich and most of them would not have understood the charity vs. justice debate of the nineteenth and twentieth centuries, a debate recently rehearsed in *Deus caritas est* (25a).[24]

## Patristic Nexus between Property, the Common Good, and Salvation

Most of the Fathers regarded property as they did usury and poverty— part of the social fabric of their times. Property, of course, included not only real estate but also assets such as cash, precious objects, and slaves. Just as pagans looked back to a Golden Age in which possessions were held in common, so, too, many early Christians regarded private property as the result of Adam's fall.[25] Before this, a universal common good obtained, which was destroyed by avarice and cupidity. Writers in the patristic period, with the exception of rigorists and those considered nonorthodox, such as Manichaeans and Pelagians, seem to have accepted the irreversibility of this postlapsarian situation, such that there was no general injunction to surrender property and no call for enforced common sharing. The vestigial and subliminal Christian idea, derived from Judaism but also mediated by Stoics like Seneca,[26] that everything in the

23. The words are those of Evelyne Patlagean, "The poor," in *The Byzantines,* ed. Guglielmo Cavallo (Chicago: University of Chicago Press, 1997), 15–42 at 22.

24. Summed up recently by Lucy Grig, "Throwing parties for the poor: poverty and splendour in the late antique church," in *Poverty in the Roman World,* ed. Atkins and Osborne, 145–61 at 154: "While the poor clearly needed the charity of the rich in order to survive, the rich needed the poor for the good of their souls."

25. On attitudes to property in the Fathers generally, see Stanislas Giet, "La doctrine de l'appropriation des biens chez quelques-uns des pères," *Recherches de science religieuse* 35 (1948): 55–91; D. J. MacQueen, "St. Augustine's Concept of Property Ownership," *Recherches Augustiniennes* 8 (1972): 187–229 (including a good discussion of pagan and early Christian views); Hengel, *Property and Riches*; Robert M. Grant, *Early Christianity and Society: Seven Studies* (London: Collins, 1978), ch. 5, 96–123; Pauline Allen, Bronwen Neil, and Wendy Meyer, *Preaching Poverty in Late Antiquity: Perceptions and Realities,* Arbeiten zur Kirchen und Theologiegeschichte 28 (Leipzig: Evangelische Verlagsanstalt, 2009); Countryman, *The Rich Christian*; Brian Matz, in this volume.

26. On Seneca's view of post-Golden Age society, see Peter Garnsey, "The Originality and Origins of Anonymus, *De Divitiis,*" in *From Rome to Constantinople: Studies in Honour of Averil Cameron*, Late Antique History and Religion 1, ed. Hagit Amirav and Bas ter Haar Romeny (Leuven: Peeters, 2007), 29–45 at 34.

beginning belonged to God[27] has implications for sharing between the haves and the have-nots, as can be seen in passages like the following from Ambrose: "since God gave the world to all, it is an act of strict justice that the rich should support the poor with some portion of what was intended for humanity as a whole."[28] Similarly Gregory Nazianzen believed that good works such as almsgiving helped to restore the original idyllic state,[29] and Augustine reminds his hearers that, when they give to the poor, they are giving what is God's rather than what is their own.[30]

While the primitive church, particularly in Jerusalem, had negative attitudes towards riches because of the perceived imminence of the παρουσία,[31] two of the earliest writers on the topic of property and wealth, Clement of Alexandria and Hermas, were writing or speaking to well-to-do audiences, so that we can expect their counsel to be a conservative one.[32] We have to remember, in Susan Holman's words, that "[s]ocial inequality was not only understood, but essential for the system to work."[33] This held even within the monastic system, to judge by the advice given by Augustine to female monastics, who are informed that it is permissible for noble women to have finer food, clothing, and bedding and that the poorer women in the monastery should not be disturbed at this because the wealthy women are being tolerated, not honored. "Otherwise," writes the bishop of Hippo, "there might result the detestable perversity that in the monastery where, as far as possible, wealthy ladies become working women, poor women become dainty and delicate ladies."[34] The static nature of this society with regard to poverty and wealth is borne out by passages in Theo-

---

27. On this see MacQueen, "St Augustine's Concept of Property Ownership," 196.

28. *Exp. in Ps. 118, sermo* 8, 22: PL 15, 1372.        29. *Hom.* 14.25.

30. *Sermo* 50.1.2.

31. See further Grant, *Early Christianity and Society*, 122–23.

32. On Clement, see Countryman, *The Rich Christian*, 47–69; on Hermas, see Carolyn Osiek, *Rich and Poor in the* Shepherd of Hermas: *An Exegetical-Social Investigation*, The Catholic Biblical Quarterly Monograph Series 15 (Washington, D.C.: The Catholic Biblical Association of America, 1983), 57, and Helen Rhee in this volume.

33. *The Hungry Are Dying*, 32. Peter Brown, *Poverty and Leadership*, 87, talks of a "frank acknowledgement of social asymmetry" in the later Roman empire. On the Cappadocians, see Mary Sheather, "Pronouncements of the Cappadocians on Issues of Poverty and Wealth," in *Prayer and Spirituality in the Early Church* 1, ed. Pauline Allen, Raymond Canning, and Lawrence Cross, with B. Janelle Caiger (Everton Park: Centre for Early Christian Studies, 1998), 375–92 at 376: the Cappadocians "initiated no wide-ranging social upheavals, and would quite possibly have been alarmed had their counsel been adopted by their audience in any comprehensive fashion."

34. Augustine, *Ep.* 211.9; WSA *Letters* 4, trans. Roland Teske (Hyde Park, N.Y., 2005), 23.

doret's work *On Providence*, where he defends inequality of wealth as being the basis of a sound economy in society, maintaining that poverty has many advantages, such as good health and an ability to withstand illness that are superior to those of the rich.[35] There were after all legitimate ways of acquiring property, although Clement suggests that it is best done by inheritance or before conversion.[36] The rigorist author of *De divitiis*, on the other hand, claims that it is avaricious not only to acquire wealth but also to maintain or increase it.[37] Nonetheless, by law one could legitimately acquire property by inheritance, gift, commerce, just conquest, and lawful possession, and none of the Fathers could properly dispute this.[38] Since the status quo was not challenged, it then remained to speak of the right attitude to property, and from Clement onwards we find an emphasis on the detachment of the owner, not of course an exclusively Christian stance with regard to wealth.

An important part of a property portfolio in classical and Christian antiquity was composed of household slaves, who were as essential to the status quo as were the poor.[39] Jean-Michel Carrié rightly points out that slavery and poverty are realities situated on completely different planes and that there is no equivalence between them.[40] With regard to the reformer Basil of Caesarea, Anthony Meredith demonstrates that despite references to slaves and their "sorry condition" in Basil's works there is no call for the abolition of slavery, even though the bishop of Caesarea, like Augustine of Hippo, regarded the institution as the result of the fall.[41] Meredith also notes that even though Gregory of Nyssa delivers a stinging attack on slavery, he "never becomes socially divisive enough as to recommend a total end to the practice."[42] Here G. E. M.

---

35. *De providenta orationes x* (*CPG* 6211), here *Oratio* 6; PG 83, 643–66.

36. *Quis dives salvetur* 26. Cf. later Augustine, *Sermo* 113.4, where it is said that wealth is not intrinsically evil and that inherited wealth or what is accumulated by dint of hard work is also legitimate.

37. E.g., 2, 3, and 4.3. See Garnsey, "Originality and Origins," 37.

38. See MacQueen, "St. Augustine's Concept of Property Ownership," 195, for more details.

39. In general on slavery, see Peter Garnsey, *Ideas of Slavery from Aristotle to Augustine* (Cambridge: Cambridge University Press, 1996) and the forthcoming study by Noel Lenski. See also Peter Van Nuffelen in this volume.

40. "*Nil habens*," 74.

41. "The Three Cappadocians on Beneficence: A Key to Their Audiences," in *Preacher and Audience*, ed. Cunningham and Allen, 89–104 at 94–95 and 102. On Augustine's views see Richard Klein, *Die Sklaverei in der Sicht der Bischöfe Ambrosius und Augustin*, Forschungen zur antiken Sklaverei 20 (Stuttgart: Steiner-Verlag, 1988).

42. Greg. Nyss, *Hom. 4 in Eccles.*, GNO 5, 334–53; Meredith, "The Three Cappadocians," 102. See

de Ste. Croix, approaching the topic from a Marxist perspective, claims in regard to the Pauline dictum "neither slave nor free" that in early Christianity such statements are true "in a *strictly spiritual sense*; the equality exists 'in the sight of God' and has no relation to temporal affairs."[43] However, we have at least one example where slavery is depicted as an actual temporal good. Much as he had defended the providentially ordained inequality between rich and poor, in an extended treatment of the division between free and slave which allegedly occurred after the Flood, Theodoret of Cyrrhus is at pains to point out that the slave, although a slave in body, is free from worries like the failure of crops, creditors, tax-collectors, and jury service. He sums up, in a vein that modern readers would find offensive:[44]

You consider only the slavery of this man; you do not consider his health. You see the work, but not the recompense involved; you complain of toil, but forget the happiness of a carefree life. You criticize his lowly state, but fail to notice how soundly he sleeps. You should see from that the providence of God and witness the equity of His rule. When sin necessitated the division of men into rulers and slaves, God joined cares to responsibility, allotting to the master sleepless nights and more than his share of sickness, whereas the slave received better health, greater zest for his food, pleasant and longer sleep calculated to free his body from fatigue and make it stronger for the toils of the morrow.[45]

We might add that nowhere in patristic socio-ethical writings do we encounter exhortations to divest oneself of one's slaves. On the contrary, in Peter Brown's words, "Christians defended with the greatest tenacity the distinction between the free and the unfree."[46]

One aspect of the patristic nexus between property, the common good, and salvation which has not found an echo in CST is the notion of a "share for the soul," a "share for the poor," or a "share for Christ." Like Clement of Alexandria, Basil of Caesarea recognized that the number of Christians who would

---

the detailed study of Richard Klein, *Die Haltung der kappadokischen Kirchenväter Basilius von Caesarea, Gregor von Nazianz und Gregor von Nyssa zur Sklaverei*, Forschungen zur antiken Sklaverei 32 (Stuttgart: Steiner-Verlag, 1999).

43. "Early Christian Attitudes to Property and Slavery," in *Church, Society and Politics*, Papers read at the Thirteenth Summer Meeting and the Fourteenth Winter Meeting of the Ecclesiastical History Society, Studies in Church History 12, ed. D. Baker (Oxford: Basil Blackwell, 1975), 1–38 at 19.

44. See, for example, the reactions of Giet, "La doctrine de l'appropriation des biens," 83–84.

45. *De providentia orationes x*, here *Oratio* 7.24; PG 83, 680A–C; *Theodoret of Cyrus on Divine Providence*, Ancient Christian Writers 49, trans. Thomas Halton (New York: Newman Press, 1988), 96.

46. *Poverty and Leadership*, 62.

give all their possessions to the poor in one, single act of self-emptying in order to be perfect was destined to remain very limited, whereas progressive or
delayed almsgiving was possible for everyone who had an interest in the salvation of their soul. Hence Basil's advice that people should give their soul the
first part of their inheritance as being the first-born, then divide the rest among
their children.[47] This idea was developed by Gregory of Nyssa into a "share for
the poor" and by John Chrysostom more tellingly still into a "share for Christ."
Nor were notions such as these confined to the East, for we find Jerome coun-
seling the childless young widow Furia to make Christ her sole heir,[48] and Augustine giving expansive advice on adding one "child" to a will.[49] Shares for the
soul, the poor, or Christ were in fact so commonplace that they had to be regulated by the *Codex Iustinianus* (1.2.25[26]): in wills where Christ was the total
or partial heir, the church or area in which the deceased lived was to be regarded as the heir and the bishop called on to collect the inheritance.[50] It is strange
that the popularity of these "shares," which endured into the Middle Ages in
many European countries, has not been recognized and taken up by CST.

## Concluding Observations

I have already spoken of the danger of anachronistic treatment of patristic socio-ethical texts. In our desire to link past with present we must firstly understand the contexts of their statements and secondly resist the temptation to wrest the Fathers' *dicta* from these contexts in order to ornament
contemporary socio-ethical debates with appeals to tradition that under these
circumstances cannot avoid being superficial and ill-considered.[51] From a pa-

---

47. *In divites* 7. Cf. Bruck, *Kirchenväter und soziales Erbrecht*, 6–7, and Holman, *The Hungry Are Dying*, 14.

48. *Ep.* 54.

49. *Sermo* 86.10–12.

50. See further Bruck, *Kirchenväter und soziales Erbrecht*, 120–21.

51. On this see, for example, Martin Hengel, *Property and Riches in the Early Church. Aspects of a Social History of Early Christianity* (Philadelphia: Fortress Press, 1974), 84: "Because they come from such a different situation, the various statements made in early Christianity can only be applied with many qualifications to our industrial society and the problems of possessions which so oppress us today." Also Countryman, *The Rich Christian*, 17: "we cannot hope to detach the social teachings of early Christian writers from their original social setting and still find them fully intelligible eighteen centuries later in a very different social milieu."

tristic point of view these are the most obvious shortcomings of all CST documents.

It is easy to spot some significant patristic omissions in CST documents: Origen, Jerome, Cyril of Alexandria, Maximus the Confessor, and John Damascene. The compilers may have considered Origen's reputation to be tarnished, although he has many sensible things to say on socio-ethical issues. The omission of Jerome, a Doctor of the Church, is less easy to explain, but admittedly he may have been subsumed into vague references to "Church Fathers." Perhaps the compilers did not like his rigorist stance. And how to account for the omission of the post-Chalcedonian touchstone of orthodoxy in both East and West, Cyril of Alexandria, particularly in view of the promulgation of the ecumenical document *Ut unum sint* by John Paul II in 1995? Again, were Maximus the Confessor and John Damascene considered to be outside patristic chronological parameters despite their first-rate importance as eastern theologians? Maximus's work, *The 400 Chapters on Love*, which reinforced in magisterial fashion the New Testament nexus between charity and love and was extremely influential in the later development of philanthropic ideals, is a sorry omission.[52]

Another missed chance relates to the Fathers' condemnations of usury.[53] In CST there are only two references to lending against interest, a practice nowadays intrinsic to the economics of individual, corporation, and state. In *Rerum novarum* 2 Leo XIII roundly condemned usury as "rapacious" and the practice of "avaricious and grasping men," and in *Centesimus annus* 35 John Paul II referred to the "largely unsolved problem of the foreign debt of the poorer countries," calling for "ways to lighten, defer or even cancel the debt," a sentiment for which he or his compilers could have had recourse to many a patristic passage, but did not.[54]

Somewhat more complicated is the work of detecting the rationale be-

---

52. On the influence of this work, see Judith Herrin, "Ideals of Charity, Realities of Welfare: The Philanthropic Activity of the Byzantine Church," in *Church and People in Byzantium*, Society for the Promotion of Byzantine Studies Twentieth Spring Symposium of Byzantine Studies, Manchester 1986, ed. Rosemary Morris (Birmingham: Centre for Byzantine, Ottoman, and Modern Greek Studies, 1990), 151–64 at 162–63 with n. 35 (lit.).

53. See in detail Brenda Ihssen's chapter in this volume.

54. See David J. O'Brien and Thomas A. Shannon, eds., *Catholic Social Thought: The Documentary Heritage* (Maryknoll, N.Y.: Orbis Books, 1998), 15 and 466, respectively.

hind the selective citation or under-citation of patristic authors' works in CST documents. Clement of Alexandria's *Quis dives salvetur*, the first patristic work dedicated systematically to the topic of wealth and salvation,[55] is cited only once.[56] Cyprian's *De opere et eleemosynis*, also an early Christian classic of socio-ethical teaching, is cited just once as well, together with two other references to the works of the bishop of Carthage, and this despite the great imbalance in the CST documents in favour of Latin writers. Perhaps the later interpretation of *De opere et eleemosynis* as a doctrine of salvation by works militated against systematic use of this treatise in CST.[57] Similarly from the eight citations of the works of Ambrose, only two derive from *De officiis* and none at all from his *De Tobia*, also a classic on the topic of social ethics devoted to a denunciation of usury, or from his treatises on the patriarchs, recently described as the first and only patristic ethics for the common man, in which Ambrose demonstrated himself as "a teacher of moderation for the many, and not merely as a teacher of asceticism for the few"—surely another regrettable omission in a CST document.[58]

At best this methodology is whimsical. It is displayed even in *Deus caritas est*, perhaps the most learned CST document. Not only do the documents betray little regard for reading ancient texts in their proper context, but also they either completely or partly neglect some of the most important patristic works on socio-ethical themes, which one would have thought were essential for the construction of an authentic CST. This is a mechanistic approach that does not seem to have a particular audience in mind, and certainly not an audience familiar with patristic literature. At the Leuven expert seminar in September 2006 from which this present volume arose my colleague Boudewijn Dehandschutter, with his customary laconic penetration of academic issues, pointed out that one of the guiding principles of documents of CST was that of *doctrina constans*, which in its turn necessitated the constant repetition in the documents of the same patristic evidence, whether apposite or not. In this as in other regards the CST documents do a disservice to patristic scholarship, a disservice which one would gratefully see remedied out of the results of this volume.

---

55. See Countryman, *The Rich Christian*, 47–48, who describes the work as the only "clear and connected" early account we have of ideas of wealth.

56. ComCST329.

57. See further Countryman, *The Rich Christian*, 197.

58. Colish, *Ambrose's Patriarchs*, 158.

# PART II

# CONTEXTS FOR PATRISTIC
# SOCIO-ETHICAL TEXTS

*Peter Van Nuffelen*

# 3. Social Ethics and Moral Discourse in Late Antiquity

The term "patristic social ethics" may convey the impression that the Church Fathers—already an immensely varied group of individuals covering at least half a millennium—shared a number of systematic views on social issues. It seems to suggest that they held a set of norms and rules, which can be reconstructed through the careful reading of their sermons, letters, and dogmatic works. On such an understanding, patristic teaching on property, poverty, or usury, takes the form of a coherent, discrete body of doctrines. Such an approach might work well for theological topics, for example, the interpretation of the Trinity—although one should not forget the impact of polemic in shaping theological doctrine of the ancient church. But it turns out to be much more problematic in the field of "social ethics." On a conceptual level, "social ethics" is a modern concern (for the Catholic Church one of the late nineteenth century), which links social justice to the structure of society and puts the pair at the heart of political thought. In the ancient world, social justice hardly played a role in ethics, which was rather concerned with how the individual could achieve happiness. This radical difference in perspective obviously does not imply that one cannot study how social issues were dealt with within the context of an ethics that focused on the individual pursuit of happiness, but it entails that such issues were dealt with in a fundamentally different way. The answer of ancient ethics to slavery tends to be the freedom of the soul, not social change.[1]

1. See Peter Garnsey, *Ideas of Slavery from Aristotle to Augustine* (Cambridge: Cambridge Univer-

An approach that projects a modern understanding of social ethics onto late antiquity will encounter another, much more serious problem. Its supposition seems to be that a single doctrine can be reconstructed from various patristic texts. But Church Fathers rarely or never wrote anything that could be termed a systematic, abstract ethical treatise. Social issues are usually addressed in sermons, which are part of a specific performative context. Sermons aim at changing the behaviour of a particular audience by instructing them; they are rarely systematic introductions to doctrine—with the exception of "theological orations" such as those of Gregory of Nazianzus. As such, they engage closely (we can presume) with the social context of the audience and its expectations. The precise nature of the "poor," for example, differs from sermon to sermon, ranging from the utterly destitute to the less well off, depending on the circumstances the speech was held in.[2] It is hazardous to reconstruct a coherent doctrine from texts that engage to such a degree with specific circumstances.

Another possible pitfall of such an approach is that it tends to assume the unique nature of Christian ethics in contrast with its "pagan" surroundings. When positing the existence of a specifically Christian doctrine on social ethics, one may be inclined to contrast it with the ideas found in classical writings. The impact of classical rhetoric on how a preacher presented his argument is then seen as rather a matter of form than of substance.[3] Apart from the fact that form and substance are not as easily separable as one might imagine, such a perspective buys into the Christian tendency to stress its own originality and to contrast its teachings with that of the "pagans." In reality, however, both interacted to a high degree.

Most scholars working on these topics are, in some way or another, aware of these problems, and will take care to contextualise their sources by setting them against the social background of the city and the specific circumstances in which the sermon was held. This paper proposes a different form of contextualisation. It proposes to sketch the discursive context of a single topic, the

---

sity Press, 1997). The difference between the modern and ancient view on ethics is explored by Bernard Williams, *Ethics and the Limits of Philosophy* (London: Fontana, 1985).

2. See Peter Brown, *Poverty and Leadership in the Later Roman Empire* (Hanover, N.H.: The University Press of New England, 2002), 46–54.

3. See M. Vinson, trans., *St. Gregory of Nazianzus: Select Orations* (Washington, D.C.: The Catholic University of America Press, 2003), xix–xxii, on the rhetorical nature of Gregory of Nazianzus's Oration 14.

care for the poor. It will analyse social ethics in late antiquity not as a series of norms and rules, but as a set of moral discourses that focus on concerns shared across social, political, and religious boundaries. It works on the assumption that sermons and speeches are not merely determined by a social context or by the restrictions of the literary genre and religious doctrine but that they are part of a moral discourse that determines the selection of topics that will be treated. On such a reading, a *topos* is not merely determined by the strictures of the panegyrical handbook, but is also used to exemplify a moral concern.

Such a reading has various advantages. It does not put a systematic doctrine at the heart of the discourse; rather, the doctrine focuses on a general moral concern.[4] It avoids the neat but misleading dichotomy between Christian and pagan ethics, and assumes on the contrary that Christians and pagans alike engaged with this shared concern, or, to put it differently and more precisely: that it surfaced in ecclesiastical as well as secular contexts. The form a particular discourse takes may differ depending on the precise context, but in the end these discourses all share a common focal point. In an earlier paper, for example, I have argued that it is possible to reconstruct a late antique discourse on the "unstained rule," which focused on the idea that it was inappropriate for a ruler to shed blood in times of peace. This expressed itself most clearly in recurring praise for emperors who refrained from capital punishment. One easily recognises in this the confluence of the traditional imperial concept of clemency and the Christian interdiction of murder. This discourse was neither single nor static. It was composed of various discourses that engaged in an original way with the shared concern that makes up the general discourse: the form each of them took depended on the specific context. Moreover, with the passing of time, the discourse started to cover a much wider array of subjects. It started out with a clear focus on capital punishment, but soon it included gladiator games as well, and in the fifth century *venationes*, in which the hunters could be hurt by the wild beasts in the arena, were also seen as incompatible with the ideal of an unstained rule.[5]

---

4. The reader may notice the common slippage in terminology in this sort of analysis: the term "discourse" may refer to the general discourse made up of all individual discourses or to an individual discourse.

5. Peter Van Nuffelen, "The Unstained Rule of Theodosius II: A Late Antique Panegyrical Topos and Moral Concern," in *Imago Virtutis,* Collection des Études classiques, ed. T. Van Houdt, et al. (Leuven: Peeters, 2004), 229–56.

I will illustrate these methodological considerations by discussing a topic that stood at the heart of Christian self-understanding in late antiquity and which has recently received much attention: the care for the poor.[6] The Christian discourse on poverty has been seen as reflecting the weakening of the classical civic sense of community, which expressed itself in elitist munificence towards the city and its institutions.[7] Peter Brown has identified it as a catalyst for the change from a classical to a medieval society.[8] The discourse of *liberalitas* and *euergesia* was to be replaced by one that focussed on Christian *caritas*. Similar arguments have been made for the transformation of the ideal of *liberalitas* as found in panegyric. On a theoretical level, *liberalitas* and *caritas* seems each other's opposite. The former is an expression of the virtue of the giver, who lavishes his generosity on his peers and friends. But it can also designate special measures to help individuals or cities which have been ravaged by a catastrophe, so as that they can return to their former standard of living.[9] Charity, on the contrary, is determined by the needs of the poor. Every other form of giving is pure vanity, according to Lactantius.[10] One gives for Christ, not for one's own glory, as Jerome stressed.[11] In late antiquity, these discourses encounter one another on the public stage. In the last pages of his study on *liberalitas principis*, H. Kloft suggested that from the fourth century onwards, Christian *caritas* profoundly influenced the traditional ideal of *lib-*

6. See Valerio Neri, *I marginali nell'occidente tardoantico: poveri, infames e criminali nella nascente società cristiana* (Bari: Edipuglia, 1998); Susan Holman, *The Hungry Are Dying: Beggars and Bishops in Roman Cappadocia* (Oxford: Oxford University Press, 2001); Brown, *Poverty and Leadership*; Pascal-Grégoire Delage, ed., *Les pères de l'Eglise et la voix des pauvres* (La Rochelle: Association Histoire et Culture, 2006); Richard D. Finn, *Almsgiving in the Later Roman Empire: Christian Promotion and Practice (313–450)* (Oxford: Oxford University Press, 2006); Christel Freu, *Les figures du pauvre dans les sources italiennes de l'antiquité tardive* (Paris: De Boccard, 2007). A fundamental study remains Evelyne Patlagean, *Pauvreté économique et pauvreté sociale à Byzance, 4e–7e siècles* (Paris: Mouton, 1977).

7. See Paul Veyne, *Le pain et le cirque* (Paris: Seuil, 1976), and Patlagean, *Pauvreté économique*. Brown, *Poverty and Leadership*, 7–8, stresses the active role played by the Christian discourse in this process.

8. Brown, *Poverty and Leadership*. For some reflections on Brown's model, see Wendy Mayer, "Poverty and Society in the World of John Chrysostom," in *Social and Political Life in Late Antiquity*, ed. W. Bowden, A. Gutterdige, and C. Machado (Leiden: Brill, 2006), 465–84, 482–83.

9. Hans Kloft, *Liberalitas principis. Herkunft und Bedeutung. Studien zur Prinzipatsideologie* (Cologne: Böhlau, 1970), 173–78; C. E. Manning, "Liberalitas—The Decline and Rehabilitation of a Virtue," *Greece and Rome* 32 (1985): 73–85, 73–74.

10. Lactantius, *Institutiones divinae* 6.11.6–8.

11. Jerome contrasts pagans, who give for their own glory, and Christians: *Breviarium in psalmos* 133 PL 26.1224. Cf. Wolfgang Schwer, "Armenpflege," *Reallexicon für Antike und Christentum* 1 (1950): 689–98, 694.

*eralitas.*[12] The care for the poor became a public virtue, part of the classical *liberalitas.* A new and unified discourse was formed, integrating *caritas* and *liberalitas,* to become the ideal to which emperors, governors and bishops alike had to conform.[13] As such, it is a good example of how an ecclesiastical discourse came to dominate the entire society.[14]

I will argue that this picture needs to be refined. Focussing my attention on the discourse on imperial munificence in late antiquity, I will suggest that this is incorrectly characterised as either dominated by *caritas* or a blend of charity and *liberalitas.* Although both can be found, classical ideas of *liberalitas* also remained alive right to the end of antiquity. A simple analysis, which considers that the public discourse on munificence was transformed in late antiquity from a classical one, with a stress on *liberalitas,* to a Christian one, with a stress on care for the poor, will not do. Rather, both *liberalitas* and *caritas* were available as modes of discourse, which were used depending on specific circumstances. Nevertheless, *caritas* and *liberalitas* are part of a shared moral discourse that, as I will suggest, focussed on care for community and the moral qualities of the giver.

## "The emperor's most beautiful garb"

Scanning through late antique panegyrics, it becomes clear that the classical idea of *liberalitas* with its focus on the remission of taxes and gifts to friends continues to exist in an unchanged form.[15] This is in particular true for texts from the fourth century, such as the *panegyrici latini*[16] and Themistius.[17] In his panegyrics for Constantius II and Eusebia, Julien equally steers clear of Christian elements.[18] A brief reference to a poor man protected from

---

12. He mainly draws on Eusebius, *Life of Constantine* 1.43, 3.58, 4.44.

13. Kloft, *Liberalitas principis,* 171–80; Brown, *Poverty and Leadership,* 80–84.

14. On this evolution, see in general Averil Cameron, *Christianity and the Rhetoric of Empire: The Development of Christian Discourse* (Berkeley: University of California Press, 1991).

15. This part is a slightly reworked version of my paper, "Le plus beau vêtement pour un empereur. L'amour des pauvres et panégyrique dans l'Antiquité tardive," *Les pères de l'Église et la voix des pauvres,* ed. P.-G. Delage (La Rochelle: Association Histoire et culture, 2006), 163–83. I thank the editor for his kind permission to reuse the material.

16. M. Mause, *Die Darstellung des Kaisers in der lateinischen Panegyrik* (Stuttgart: Steiner, 1994), 175.

17. Themistius, *Oration* 1.17b–18a, 3.46d–48a, 4.58bd, 8.112a–115d, 18.220c–223b, 19.229b. Cf. L. J. Daly, "Themistius' Concept of Philanthropy," *Byzantion* 45 (1975): 22–40.

18. Julian, *Oration* 1.6, 1.11, 1.35–36, 2.8, 2.19.

the greedy rich by imperial justice is nothing but a traditional trope.[19] Ambrose, a Christian bishop, merely praises Valentinian II for not raising any new taxes.[20] Alluding in various instances to imperial *benificia*,[21] Symmachus does refer once to poverty, but his eighth discourse is actually a letter of recommendation for an impoverished aristocrat. In passages dedicated to imperial *liberalitas*, Claudian occasionally refers to the "poor," but these are not the needy but the less rich.[22]

These are all texts from the fourth or early fifth century, which seems to confirm Peter Brown's argument that the Christian discourse only started to dominate Roman society from the end of the fourth century onwards.[23] There is obviously truth in his point: a Christian stress on charity and the poor comes much more to the fore in panegyrics from the fifth century onwards. Nevertheless, later authors can still draw on the classical ideas and concepts, as we see in Ennodius's praise of Theodoric (474–526).[24] Moreover, a Christianising vocabulary may actually hide classical concepts, as will see shortly. Before we can fully understand such "survivals," I will illustrate the various forms that the "Christianised" ideal of care for the poor could take by confronting two Justinianic texts: Procopius's *Secret History* and Agapetus's *Ekthesis*.

Greed, a vice despised as much by Christians as by pagans, is one of the red threads that runs through the *Secret History* (traditionally dated to 550). Introduced as a motive for Belisarius' actions in chapter 5 (2–4), it is depicted in the next chapter by Procopius as the driving force of Justinian's actions and linked to that other supreme injustice, murder: "For he used to proceed with the lightest of hearts to the unjust murder of men and the seizure of other men's money, and for him it was nothing that countless thousands of men should have been destroyed, though they had given him no grievance." "Some he killed without any just cause, while others he left in the grip of poverty, making them more wretched than those who died, so that they implored him to resolve their present misery by a most pitiable death. In some cases, however, he destroyed both property and life" (6.20, 24).[25] Lacking in all the du-

---

19. Julian, *Oration* 3.31.                    20. Ambrose, *De obitu Valentiniani* 21.

21. Symmachus, *Oration* 1.11, 4.2.

22. Claudian, *Probus* 42–54, *On the fourth consulship of Honorius* 412–17, *On the sixth consulship of Honorius* 60–62.

23. Brown, *Poverty and Leadership*, 7.                    24. Ennodius, *Panegyric of Theoderic*, 19, 57, 74.

25. All translations are by H. B. Dewing, *Procopius. The Anecdota or Secret History* (London: William Heinemann, 1935).

ties of traditional imperial beneficence, Justinian became the "creator of poverty for all" (8.32): no remission of arrears (23.1) or lowering of taxes (18.10–12, 20.1–2), no *largitiones* when a new consul was created (26.12–6). General poverty was the ineluctable consequence (25.25). But Justinian did not care: he totally lacked the normal sentiment of pity in face of poverty (15.28). This is clearly illustrated by Procopius's insistence on the lack of interest the emperor showed for the poor: he made access to water and bread difficult and expensive for the poor of Constantinople (26.25), whereas his emissary Alexander abolished the support given to the beggars who gathered around S. Peter in Rome (26.29–30). Similar measures were taken in Alexandria (26.40–44). Justinian acted in total contradiction to what was expected of a Christian: dominated by his own greed, he abolished traditional means of support for the poor, which lead to a general impoverishment of society. Indifferent to their fate, and feeling no pity, he let the poor die without qualms. Procopius has thus turned Justinian into a perfect counterimage of the ideal that Eusebius had sketched of Constantine.[26]

Agapetus's *Ekthesis*, composed by a deacon from Constantinople and dated between 527 and 533, instructs the emperor on how to behave in imitation of God.[27] Although its seventy-two brief chapters may give an unstructured and incoherent impression, it is relatively easy to detect in them a thoroughly Christian image of the care for the poor. Chapter 7 stresses that possessions can only serve to give away. Their aim must be to do well (*eupoiia*), and the emperor will be rewarded with divine favours. More than once, pity is put forward as a sentiment indicative of a true imitation of God (37, 58, 63). Chapter 44 explicitly states that the act of giving must be determined by the needs of the receiver. This is an explicit affirmation of Christian teaching and an implicit rejection of the classical idea of *liberalitas*, which tended to stress the giver. These earlier chapters have introduced all the basic notions of Christian charity, and towards the end of his work Agapetus heavily stresses its importance for the emperor. He remarks that the poor are unavoidably attracted by the imperial majesty and that the emperor is obliged to help them. The love of the poor, Agapetus insists, thus means garbing oneself in the true purple: not the one of earthly majesty but that of divine imitation (52, 60).

26. See the references in n. 12.

27. See Alexander Demandt, "Der Fürstenspiegel des Agapet," *Mediterraneo Antico* 5 (2002): 573–84, 575.

Both Procopius and Agapetus use a Christianised discourse on imperial munificence, but the respective forms it takes differ fundamentally. In Agapetus, classical *liberalitas* is totally eclipsed by Christian charity and even implicitly rejected. His message is simple and straightforward: one has to give to the poor. For Procopius, on the contrary, Justinian did not perform any act of *liberalitas*, which caused general poverty. Faced with such a situation—moreover of his own making—the emperor refused to support the poor. Procopius does not exclude deeds of classical *liberalitas* from Christian *caritas*, but he has rather joined them in a single, coherent form: Justinian's refusal of *liberalitas* also expresses itself in a lack of *caritas*. The cases of Procopius and Agapetus show that it would be mistaken to assume that by the sixth century Christian charity had supplanted classical ideas about *liberalitas*, or that there existed a standard synthesis of both.

Variety was even greater than the previous pages have suggested. It did happen that language was Christianised, without the underlying actions really having changed. For a first example we have to return to the fourth century. Ausonius's *gratiarum actio* is a curious mix of archaism and innovation. *Liberalitas* is obviously the central point in this speech, which thanks the emperor Gratian for bestowing the consulship of 379 on him. Chapters 15 to 17 detail the emperor's acts of munificence. After a reference to the remission of taxes, Ausonius praises Gratian's care for his soldiers. Ausonius singles out that the emperor paid for the clothing of poor soldiers and that he acted out of "true pity and without any display" (17). These words clearly qualify Gratian's acts as Christian charity. Nevertheless, Ausonius is not talking about the poor, but about soldiers. Moreover, the beginning of the chapter compares Gratian to Trajan, who always cared for his friends. This rather suggests that Gratian tended to extend his circle of friends to his soldiers, which is a much more traditional form of praise. Ausonius thus seems to have disguised this traditional form of *liberalitas* as Christian charity.

A second example of this tendency to describe *liberalitas* as caritas is to be found in the closing scene of the second book of Corippus's panegyric on Justin II (567). The poet describes how creditors, whom Justinian had forced to lend him money, line up in front of the emperor. They move Justin to pity and he pays immediately all the debts. The sentiment of pity is clearly Christian, and Corippus depicts the creditors as exasperated poor, which they hardly are.[28] Again an act of imperial munificence is dressed up in the vocabulary of charity. By the sixth century, demands for favours are often expressed in the language of charity.[29]

This brief overview suffices to show that it is too easy to claim that the ancient ideal of imperial munificence was simply replaced by a new ideal, dominated by Christian charity and care for the poor. A brief typology may help us to understand the various ways in which the new Christian concern for care of the poor interacted with a more traditional discourse that focused on imperial *liberalitas*. There are two extreme sides in the spectrum. On the one hand, classical *liberalitas* simply continues its existence, as we have seen for Symmachus or Ennodius. On the other hand, Christian charity can totally replace the classical ideal in some instances, as was illustrated by Agapetus. In between these extremes, there are various possibilities. There is firstly the case of Ausonius and Corippus, who use the vocabulary of charity to describe imperial munificence. Procopius, on the contrary, has integrated Christian charity and care for the poor into more classical ideas on imperial evergetism. Thus, the discourse on imperial munificence in late antiquity was not monolithic nor a mere blend of old and new elements. Old and new elements existed side by side. They could be integrated in some cases, but many authors preferred to reject *liberalitas* in favour of *caritas* or vice versa. All authors agree that the emperor has to take care of his subjects, but the precise form that is supposed to take can differ greatly.

I do not wish to deny that the Christian discourse on charity had a huge attraction, even to the point that *liberalitas* was disguised as *caritas*. Even so, the latter never fully displaced the former. Seen in a diachronic perspective, it is evident that Christian charity became more important with the progressive Christianisation of the empire. Nevertheless, *liberalitas* never disappeared and even clerics and faithful Christians were able to draw on it. The Church historian Evagrius Scholasticus, writing at the end of the sixth century, could say of

---

28. Corippus, *Praise of Justin* 2.361–405, spec. 366 (*miserere, perimus*), 376 (*vix nobis vitae constant alimenta diurnae*), 379–80 (*flere diu tantos lacrimis non passus acerbis condoluit miserans*).

29. See the correspondence of Dioscorus of Aphrodite in Egypt: P. Diosc. 8 l. 5 = P.Cair.Maspéro II 67185; P. Diosc. 10 l. 45-50 = P.Cair.Maspéro I 67097; P. Diosc. 11 l. 51 = P.Cair.Maspéro III 67317 + P. Berol. inv. 10580; P. Diosc. 13 l. 17 = P. Lond. Lit. 100F; P. Diosc. 14 l. 38 = P.Cair.Maspéro I 67120. Cf. J.-L. Fournet, *Hellénisme dans l'Egypte du VIe siècle: la bibliothèque et l'oeuvre de Dioscore d'Aphrodité* (Cairo: Institut français, 1999).

the emperor Tiberius: "He did not consider what those in need ought to receive, but what befitted a Roman Emperor to give, and he regarded as adulterated the gold which had come in as the result of tears." He thus remitted taxes.[30] Just like Agapetus, Evagrius remained aware of the conceptual distinction between the two forms of munificence, as expressed by Lactantius.

The late antique discourse on imperial munificence is thus best analysed as composed of various discourses, which each have a slightly different take on evergetism while still sharing basic general concerns. This variety precludes the possibility of explaining the late antique discourse on imperial munificence as simply the result of the Christianisation of the empire and the infusion of Christian elements into a classical discourse, or even the replacement of a classical ideal by new Christian concerns. I suggest that the social position and context of orator and audience provide the main explanation for why an orator models his discourse in a certain way.

First one must admit that the care for the poor was seen as a specifically Christian virtue and recognised as such by pagan authors. This becomes clear in the polemic by the Antiochean orator Libanius (ca. 314–393) in his *Oration for the Temples*. Addressing his speech to Theodosius I, he wants to show that the destruction of rural sanctuaries entails consequences that go against Christian ideals. Twice his attack is aimed at the care for the poor. In chapter 10, Libanius suggests that the demolitions of temples demoralises local farmers, who abandon their fields and thus become even poorer than they already are. Chapter 20 is more explicit. The orator argues that the Christians, by destroying the temples, chase away temple staff that took care of the poor, elderly, women, orphans, and handicapped.[31] Libanius's attack in this chapter has two aims. First, he accuses the Christian of behaving in an unchristian way. By closing the temples, they obstruct charity to the poor. Second, he disputes the specifically Christian character of the care for the poor by asserting that pagans

---

30. Evagrius, *Historia ecclesiastica* 5.13, in *The Ecclesiastical History of Evagrius Scholasticus*, trans. Michael Whitby (Liverpool: Liverpool University Press, 2000), 273. A different reading of this passage is possible. It might be an implicit critique of the emperor, known for his donations to the point that he exhausted the treasury (John of Ephesus, *Historia ecclesiastica* 3.11, 3.14, 5.19). In that case, Evagrius might be hinting at the dangers of the classical ideal *of liberalitas:* see Michael Whitby, "Evagrius on Patriarchs and Emperors," *The Propaganda of Power: The Role of Panegyric in Late Antiquity*, ed. Mary Whitby (Leiden: Brill, 1998), 321–44, 327–28.

31. See also Libanius, *Oration* 2.30.

as well take care of them. This argument actually confirms the Christian nature of charity. Libanius was undoubtedly well aware of the fact that the care for the poor was a central virtue among Christians: in his panegyrics, he does praise Christian emperors for their charitable behaviour.[32] This explains his decision to use the care of the poor as part of his argument in a discourse addressed to an emperor of whose Christian credentials he was well aware. By arguing that the destruction of temples harmed the poor, he could hope to influence Theodosius or, at least, he could accuse his Christian adversaries of inconsistency—they claim to care for the poor but actually destroy institutions that support them. One should not conclude from this passage that pagan temples performed charity on the same scale as Christian churches—that is merely what Libanius's rhetoric wants us to believe.[33]

In comparison with paganism, the care for the poor thus appears as a Christian virtue. But when one looks at it from within the Church, it is in the first place an ecclesiastical and episcopal activity. The state explicitly recognised that *caritas* was the specific task of the church.[34] Bishops were supposed to intervene with emperors and kings in favour of the poor.[35] This helps to explain why the deacon Agapetus substituted Christian charity entirely for classical munificence in his *Ekthesis*: he projected an ecclesiastical ideal onto the monarch. The reluctance one notes in pagan authors to praise emperors for their charity (with notable exceptions such as the vociferous but unprincipled Libanius) is also explained by the explicitly Christian character of the care for the poor.[36]

---

32. Libanius, *Oration* 20.38, 33.33, 49.122b, 159.

33. This is confirmed by Julian's *Letter* 84, in which he contrasts Jewish and Christian charity with its lack among pagans. But the authenticity of this letter has been disputed: see Peter Van Nuffelen, "Deux fausses lettres de Julien l'Apostat ("La lettre aux Juifs, Ep. 51 [Wright], et la lettre à Arsacius, Ep. 84 [Bidez])," *VC* 56 (2002): 131–50; Peter Van Nuffelen, *Un héritage de paix et de piété. Etude sur les Histoires ecclésiastiques de Socrate et de Sozomène* (Leuven: Peeters, 2004), 142, n. 281; Jean Bouffartigue, "L'authenticité de la letter 84 de l'empereur Julien," *Revue de philologie* 79 (2005): 231–42.

34. *Codex Theodosianus* 16.2.6 (326), *Codex Justinianus* 1.2.12 (454); Eusebius, *Life of Constantine* 4.28.

35. E.g., *Life of Shenoute* 76, CSCO 41, 38; Gregory of Nazianzus, *Epitaphios of Basil* 34–37; Ennodius, *Life of Epiphanius* 181. See Brown, *Poverty and Leadership*, 45.

36. One should note that charity was very often seen as a virtue especially appropriate for empresses: for example, Helena (Eusebius, *Life of Constantine*, 3.44); Flacilla (Gregory of Nyssa, *Epitaphios logo* GNO IX p. 480.21–23); see also Kenneth Holum, *Theodosian Empresses: Women and Imperial Dominion in Late Antiquity* (Berkeley: University of California Press, 1982), 23–30; Hartmut Leppin, "Das Bild der kaiserlichen Frauen bei Gregor von Nyssa," *Gregory of Nyssa. Homilies on the Beatitudes*, ed. H.R. Drobner—

The fact that charity was seen as a Christian and ecclesiastical virtue does
not entail that Christian authors praise emperors by default for charity. On
the contrary, we often notice that their accounts of imperial munificence are
entirely couched in terms of classical *liberalitas*. A comparison between the
panegyrics of Procopius of Gaza (460–70 to 520/30) and Priscian of Caesarea
(first half of the sixth century) will help us to understand how the specific circumstances shaped their descriptions of imperial munificence. Both wrote a
panegyric of the emperor Anastasius (491–518), Procopius ca. 503/4, Priscian
probably in the early months of 502.[37]

In the opening chapters of their respective panegyrics, both orators briefly describe the problems that faced the empire at the accession of Anastasius.
Procopius summarises that "at that time, life was unhappy for most citizens of
the empire." A little later, he adds: "Strange, unnatural things happened then:
the fact that one was rich upset those with possessions."[38] Priscian opens his
panegyric by describing the Isaurian raids (which Procopius refers to in paragraphs 7–10). He stresses that their violence affected the poor: "Being of lowly status was of no avail, although it is the usual safeguard under mischievous
rulers. . . . When there was nothing to steal, they attacked the persons, locking
them in chains and beating them merciless" (31–7). Priscian takes a perspective
clearly different from Procopius: whereas the latter seems to focus on the well
off, he pays more attention to those of a lower status. This difference in emphasis returns in the description of Anastasius's famous abolition of the *chrys-*
*argyron* tax (498). Procopius describes how those who worked independently,
that is, the farmer, fisherman, merchant, and even the prostitute, suffered from
this tax. Although he suggests that they "lacked the daily minimum," these are
clearly not the absolute poor. He sees Anastasius's action as expressing a desire
for *euergesia* and *philanthropia* (13). Contrary to Procopius's more classical approach, Priscian's is dramatic and profoundly Christian: "Continuously aspiring for the supreme recompense in heaven, Anastasius despised richness, and

---

A. Viciano (Leiden: Brill, 2000), 487–506); Eudocia (Cyril of Scythopolis, *Life of Euthymius* 35; *Life of*
*Peter the Iberian* 123; *Pascal Chronicle* a. 444); Pulcheria (Sozomen, *Historia ecclesiastica* 9.1.9); Theodora
(John Lydus, *De magistratibus* 3.69–70).

37. See Fiona Haarer, *Anastasius I: Politics and Religion in the Late Roman World* (Cambridge:
Francis Cairns, 2006), 272–78. For earlier discussions, see Alain Chauvot, *Procope de Gaza, Priscien de*
*Césarée: Panégyriques de l'Empereur Anastase Ier* (Bonn: Habelt, 1986), 95–107.

38. Procopius of Gaza, *Panegyric* 5.

as such, he became a benefactor for all. Indeed, those who had hardly anything to live on, those poor people, paid their tax whilst weeping, a tax that was extorted from them in tears and complaints" (229–33). Priscian stresses much more the painful and poor condition of the taxed individuals, and depicts Anastasius as acting out of Christian motives, not classical philanthropy.

One might want to explain the contrast between Priscian and Procopius by thinking that the former underwent a much stronger Christian influence. But Procopius of Gaza also wrote commentaries on the Old Testament, whereas the Constantinopolitan Priscian is better known for his *Institutio de arte grammatica*. If Christian character was the main cause, Procopius should have written Priscian's oration. A contrast in implied audience might be the better explanation. Procopius gave his speech during a local celebration in Gaza, when a statue of the emperor was set up. He addresses the citizens of Gaza (1). An important part of the speech is thus dedicated to what has happened to the cities, which are presented by Procopius as the essential building blocks of the empire. He stresses, for example, the public works Anastasius paid for. The panegyric is at once a praise of the emperor and a celebration of city life. This may explain the absence of the theme of the care for the poor. Beggars, widows, and orphans live in the margins of the city; their presence is tolerated, but they do not constitute a central focus of city life, and definitely not during a communal celebration. Priscian, on the contrary, probably addressed himself to Anastasius directly: it is not unlikely that he read his panegyric in court. Before an audience that thought of itself as the *caput imperii*, the orator could hardly limit his perspective to that of a single city, but had to present the emperor as guardian of all his subjects, including the very poor. Undoubtedly, he also felt obliged to depict Anastasius in line with the Christian ideals then current. In such a context, Christian charity could not be absent.

## Shared Themes of *liberalitas* and *caritas*

The foregoing analysis confirms some of the assumptions I sketched in the introduction. The care for the poor is indeed perceived mainly as an ecclesiastical virtue, and often stressed in opposition to classical ideas about evergetism. It is also clear that it becomes much more prominent with the passing of time. But I hope that my argument has also shown that some of the beliefs held about the impact of this new discourse on classical *liberalitas* should be nuanced. *Caritas* did not supplant *liberalitas* in the public discourse, nor were the two by definition fused into a new, original synthesis. Right to the end of antiquity, authors could draw on both discourses in an unmixed form and, as shown by the passage of Evagrius, in full awareness of how they differed. The survival of classical *liberalitas* was not simply a function of the persistence of the traditional civic elite which clung to old ideals, and definitely not the expression of pagan ideas. Much depended on the precise circumstances in which a panegyric was held, as is illustrated by the fact that Procopius of Gaza hardly cares for the poor in his speech during a civic celebration. It is not just social position or belief of the orator that determine his take on things, but also the circumstances and audience of his speech.

The foregoing should not be taken to suggest that *caritas* and *liberalitas* coexisted as two separate discourses, which had little to do with one another. On the contrary, they constantly interacted. This is most evident in the way an individual author may blend them, but it is also true when only *caritas* surfaces. Agapetus's insistence on the precise nature of Christian giving, for example, can only be understood as an argument against more classical forms of munificence. Rather than taking *caritas* and *liberalitas* as separate discourses with their own tradition and topoi, we should consider them to be part of a shared discourse on munificence. This discourse is not defined by a blend of *liberalitas* and caritas; rather both ideals define the two poles of the discourse. Depending on the personality and background of the orator and the precise circumstances, one could be drawn more to the front of the scene. But even then the other echoes in the background.

It remains true, however, that Christian charity was often constructed in opposition to the classical conception of *liberalitas*. Basil of Caesarea, for example, opposed his own new city for the poor (his *basileias*) to the boastful city of Caesarea.[39] Such sentiments seem to argue against the idea that there was any common ground between Christian care for the poor and classical evergetism. For the most part this is rhetoric and polemic: as a radical virtue, charity is constantly contrasted—with pagans, our greed, our indifference. The theological identification of the poor as a figure of Christ already implicitly contrasts divine love with our human limitedness. Of a divine nature, it

39. Basil of Caesarea, *Homily on the Rich* 4: PG 31.289.

can never be fully realised on earth. As such charity is in constant need of definition by opposition. This should not conceal, however, that Christian sermons on poverty share important underlying themes with *liberalitas*, which belie its self-proclaimed uniqueness.

Christian poverty sermons often seem to deny the focus of *liberalitas* on the local community and the giver. They tend to stress the poor as the embodiment of Christ, and as such he already transcends the borders of a community. Moreover, as we have seen, in Christian *caritas*, giving is not to be done for the glory of the donator but for that of Christ. As such the Christian care for the poor seems universal and to transcend the frontiers of the community: every poor, citizen or stranger, deserves our pity and help.

But that reading is one-sided. It has often been remarked that the poor remain largely anonymous in patristic sermons, and are described, in general terms, rather by their condition than by their personality.[40] This shifts the focus of the sermons to the audience, which is exhorted to feel pity and to relieve the plight of the poor. Arguments revolve around the virtues and vices of the audience: the focus is on the giver, much more than on the receiver.[41] Moreover, giving to the poor is duly rewarded by God. Significantly, Gregory of Nazianzus makes it the touchstone of one's religious nature (*Oration* 14.40). Arguments in favour of *caritas* thus start to resemble very much those about *liberalitas*, with its stress on the giver and his moral status. Admittedly, the appeal of the poor and the idea that the poor have a right to exert on the rich is much stronger developed in Christian discourse, but it was nevertheless far from absent in the classical discourse on munificence. *Liberalitas* also meant acceding to demands of tax remission and material relief, and supporting those who were struck by catastrophe. Giving to the poor thus quickly transforms into a public duty. Although the gospel commands otherwise, almsgiving, for example, is often publicly and emphatically enacted.[42] Rather than being an ethical practice aroused by a Levinasian appeal of the "vis-

---

40. Brown, *Poverty and Leadership*, 45–46.

41. See, for example, Gregory of Nyssa, *Comm. in Eccl. Homilia,* GNO V p. 346.15–20; Gregory of Nazianzus, *Oration* 14.1–5. See Mary Sheather, "Pronouncements of the Cappadocians on Issues of Poverty and Wealth," *Prayer and Spirituality in the Early Church*, ed. Pauline Allen, Raymond Canning, and Lawrence Cross (Everton Park: Centre for Early Christian Studies, 1998), 175–392, 379.

42. Lucy Grig, "Throwing Parties for the Poor: Poverty and Splendour in the Late Antique Church," in *Poverty in the Roman World*, ed. Margaret Atkins and Robin Osborne (Cambridge: Cambridge University Press, 2006), 145–61. See also Finn, *Almsgiving*, passim.

age," care for the poor becomes a public duty performed for one's own salvation and public esteem. Both *liberalitas* and *caritas* thus seem to be subject to a double dynamic: they are the replies of virtuous souls to a spectacle of destitution.

The main difference seems to be that Christian charity shifts the focus of the act of giving to a specific segment of society, moreover one that was hardly of any concern for *liberalitas*. As stated above, the Christian stress on care for the poor has been seen as undermining the civic sense of community. To a certain degree this is true, in the sense that the focus on the poor catapulted a new category of people to the front of public discourse. But the Christian sermons on the poor do not simply shift attention away from civic communities; in their specific way, they are also concerned with restoring social communities. This becomes already clear in the first Christian text to include care for the poor among the imperial virtues. In his *Life of Constantine*, Eusebius of Caesarea praises the emperor for his care for the poor. "He made all sorts of distributions to the poor, and apart from them showed himself compassionate and beneficent to those outside who approached him" (43.1).[43] Eusebius then lists the measures taken by Constantine: gifts of food, alms, and clothing for the poor; grants of land and office to impoverished members of the elite; care for orphans and widows; dowries for orphaned girls. Classified as care for the poor, these measures actually aim at the reconstruction of the social fabric. The poor are taken care of, and those impoverished are again raised to their original station.[44] This is implicitly contrasted with Licinius, who is described as wrecking the East with high taxes and other injustices (1.54–55).

Eusebius' *Life of Constantine* is too idiosyncratic a work to allow general conclusions, but a similar tendency can be observed in Gregory of Nazianzus's famous Oration *On the Love of the Poor* (Oration 14).[45] Gregory's description of the poor sounds at first sight very general:

We must open our hearts, then, to all the poor, to those suffering evil for any reason at all, according to the Scripture that commands us to rejoice with those who rejoice and weep with

---

43. Averil Cameron and Stuart Hall, trans., *Eusebius. Life of Constantine* (Oxford: Oxford University Press, 1999), 87. See also Eusebius, *Life of Constantine* 4.4, 4.44.

44. See also Helena's actions described in 3.44.

45. One can note that love for his subjects is also an important quality for the emperor and which is described by Themistius as binding a community together (*Oration* 3.14).

those who weep (Rom. 12.15). Because we are human beings, we must offer the favour of our kindness first of all to other human beings, whether they need it because they are widows or orphans, or because they are exiles from their own country, or because of the cruelty of their masters or the harshness of their rulers or the inhumanity of their tax-collectors, or because of the bloody violence of robbers or the insatiable greed of thieves, or because if the legal confiscation of their property, or shipwreck—all are wretched alike, and so all look towards our hands, as we look towards God's, for the things we need (14.6).[46]

The poor as detailed by Gregory are, however, those whose social position has been affected by external conditions. These are not the poor born from poor, but individuals who for some reason have seen their community wrecked or who have dropped down the social ladder.[47] Gregory singles out the lepers to arouse the pity of his audience and make them repent. Their example is not only suitable for its obvious biblical resonance, but also because they are the extreme example of outcasts: whereas the other that were enumerated might find some refuge somewhere, lepers "are driven away from the cities, driven away from their homes, from the market-place, from public assemblies, from the streets, from festivals and private celebrations, even—worst of all sufferings!—from our water" (14.12). They are thrown out of the civic community. The care for the poor, thus, does not do away with the local community in favour of an abstract notion of man; it is also an attempt to restore the fabric of social life or at least to minimise the impact of catastrophe.[48] Society as depicted by late antique Christian sources always seems in danger and under threat of dissolution; constant reminder of one's duties towards God and one's fellow human beings is needed to maintain its existence.[49]

This concern with the coherence of the community becomes clear in the patristic concern with usury.[50] There might be sound theological and biblical reasons for rejecting usury (see Dt. 23.19–20), but in many texts the disrup-

46. Brian E. Daley, trans., *Gregory of Nazianzus* (London: Routledge, 2006), 78.

47. See also Gregory of Nyssa, *Oration 1 On the Love of the Poor*, GNO IX p. 96–98; cf. Johan Leemans, "'Les pauvres ont revêtu le visage de notre Sauveur.' Analyse historico-théologique du premier sermon de Grégoire de Nysse De l'amour des pauvres," in *Les pères de l'Eglise et la voix des pauvres*, ed. Pascal-Grégoire Delage (La Rochelle: Association Histoire et Culture, 2006), 75–87.

48. See Susan Holman, "Constructed and Consumed: The Every Day Life of the Poor in 4th C. Cappadocia," in *Social and Political Life in Late Antiquity*, ed. W. Bowden, A. Gutteridge, C. Machado (Leiden: Brill, 2006): 441–64, 444, on Basil's sermons; Wendy Mayer, *Poverty and Society*, 470–71.

49. Salvianus of Marseille's *De gubernatione Dei* is a long reminder of a Christian's duties and the disruption that threatens when one does not fulfill them. See also Gregory of Nazianzus, *Oration* 16.18–20.

50. See for further details Brenda Ihsen's paper in this volume.

tive effect of usury on a community is stressed.[51] It is interesting to note that, exceptionally, some authors accepted usury in special circumstances and then to individuals from *outside the community*.[52] This is hardly surprising given the stress on usury as a disruptive force within a community. Significantly, a Diocletianic rescript, incorporated in the *Codex Justinianus* (2.12.20) punished usurers with *infamia*, that is, the loss of status and concomitant legal rights: they were thrown out of the community.

Patristic authors were also prone to adopting the language of benefaction. Gregory of Nazianzus describes God as the supreme benefactor, whom we can never outdo (14.22, 27). He gives to all alike (14.24). Gregory even exhorts us to vie with each other in beneficence: "Become more eminent than your neighbour by showing yourself more generous; become a god to the unfortunate, by imitating the mercy of God" (14.26). The last argument pointedly resonates with Christian ideas about the imitation of God, but its formulation recalls immediately panegyrics that praise the emperor for imitating God by copying his actions.

## Conclusion

My argument does not aim at denying the transformative impact *caritas* may have had on the Roman emperor and that it was indeed a new concept and idea injected by Christianity into the public discourse. [53] But even as a new, transformative power, Christian care for the poor became embedded in late antiquity society. It not only transformed society, but was also transformed by it.[54] This becomes clear in the fact that the care of the poor very soon took on the form of patronage—an essential feature of ancient society.[55] Although

51. E.g., Gregory of Nyssa, *Contra usuriarios* PG 46.445, *Comm. in Eccl. Homilia* 4, GNO V p. 334–53; John Chrysostom, *Hom. in princ. Actorum* 4: PG 51.97. See also Procopius of Caesarea, *Anecdota* 21.13.

52. Clement of Alexandria, *Stromata* PG 8.1024–5; Ambrose, *De Tobia* 15.51 PL 14.779.

53. Brown, *Poverty and Leadership,* 7–8, 86

54. Brown, *Poverty and Leadership,* tends to stress the former aspect, e.g., when he suggests that through the Bible a Near-Eastern model of poverty and society infiltrated ancient society (71).

55. Jens-Uwe Krause, "Das spätantike Städtepatronat," *Chiron* 17 (1987): 1–80; F. E. Consolino, "Sante o patrone? Le aristocratiche tardoantiche e il potere della carità," *Studi Storici* 30 (1989): 969–71; Claude Lepelley, "Le patronat épiscopal aux IVe et Ve siècles: continuités et ruptures avec le patronat classique," in *L'évêque dans la cité du IV au Ve siècle,* ed. E. Rebillard and C. Sotinel (Rome: Ecole française de Rome, 1998), 17–33.

coming from a different perspective, my argument also wants to stress the embedded character of Christian discourse. Contrary to views that see Christian charity as an opposite of *liberalitas* and that argue that it totally replaced the latter as the dominant public virtue in late antiquity (or that charity at least became the dominant component of a new public ideal), I have suggested that *liberalitas* was never fully eclipsed and that the blended discourse never became the dominating form. Rather, *liberalitas* and *caritas* continued to exist as two poles of a shared discourse. This coexistence is partially explained by rhetoric: because of its radical nature, *caritas* needed a concept to contrast itself with. Right up to the end of late antiquity, we encounter authors that are able to contrast precisely *caritas* and *liberalitas*: the latter is giving for one's own glory, the former for that of Christ. Charity kept *liberalitas* alive to contrast itself with. But that was not the only reason. It depended on the precise circumstances of the speech (audience, occasion, orator) whether an orator would strike the note of *liberalitas* or *caritas*. But contrary to the habitual rhetorical opposition between both forms of giving, they did share common concerns. I have suggested that the care for the poor, although it seems to claim universality and to focus on the poor, is actually part of a concern for the wider local community (though that was now conceived much more inclusive that it used to be) and that it usually focused on the disposition of the giver and his salvation. Giving to the poor was rarely done with the left hand not knowing what the right did: very soon it had become a public virtue.

*Helen Rhee*

# 4. Wealth, Poverty, and Eschatology

*Pre-Constantine Christian Social Thought
and the Hope for the World to Come*

Christian eschatology and otherworldliness have been used and misused throughout history. On the one hand, they were used by Christians to justify maintaining the socio-political or religious status quo resulting in either a tragic neglect of social injustice or a passivity toward social reforms in the present age.[1] On the other hand, they were used to justify socio-political and religious radicalism and violence to the point that Christianity may be seen in some quarters as a militant opponent of social process and tolerance.[2] While it is true that the eschatological orientation and "otherworldliness" of early Christian teachings did not directly deal with or call for the larger social change and reform, and while it is also true that there was no lack of the marginal millenarian sects that reaped tragic consequences in efforts to establish God's kingdom on earth by force, such as the revolutionary Anabaptists of Münster in the sixteenth century, the very eschatological perception of reality and apocalyp-

---

1. See, for example, criticism of the early Christians in G. E. M. de Ste. Croix, "Early Christian Attitudes to Property and Slavery," in *Church, Society and Politics,* ed. D. Baker (Oxford: Basil Blackwell, 1975), 24–38.

2. See, for example, I. Gruenwald's critique of apocalyptic determinism and its ethical dehumanization leading to violence, "A Case Study of Scripture and Culture: Apocalypticism as Cultural Identity in Past and Present," in *Ancient and Modern Perspectives on the Bible and Culture: Essays in Honor of Hans Dieter Betz,* ed. A. Y. Collins (Atlanta: Scholars Press, 1998), 252–80.

tic framework did *constructively* guide and shape Christian social thought and concrete Christian practices.[3]

Indeed, this study argues both that early Christian (here, pre-Constantine) social ethics could not have existed without a robust eschatology and that early Christian eschatology was shaped by its understanding of social ethics. This study focuses on the tension between the rich and the poor, one of the major social challenges in the early Christian communities. As the patristic writers responded to the challenges and issues involving both attitudes toward and use of wealth, they consistently resorted to eschatological language to paint "a comprehensive picture of what is wrong and why, and of how life ought to be organized" toward the ultimate salvation and judgment of the individuals and the communities.[4] Having said this, the paper begins by reviewing the functional relationship between eschatology and ethics in early Christianity. Following that, the paper evaluates two ways in which eschatology shaped early Christian social ethics: 1) it placed divine judgment at the center of discussion, and 2) it fostered dualistic visions with respect both to the Christian's true home and to the Christian's true wealth.

## Patristic Eschatology and Ethics

Eschatology, broadly understood as a study or doctrine of last things, refers to the entire range of beliefs and notions concerning the end of history and final transformation of the world. The life in this present age, imperfect and impermanent, will be brought to an end in which the sovereign God will judge the righteous and the wicked and make all things new.[5] Ancient Jews in the exile and under the Greek and Roman occupations looked forward to the end where God's reign would be established, and early Christians inherited, transformed, and appropriated for their own purpose the Jewish eschatological expectations of the prophetic and apocalyptic traditions of the

---

3. See J. Viner, "The Economic Doctrines of the Early Christian Fathers," in *Religious Thought and Economic Society: Four Chapters of an Unfinished Work by Jacob Viner,* ed. J. Melitz and D. Winch (Durham, N.C.: Duke University Press, 1978), 9–18.

4. W. A. Meeks, *The First Urban Christians: The Social World of the Apostle Paul* (New Haven: Yale University Press, 1983), 173.

5. For an overview of patristic eschatology, see B. E. Daley, *The Hope of the Early Church: A Handbook of Patristic Eschatology* (Peabody, Mass.: Hendrickson, 2003).

Second Temple period. With a conviction in the death and resurrection of Jesus Christ, early Christians, both Jews and Gentiles, believed that the eschaton invaded the present age and that they were indeed living in the last days where God's kingdom would be ushered in; with a belief in the imminent return of Christ (παρουσία), they looked forward to the final judgment where God (through Christ) would vindicate the righteous and punish the sinners. In the pre-Constantine era, eschatological concerns were still alive within various Christian communities in varying degrees. Regardless of different nuances and understandings of the eschaton, for early Christians, the end (which is the beginning of the new era) was not only the restoration of the pristine past and the *telos* of history, but also the fulfillment of future hope in a perfect, just world ruled by God. The eschatological vision for the perfect world to come might take a messianic figure, millennial kingdom, cataclysmic events, or apocalyptic transformations veiled in mysterious symbols, images, and code words. Regardless of the varieties of the eschatological vision, it created an alternative reality by which the present world should be perceived and understood, and projected the hope for the ultimate judgment into this world.

Eschatology in the pre-Constantine period then carried a significant social and moral function in the corporate lives of early Christian communities that shared that vision. It provided social and moral critique and judgment on the present society and status quo on the one hand and put forth an alternative vision and reality of the other world.[6] It not only created a Christian identity distinct from the dominant world but also connected this unique sense of group identity and solidarity to the particular behaviors within the community and vis-à-vis the outsiders. For instance, the eschatological scenario of the *Didache* (16.3–8) with a double call to be vigilant and to assemble frequently (16.1–2) functions as a warning to its Jewish Christian community to reinforce righteous living expected in this present age for the retribution at the end of time.[7] And the second century apologists, in response to the pa-

---

6. See, for example, Tertullian, *Ap.* 47.12; *De pat.* 7; *Ad mart.* 2.5–6; and Lactantius' sharp critique of the Tetrarchy in *Mort. pers.* 7.3 and *D.I.* 7.24.7–8.

7. For a helpful comprehensive study on the *Didache*, see, for instance, H. van de Sandt and D. Flusser, *The Didache: Its Jewish Sources and Its Place in Early Judaism and Christianity* (Minneapolis: Fortress Press, 2002); K. Niederwimmer, *The Didache: A Commentary,* Hermeneia, trans. L M. Maloney (Minneapolis: Fortress Press, 1998); J. A. Draper, ed., *The Didache in Modern Research,* AGJU 37 (Leiden: Brill, 1996).

gan charges of Christian immorality, frequently based superiority of Christian morality on the Christian hope for eternal life and resurrection, and God's eschatological judgment: "it is alike impossible for the wicked, . . . and the virtuous to escape the notice of God, and . . . everyone goes to eternal punishment or salvation in accordance with the character of his acts. If all people knew this, no one would choose wickedness even for a while."[8] Characteristically, the patristic eschatological emphases were influenced by and responded to practical conflicts, issues, and dilemmas in the life of a believer and the community.[9] In so doing, patristic eschatology linked ethical behaviors in this world to the ultimate salvation and judgment of God. Whether early Christians understood the Parousia literally or figuratively and despite the fact that the imminent Parousia was apparently delayed,[10] early Christians "must live in a community of corporate thought and action befitting those who were called to the superabundant society of the future."[11] Therefore, "various elements of early Christian ethics can best be understood as efforts to capture in the present the conditions of the future."[12]

## Judgment, the Rich, and the Poor

We turn now to an exploration of the first of two, broad ways in which eschatology shaped early Christian socio-ethical thought. It placed divine judgment at the center of any discussion about social ethics. "The issue of poverty and wealth is inextricably bound up with the question of divine justice and judgment."[13] The link among eschatology, judgment, and the issue of wealth

8. Justin, *1 Ap.* 12.1–2; see also, Athenagoras, *Legatio* 33.1–3; *De resurrectione* 18.1–2, 4–5: "Each man will be examined in these matters individually, and reward or punishment will be distributed in proportion to each for lives lived well or badly."

9. E.g., The Shepherd of Hermas, *1 Clement*, and *The Didache*.

10. Note D. E. Aune's point that "[A]wareness of the delay of the Parousia has in no demonstrable way muted, altered, or transformed imminent eschatological expectations [in early Christianity]" and that "the expectation of the future Parousia was functionally drawn into the present experience of early Christians," in "The Significance of the Delay of the Parousia for Early Christianity," in *Current Issues in Biblical and Patristic Interpretation,* ed. G. F. Hawthorne (Grand Rapids, Mich.: Eerdmans, 1975), 102, 107.

11. R. C. Petry, *Christian Eschatology and Social Thought* (New York: Abingdon Press, 1956), 77.

12. J. G. Gager, *Kingdom and Community: The Social World of Early Christianity* (Englewood Cliffs, N.J.: Prentice-Hall, 1975), 49–50.

13. G. W. E. Nickelsburg, "Revisiting the Rich and the Poor in *1 Enoch* 92–105 and the Gospel according to Luke," in *Society of Biblical Literature 1998 Seminar Papers Part Two* (Atlanta: Scholars Press, 1998), 588.

and poverty essentially takes the form of the vindication of the righteous and the condemnation of the wicked and is deeply rooted in the Jewish theological and cultural tradition of "the righteous poor" and "the wicked rich."[14] This particular tradition sprang from Yahweh's deep concern for the poor in the Torah and developed over the whole history of Israel particularly during the monarchy and exilic and postexilic period in the prophetic, wisdom, and apocalyptic traditions.

The Torah reveals Yahweh's special care and protection for the poor by establishing social obligation toward the poor. Since Israel's land belongs to God, the Torah declares as Yahweh's will that there should be no poor in the covenant community (Deut 15:4).[15] Under the monarchy, the economic and urban development created a small group of aristocratic and plutocratic landowners at the expense of the impoverishment of the larger population.[16] "In the Day of the Lord," God would surely bring his judgment upon the rich who violated the core of God's law and the whole people of Israel (Isa 5:8–9.; Amos 5:11–13; Mic 6:13–16); the rich would go down to the Sheol (Isa 5:14), and the destruction of the kingdoms of Israel and Judah was God's punishment for their oppression of the poor and needy (Ezek 22:29; cf. Isa 5:13). Such prophetic oracles

14. For a concise survey of this rich tradition in Jewish and early Christian literature, see P. U. Maynard-Reid, *Poverty and Wealth in James* (New York: Orbis Books, 1987), 24-37; E. Bammel, "πτωχός," *TDNT* 6:885–915; M. Hengel, *Property and Riches in the Early Church: Aspects of a Social History of Early Christianity* (Philadelphia: Fortress, 1974), 12-41; H.-H. Esser and C. Brown, "Poor" ("πτωχός), *NIDNTT* 2:821–29; C. Osiek, *Rich and Poor in the Shepherd of Hermas: An Exegetical-Social Investigation*, CBQMS 15 (Washington D.C.: The Catholic Biblical Association of America. 1983), 15–38; M. Dibelius, *James: A Commentary on the Epistle of James*, rev. H. Greeven, trans. M. A. Williams (Philadelphia: Fortress, 1976), 39–45; E. Nardoni, *Rise Up, O Judge: A Study of Justice in the Biblical World* (Peabody, Mass.: Hendrickson, 2004), precisely relates this tradition to the broader issue of biblical justice and ethics.

15. The Book of the Covenant (Ex 20:22–23:19) institutes the sabbatical year for debt servitude (21:2), grants the poor the produce of the land in the fallow year (23:10 –11), and forbids the exploitation of (22:22–27) the poor and perversion of justice against them (23:6). See also Esser and Brown, *NIDNTT* 2:822. The community is obliged to open their hands to the poor and needy (Deut 15:11), especially the Levites, foreigners, widows, and orphans, for they are the landless or socially helpless and God loves them (see Ex 22:21–24).

16. Maynard-Reid, *Poverty and Wealth*, 26–7; F. Hauck and W. Kasch, "πλοῦτος," *TDNT* 6:324. The prophets saw this process not only socially but also theologically because it ran contrary to Yahweh's will for Israel (Amos 2:10; Mic 6:3–4; Jer 2:6–7; cf. Deut 15:4), and they denounced the wealthy and powerful (the same people) as such for their social and economic injustice and oppression of the poor in particular. The rich oppress the poor and crush the needy (Amos 4:1) with their avarice and covetousness for amassing more wealth, and ruthless acquisition of the land at the expense of the poor (Mic 2:2; 3:2–3); the wealthy are equivalent of the wicked who are "full of violence," dishonesty, and falsehood (Mic 6:9–12; cf. Isa 53:9).

can be juxtaposed with the lament psalms in which may be found the Psalm-ists' self-identification with the poor and needy (e.g., 40:17; 69:30; 86:1; 88:16; 109:22). The poor are the victims of the "wicked" *(rash'im)*; material poverty is frequently either the cause or the result of the injustice they suffer (10:3–11; 31:15; 35:10; 37:14; 94:3–7; 109 passim).[17]

In the Second Temple period, there is a more explicit development of the notion "the pious poor and the wicked rich," especially in the apocryphal and pseudepigraphical literature. While the traditional piety of caring for the poor as an essential religious duty continued in wisdom tradition (Sir 3:30–31; 4:1–10; Tob 1:8; Wis 19:14–15), the issue of poor and rich in this literature (in-cluding wisdom literature) was linked with and subsumed under the prevail-ing apocalyptic and eschatological framework, which envisioned the struggle between the righteous and the wicked, and God's final vindication of the righ-teous and judgment of the wicked.[18] In this struggle, the righteous were iden-tified as those who are poor and the wicked as the rich; this eschatological conflict between the righteous poor and the wicked rich (see Jub 23:19) in-volved the "great reversal" of their earthly fortunes in the Last Day. This theme is most conspicuously depicted in *1 Enoch*.

Written in the first century BCE., *1 Enoch* (Ethiopic), which significant-ly influenced early Christian literature, portrays a bitter struggle between the "righteous" (δίκαιοι, εὐσεβεῖς) and the "sinners" (ἁμαρτωλοί).[19] In one of the five main sections, the "Epistle of Enoch" (*1 Enoch*, 91–105), where this dual theme is expounded, the righteous are the ones who are persecuted, op-pressed, hated, abused, robbed and devoured (95:7; 103:9–15) by the rich and

17. See Bammel, *TDNT* 6:892. Being helpless and lowly, they cry out and turn to God for help in times of distress and appeal to God's righteousness and salvation (9:12; 22:24; 34:18). God is portrayed as the just defender and protector of the poor from their enemies (10:17–18; 64:1, 10; 70:5; 140:12), provid-er for the needy (12:5; 34:7; 68:10), deliverer of the oppressed and the righteous (72:12–14; 82:1–4), and lifter of the poor and lowly for his glory (113:7–9; 145:14). The notion of poverty is then extended to the spiritual level and the poor are identified as the humble, the afflicted, the oppressed, and the righteous who turn to God, depend on his help, and enjoy his special favor. Thus, "poor" and "pious" form a paral-lel concept (86:1–2; 132:15–16) as "friends of God" (41:1) and the enemy of the poor is also the enemy of God (107:39–41; 109:31). See also M. Dibelius, *James*, 39.

18. See Hauck and Kasch, *TDNT* 6:325.

19. Nickelsburg, "Riches, the Rich, and God's Judgment in I Enoch 92–105 and the Gospel accord-ing to Luke," *NTS* 25 (1979): 326–32, provides a succinct study of the wicked rich in *1 Enoch* 92–105. For the best available study of *1 Enoch*, see G. W. E. Nickelsburg, *1 Enoch 1: A Commentary on the Book of 1 Enoch, Chapters 1–36; 81–108,* Hermeneia (Minneapolis: Fortress Press, 2001).

mighty (e.g., the Maccabees and the Sadducees), who are deceitful, unrighteous, and ungodly (94:6–8; 96:7), and trust their own wealth for future security; the self-indulgent and godless wealthy gain their wealth unjustly, and
these foolish sinners will perish with their possessions (98:1–10). They are
doomed to destruction on the Day of Judgment because of their wicked deeds
(99:1; 100:4, 9; 102:5).[20] The writer juxtaposes a series of woes and indictments
to the rich (e.g., 94:6–8; 95:4–7; 96:4–8; 97:7–8; 98:9–16; 99:1–16) account-
ing their sins and divine judgment with a series of exhortations to the righteous calling them to courage and hope because of divine vindication and
promise of eternal life in the coming judgment (e.g., 94:6–11; 96:4–8; 97:3–
10; 99:1–16; 100:7; 102:4–5; 104:2).[21] Despite the absence of the term "poor,"
the identification of the righteous with the poor appears obvious as the sinners are singled out as the rich; they are the helpless and precarious victims of
the very socio-economic exploitation and injustice by the rich and powerful
sinners who prosper and enjoy in this life.

Death is a great equalizer of earthly fortunes and it is God's just judgment
that brings about the reversal of their twisted fortunes. Rewards and punishments at the judgment are primarily "otherworldly" in a sense that they are
postmortem phenomena.[22] However, the rewards and punishments are also
"this-worldly" according to the "Apocalypse of Weeks" (93:1–10; 91:11–17). The
righteous execute a righteous judgment on the oppressive sinners with a sword
and acquire possessions *through their righteousness* in the eighth week of righteousness *in this life*. At least in "Apocalypse of Weeks," the "this-worldly" reversal seems to constitute a core part of the divine judgment executed by God's
righteous people.[23] This recovers the ancient Deuteronomic tradition, in which
wealth, honor, and prosperity are still signs of God's favor and justice while deprivation and poverty are God's punishment. The moral exhortation to the
pious righteous, who are Enoch's main audience, is to love and walk in righ-

---

20. See Osiek, *Rich and Poor*, 20.

21. See Nickelsburg, "Riches, the Rich, and God's Judgment," 327.

22. The Day of Judgment is the day of cursing and retribution for the sinners (102:5, 11), but of
goodness, joy, and glory for the righteous (103:3). What the wealthy sinners have and enjoy in this life
will be taken away from them (103:5–8) while what the righteous lack in this life will be recompensed
abundantly (102:4–11; 103:1–4, 9–15; 104:1–4).

23. In the later, Christian *Acts of Thomas*, both the premortem and postmortem rewards and punishments are "this-worldly" in another sense: prosperity, wealth, honor, and satisfaction, on the one hand,
and deprivation, grief, toil, and tribulation, on the other, are both described as heavenly and earthly riches.

teousness, fear God, and wait for the day of judgment of sinners while on earth (91:4; 94:1, 19; 101:1; 102:5).

In this light, the Qumran community also seemed to use the term "poor" for self-designation of the sect.[24] The community renounced private property as its rule (1QS 3:2; 5:1) and practiced communalism (1QS 1:12; 5:2; 6:17; 7.6; see also Josephus, *War* 2.8.3) as a way of erasing distinctions between rich and poor in expectation of eschatological salvation and in attempt to mirror the form of life which God would bring about with the coming age.[25] Earthly wealth and possession is the most obvious sign of imprisonment to this world and thus something "wicked" and unclean from which the members of the community should abstain (CD 6:15; 1QS 5:20; 8:23; see also Josephus, *Bell.* 2:122). While the members are exhorted to strengthen the poor and needy in the community (CD 6:16, 21; 14:14), they themselves constitute the "congregation of the poor" who endured and survived the persecution and violence of the Wicked Priest and the Jerusalem priests (1QpHab 12:3–10; 4QpPs 2:10); whereas the poor will inherit the land as the "congregation of his [Yahweh's] elect," the wicked will no longer exist (4QpPs 2:4–5, 9). Therefore, God is praised as the one who delivers the life of the poor (1QH 2:32–35; also 3:25) and rescues the soul of the needy from the powerful wicked (1QH 5:12–18). Thus, the Qumran writers use the term "poor" to denote their sectarian identity and the title of honor as the object of God's mercy and eschatological dealings.

In the first century CE, the early followers of Jesus believed that, with the coming of Jesus, the eschatological new age had indeed dawned, and they inherited the tradition of poverty-piety from their Jewish, eschatological context. Jesus' attitude toward poverty and wealth is frequently depicted in the Synoptic Gospels and the epistle of James often alludes to this Jesus tradition.[26] While Jesus does associate with the wealthy and powerful (see Matt 27:57), he frequently warns against the acquisition of wealth. In particular, the Gos-

---

24. Bammel, *TDNT* 6:897; Esser, *NIDNTT* 2:824. L. Keck, "The Poor among the Saints in Jewish Christianity and Qumran," *ZNW* 57 (1966): 54–78, argues that although the Qumran community used this term as a self-description, it was not a technical name for the community.

25. Bammel, *TDNT* 6:898.

26. For Jesus' attitude to wealth in the Synoptics, see Hauck and Kasch, *TDNT* 6:327–28; F. Selter, "πλοῦτος" *NIDNTT* 2:840–45. See also P. H. Davids, "James and Jesus," in *Jesus Tradition outside the Gospels,* GP 5, ed. D. Wenham, (Sheffield: JSOT Press, 1985), 63–84.

pel of Luke expresses favor for the poor and disapproval for the rich and for wealth.[27] The theme of the "great reversal" in judgment and salvation is carefully woven together throughout the Gospel, especially in the unique Lucan materials.[28] Without idealizing poverty, the Lucan Gospel portrays the poor as the object of God's eschatological salvation and the rich as the ungodly ones who are alienated from God because of their present comfort and reliance on wealth.

Although the early Christian groups did not formally identify themselves as the "poor," in general they belonged to the socio-economic category of "the poor,"[29] and they experienced oppression and maltreatment by the rich and powerful in one way or another.[30] So, in the epistle of James, the theme of the rich and the poor is interwoven with James' communal concerns and eschatological outlook (see 1:9–12, 2:1–7, and 5:1–6)[31] and is strategically placed throughout the epistle.[32]

---

27. On this see Bammel, *TDNT* 6.906–7; Osiek, *Rich and Poor*, 24–32; Nickelsburg, "Riches, the Rich, and God's Judgment," 332–40.

28. E.g., Mary rejoices that God has exalted the lowly and hungry but sent the rich away empty, quoting Isa 61:1. Jesus, at the beginning of his ministry, proclaims the good news to the πτωχοῖ as his specific mission (Lk 4:18a) and commands the host of the feast to invite not the relatives or rich neighbors but the poor and disabled, pointing to the latter's place at the great eschatological banquet (14:13, 21). In the Sermon on the Plain, eschatological blessings pronounced to the poor are coupled with woes to the rich who have already received their reward (6:20–26). The parable of the rich fool (12:16–21) shows the folly of the rich man's avarice and luxury and of trusting wealth as a means of future security, which is a sign of his spiritual "poverty" toward God and thus a basis of God's condemnation. This theme is dramatized in the parable of the Rich Man and Lazarus (16:19–31), where eternal torment is the destiny of πλούσιος as such, who enjoyed good things in life, whereas consolation of Abraham is the destiny of Lazarus as πτωχός who suffered bad things on earth (v. 25). Whereas both the rich fool and the rich man fail to care for the poor and consider God while on earth, Zacchaeus, a "sinful rich publican," as an exceptional model, receives salvation through almsgiving to the poor and making restitution for ill-gotten wealth (19:1–10).

29. This can be said of Jesus and his disciples (Matt 8:20), the Jerusalem church (Gal 2:10; Rom 15:26) or Pauline communities (1 Cor 1:26–; 2 Cor 8:1–). See also L. E. Keck, "The Poor among the Saints in the New Testament," *ZNW* 56 (1965): 100–29. "The poor" or poverty was not "a technical designation" but "an actual description" of the early church (110). See also S. J. Friesen, "Poverty in Pauline Studies: Beyond the So-called New Consensus," *JSNT* 26 (2004): 323–61.

30. See Lk 12:12; 22:3; Acts 4:1–3; 8:1–3; 12:1–4; 2 Cor 11:23–27; Heb 10:32–34. In particular, the Jewish Christians in Jerusalem were not exempt from the socio-economic plight in Palestine and suffered from financial pressure and impoverishment, as attested by the Pauline collection (1 Cor 16:3; Rom 15:26, 31). The Jacobean audience may have belonged to these "saints" who were struggling with oppression by the wealthy upper class in apocalyptic hope of Christ's Judgment but struggling also with a desire to become part of them in this world (2:1–7; also 4:1–5).

31. Thus R. W. Wall, "James as Apocalyptic Paranesis," *Restoration Quarterly* 32 (1990): 11–22.

32. In particular, the community's partiality toward the ones with "gold rings and fine clothing"

Divine judgment and the great reversal theme continue with standard expectations and further developments in Christian apocalyptic literature. In the *Apocalypse of John*, the "unrighteous rich" *topos* takes a form of the cosmic powers of evil, manifested chiefly in the socio-economic and religio-political systems of Roman empire (Babylon).[33] In the second century *Fifth Ezra*, God's people, Israel (i.e., Christians), are exhorted not to be anxious about the day of the judgment because "others will weep and be sorrowful, but thou shalt be

---

over against the "poor" (2:1–4) prompts James to harshly remind them in diatribe of whom God has chosen as his elect and who their real enemy is (2:5–7). It is the poor that God has chosen to be pious and heirs of his kingdom; it is the rich that oppress with legal assault and persecute the very poor (the community members) God has chosen. Hence, by favoring the rich, they dishonored the poor (2:6); and the community's action of dishonoring the poor not only betrays their core faith and hope in the God of "the pious poor" but also places themselves in the ironic position of the wicked rich who will be judged by God (the identity of the rich as the outsiders becomes obvious in their blaspheming of Christ, v. 7). The eschatological element is still apparent; while it is the rich people's doom that was emphasized in 1:9–12, here it is the poor people's destiny as the heirs of God's promised kingdom is emphasized. However, this eschatological motif is subsumed under the practical admonition to the community—showing their faith in God by taking care of the poor (2:14–16; cf. 1:26–27).

The most biting attack on the rich is reserved for 5:1–6. In this text, indeed the eschatological framework dominates the scene, especially in light of 5:7–11. James's adaptation of the prophetic imageries and rhetorical diatribe heightens the literary vividness of the sure fall of the rich: they are hoarding their wealth whose remain will only destroy them (5:2–3b); they are laying up their treasure in the last days (5:3c) and feasting on the day of slaughter (5:5b); the cries of the defrauded poor have already reached the ears of the Lord of hosts (5:4b). Therefore, the readers need to be patient and endure the present suffering until the coming of the Lord, who will come soon as the Judge, says James (5:7–11). The pronouncement of the imminent destruction of the rich is joined by the practical exhortation to the community again with God's vindication and the eschatological reversal of the members' present predicament. In light of this thematic context, it becomes plain that the indictment against the rich in 5:1–6 is addressed not to the rich—the outsider—but to the poor—the insider—for their encouragement and awareness. See also Wheeler, *Wealth as Peril and Obligation: The New Testament on Possessions* (Grand Rapids, Mich.: Eerdmans, 1995), 103.

33. For ideological analysis of wealth imagery in John's Apocalypse, see R. M. Royalty, *The Streets and Heaven: The Ideology of Wealth in the Apocalypse of John* (Macon, Ga.: Mercer University Press, 1998). For a detailed study of the Revelation's economic critique of Rome, see R. Bauckham, "The Economic Critique of Rome in Revelation 18," in *Images of Empire*, JSOTSS 12, ed. L. Alexander, (Sheffield, U.K.: Sheffield Academic Press, 1991), 47–90. The mighty and oppressive Babylon with her self-indulgent luxury, commerce, and earthly riches comes under the divine woe and cataclysmic judgment (chs. 17–18) whereas the New Jerusalem, "the focus of eschatological hope" (Royalty, *The Streets of Heaven*, 71), adorned with magnificent wealth (jasper, crystal, pure gold, pearls, etc.), is reserved for those who are afflicted, persecuted, and yet persevere through the tribulation and injustice of evil powers of Rome/Babylon, the group that corresponds to the "righteous poor" (21:1–26; 2:9). At the judgment, these "righteous poor" will live in the new heaven and new earth as the place of abundance (22:2), and worship the Lord God Almighty, the righteous judge, in the heavenly throne room characterized by the same kind of stunning material opulence as the New Jerusalem (4:3–6).

gay and rich" (27); meanwhile, they are commanded to "do right to the widow, assist the fatherless to his right; give to the needy; protect the orphan, clothe the naked; tend the cripple and the feeble, laugh not at the lame, defend the frail " (20), and be "ready for the rewards of the kingdom" (35). While there is no evident identification of "Israel" as the poor here as in Isaiah, the focus is to ensure their present social responsibility in anticipation of their future reward. In *Sixth Ezra*, God's judgment on Asia, one of Israel's enemies, comes in the form of widowhood, poverty, famine, sword, pestilence, hunger, and deprivation of its treasure and splendor (49, 57), which represent the "typical" this-worldly descriptions of apocalyptic judgment. In the Christian *Sybilline Oracles*, the wrath of God will be poured out to those sinners including presbyters and reverend deacons who had more regard for wealth than for people and did injustice to others (II.260–72).[34]

A further judgment theme in the second and third century apocalypses is that of distinctive "tours of hell" in which sins and eternal punishments are matched measure for measure.[35] In *Apocalypse of Peter* and *Apocalypse of Paul*, those who trusted in their wealth (Eth. 9; Gk. 30; *Apoc. Paul*, 37) and did not have mercy on widows and orphans (Eth. 9; Gk.30; *Apoc. Paul*, 35, 40) are clad in filthy rags and suffer in torment. Those who lent money and took usury are thrown into a place saturated with filth (*Apoc. Pet.*, Eth.10; Gk.31). In the early third century *Acts of Thomas*, those hung up by the hands in chasm are those "who took that which did not belong to them and have stolen, and who never gave anything to the poor, nor helped the afflicted; but they did so because

---

34. Also, God's wrath will be poured out on the inordinately proud and usurers heaping up usury out of usury who wrought harm to orphans and widows, and those who gave to widows and orphans from ill-gotten gains. They will eternally burn in a mighty fire and gnash with their teeth, and God will turn away his face from them. On the other hand, those who think and practice justice, noble works, piety, and righteousness are destined to the new age of eternal bliss where there are threefold springs of wine, milk and honey, abundant fruits, common wealth ("unapportioned wealth"), neither paupers nor the rich, neither slaves nor kings, and neither buying nor selling (II.313–30). This portrait of the new age at the judgment is repeated elsewhere: with the resurrection of the dead, there will be common sharing of life, riches, and earth, abundant crops and fruits, and springs of sweet wine, white milk, and honey (VIII.180, 205–12); no slaves, no kings, no ruler judging for money (VIII.107–21). The coming new age has no social distinctions or disparities, and no private property—only social equality, abundance, and common sharing of that abundance. This could be taken as an implicit critique of the contemporary social inequalities and private properties as the culprit. The idea of common ownership in the Golden Age and the New Age will become popular among the Church Fathers in the fourth and fifth centuries.

35. See M. Himmelfarb, *Tours of Hell: An Apocalyptic Form in Jewish and Christian Literature* (Philadelphia: Fortress Press, 1983), particularly 68–126.

they wished to get everything, and cared neither for law nor right" (56). In these cases, the particular sins that merit corresponding punishments in hell are greed, trust in wealth and, most importantly, ignoring the traditional responsibilities of caring for the poor, widows, and orphans. The use of wealth and possessions, rather than the wealth or possessions themselves, is the issue. The clear message is that *individual believers* are obliged to use their wealth to the right end in light of the coming judgment.[36]

Having said this, it was nevertheless the case that, during the second and third centuries, a move was underway to tone down rhetoric both of the wicked rich and of the pious poor. Christianity attracted a greater number of the wealthy and those with high, social status. Rich and poor alike participated in the Christian assemblies with the former taking an indispensable and substantial role. Therefore, while social tensions between them occasionally led to social crises within the church (e.g., neglect of the poor by the rich as in the case of the Shepherd of Hermas), the great reversal theme diminished. Instead, moral and eschatological discourses shifted their focus to moving the rich to change their behavior so that *both* the rich and the poor will pass the coming judgment and receive the heavenly reward together. The notion of "redemptive almsgiving" appearing in Second Temple sapiential texts, such as Tobit and Sirach (Ecclesiasticus), receives renewed significance in this context.[37] Hence, the symbiosis or reciprocity theme becomes more dominant than the reversal theme in the second- and third- century Christian writings.[38] Although denunciation of avarice in an apocalyptic framework remained strong, the righteous rich may find hope of eternal life through generous almsgiving.

36. Note a shift in the punishment of the wicked in these works compared to John's Apocalypse, the *Fifth* and *Sixth Ezra*, and the Christian *Sybilline Oracles*: from punishment of wicked nations to individual retribution, and from punishment for the mistreatment of Israel (i.e., people of God) to punishment for individual sins against God's commandments. This would be an example of Aune's observation that "the experience of salvation as conveyed by the doctrine of the immortality of the soul upon personal death became, therefore, a functional substitute for the experience of salvation that was expected to occur upon the event of the Parousia of Jesus," in "The Significance of the Delay of the Parousia," 108.

37. R. Garrison, *Redemptive Almsgiving in Early Christianity* (Sheffield, U.K.: JSOT Press, 1993), thinks that the early Christian notion of "redemptive almsgiving" emerged as an antidote to anxiety about delay of Parousia and the ensuing problem of postbaptismal sin despite Christ's death as sufficient atonement for sin. This, though it has its merit, seems to be a bit too narrow understanding of "redemptive almsgiving."

38. E.g., *Hermas*; Clement of Alexandria, *Who Is Rich Man That Is Saved?* See the section, "Eschatological Visions, Dualism, and Use of Wealth."

Consequently, future rewards and punishments now corresponded to distinctions between the righteous and unrighteous rich rather than to distinctions between the pious poor and oppressive rich.

The second-century homily known as *Second Clement* evokes apocalyptic imagery and language when exhorting almsgiving. Since "the day of judgment is already 'coming as a blazing furnace,' and 'some of the heavens will dissolve,' and the whole earth will be like lead melting in a fire," every human work will be exposed (16.3). Therefore, "renunciation" or "hatred" of the earthly things turns out to be none other than almsgiving: "almsgiving is good, as is repentance from sin. Fasting is better than prayer, while almsgiving is better than both, and 'love covers a multitude of sins' . . . almsgiving relieves the burden of sin" (16.4).[39] *Second Clement* is the first Christian text explicitly to link 1 Pet 4:8 to almsgiving, and almsgiving to pardon of sin. Almsgiving is the ultimate antidote to love of money, the prime act of love and righteousness, and thus the surest way to get ready for the imminent judgment (see 12:1; 18:2).[40]

Cyprian of Carthage is even clearer in articulating the eschatological significance of almsgiving. The Decian persecution of 250 and 251 CE caught the churches off-guard and indeed demoralized them to internal chaos and crisis that generated eschatological anxiety. Cyprian's *On the Lapsed* sees the persecution as God's testing of his household that has been growing complacent in the years of peace. It is a divine wake-up call to their languid and sleeping faith (5). He attributes the cause of persecution, indeed God's testing, primarily to the faithful's "insatiable greed" *(insatiabili cupiditatis)* and preoccupation with accumulating their wealth to the neglect of generous charity for the needy (6).[41] To this the "apostolic solution" is given: scorn worldly possessions; abandon

---

39. See Sir 3:30; Tob 4:10; 12:9.

40. As in *Hermas*, double-mindedness is a major problem here, for it prevents serving God with a pure heart and enduring in hope for the heavenly reward. There is an implicit reversal theme in addressing the present hardship of God's servants as opposed to wealth of the unrighteous, but there is no correlation throughout the text between "the poor" and God's servants on the one hand, and "the rich" and the unrighteous on the other. God will punish the unrighteous whereas the righteous will receive their reward in the life to come (20:1–4).

41. Too many bishops "took up the administration of secular business; they left their sees . . . and toured the markets in other territories on the look-out for profitable deals" (6). While members in their church went hungry, "they wanted to have money in abundance, they acquired landed estates by fraud and made profits by loans at compound interest" (6). The church's failing in this persecution (i.e., massive apostasy) revealed "the true nature of our malady," which was "a blind attachment to their patrimony," their enslavement to their earthly riches and property (11, 12).

them for the Kingdom of God and heavenly compensation (12). Cyprian frames both the problem and solution in apocalyptic dualism. As the sign of true repentance, the (wealthy) lapsed should apply themselves to "good deeds [*iustis operibus*] which can wash away [their] sins, be constant and generous in giving alms, whereby souls are freed from death" (35). In his *On Works and Alms*, which was written during a deadly and devastating plague after the persecution (252–54 CE), Cyprian capitalized on the appeal of heavenly reward and the contrast between earthly and heavenly riches to entreat the rich members of his church. Quoting Tobit 12:8–9, Cyprian stresses salvific efficacy of almsgiving and connects it to the day of the judgment (5, 9). In proportion as Christians grow rich in this world, they become poor to God (13). The rich members should "make Christ a partner with [them] in [their] earthly possessions, that He also may make [them] a fellow-heir with Him in His heavenly kingdom" (13).

According to Abraham Cronbach, the difference between charity and social justice lies in the fact that "charity seems to signify the relieving of poverty without regard to what people may have done to cause the poverty, while social justice holds people—that is, people other than the sufferer—accountable and directs its course accordingly."[42] In one sense, the early Christian vision for eschatological judgment and great reversal could be seen as a way and call to bring about social justice *in this world* insofar as it identifies those responsible for social injustice ("the wicked rich") and anticipates the fate of everyone in the world to come. On the other hand, the increasing shift from the great reversal to salvific almsgiving could be seen as steering a focus from social justice to charity. Nonetheless, the cumulative effect of ethical paraenesis and eschatological judgment is that they serve as a boundary maker for early Christians as God's eschatological people—they will be judged by what they do to those who are helpless, lowly, and poor.

## Eschatological Visions, Dualism, and Use of Wealth

We turn now to a second way in which eschatology shaped early Christian socio-ethical thought in the pre-Constantine era. It fostered dualistic visions with respect both to the Christian's true home and to the Christian's

---

42. A. Cronbach, "The Social Ideals of the Apocrypha and the Pseudepigrapha," *Hebrew Union College Annual* 18 (1944): 143.

true wealth. These visions may be seen in two important texts: Hermas's Shepherd and *Acts of Thomas*. In the former is a particular concern to explore a dualism between a Christian's earthly and heavenly residence. The latter juxtaposes earthly and heavenly wealth.

Scholars still debate Hermas's literary genre, to what extent it is a "genuine" apocalypse, pointing out its lack of revelation about eschatological future, end-time cataclysm, or pessimism in history and the present world order. Its content is largely paraenetic on repentance while it retains an apocalyptic form and style such as visions, parables, allegories, and eschatological urgency, and warnings.[43] However, as Carolyn Osiek has shown, Hermas can be legitimately categorized as apocalyptic literature by its function.[44] Apocalyptic literature addresses a crisis of some sort, whether political, spiritual, or historical, and whether real, perceived, or imagined, by constructing an alternative vision and exhorting concrete behaviors based on that alternative perception of reality.[45] Hermas serves the same function of apocalypse as it deals with an internal crisis of the local Christian community utilizing apocalyptic form and style.

In a series of the visions of a cosmic tower (the eschatological church), Hermas discovers that wealth is a problem insofar as it ties the rich person to the present world. The rich person's faith dissolves in times of persecution (*Vis.* 3.6.5), and he or she is preoccupied with security and well-being to the neglect of his or her social responsibility to care for the needy (*Vis.* 3.9.2–6). Eschatological salvation and wealth cannot go together unless the latter is "cut away" from the rich; and in light of the coming judgment, a major warning is directed to those "who exult in [their] wealth" lest they "together with [their] good things be shut outside the door of the tower" (*Vis.* 3.9.5–6).

Later in Hermas's text, *Similitude* 9, it becomes clear that rich persons are integral to the construction of the cosmic tower. They are round stones who must be transformed into useable, square stones, a transformation that involves

---

43. See P. Vielhauer and G. Strecker, "Apocalypses and Related Subjects: Introduction" in *Writings Relating to Apostles, Apocalypses and Related Subjects*, ed. W. Schneemelcher in *New Testament Apocrypha*, vol. 2, rev. ed., trans. R. McL. Wilson (Louisville: Westminster John Knox, 1991, 1992), 544–60; N. Brox, *Der Hirt des Hermas*, Kommentar zu den Apostolischen Vätern 7 (Göttingen: Vandenhoeck & Ruprecht, 1991), 36–37.

44. C. Osiek, "The Genre and Function of The Shepherd of Hermas," in *Early Christian Apocalypticism: Genre and Social Setting*, Semeia 36, ed. A. Y. Collins, (Decatur, Ga.: Scholars Press, 1986), 113–21.

45. See Osiek, "The Shepherd of Hermas," 115–118; Osiek, *The Shepherd of Hermas: A Commentary*, Hermeneia (Minneapolis: Augsburg Fortress, 1999), 12.

"cutting away" their wealth. Yet, the fact remains that rich persons have the opportunity to be transformed and that some will take advantage of that opportunity while the tower is being constructed. Indeed, the tower will not be complete until the master comes and tests the building (*Sim.* 9.5.2); only the completion of the tower with the master's visit brings the eschaton (*Vis.* 3.8.9; *Sim.* 9.5.1). The rich have a short window of opportunity to be cleaned up and cut off from "this world and the vanities of their possessions" (*Sim.* 9.31.2); the urgency to repent and change lies in the fact that the master might come suddenly and unexpectedly (*Sim.* 9.7.6). Indeed, the danger of wealth has to do with its distraction and entanglement with this world through business affairs and with the rich avoiding their responsibility; however, those who repent "quickly" will enter the Kingdom (*Sim.* 9.20.1–4). Interestingly, Hermas relates that, although wealth must be cut away, it should not be eliminated completely. Instead, some wealth is left "so that they might be able to do some good with that which was left to them, and they will live to God" (9.31.5). Thus, the goal is not to denounce wealth or the rich as such but to move the rich into concrete behaviors for the good of the community (and for their own good).[46] Here the paraenetic nature of eschatological visions and warnings is clearly shown.

The point of the cosmic tower may be seen as well in Hermas's parable of a cosmic willow tree in *Similitude* 8. Among the willow tree's various branches, there are some leaves that are half-withered and half-green and there are some leaves that are two-thirds withered and one-third green. The former leaves represent *believers* preoccupied with business. the latter leaves represent *believers* who became wealthy, acquired honor and status among the pagans, lived according to their standards, and failed to "do the works of faith" (*Sim.* 8.8.1; 8.9.1). In both cases, the problem for these believers is double-mindedness *(dipsychia)*. Double-mindedness, a major issue and concern in Hermas, is a typical characteristic of those with "a divided allegiance . . . doubt, uncertainty with regard to God and salvation, and with regard to their own affairs."[47] It is this

---

46. See Hermas's comments about communal responsibility, including "serving widows, looking after orphans and those in need, delivering God's servants form distress, being hospitable . . . becoming more needy (*endeesteros*; cf. Mandates 11:8) than all other people, . . . not oppressing debtors and all those in need" (Mandates 8:10).

47. J. Reiling, *Hermas and Christian Prophecy: A Study of the Eleventh Mandate*, NovTSup 37 (Leiden: Brill, 1973), 22–32; quoted by C. Osiek, *The Shepherd of Hermas*, 31.

double-mindedness, "an earthly spirit from the devil" (*Man.* 9.11), that absorbs them in "all the vanities of this life" (*Man.* 9.4) and therefore prevents them to turn to God "unhesitatingly" (*Man.* 9.2, 4, 6). It invariably causes dissension and division for it leads those affected to disassociate themselves from their Christian community and to ignore acts of charity and hospitality (i.e., "the works of faith") in favor of their own affairs. Ultimately, double-mindedness is a manifestation of pride (see *Sim.* 8.9.1), and it has communal consequences. Therefore, once again, the call is to swift repentance so that "their home may be within the tower" (*Sim.* 8.8.3; 8.9.4), but "for those who do not repent, persist in their pleasures, death is near" (*Sim.* 8.9.4).

The sum of this tension between this world and the world to come, a dualism that is both temporal and spatial, is expressed in a parable of two cities (*Sim.* 1.1–11). This parable, according to Osiek, is "the author's clearest articulation of his view of the Christian's place in society."[48] It portrays Christian existence in terms of a dual residence, one in a foreign city and one in the city of eschatological destiny, and each are governed by a law incompatible with the other. Acquiring fields, buildings, and other properties in the temporary, earthly (and, therefore, foreign) city is a sure sign of foolishness and double-mindedness, for the lord of the foreign city will inevitably expel Christians who claim they are subject to the laws of their eschatological city (see *Sim.* 1.1–4). Christians cannot keep the law of their eschatological city by retaining possessions in the foreign city, so it is to their best interest that they be self-sufficient (αὐτάρκεια), free and prepared to leave the land at any time (*Sim.* 1.5–6). "Instead of fields, buy souls that are in distress, as anyone is able, and visit widows and orphans, and do not neglect them; and spend your wealth and all your possessions, which you received from God, on fields and houses of this kind" (*Sim.* 1.8). Once again, these divine commandments articulate the classic (Jewish and) Christian acts of charity as a way of converting earthly temporal riches into heavenly spiritual riches—since it is God's intention and purpose for earthly wealth. God makes one rich for this reason, that is, for performing "ministries" or "services" (διακονίαι), and therefore "it is much better to purchase fields and possessions and houses of this kind" (*Sim.* 1.9). This eschatological motif does not renounce material wealth but affirms it as

48. Osiek, *The Shepherd of Hermas*, 158.

God's gift, relativizes its earthly significance, and channels it to its proper use of amassing spiritual wealth through acts of charitable ministry.

Whereas in Hermas's Shepherd the expressed dualism was between the proper orientation of the Christian towards their true, heavenly home and the double-mindedness that too often directed their gaze towards the earthly home, in *Acts of Thomas* the expressed dualism is between the eschatological significance of earthly and heavenly wealth.[49] Riches in this world—gold, silver, and jewelry—are corruptible, transient, and attend to bodily pleasures (36, 37, 116, 117), but riches in heaven—the Kingdom of God (66) and eternal life (130, 136)—are incorruptible, everlasting and nourish the soul. The former are "entirely useless" in the world above and so must be "left behind," but the latter are indispensable and sufficient for the life above (66). Only those who despise earthly treasures will find the everlasting treasures in heaven (130).

The *Acts* employs opulent imagery and acquisitive language to describe heavenly riches. In a famous "Hymn of the Pearl" sung by Thomas, the heavenly palace is described as a place of wealth and luxury adorned with gold, silver, and precious stones (108). In the story of Thomas building a palace for king Gundaphorus, heaven is described as full of palaces and mansions.[50] When Gad, the king's brother, dies, he sees different palaces in heaven, including that built by Thomas for the king. It is so desirable that Gad bargains to buy it from the his brother upon returning to life on earth (22–24). Heavenly riches are much to be coveted and desired. Indeed, the ascetic Thomas is unashamed to

---

49. Elsewhere, I have compared the dualism of earthly and heavenly riches and the dualism of earthly and heavenly marriage. See H. Rhee, "Wealth and Poverty in the *Acts of Thomas*," presented at the Prayer and Spirituality in the Early Church Conference V, Melbourne, Australia, 2008.

50. At the request of the king to build an earthly palace, Thomas takes all the money given by the king and distributes to the poor and needy in the cities and villages. As he keeps providing alms for the poor (the afflicted), orphans and widows with king's gold and silver, Thomas assures the king that his palace is being built. When the king finds out what has been happening and demands an explanation, Thomas's answer only enrages the bewildered king further: "Now you cannot see it, but you shall see it when you depart this life" (21). This is the context in which Gad, the king's brother, dies, witnesses the magnificent heavenly place belonged to the king, and attempts to persuade the king to sell it to him upon returning to earth. Only then the king realizes Thomas's words and actions, seeks forgiveness from Thomas's God, and finally joins him in serving God. Almsgiving here not only obtains one's "eternal benefits" but even works vicariously for an inadvertent giver of alms (24). Hence the prayer of the king: "I may become worthy to be an inhabitant of that house for which indeed I have done nothing, but which you [Thomas], labouring alone, have built for me with the help of the grace of your God" (24). This episode may bear the strongest testimony to salvific efficacy of almsgiving even on behalf of an unbeliever.

preach to Tertia, the king's wife, a heavenly, prosperity gospel: "if you truly believe in him, . . . he will make you great and rich and an heir to his Kingdom" (136). Heavenly reward far outweighs any earthly compensation.

As in Hermas's *Shepherd*, the surest means of acquiring heavenly riches in *Acts of Thomas* is almsgiving, or acts of service. The *Acts* presents a consistent pattern of conversion resulting in almsgiving and vice versa, which is typical in Christian social thought by this time.[51] Thomas' ascetic message of renouncing the world and turning to God who will judge the world leads the people to mass conversion (59). The people bring their money to serve the widows, and they leave their homes and patrimonies (59, 61). Yet, this call is not necessarily meant to be voluntary poverty, or renunciation in an absolute sense. The call for material renunciation is not as consistent or radical as that of sexual renunciation in *Acts*. Upon their conversion, the king and his brother Gad faithfully follow Thomas, "providing for the poor, giving to all, and relieving all" (26); however, there is no mention of them giving *all* and distributing *all* of their possessions to the poor. So, too, in the conversion of Siphor, a captain of King Misdaeus in India and "one of the wealthiest in India" (62), it does not mention the entire dispossession of his wealth. The same is true of other wealthy people in *Acts*. The danger of earthly riches is real and serious, but ultimately "neither shall riches help the rich, nor will poverty save the poor from judgment" (83). Unlike the universal call to sexual renunciation necessary for heavenly marriage, the call to material renunciation is neither universal nor necessary for heavenly riches but is relativized.

The only exception may be Thomas, who fills the role of a mediator and revealer of the one true God, Jesus Christ.[52] Jesus Christ, the "true riches" (136, 145), is "Lord of undefiled possessions" (156), a giver of great gifts and abundant riches (120, 142, 149, 159). At the same time, he is also the "poor one" (156) and ascetic (143); he is "hope of the poor" (10), "hope of the weak and trust of the poor, refuge and shelter of the weary" (156); he is "the support of the orphans and the nourisher of the widows and rest and repose to all who

---

51. See, for example, H. Rhee, "Wealth and the Wealthy in the *Acts of Peter,*" presented at XV International Conference on Patristic Studies, Oxford, U.K., 2007; see also "almsgiving as the marker of the doctrinal orthodoxy" in apocryphal acts, in R. Finn, *Almsgiving in the Later Roman Empire: Christian Promotion and Practice 313–450* (Oxford: Oxford University Press, 2006), 129–31.

52. See M. Hengel, *Property and Riches*, 51–53.

are afflicted" (19). As an imitator of Christ, Thomas lives a life of poverty on earth so that he can obtain heavenly riches (61). Just like his Lord, Thomas is known for his poverty (66, 96, 136, 139, 149), ascetic practices and preaching (3, 5, 28, 100, 136), and generosity to the poor (19, 20, 62). In fact, it is this imitation of Christ that accords him spiritual authority and mediating power as an apostolic "stand-in" for his "new God," Christ. Thomas regards his earthly poverty as a necessary condition for gaining his heavenly wealth. Therefore, he can claim his heavenly riches with certainty: "for my recompenser is righteous; he knows how I ought to receive my reward; for he is not grudging nor envious, but is rich in his gifts; . . . for he has confidence in his possessions which cannot fail" (159). In this sense, renunciation of earthly riches does serve as an ideal of imitating Christ and affords one a unique status and power for securing heavenly wealth.

## Conclusion

This study has stressed the close mutual impact and effect of eschatological expectations and social messages on the issue of wealth and poverty in pre-Constantine Christianity. Eschatology served at least two important social functions. On the one hand, it provided a conceptual and practical framework of divine judgment. A coming "great reversal," a separation between the "oppressive" rich and the "righteous" poor, was expected to bring about right conduct in this world. In the Jewish apocalyptic texts and the earlier Christian texts, the association of the wicked rich with the threat of the judgment and the pious poor with the promise of justice and reward featured prominently. However, it is also in the apocalyptic framework that the rich and the poor are exhorted to support and to benefit each other through their respective services in anticipation of the coming judgment. In this context, we discussed how our sources interpret and reformulate definitions of wealth and poverty, and the rich and the poor.

The eschatological visions and moral exhortations are also brought together to bear on the *present* earthly issues of social dissonance and stratification in the Christian communities (Hermas) and even of disaster relief for the wider communities *(On Works and Alms)*. The danger of wealth has mainly to do with its earthly attachment obscuring the desire for gaining heavenly riches. While avarice and luxury are universally denounced in apocalyptic critique, one can discern ambiguity about renunciation of wealth and Christian commercial activities; renunciation is held as an ideal but relativization of wealth is practiced through almsgiving. We have also seen how the Christian, eschatological hope offered an alternative reality and identity markers in Christian social contexts and how the eschatological discourses both encouraged and constructed Christian social ethics.

*Wendy Mayer*

# 5. The Audience(s) for Patristic Social Teaching

## *A Case Study*

When we reflect on the audience of social teaching by the Fathers of the Church, it is not unnatural to look first to the most overt of patristic media for the delivery of moral instruction—the sermon. In a book titled *The Media Revolution of Early Christianity*, however, the author, Doron Mendels, challenges us to broaden our perspective. He proposes that Eusebius's *Ecclesiastical History*, an overtly nonethical text, nonetheless has at its core the message that the Catholic Church represents the right order in society. This message, he argues, permeates the stories recorded, and is demonstrated "in many ways, such as helping the sick and setting a moral example by maintaining purity within family life . . . and in embodying such virtues as honesty, peace, simplicity, love of neighbor, and love of God."[1] By emphasizing that "in many fields of life Christians . . . provided an outstanding moral example," Eusebius, he contends, shows how they "contributed by their pure behaviour to the welfare of society."[2] Mendels identifies the audience at which this message is aimed as the broader gentile Graeco-Roman community, rather than Jews, reasoning that

---

1. D. Mendels, *The Media Revolution of Early Christianity: An Essay on Eusebius's* Ecclesiastical History (Grand Rapids, Mich.: Eerdmans, 1999), 208–9. Mendels does not argue that this is the only message at the core of the *Historia ecclesiastica*, viewing it rather within the framework of mission.

2. Mendels, *Media Revolution*, 211.

the latter would have been uninterested, since they adhered to the same moral values.[3] Similarly, Richard Finn, in his study of almsgiving in the later Roman empire, shows how not just sermons but texts such as the *Acts of Peter* and the *Acts of Thomas* give prominence to the practice of almsgiving, in this instance using it "as a marker of the doctrinal orthodoxy recognized by their authors and redactors."[4] The *Apostolic Constitutions* is yet another type of nonhomiletic text that constitutes a source of instruction concerning good ecclesiastical and social order.[5] Like the apocryphal Acts just mentioned, this too has its own peculiar audience. It was compiled in the Syrian milieu as an alternative body of canonico-institutional material with its own (apostolic) claim to orthodoxy. Joseph Mueller, who has recently produced a monumental study of its Old Testament ecclesiology, proposes that the *Apostolic Constitutions* is not just a compilation of earlier sources, but has its own literary integrity and that it emerges in opposition to the pro-Nicene canonical material that was assembled by Meletius, bishop of Antioch, and promoted by the emperor Theodosius I. It is this anti-imperial and anti-Nicene stance, and its rapport with Bible and tradition, Mueller argues, that explains the text's particular reading of the Old Testament. It also explains why citations of the Old Testament are more frequent in the *Apostolic Constitutions* than in its sources.[6] The point to be made here, firstly, is that not just sermons, but a wide variety of media were utilized by the early Christians to convey social ethical teaching. A second, more important point is that each medium and each text within that medium had their own specific interests in promoting social teaching, and that those interests were intimately connected both with the community within which it was produced and with its target audience.

3. Ibid., 210.

4. R. Finn, *Almsgiving in the Later Roman Empire: Christian Promotion and Practice (313–450)* (Oxford: Oxford University Press, 2006), 130.

5. *Const. ap.* 4.1–2, in particular deals with helping others in need, giving, the proper use of money and other social teachings. On the moral instruction contained in church orders in general see Finn, *Almsgiving*, 126.

6. J. G. Mueller, *L'Ancien Testament dans l'ecclésiologie des pères. Une lecture des* Constitutions Apostoliques (Turnhout: Brepols, 2004), esp. 121–26. For a discussion of the relationship of *Const. ap.* to other "church orders" produced within the first four centuries of Christianity, see J. G. Mueller, "The Ancient Church Order Literature: Genre or Tradition?" *Journal of Early Christian Studies* 15 (2007): 337–80; and P. Bradshaw, *The Search for the Origins of Christian Worship* (London: SPCK, 1992), 80–110. Finn, *Almsgiving*, 126, argues that *Const. ap.* and the sources on which it draws were directed towards a limited clerical audience.

Bearing those points in mind, the texts that allow us to scrutinize the community that produced them and the audience towards which they were directed in the greatest detail remain sermons. In the remainder of this article a focused study of patristic preaching, with particular attention to the homiletic oeuvre of John Chrysostom and the topics of the proper use of wealth and care for the poor, will be employed to illustrate particular points regarding the relationship of context, message, and audience.[7] At the conclusion, reflection will be offered on the relevance of these issues more generally for contextualizing patristic social thought.

A point that Mendels makes in his discussion of the media strategy adopted by Eusebius is that he accommodates his message to the conceptual world within which his intended audience was raised. That is, Eusebius makes it easy for his audience to identify with his claim for the universal benefit to society of Christian virtues by normalizing it to the Greek literature and philosophical virtues familiar to an educated Greek-speaking audience.[8] This same point can be made of the social teaching offered in the homilies of John Chrysostom. On the topic of slavery, for instance, John will on one occasion use a Stoic model to argue that slavery is an *adiaphoron*, which has no bearing on the inner virtue of the Christian.[9] On another occasion he construes slavery within a Platonic framework to argue that the slave is a model of a properly philosophical life that every Christian should emulate.[10] On yet another occasion he invokes an Aristotelean view of slaves, when he argues that they are passionate, not open to impression, intractable, and not very apt to receive instruction in virtue. This

---

7. Not included in this discussion are the technical details of the social structure and gender and age composition of the audience in general, which are topics I have dealt with in detail elsewhere. See W. Mayer, "Female Participation and the Late Fourth-Century Preacher's Audience," *Augustinianum* 39 (1999): 139–47; Mayer, "Who Came to Hear John Chrysostom Preach? Recovering a Late Fourth-Century Preacher's Audience," *Ephemerides Theologicae Lovanienses* 76 (2000): 73–87; and Mayer, "John Chrysostom: Extraordinary Preacher, Ordinary Audience," in *Preacher and Audience: Studies in Early Christian and Byzantine Homiletics*, ed. M. Cunningham and P. Allen (Leiden: Brill, 1998), 105–37.

8. Mendels, *Media Revolution*, 208.

9. *In 1 Cor. hom.* 19 (PG 61, 155–7). John concludes (157): "Christianity is like this: in slavery it bestows the gift of freedom. Indeed, just as the body which is invulnerable demonstrates that it is invulnerable when it is struck by an arrow and suffers no harm, so the person who is strictly free is revealed when, even though he has masters, he is not enslaved. It is for this reason that Paul bids 'remain a slave.' If it is impossible for a person who is a slave to be a Christian, as they ought, Greeks will condemn true religion as substantially weak, just as, if they learn that slavery in no way harms the true religion, they will marvel at its teaching." See also *In Joh. hom.* 80 (PG 59, 436).

10. *In 1 Tim. hom.* 16 (PG 62, 589–90).

is through ill breeding and the fault of their masters, rather than nature, he allows, but nonetheless serves to underline his main point: that if Christianity can impose restraint upon a class inherently so self-willed, it makes the power of the true philosophy that has so reformed them all the more admirable.[11] John's approach to teaching his audiences about the proper attitude towards poverty and the use of wealth is not dissimilar.[12] On more than one occasion John used the Stoic idea of indifferents *(adiaphora)* to explain to his audience that poverty and wealth are in themselves neither good nor evil. Those values attach rather to how a person endures the one or uses the other.[13] Wealth used for the benefit of others becomes a good; when directed towards appropriating what belongs to others, towards greed and violence, it is converted into the opposite. This same basic Stoic understanding of poverty and wealth, allied with one of the Cynic paradoxes—that poverty is wealth—is utilized by John in his second homily on the parable of Lazarus and the rich man to explain why one should not consider the rich blessed nor despise the poor.[14] In the case of Lazarus, it is not the rich man who is truly rich, but the man who is to all intents and purposes utterly poor. The use of this paradox serves his message that it is not our lot here on earth that really matters but what happens when we face God's judgment after death. It is then that the masks are stripped away and the true nature of the rich person and the poor person are revealed.[15] This approach, of

11. *In Titum hom.* 4 (PG 62, 685). I am indebted to Noel Lenski (University of Colorado, Boulder), who is in the process of writing a book on slavery in late antiquity, for these observations ("John Chrysostom on Slavery," lecture, Center for the Study of Early Christianity, The Catholic University of America, March 9, 2006). Lenski makes the point that when he talks about slavery, John displays his own conformity to his cultural setting. He has no interest in teaching that an institution that is a normative element of Graeco-Roman society and integral to its economy is an injustice that should be overcome. His reflections on the topic assume that it is an immutable social structure that may be open to abuses that can be corrected, but on the whole slavery is more useful to him as a source of exempla for promoting other ideas about the moral way to live one's life.

12. For a detailed study on the philosophical underpinnings of his discourse on these topics see G. Viansino, "Aspetti dell'opera di Giovanni Crisostomo," *Koinonia* 25 (2001): 137–205.

13. See, e.g., *De peccata fratrum non evulganda* (PG 51, 355–56); *De Lazaro conc.* 2 (PG 48, 981); *Illud Isaiae: Ego dominus deus feci lumen* (PG 56, 147–48). Cf. *De Lazaro conc.* 3 (PG 48, 1002), where the same idea underlies the argument that not even wealth can benefit the person who is lazy, while not even poverty can harm the person who is alert. It is neither poverty nor sickness that compels a person to curse God, but rather disposition or dereliction of virtue.

14. On the paradoxes, see W. D. Desmond, *The Greek Praise of Poverty: Origins of Ancient Cynicism* (Notre Dame, Ind.: University of Notre Dame Press, 2006), 24.

15. *De Lazaro conc.* 2 (PG 48, 981 and 986). Although note that John exploits the paradox to greater effect in relation to the practice of voluntary poverty (asceticism) in *In Matt. hom.* 47/48 (PG 58, 486).

formulating the Christian message within the hearer's own framework of symbols and ideas, is one that had been adopted from the very beginning of Christianity.[16]

This same basically Stoic framing of wealth and poverty is employed by John not just when he is preaching to a lay audience, but also in a lengthy letter that he writes to the deaconess Olympias and her ascetic community on the topic that no one can in reality be harmed except by their own self.[17] There, as part of his broader message concerning the proper exercise of virtue, he seeks to teach that wealth is to be shunned and cast off, while poverty is in itself not harmful, if one endures it nobly and with true philosophy.[18] In this instance the level of education and social standing of his immediate audience is clear. Olympias was raised at the highest level of society and a significant number of her companions were either members of her own family or women from families that were of senatorial status.[19] Olympias is at this point in exile in Asia Minor.[20] Since a large number of the women in Olympias's ascetic community at Constantinople were former servants—she is said to have brought fifty from her own household into the community with her—and since she is unlikely to have gone into exile without them, this raises an interesting question about the audience to which patristic ethical teaching was addressed.[21] In general slaves would not have had the level of education expected of Olympias and her peers and therefore on the face of it were excluded from

16. See Mendels, *Media Revolution*, 206–8.

17. On the strong Platonic, Cynic, and Stoic resonances in this letter, which is in effect a treatise, see A.-M. Malingrey, *Lettre d'exil* (SC 103: Paris, 1964), 19–26.

18. *Quod nemo laeditur sed a seipso* 10 (SC 103, 106–8).

19. See W. Mayer, "Constantinopolitan Women in Chrysostom's Circle," *VC* 53 (1999): 267–8; and Mayer, "Poverty and Generosity towards the Poor in the Time of John Chrysostom," in *Wealth and Poverty in Early Christianity,* ed. S. Holman (Grand Rapids, Mich.: Baker Academic, 2008). That women in families of this status had tutors is suggested by the fact that the empress Eudoxia was tutored by Pansophius, who was later consecrated bishop of Nicomedia (Soz., *HE* 8.6.6). At that stage she was being raised as a foster child in the household of Promotus, military commander for the eastern empire. See Mayer, "Aelia Eudoxia (wife of Arcadius)," in *De Imperatoribus Romanis: An Online Encyclopedia of Roman Emperors,* available at www.roman-emperors.org (accessed 2002).

20. On the date of the letter (winter 406/407 CE), see *Ad Olymp. ep.* 17.4.c (SC 13bis, 384), where John in his final surviving letter to Olympias says that he has sent what he recently wrote on the topic that no one can be harmed except by oneself. On the date of that letter (spring 407), see R. Delmaire, "Les «lettres d'exil» de Jean Chrysostome. Études de chronologie et de prosopographie," *Recherches Augustiniennes* 25 (1991): 148; on the date Olympias went into exile (405), see ibid., 85.

21. *Vita Olymp.* 6 (SC 13bis, 418).

the message that the letter conveyed. They may well have been intended, however, to be a secondary audience, not through hearing the written message,
with which they would not readily have identified, but through seeing the
message exemplified in the behaviour of the women within their ascetic community to whom the message was directed. This possibility is raised by Mendels, who argues that, if we see the bulk of patristic texts prior to Constantine's conversion as mission-oriented, then for the gentiles who could not read
or who were not interested in "listening to the Christian 'charter,' the personal moral stance radiated by the Christian organization became an important
media asset."[22] Decades after the conversion of Constantine, we see this same
point made by John Chrysostom. For a preacher, the imprinting of right moral behaviour upon the Christian community served an important secondary
purpose. It was to their behaviour, he constantly told his audience, that non-
Christians looked when they assessed the effectiveness of Christian teaching
and the value of Christianity as a religion.[23] Through their behaviour Christians communicated a significant moral and social message to the wider community. When we assess John's social ethical teaching on the giving of alms,
on voluntary poverty, usury, and similar topics we should always keep this secondary audience in mind.

Christians who demonstrated through their actions the type of social ethical behaviour that John was trying to inculcate could as readily become an effective teaching tool not just for the non-Christian community but for other
Christians. In his first sermon on Genesis John states that he wanted to add
some arguments about charitable giving, but deems it pointless when there is a
far more persuasive exemplum present in the church in the form of their bishop, Flavian. Once again, his actions are more powerful than any word. This is a
man, he tells his audience, who has taken the house he inherited from his fam-

---

22. Mendels, *Media Revolution*, 209.
   23. E.g., *In Col. hom.* 10 (PG 62, 368): "For what if he (your master) is a Greek, while you are a
Christian? It is not the mask (role), but the actions that are examined"; *In Titum hom.* 4 (PG 62,685): "If
[a Greek master] were to see his slave who had been instructed in the virtuous way of life in Christ dis-
playing greater self-control than their own philosophers . . . he would in every respect admire the power
of the Gospel. For it is not from doctrines that Greeks assess doctrine, but from a person's actions and
their way of life." The same thought underlies John's instructions on the correct way to return to the
city after celebrating the festival of a martyr (*Hom. in martyres*; PG 50, 665–66): "the person returning from viewing martyrs should be recognisable to all—through their gaze, their appearance, their gait,
their compunction, and their composed thoughts."

ily and devoted it to the care of strangers to such a degree that it can scarcely be said to belong to him.[24] Yet precisely because it is almost literally theirs, it is to be thought of as his possession more than ever. The lesson this teaches is that what we possess is especially ours, when we use it not for our own benefit, but for the benefit of the poor.[25] By exploiting the convenience of being able to point to a living example the message is communicated in multiple ways. John communicates it to his immediate audience through his sermon; Flavian communicates it to the rest of the audience and to the wider Christian community through his actions; Flavian's actions and the altered behaviour of the audience are then expected to communicate the message to the wider, non-Christian community. There may in fact be another dimension here. John is careful to add that the actions he holds up for emulation are not indiscriminate. The strangers towards whom the bishop extends his charity are people who have been driven to Antioch from elsewhere on account of the true, that is, Nicene faith.[26] This reminds us that at Antioch at the time that this sermon was preached there were at least three separately worshipping Christian communities: an Arian or Anomoean community, a Nicene community led by Bishop Evagrius, and a larger Nicene community into which John had been baptized and in which he served as a priest.[27] It was this latter community, of which Flavian was bishop, within which John preached. When we talk, then, of the Christian community to whom the message was directed or by whose actions it was further disseminated, we need to take care to discriminate. It may be that one of the secondary target audiences of social ethical teaching was not just the wider non-Christian community, but heterodox Christian groups.

There is also a tertiary audience that needs to be brought into consideration. John's success as an instructor of social ethical behaviour and as an exegete of the Gospels of Matthew and John and of the Pauline epistles, whose

24. Despite the use of the term οἰκία, which tends to denote the physical building (LSJ s.v. οἰκία), it is clear that Flavian's largesse is assumed to include the expenditure necessary to support the care of the inmates, which would have included the dole and slaves that went with the property.

25. *Sermo 1 in Gen.* (SC 433, 170).

26. SC 433, 170.267–68.

27. For a neat summary of the Meletian schism at Antioch and John's place in it, see A. J. Quiroga Puertas, "Elementos hagiográficos en las 'Homilías de las estatuas' de Juan Crisóstomo," *Collectanea Christiana Orientalia* 4 (2007): 145–46.

content often prompted John's ethical instruction, was so great that texts that had been intended primarily for the specific communities of Antioch and Constantinople were transmitted to other geographic areas. They were also translated into other languages. We find them, too, re-used in their original or in other forms by Greek- and other language-speaking communities in later centuries. The most extreme example of this latter practice are the forty-eight Eclogues, each of which is a pastiche of genuine Chryosostomic exegesis and teaching derived from multiple homilies, treatises, and letters, reshaped to suit the needs of a Greek-speaking community in what appears to have been the tenth century.[28] In regard to the broad transmission of John's genuine works which contain social teaching, an early example is the translation into Latin by Anianus of Celeda of the series of homilies which comprise his commentary on Matthew and which contain a great deal of material about almsgiving, voluntary poverty, and the proper use of wealth. The translation was completed by c. 420 CE.[29] The translator, Anianus, was closely engaged in the Pelagian controversy. Pelagius in turn held strong views against the holding of wealth.[30] This raises the issue of how John's social teaching was received when it was read aloud in communities beyond those for which it had originally been intended.[31]

The transmission of John's social teaching into other languages and language communities also reminds us that both in Antioch and Constantinople, John on occasion preached to congregations who were either bilingual or who comprised a mixed audience of whom only a portion spoke and understood Greek, while another portion spoke and understood only Gothic or Syriac.[32]

---

28. See S. J. Voicu, "Pseudo-Giovanni Crisostomo: I confini del corpus," *Jahrbuch für Antike und Christentum* 39 (1996): 109–10 regarding the connection between the Eclogues and Theodore Daphnopates. The composite sources for each are listed by J. A. de Aldama, *Repertorium Pseudochrysostomicum* (Paris: CNRS, 1965), passim (for inventory numbers, see *CPG* 4684).

29. His translation of only the first twenty-five survives in the manuscripts. See R. Skalitzky, "Annianus of Celeda, his text of Chrysostom's Homilies on Matthew," *Aevum* 45 (1971): 208–33.

30. See B. Neil, "On True Humility: An Anonymous Letter on Poverty and the Female Ascetic," in *Prayer and Spirituality in the Early Church* 4, *The Spiritual Life,* ed. W. Mayer, P. Allen, and L. Cross (Strathfield: St. Paul's Publishers, 2006), 233–46, esp. 238.

31. For some discussion on this point, see K. Cooper, "An(n)ianus of Celeda and the Latin readers of John Chrysostom," *Studia Patristica* 27 (1993): 249–55.

32. See *Cat.* 8 (SC 50bis, 247–60), *De statuis hom.* 19 (PG 49,187–98), and *Hom. habita postquam presbyter Gothus* (PG 63, 499–510). In the first two instances less well-educated Syriac-speakers from rural areas of Syria were present; in the third the congregation was comprised largely of Nicene Goths to

At Constantinople, which in the late fourth century as the capital of the eastern half of the Roman empire, attracted visitors from various regions of the western half of the empire as well as from all over the east and Egypt, Latin-speakers, Syriac-speakers, Gothic-speakers, and Greek-speakers could all be present on the same occasion.[33] Regardless of the composition of his audience John never deviated from preaching in Greek. This raises the possibility that the non-Greek-speaking sectors of the audience either failed to receive his message altogether, because they could not understand it or that for their benefit there was provided simultaneous translation. Even if they had access via simultaneous translation, since his preaching was accommodated to the symbols, ideas and cultural norms of a Greek-speaking and Greek-thinking audience, we must ask to what degree a Latin-, Syriac- or Gothic-thinking and speaking group would readily have identified with or accepted his social message.

Thus far we have defined John's primary target audience as Greek by language and education and, at Antioch at least, as belonging to the larger of two separately worshipping Nicene Christian communities. Those communities were in competition with, in turn, a separately worshipping Arian community and a vibrant Jewish community.[34] While the notoriety of his career at Constantinople may give the impression that there John presided over a city that was uniformly Nicene, caution too must be exercised in this instance. In one of the first sermons that he preached in that city he indicates that the Nicene community was as yet quite small, comparing it unfavourably to the size of the community to whom he had preached in Antioch.[35] He in fact states that the church building in which he preaches is surrounded by heretics.[36] This is not unsurprising when we consider that until 381 the churches of Constantinople had for some fifty years been in the possession of the Arian community, that Anomoean monks had long been working in the city, that a large portion of the military command infrastructure and troops stationed near the city

whom the lessons had been read and a sermon preached in Gothic. Since John preached his own sermon in Greek, either the congregation was bilingual or the sermon was translated simultaneously.

33. See *Hom. dicta postquam reliquiae martyrum* (PG 63, 472).

34. The active status or otherwise of the various Graeco-Roman cults in Antioch at this time is difficult to determine. For the most recent analysis of how identity worked for an adherent of Graeco-Roman "religion" at this time, see I. Sandwell, *Religious Identity in Late Antiquity. Greeks, Jews and Christians in Antioch* (Cambridge: Cambridge University Press, 2007).

35. *Contra anomoeos hom.* 11 (SC 396, 286–88).

36. SC 396, 288.18–23.

were Arian, because as Goths that was the version of Christianity under which they had been converted, and that the Novatian community, a rigorist sect of Christianity, continued to possess churches in the city and enjoy the patronage of the eastern emperors even after Theodosius I had declared Nicene Christianity the approved religion.[37] One other primary target audience we identified were the educated women who belonged, even in exile from Constantinople, to Olympias's ascetic community. We identified a secondary audience in the form of the wider non-Christian community and perhaps also one or more of the local heterodox Christian communities. A number of tertiary audiences were also identified in the form of Christian communities elsewhere in the world to whom John's social teachings were transmitted, often in translation, or communities who centuries later extracted what they deemed valuable from his teachings and reformulated it to suit their own purposes. Having pursued the question of audience in ever broadening circles, we now reverse direction to narrow down the focus and to turn to a more minute examination of John's audiences in each city and to explore further how this impacted on his social teaching.

Of his extant sermons the most direct that John ever preached at Constantinople on the topic of wealth is unarguably the homily that he delivered while the most powerful and feared public official in the eastern empire, the consul-eunuch Eutropius, cowered at the altar of the episcopal church, in fear of being handed over to the emperor's troops for execution. Because of the presence of the fugitive and the shock of his deposition, the church was full to overflowing. On the day following this newsworthy event, people from every sector of society jostled to be present. He likens the breadth and size of the crowd to the attendance at Easter.[38] Men who would normally forego church to conduct business, and women who might otherwise have been engaged in running the household are among those present. The exception to his audi-

---

37. See W. Mayer, "Cathedral Church or Cathedral Churches? The Situation at Constantinople (c.360–404 AD)," *Orientalia Christiana Periodica* 66 (2000): 49–68; D. Caner, *Wandering, Begging Monks: Spiritual Authority and the Promotion of Monasticism in Late Antiquity* (Berkeley: University of California Press, 2002), ch. 5; G. Dagron, "Les moines et la ville. Le monachisme à Constantinople jusqu'au concile de Chalcédoine (451)," *Travaux et Mémoires* 4 (1970): 229–76; J. H. W. G. Liebeschuetz, *Barbarians and Bishops: Army, Church, and State in the Age of Arcadius and Chrysostom* (Oxford: Oxford University Press, 1990); and A. Cameron and J. Long, with L. Sherry, *Barbarians and Politics at the Court of Arcadius* (Berkeley: University of California Press, 1993).

38. *In Eutropium* (PG 52, 394.40–50).

ence is the imperial household (he carefully invokes the absence of the emperor, who remains not too far away from the church in the palace). Also absent is the army, who is baying for Eutropius's blood.[39] In these circumstances, when John has the entire city as it were hanging on his word, we find the same techniques employed in the service of his message that we observed in his first sermon on Genesis. Initially he addresses his lesson solely to Eutropius. Wealth and power are empty and fleeting, as he has so frequently tried to teach him.[40] Only this time there is no need to take John's word for it. By his very circumstances Eutropius can no longer avoid the truth of the message that wealth is not just difficult to hold on to, but that it can even become the death of the person who possesses it. From this single, almost literally captive member of his audience, John then turns to everyone else who is present. Eutropius at this point becomes John's co-teacher in his message concerning poverty and wealth.[41] His fate, his presence, the consequences of his actions are woven into John's instruction as a powerful demonstration of the truth of his words and an effective medium for communicating his message. Simply from seeing this most powerful and rich of all men brought so low, a rich person would have their arrogance and conceit knocked out of them and would depart reflecting on human affairs in the philosophical way that they ought. A poor person would be comforted, no longer despising their state, realizing that their poverty affords them security. Slaves would, presumably, reflect on their own situation in a similar way.[42] These are in essence the same messages that poverty and wealth are masks and that in poverty there is true wealth that we have seen transmitted in other sermons.

What is more significant here is that John draws an even more powerful message from action about forgiveness of one's enemies and about social justice. The church, which has so generously and compassionately given Eutropius sanctuary, is the same church of which Eutropius had long been an enemy and from whom he had by legislation taken away the right of sanctuary.[43] Eutropius, John makes a point of saying, is the first person to break his own law.[44] By his actions he shows that he has learnt the lesson that Christians forgive

---

39. PG 52, 395–96.

40. PG 52, 392: "Haven't I said to you constantly that wealth is a runaway slave? But you wouldn't put up with us. Didn't I say that it's an ungrateful servant? But you didn't want to be convinced."

41. PG 52, 393–95.                    42. PG 52, 394.60–395.22.

43. PG 52, 392 and 394.25–30.          44. PG 52, 394.29–30.

their enemies. It is the audience, who are angry towards their bishop for giving so despised a public figure sanctuary, who have failed to learn to put into action the precept that they pray regularly in the Lord's prayer.[45] By standing up to the anger of the government, the military, and popular rage, the church demonstrates the truth of Jesus' own command concerning forgiveness. As the Gospel of John shows, when Jesus welcomed the prostitute who touched his feet, he was in no way harmed, but on the contrary transmitted his own purity to her.[46] By the time he has finished the sermon, the audience has been moved to tears.[47] By exhibiting forgiveness and begging the emperor to let Eutropius, whom they hated, live, John argues, the audience will have taught an important lesson about compassion not just to the emperor, but to the entire population of Constantinople and ultimately, as news of their behaviour spreads, to the entire Graeco-Roman world.[48] In this homily thus, while John begins by addressing his message to a single person, Eutropius, the audience he targets keeps expanding. Through the actions of Eutropius his message about the proper way to regard wealth is directed towards the full range of people in his audience; to that same audience, through his own actions he, as representative of the church and their bishop, teaches them about forgiving their enemies; by adopting his teaching, together he and the audience can then focus their message on the government, via the emperor; and through the success of that Christian social action they will then persuade the entire known world of the effectiveness of Christian ethical teaching. The ripple effect of just this one Christian precept (forgiveness of one's enemies), he argues in this sermon, can be powerful indeed. This is an exceptional primary audience and an exceptional occasion, but it serves to show that John knew how to exploit the parameters of his audience and the circumstances available to him to their fullest extent in the service of communicating important Christian ethical concepts.

A different point is illustrated when we look more minutely at his audience at Antioch. Here it is interesting to observe that in promoting the Christian ethic of using one's possessions not for oneself, but for the care of others in need, John was aware that the Christian ethos he was trying to inculcate often conflicted with social views prevalent in the Graeco-Roman empire and more locally at Antioch. As I have argued elsewhere, in a world in which the notion

---

45. PG 52, 393–94.                           46. PG 52, 394/10–25.
47. PG 52, 395.20–28.                        48. PG 52, 396.

of "limited good" permeated the way in which people viewed their own possessions in relation to the possessions of others, any person who could not support themselves and needed assistance from others to survive was treated with considerable suspicion.[49] At the same time the apostolic teaching that it was the duty of the lay Christian community to care for widows and orphans had by the late fourth century become institutionalized to the point that the Christian community at Antioch believed that it was the duty of the church and its clergy to care for the poor in society, rather than being their own personal responsibility. John was obliged to negotiate his way delicately between these two systems of belief in order to communicate his message. We see one example of how John tackled this issue in his twenty-first homily on 1 Corinthians. There once again the message is that one's beliefs are clearly expressed in one's actions. In relation to the dominical command expressed in Matthew 19:21 ("If you wish to be perfect, go and sell what you own and give the money to the poor"), John argues that Christ left the choice open, giving us the opportunity to do even more than he commanded. Yet what does his audience do? Not only don't they aspire to do more, but they fall far short of Christ's instruction. What they effectively say is: "Let moths eat what we've stored away, but let the poor person not eat; let time destroy our possessions, but don't let Christ be fed, even though he is hungry." To the imagined objection that no one in his audience would say that, John points out that the serious thing is that these sentiments aren't expressed in words, but are communicated clearly in how his audience behaves.[50]

As the homily progresses he leads his audience carefully through the inhumanity behind their reasons for not giving. The first is the common social belief that the indigent poor are not really as pitiful as they appear, but exaggerate their appearance to induce giving. Even if this is a genuine strategy

---

49. See Mayer, "Poverty and generosity" (n. 19). For the original statement of this cultural anthropological model, see G. M. Foster, "Peasant Society and the Image of Limited Good," *American Anthropologist* 67 (1965): 293–315; and Foster, "A Second Look at Limited Good," *Anthropological Quarterly* 45 (1972): 57–64. For the range of criticisms which initially greeted this model, see J.R. Gregory, "'Image of Limited Good,' or Expectation of Reciprocity?" *Current Anthropology* 16 (1975): 73–92. The model has gained currency in New Testament studies. See, e.g., B. Malina, *The New Testament World. Insights from Cultural Anthropology* (Atlanta/London, 1981); R. L. Rohrbaugh, ed., *Using the Social Sciences in New Testament Interpretation*, (Peabody, Mass., 1996); and J. H. Neyrey and R. L. Rohrbaugh, "'He must increase, I must decrease' (John 3:30)' A cultural and social interpretation," *CBQ* 63 (2001): 464–83.

50. *In 1 Cor. hom.* 21 (Field 1847: 251).

employed by beggars, John argues, it says more about the hardheartedness of those who won't help them out, and so force them into this shameful practice. Contrary to their belief, disgrace and shame attaches to those who refuse to give, rather than to the beggars who are obliged to go to extremes to excite pity in those whom they solicit.[51] Even more pathetic is the fact that beggars are driven to entertain passersby by mutilating themselves and performing ever more extreme acts and that it is this rather than their indigent state that induces a willingness to give that is proportionate to their entertainment value.[52] Here we observe John attempting to address the incompatibility between the Christian ethic and the concept of "limited good." In a world where the person who is approached by a beggar believes that both what they possess and what is available within their society is limited, it follows that the act of giving without return dangerously diminishes the giver's own resources. Since reciprocity is a key concept within this framework, the person who needs to take from others to survive is accorded the same social value as a thief and their actions are conceived of as socially destabilizing. This explains why beggars who entertain were not perceived in this way, since they provided a service in return for the money, clothing or food that they received from their audience. This same belief, that those who take without return consume finite resources, underlies the widespread suspicion of refugees who had been driven to Antioch in a time of regional crisis, which John addresses in a different homily on almsgiving.[53] In the case of his homily on 1 Corinthians John's recourse to countering this belief and to the complaints of his audience that the church provides for the poor in any case—the argument that personal giving to the poor mitigates a person's sins—may well have fallen on deaf ears.[54] In other sermons at Antioch he worked more explicitly within the framework of "limited good," exploiting Luke 12:33 to argue, perhaps more persuasively, that almsgiving is a "commercial transaction" whereby goods deposited with the Lord here in the person of the poor are secured as treasure in heaven.[55]

To sum up, in the course of exploring the context in which patristic social teaching occurred by asking questions about its audience, a number of is-

---

51. Field 1847: 252–53.                      52. Field 1847: 253–54.

53. *De eleemosyna* (PG 51, 270).            54. *In 1 Cor. hom.* 21 (Field 1847: 255–56).

55. E.g., *De eleemosyna* (PG 51, 266); *De statuis hom.* 16 (PG 49, 170). Cf. *In Joh. hom.* 77 (PG 59, 418); *In Rom. hom.* 7 (PG 60, 452).

sues have come to our attention. In the first instance, setting patristic teaching within its own particular context can be seen to be essential, giving greater depth to our understanding of the injunction in question. In this respect understanding the agenda of the author, the specific community that gave birth to the text, and the particular nature of the target audience are all important for understanding the framing of the social message. So, too, is an understanding of the social concepts prevalent among the audience to which it was directed. Equally important has been the recognition that the reception of the message was almost certainly intended to function at a number of levels. The immediate target audience is usually not the only one, just as the message itself could be mediated not only via the text, but also via behaviour that exemplified the social teaching or the behaviour that the social teaching subsequently modified. For John Chrysostom, above all, social teaching and action go hand in hand and it is through the behaviour that results that we effectively communicate the power of the Christian gospel. One wonders if in this respect Mendels's analysis cannot be more broadly applied—that is, that, whatever the primary audience of patristic social teaching, one of its secondary aims is missiological.[56] While there is inevitably a vast gap between the patristic world and the world in which CST is situated, there are also points, one suspects, that remain in common.[57]

---

56. That is, from the apostolic period to at least the mid-fifth century, social ethical teaching served to establish identity within Christian communities as well as to define their identity in relation to other forms of Christianity and other religions. Within such a context it was important to convert those outside a particular Christian community to belief in the rightness and superiority of one's doctrine.

57. A significant difference lies in the emphasis in the Graeco-Roman context on personal rather than civic virtue, which is independent of the circumstances in which a human being finds themselves, as opposed to contemporary concern with the dignity of the human being and the right of each human being to live in a free and just society.

# PART III

# ISSUES IN PATRISTIC AND CATHOLIC SOCIAL THOUGHT

*Susan R. Holman*

# 6. Out of the Fitting Room

*Rethinking Patristic Social Texts on*
*"The Common Good"*

## Introduction: Garbing the Fathers

The Leuven Expert Seminar dialogue on "The Church Fathers and Catholic Social Thought" offered an extraordinary opportunity to explore what patristic sources might offer in the ongoing construction of modern Catholic social thought, and particularly how they might encourage religious dialogue for justice and goodness internationally. In this chapter, I apply this challenge to explore the use of patristic ideas as they relate specifically to the ethical rhetoric of "the common good."

Unlike the heterogeneity of Protestant social action rhetoric and the intentional mystery of Orthodox theologies, Catholic social teaching is very systematic.It may not be amiss, therefore, in light of the ecumenical potential of the topic, to introduce a creative metaphor with which to address patristic ideas of the "common good" with their concerns for the quality of the human image. Thus in this essay, I invite the reader to think through this process

Earlier versions of several sections of this paper were presented at the Research Group on Piety and Charity at the Institute of Advanced Study, Hebrew University, Jerusalem, in February, 2007, and at the Fifteenth International Conference on Patristic Studies, Oxford, U.K., in August, 2007. I am grateful to the organizers of these conferences and to those who participated in the discussions, especially Amitai Spitzer in Jerusalem and Richard Finn, O.P., at Oxford. The final text benefits from further conversations at both the Leuven expert seminar and Patristica Bostoniensia.

with me by envisioning as a somewhat playful analogy the image of the fitting room, that space in a shop where we try on a new suit or coat before deciding on its purchase.

In trying on ethical ideas that might have practical relevance today, the historian or theologian may be tempted to take ancient texts and cut and tuck them to make them fit our very differently shaped culture, dressing them up with current fashions into recognizably modern forms. Some will fit into street clothes; others clearly may not. There may be nothing wrong with either the fashion or the shape of the body that wears it—that is, neither our modern ideas nor our historical texts—but it should not surprise us if we face difficulties in trying to fit one to the other. There will always be some discrepancies between ancient and modern shapes of Christian ethics, discrepancies that challenge easy application and tempt us to pin down, trim off, and toss out what we don't think fits. Indeed, the Leuven project's first study—reviewing how official Catholic social teaching documents used ancient sources—revealed how this is commonly done—not that Catholic social teaching documents have intentionally warped the patristic fabric they use, but rather that they have occasionally assumed it must fit, uncritically taking just those bits that usefully applied to certain gaps.[1]

This study and others emphasize that patristic contributions to present ethical dialogue have historical integrity only when their texts are used in a way that respects or at least respectfully recognizes the original context.[2] The patristic authors are not fabric that we may cut and stitch to fit, but rather are part of a vibrant living body, the body of Christian tradition itself. Further, they offer us not one monolithic model, but a community of diverse voices. In

---

1. Brian Matz, "Patristic Sources and Catholic Social Teaching, a Forgotten Dimension: A Textual, Historical, and Rhetorical Analysis of Patristic Source Citations in the Church's Social Documents," in *Annua Nuntia Lovaniensia* 59 (Leuven: Peeters, 2008), cited in Brian Matz with Johan Leemans and Johan Verstraeten, "Position Paper: The Church Fathers and Catholic Social Thought with a Case Study of Private Property" (predistributed seminar paper, 2007), 5–9.

2. I have discussed this elsewhere; see, e.g., Susan R. Holman, "The Entitled Poor: Human Rights Language in the Cappadocians," *ProEcclesia* 9 (2000): 476–89; Holman, "Healing the World with Righteousness? The Language of Social Justice in Early Christian Homilies," in *Charity and Giving in Monotheistic Religions,* Studien zur Geschichte und Kultur des islamischen Orients, ed. Miriam Frenkel and Yaacov Lev (Berlin: de Gruyter, 2009), 89–110. On context, see also Holman, "God and the Poor in Early Christian Thought," in *God in Early Christian Thought: Essays in Memory of Lloyd G. Patterson,* Supplements to Vigiliae Christianae 94, ed. Andrew B. McGowan, Brian E. Daley, S.J., and Timothy J. Gaden (Leiden: Brill, 2009), 297–321.

bringing them into modern dialogue, we need not force them to parrot cultural views on Christian ideals that perfectly match our own. This would be dishonest, since they may sometimes include views on issues such as slavery, human rights, gender roles, punitive norms, and other behaviors that we reject as unequal or unjust. How then can we envision what might be called a "conceptual bridge" to enable patristic and modern views on the common good to walk together respectfully, and emerge from the fitting room of our theological imagination suitably garbed to work together? Perhaps we might begin, I suggest, by intentionally recognizing them as revered but fallible human representatives of a wide diversity of Christian social ethics. As part of living Christian tradition, their texts shape where we are today, both our exegesis and application, regardless of where we place ourselves within that tradition, whether Protestant, Catholic, Orthodox, or some alternative medley. If we let them escape unscathed from our fitting rooms, we are more able to meet them as a crowd of old friends, esteemed colleagues, and suspicious characters in garbs that range from gilded to gaudy to ragged. At such meeting points, we will find that, in terms of social thought, they still share certain goals with us: a keen concern to right injustice, and a passion for ethical use of the natural and material world to relieve poverty, destitution, hunger, disease, and the sorrows, griefs, and outrage that follow any violation of human dignity. Perhaps the leading question to shape our own actions is not so much "Does their view fit ours, and, if so, how?"—though certainly we must ask this at some point. But perhaps we might also ask the question that we ask so regularly of our own ecumenical present, that is, "How do we walk together?" How might we draw from their wisdom, respecting nuances of diversities in a manner that supports what we honestly believe to be true about goodness and justice? While I offer elsewhere an extensive systematic response to this question, the present essay draws on this metaphor and these questions to explore the relevance of patristic texts to one specific ethical concept, that of the common good.[3]

---

3. For the broader discussion, see now Susan R. Holman, *God Knows There's Need: Christian Responses to Poverty* (New York: Oxford University Press, 2009); and Holman, "On the ground: Realizing an 'altared' *philoptochia*," in *Philanthropy and Social Compassion in Eastern Orthodox Tradition*, ed. Matthew Pereira (New York: Theotokos Press, forthcoming).

## Constructing "the Common Good"

Modern dialogue on common good in Catholic social teaching is based on Aquinas's interpretation of Aristotle's political justice. For Aquinas, justice was "the premier moral virtue" that "directs a person's actions toward the good of fellow human beings."[4] Common good is thus inseparable from and dependent upon justice. Figures 6-1 and 6-2 offer diagrammatic models for this. Figure 6-1 shows David Hollenbach's diagrammatic model of the common good in Catholic social teaching and figure 6-2, discussed further below, is my own experimental substitution of Hollenbach's modern terminology with patristic terminology within the same relational dynamics. Figure 6-1 makes quite clear that the "common good" in Catholic social teaching is not just a general phrase about an ideal image but a specific construct about social relationships.[5] In our theological fitting room, that is, the "common good" is a sort

4. David Hollenbach, S.J., "Commentary on *Gaudium et spes (Pastoral Constitution on the Church in the Modern World)*," in *Modern Catholic Social Teaching: Commentaries and Interpretations*, ed. Kenneth R. Himes, Lisa Sowle Cahill, Charles E. Curran, David Hollenbach, S.J., and Thomas Shannon (Washington, D.C.: Georgetown University Press, 2005), 279. In a footnote Hollenbach comments (290, n. 19) that "Thomas Aquinas called the form of justice that orients citizens to the service of the common good both 'general justice' and 'legal justice.' See *Summa Theologiae* II-II, q. 58, art. 6. Pius XI called it 'social justice' in *Divini redemptoris* no. 51, and the U.S. bishops called it 'contributive justice' in *EJA* 71." Eleonore Stump's study of Aquinas does not address his views on mercy, but it might be usefully compared with her broader contrast between "ethics of justice" and "ethics of care." In my view, Greek patristic texts do not support this philosophic tendency to place mercy in inherent tension with justice; see discussion.

5. For my understanding of modern Catholic social teaching and how it relates to this issue, in preparing this paper, I am most indebted to the following sources: John A. Colmen and William F. Ryan, eds., *Globalization and Catholic Social Thought: Present Crisis, Future Hope* (Ottawa: Novalis, 2005), esp. Johan Verstraeten's contribution, "Catholic Social Thinking as Living Tradition that Gives Meaning to Globalization as a Process of Humanization," 28–41; Joseph Gremillion, ed., *The Gospel of Peace and Justice: Catholic Social Teaching since Pope John* (Maryknoll, N.Y.: Orbis, 1976); Kenneth R. Himes, ed., *Modern Catholic Social Teaching: Commentaries and Interpretations* (Washington, D.C.: Georgetown University Press, 2005); David Hollenbach, S.J., *The Common Good and Christian Ethics*, New Studies in Christian Ethics (Cambridge: Cambridge University Press, 2002); Mary M. Keys, *Aquinas, Aristotle, and the Promise of the Common Good* (Cambridge: Cambridge University Press, 2006); André Laks and Malcolm Schofield, eds., *Justice and Generosity: Studies in Hellenistic Social and Political Philosophy. Proceedings of the Sixth Symposium Hellenisticum* (Cambridge: Cambridge University Press, 1992); Patrick D. Miller and Dennis P. McCann, eds., *In Search of the Common Good, Theology for the Twenty-first Century* (New York: T. & T. Clark, 2005); David J. O'Brien and Thomas A. Shannon, eds., *Catholic Social Thought: The Documentary Heritage* (Maryknoll, N.Y.: Orbis, 1992); and Eleonore Stump, *Aquinas* (London: Routledge, 2003), esp. ch. 10, "A Representative Moral Virtue: Justice," 309–38. I am grateful to Ian Deweese-Boyd for drawing my attention to Stump's reference to Basil of Caesarea, and to Maria McDowell, Paul Kolbet, and Robert J. Daly, S.J., for their discussion of the work of David Hollenbach.

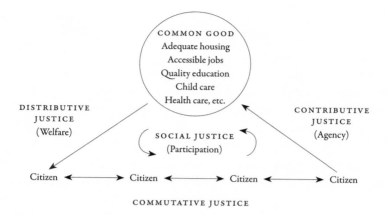

**FIGURE 6-1.** The Modern Model of the "Common Good" in Catholic Social Ethics.
Source: David Hollenbach, S.J., *The Common Good and Christian Ethics,* New Studies in Christian Ethics (New York: Cambridge University Press, 2002), 196. Reprinted with the permission of Cambridge University Press.

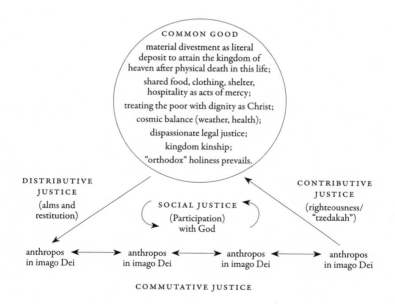

**FIGURE 6-2.** Patristic Concepts of the Common Good within Hollenbach's Framework.
Note: The terms in the "common good" box describe how this ideal was concretely defined and measured within society according to most patristic texts on social justice.

of formal moral suit one dons to delineate that conceptual system for measuring Christian social justice. As I will argue, patristic sources did share with us some aspects of this system, making "common good" a useful concept for comparative dialogue. And the better we understand their different terminology, the more effectively we can work together with our patristic mothers and fathers in applying the cloth to the oozing and bleeding social crises of our own world.

The authors of what we now call patristic texts lived, chronologically, at the historical midpoint between Aristotle and Aquinas. Since we know that Aristotle discusses the common good, and since we know that our authors were influenced—to varying degrees—by Greek philosophy, in crafting an integrated interpretive method, we may approach the texts with three practical questions: First, how do the authors themselves describe "the common good"? Second, is there any hint that patristic views on these issues were influenced by Aristotle? And third, as we bring to the texts our own concepts of common good: which of these do our sources share, how do they discuss them, and what are the obvious differences? In other words, "Does their view fit ours and if so, how?"

### Common Good in a Word: Patristic Use of κοινωφελής

First, how do the texts themselves speak of common good? Here we are helped by the fact that the patristic concept of "the common good" presents itself neatly in a single Greek word, κοινωφελής.[6] κοινωφελής meant "common good" in the obvious sense of that which is good for all persons in a society. The word was used across the spectrum of ancient Greek texts to describe political, theological, and social ideals. Early Christian texts that use it include monastic *typica*, patriarchal registers, catena, a few legal novels, histories, and sermons. From late antiquity, we find it in *1 Clement*, Clement of Alexandria, Origen, Eusebius, Libanius, Gregory of Nyssa, Basil of Caesarea, John Chrysostom, and even a very late Greek translation of a sermon on penitence attributed to Ephrem. I will focus here only on Basil's use of this word as a place to launch the discussion. Basil's prominence in medieval discussion of common

---

6. I do not suggest that this is a "definitive" technical term, only that its existence illustrates that the generic concept—as a concept—was present in patristic thinking. Obviously the ideas inherent in this word could be expressed using other words and phrases (see discussion below).

good is suggested by the fact that he is the only patristic author whom Eleonor Stump quotes in her recent chapter on Aquinas's view of social justice. Other patristic scholars may wish to take this further in their own work on other patristic authors.

Basil used κοινωφελής only twice. In *Homily* 6, condemning stockpiling, he says, "riches grow useless left idle and unused in any place; but moved about, passing from one person to another, they serve the common good (κοινωφελὲς) and bear fruit."[7] Here material possessions are imaged as a living substance that can grow in a healthy way only through a kinetic rotation process. This image is at the root of most patristic texts on redemptive almsgiving, and is one Basil frequently contrasts with unnatural processes, like stagnation, here in stockpiling grain, and in the destructive multiplication of usury, condemned in his second homily on Ps. 14/15. His use of κοινωφελής in *Homily* 6 is especially relevant to modern Catholic social teaching because we know that Aquinas quoted from this sermon (though not this particular passage) in his own discussion of justice as it relates to ownership and redistribution to those in need.[8]

Basil's second use of the word is in *Ep.* 265, to three Egyptian bishops exiled in Palestine. There he writes, "We have learned of the orthodoxy of your faith and . . . your care for the brethren, and that not . . . carelessly do you furnish the means which are of common benefit (κοινωφελής) and indispensable to salvation."[9] The context is the bishops' zeal at refuting Apollinarius and does not at all refer to material justice. Yet Basil's two examples echo precisely the two uses that we find dominant in the other Christian authors: first, social harmony in terms of doctrinal "orthodoxy"; and, second, to note actions that repair material injustices. John Chrysostom most often assumes the second meaning, as we might expect. In his seventy-eighth homily on Matthew, Chrysostom praises the apostles, saying that since they "did all things for the common good, they attained to heaven. For nothing is so pleasing to

7. Basil, *Hom.* 6.5, trans. Toal, 3:329, slightly revised.

8. In *Summa Theol.* IIaIIae.32.5 ad 2, Aquinas quotes from Basil's *Hom.* 6.7, which Eleonore Stump translates as, "It is the hungry man's bread that you withhold, the naked man's cloak that you have stored away, the shoes of the barefoot that you have left to rot, the money of the needy that you have buried underground." Cited and briefly discussed in Eleonore Stump, *Aquinas*, 323, and 543, n. 88.

9. Basil, *Ep.* 265, trans. Deferrari, *Letters*, vol. 4, 106–7, dated 377, addressed to Eulogius, Alexander, and Harpocration.

God as to live for the common advantage. For this end God gave us speech, and hands, and feet, and strength of body, and mind, and understanding, that we might use all these things, both for our own salvation, and for our neighbor's advantage."[10] Several late Byzantine sermons also repeat this explicit association of κοινωφελής. For example, the tenth-century collection of Symeon Metaphrastes quotes the passage from Basil's *Hom.* 6.5 verbatim. And the fifteenth-century *Tractatus de primo servitu Dei* of Gennadius Scholarius II, the first patriarch of Constantinople under Islamic rule, uses the word in an extensive appeal to help the needy based on the material models of Matthew 25. While late for our purposes, Gennadius's example offers clear evidence that κοινωφελής remained in the Eastern church a term closely connected with social justice to the poor.[11]

### Common Good, Civic Identity, and the
### Question of Aristotelian Influence

Hollenbach's diagram reminds us that common good is, primarily, about the relationship of the individual to his or her civic or political community, whatever words are used. The context of κοινωφελής points us to an ethic of common good that builds on issues of community identity that are defined variously, as in Aristotle, with such terms as *polis*, *koinonia*, and related images. Thus we may next ask: Do we find any explicit evidence of Aristotelian influence in patristic texts on social issues? There is much debate over how Aristotelian ideas were mediated through the sources available.[12] Yet I suggest that

10. E.g, *In Matthaeum*, Hom. 78.3 (7.775A) (PG 58.714); trans. George Prevost, *NPNF* 1, 10: 472; *In Joannem* 59, 101, l. 7 (= Hom 15.3 in John): "But how may we become imitators of Christ? By acting in everything for the common good and not merely seeking our own" (trans. G.T. Stupart, *NPNF* 1, 14:53); relating to upright living rather than explicit care for the poor in *De Babyla contra Julianum et gentiles*, sec. 47, l. 2; also alluding to it as imitating God in *De laudibus sancti Pauli apostoli*, hom. 3, sec. 1, ln. 10; on preaching for the moral benefit of all, in *De Davide et Saule*, the 3rd homily on David and Saul, in *St. John Chrysostom, Old Testament Homilies, Vol. 1: Homilies on Hannah, David and Saul*, trans. Robert Charles Hill (Brookline, Mass.: Holy Cross Orthodox Press, 2003), 41–42 (a text repeated verbatim in the spurious Chrysostom homily, *Contra theatra*, vol. 56, 544, l. 24); and as it relates to the heavenly *politeias* in the spurious Chrysostom homily, *In sanctum pascha (sermo 6)*, chapter 9, sec. 1, ln. 2.

11. *Sermones de moribus a Symeone Metaphrasta collecti*, PG 32.1168, l. 23. Gennadius Scholarius II's *Tractatus de primo servitu Dei*, chapter 9, is available through the TLG. In his day there was a revival of Greek and Latin learning in Constantinople. My source for the historical information about Gennadius is, Warren Treadgold, *A History of the Byzantine State and Society* (Stanford: Stanford University Press, 1997), 800, 827, 830.

12. I.e., whether they reached them through whole treatises, catena, commentaries, popular oral wisdom, etc.

Basil offers us one particular sentence, on political ideals of civic and social harmony as it relates to the poor, that is suspiciously Aristotelian. Let us look at this sentence, its possible sources, and, most crucially, how Basil turns it to his own purposes.

In chapter 6 of his first homily on Psalm 14, Basil makes several biblical allusions and then says,

> The Word orders us to share (κοινωνικός) and to love one another, in natural kinship (τῇ φύσει οἰκεῖον). After all, humankind is a civic and sociable (or gregarious) animal (πολιτικὸν γὰρ ζῷον καὶ συναγελαστικὸν ὁ ἄνθρωπος). Liberality for the purpose of restoration is a necessary part of the common life (κοινὴ πολιτεία) and helping one another upwards.[13]

I suggest that the sentence I translate, "Humankind is a civic and sociable animal," points to an Aristotelian source, although it is up for grabs how Basil learned his Aristotle.[14] Let us consider how Basil's version differs from Aristotle and what mediating texts might stand between the two authors.

In Aristotle's *Politics* 1.1.9, we find, "Humankind is by nature a civic animal," or, in the Loeb translation, "Man is by nature a political animal."[15] This sounds very similar, but Basil's sentence and Aristotle's are not literally identical. In particular, Basil's appeal to *politikon* and the *koine politeia* includes the rare word, συναγελαστικὸν, sociable or gregarious, literally a zoological tendency to move about in flocks. We can find several early Aristotelian fragments that use this word but never in relation to *anthropos* and *politikon*. The only extant text in which Basil's full spectrum of terms occurs in a single sentence (though not in the same word order)—*and* refers to Aristotle—is in Eustratius's eleventh or twelfth century *Commentary* on the *Nicomachean Ethics*.[16] This is highly suggestive, but it seems somewhat late to be absolutely conclusive.

Yet if we stop looking for a text explicitly identified with Aristotle, we

---

13. Basil, *Hom Ps. 14/15a*, PG 29.261CD, my translation. For a translation of all of chapter 6 and discussion of context, see Holman, *The Hungry Are Dying*, 112.

14. For some discussion of this debate, see, e.g., Stephen M. Hildebrand, *The Trinitarian Theology of Basil of Caesarea: A Synthesis of Greek Thought and Biblical Truth* (Washington, D.C.: The Catholic University of America Press, 2007).

15. ὁ ἄνθρωπος φύσει πολιτικὸν ζῷον. Aristotle, *Politics*, LCL 264, trans. H. Rackham, (Cambridge, Mass.: Harvard University Press, 1932), 1253a.

16. *In Aristotelis ethica Nicomachea vi commentaria*, 342, l. 27, where the sentence begins, ἢ οὖν οὕτως ἢ ὅτι ἐπεὶ κοινωνικὸν ὁ ἄνθρωπος φύσει καὶ συναγελαστικόν, ἑπόμενος ὁ φιλόσοφος τῇ τοιαύτῃ φύσει τοῦ ἀνθρώπου φησίν.

quickly find three identical examples of a sentence that includes the word συναγελαστικόν and can be translated, "For humankind is a naturally sociable animal, and made for citizenship."[17] This first appears in a fragment of Posidonius.[18] It is repeated, verbatim, by the fourth-century Christian, Nemesius of Emesa, which R. W. Sharples and P. J. van der Eijk translate, "For man was naturally born to flock together and be a creature living in a social community."[19] This same statement is one of the many sentences that the Byzantine monk-physician, Meletius, copied verbatim from Nemesius several centuries later.[20] In each of these three identical texts, it is part of a larger, also identical, passage that defends the necessary interdependence and social benefits of civic life.[21] Basil is alone in the way he orders the individual words, and unique in placing the sentence I have quoted—but not the rest of the identical text—within a context referring to Christian scripture. Basil alone cites this sentence immediately after mentioning natural kinship and just before his defense of material restoration, common *politeia*, and the eschatological goal of social behavior and the common good that is, for him, the spiritual journey of "helping one another upwards."

17. φύσει γὰρ συναγελαστικὸν καὶ πολιτικὸν θῷον γέγονεν ὁ ἄνθρωπος.

18. Posidonius, *frag.* 309a, l. 138, in *Posidonius: Die Fragmente,* ed. W. Theiler (Berlin: de Gruyter, 1982), 1:227.

19. Nemesius, *De natura hominis,* in *Nemesius Emesenus de Natura Hominis: Graece et Latine,* Christian Frideric Matthaei (Magdeburg: Gebauer, 1802), 52, §19; for Eng. trans. see R. W. Sharples and P. J. van der Eijk, ed. and trans., *Nemesius: On the Nature of Man,* Translated Texts for Historians 49 (Liverpool, U.K.: Liverpool University Press, 2008), 44 and n. 225. Sharples and van der Eijk explicitly identify the occurrence of this line in Nemesius's with both Aristotle (*Politics* 1.1.1253a2, 7) and Basil (*Homilies on the Psalms 14.6,* PG 29.261C). For another Eng. translation, see William Telfer, ed. and trans., Nemesius, *On the Nature of Man 5* in *Cyril of Jerusalem and Nemesius of Emesa,* Library of Christian Classics, (Philadelphia: Westminster Press, 1955), 243. W. W. Jaeger (*Nemesios von Emesa* [Berlin, 1914], 126, n. 1 and 127) identifies Posidonius as the source of many of Nemesius's extensive citations, including this one.

20. J. A. Cramer, ed., *Anecdota Graeca e codd. manuscriptis Bibliothecarum Oxoniensium* (Oxford: Typographeo Academico, 1836), 3:19, l. 10.

21. The following is Sharples and van der Eijk's translation of the final two paragraphs in Nemesius's chapter 5, illustrating both the context of this sentence and a piece of the larger whole that is replicated identically in these three texts: "On account of the crafts and the sciences and the useful things that arise from these we have need of each other. Because we have need of each other we come together in numbers and share what is useful for life in our co-operative activities; this coming and living together they call a city. This was so that we should enjoy the benefit of each other from near and not from afar. For man was naturally born to flock together and to be a creature living in a social community: for no one man is self-sufficient in all things. So it is clear that cities were formed for co-operative activities and for learning" (trans. Sharples and van der Eijk, *Nemesius: On the Nature of Man,* 44).

Despite Basil's tinkering, the obvious similarities of these texts, and the linked use of the words, φύσει, συναγελαστικόν, πολιτικόν, ζῷον, and ὁ ἄνθρωπος, seem clearly to argue for a common source, one that almost certainly goes back to Aristotle, but perhaps mediated through a later philosopher, like Posidonius. It is fairly clear that Basil is consciously quoting something and not composing this sentence *de novo*.[22] Nor could I identify any other patristic use of συναγελαστικόν in a similar discussion. Thus we seem here to have a clear example of Aristotelian influence in how patristic texts defined civic identity.

### Common Good in Modern Terms? Patristic Justice, Mercy, and the Appeal to "Common Nature"

These two examples—a word and a sentence—are relevant to us because they show us that concepts familiar to our own concerns were shared by the patristic imagination apart from preconceived notions that we might bring to these texts. Since they demonstrate shared concerns with ours, let us now bring our own agenda to the patristic sources and consider how certain broad ideals may or may not fit our own applications. In preparing for the seminar, contributors were asked to consider a number of application questions, offered in the organizers' position paper's case study on property. Three of these are worth revisiting in this context. First: what is the end [= ultimate goal] of [in this case, the common good] for patristic authors? Second: for whom does [the common good] exist? And third: how does one cultivate a right attitude towards it? Holding these questions in mind, I turn now to the issue of justice, and particularly how, in biblical and patristic texts, social justice is inseparable from individual action and mercy, again limiting the discussion to Cappadocian examples.[23] Bound into these concepts in the Cappadocian texts, we find as a consistent thread an appeal to *common nature*, with regular if perhaps qualified allusions to equality. These terms sound quite modern, or at least very useful for the modern reader, and merit careful attention.

We know from many texts that for Basil, as for Aquinas, "the common

---

22. For example, the only other Basilian use of συναγελαστικόν that I can find is in a sermon among the *spuria*, in which the word similarly modifies ζῷον but is otherwise used differently, there contrasted with ἰδιαστικόν and μοναστική and nothing to do with philanthropic social justice to the needy. Ps.-Basil, *Homilia in illud: Ne dederis somnum oculis tuis* (PG 31.1505, l. 47).

23. See, e.g., Moshe Weinfeld, *Social Justice in Ancient Israel and in the Ancient Near East* (Jerusalem: Magnes Press, 1995), esp. 25–44.

good" is by nature relative to one's definition of justice, but this justice op-
erated on the individual moral as well as the community level. For example,
many of Basil's sermons on virtues pointedly define the healthy community
in terms that cultivate individual ideals such as detachment, self-control, and
ascetic self-reflection, and appeal to individual, personal gain in heaven as the
leading motive for imitating God's natural beneficence and the common sharing seen among the animals. His sermons on fasting, for instance, explicitly relate communal ideals with personal piety. Not only does the wise abstinence
of fasting build one's treasure in heaven, he says, but the one who practices the
proper detached control of liturgical fasting incidentally "ensures dignity to
the city, right ordering in the courts, household peace and salvation; (*De jejunio* 1.11, PG 31.184B); "it is no less useful to the public, for it maintains good
order among the population" (*De jejunio* 2.5; PG 31.192B) and "greatly benefits
the household, the marketplace, night and day, city and wilderness." (*De jejunio* 2.7, PG 31.196A); ultimately resulting in the "crown of justice" (*De jejunio*
2.1, PG 31.185B). The justice of the common good, for Basil, is ultimately rooted in God's goodness for, he says (in *Hom.* 20), "You have not known God by
reason of your justice, but God has known you by reason of His goodness."[24]
Common goodness is therefore based not only on ideals of harmonious community, but on all that goodness means for the individual within the very nature and person of God.

Gregory of Nyssa, calling for a just distribution of goods to the destitute
sick, appeals to the legal image of equal inheritance between brothers. He
identifies the homeless strangers as "kin" (συγγένειαν) and "of your own race"
(ὁμόφυλον),[25] and says, "Share with the poor who are the most-loved by God"
because "all belongs to God, our common father, and we are brothers of the
same race (ὁμόφυλοι).[26] His second sermon on the love of the poor emphasizes

---

24. Basil, *Hom.* 20, *On humility* (*Hum.*), in *Saint Basil: Ascetical Works,* trans. M. Monica Wagner
(New York: Fathers of the Church, 1950), 480.

25. "You see a human being and in him you have no respect for [one who is] kin? No, you do not
pity a being of your own race" (*Paup.* 2; PG 46.476, van Heck p. 115, ll. 8–10). Ἐν τοιούτοις τοίνυν βλέπων
τὸν ἄνθρωπον οὐκ αἰδῇ τὴν συγγένειαν; οὐκ ἐλεεῖς τὸν ὁμόφυλον .

26. "But share with the poor who are the most-loved by God; all belongs to God, our common father, and we are all brothers of the same race. And it is best and more just that brothers reap an equal part
of the heritage [but since things are ordered otherwise, and one or another monopolizes the greater part,
at least let the others not be entirely frustrated" (*Paup.* 1; PG 46.465, van Heck, 103, ll. 21–25). ἀλλὰ μέρος
ἔστω καὶ τῶν πενήτων τῶν ἀγαπητῶν τοῦ θεοῦ· πάντα γὰρ τοῦ θεοῦ, τοῦ κοινοῦ πατρός· ἡμεῖς δὲ ἀδελφοὶ ὡς

that lepers are "human beings ashamed to answer this common name and fear dishonoring the common nature";[27] since "all humanity is governed by a single nature,"[28] Gregory says, "You belong to the common nature of all";[29] "let all therefore be accorded common use."[30]

Nazianzen uses similar language, exhorting his audience to imitate the ἰσότης of God, which translators render equality, evenhandedness, or "the justice of God."[31] He also uses ἰσονομία, a Greek political term meaning "equality of rights." Appealing to Eden he says, "I would have you look back to our primary equality of rights, not the later diversity.... As far as you can, ... cover the shame of your race (genos), ... offer relief to human need" (Or. 14.26).[32] He also appeals to "same" or "equal" race (syngenēs[33] or homophylos[34]). And

---

ὁμόφυλοι· ἀδελφοὺς δὲ τὸ μὲν ἄριστον καὶ δικαιότερον κατ᾽ ἰσομοιρίαν μεταλαγχάνειν τοῦ κλήρου. All translations of Nyssen's De pauperibus amandis sermons are mine.

27. "Human beings, I say, who are ashamed to answer to this common name, and who fear dishonoring the common nature by carrying the title" (Paup. 2; PG 46.480, van Heck, 118, ll. 6–9). ἄνθρωποι, οἱ καὶ ὀνομάζειν ἑαυτοὺς ἀπὸ τῆς κοινῆς προσηγορίας αἰσχύνονται· ὡς ἂν μὴ τῇ κοιμωνίᾳ τοῦ ὀνόματος τὴν κοινὴν φύσιν δι᾽ ἑαυτῶν καθυβρίσειαν.

28. "Sympathy (συμπάθεια) toward the unfortunate is, in this life, profitable for the healthy. For it is good (καλός) for the soul (nous) to provide mercy to others who have fallen on misfortune, for all humanity is governed by a single nature" (Paup. 2; PG 46.488, van Heck 126, ll. 8–10): [...] καλὸς γάρ ἐστι τοῖς νοῦν ἔχουσιν ἔρανος ἐλέου ἐν ταῖς ἑτέρων δυσπραγίαις προαποκείμενος. Ἐπειδὴ γὰρ μιᾷ φύσει διοικεῖται πᾶν τὸ ἀνθρώπινον.

29. "Remember who you contemplate: a human person like yourself whose basic nature is no different from your own [in condemning the sickness of this body you may be condemning yourself and all nature]. For you yourself belong to the common nature of all. Let all therefore be accorded common use." (Paup. 2; PG 46.476, van Heck, 115, ll. 21–23, 26–28); Greek: γνῶθι τίς ὢν περὶ τίνων βουλεύῃ· ὅτι περὶ ἀνθρώπων ἄνθρωπος, οὐδέν ἰδιάζον ἐν σεαυτῷ παρὰ τὴν κοινὴν κεκτημένος φύσιν ... μετέχεις δὲ καὶ σὺ τῆς φύσεως παραπλησίως τοῖς πᾶσιν. Οὐκοῦν ὡς ὑπὲρ κοινοῦ τοῦ πράγματος ὁ λόγος ἔστω.

30. Οὐκοῦν ὡς ὑπὲρ κοινοῦ τοῦ πράγματος ὁ λόγος ἔστω (GNys Paup. 2; PG 46.476).

31. Gregory of Nazianzus, Or. 14, trans. M. F. Toal, The Sunday Sermons of the Great Fathers (Chicago: Regnery, 1963), 4:55.

32. Brian Daley, S.J., trans., Gregory of Nazianzus, The Early Church Fathers (New York: Routledge, 2006), 90.

33. Twice: (1) Or. 14:5: καὶ τῇ περὶ τὸ συγγενὲς εὐσπλαγχνίαν τε καὶ συμπάθειαν (PG 35.864), trans. Daley: "compassion and sympathy for our own flesh and blood" (78); and (2) Or. 14.8: θεραπευτέον, ἀδελφοί, τὸ συγγενὲς καὶ ὁμόδουλον (PG 35.868), trans. Daley: "brothers and sisters, we must care for what is part of our nature and shares in our slavery" (79).

34. In 14.28 he writes, Πόση γὰρ ὀφείλεται τοῖς ὁμοφύλοις καὶ ὁμοτίμοις ἡ καὶ μέχρι τῶν ἀλόγων ἀπαιτου μένη? (Or. 14.28, PG 35.896, l. 35–36, transliterated from the TLG. Daley notes, "It's interesting that Gregory is using philanthropia here to make his point. This, of course, is the word that really dominates this oration, especially in the first five chapters or so, where he identifies it as the chief of virtues, a reflection of God's creative love. But here, he's talking about kindness to animals with a term that basically means 'love of humans.' So the irony in what he's saying is increased: we show philanthropia (and should!) to animals that are not humans, when they are in trouble; how much more should we show it to

we see similar examples in Asterius of Amasea,[35] who in one sermon is out-raged "that we who are created with equal honor (ὁμοτίμως) live so unequally (ἀνίσως) with members of the same race (μετὰ τῶν ὁμοφύλων).[36]

We also find this theme in an anonymous fourth-century homily "On Mercy and Justice,"(περὶ ἐλέους καὶ κρίσεως)[37] that is attributed variously to Basil and three other fourth-century bishops.[38] This sermon closely pairs so-

---

the anthropoi that are homophyleis and of equal dignity with ourselves, precisely because they ARE an-thropoi" [personal communication]. And in 14.14 Gregory writes, οἱ τὸ κατ᾽ εἰκόνα καὶ λαχόντες ὁμοίως ἡμῖν, καὶ φυλάσσοντες ἴσως (10) ὑπὲρ ἡμᾶς, εἰ καὶ τὰ σώματα διεφθάρησαν (PG 35.876, ll. 9–11, which Daley translates, "They have been made in the image of God in the same way you and I have, and perhaps pre-serve that image better than we, even if their bodies are corrupted" (83).

35. Asterius provides us with a virtually identical appeal to created equality, which he contrasts with the anomaly *(anomalia)* of injustice. "Covetousness is the mother of inequality, unmerciful, hat-ing mankind, most cruel. On account of it, the life of mankind is full of abnormality" (Πλεονεξία μήτηρ τῆς ἀνισότητος, ἀνηλεής, μισάνθρωπος, ὠμοτάτη. Διὰ ταύτην ὁ τῶν ἀνθρώπων βίος ἀνωμαλίας γέμει) (*Hom.* 3, "Against Covetousness," ch. 12.1 in *Ancient Sermons for Modern Times by Asterius, Bishop of Amasia, circa 375–405 A.D.,* trans. Galusha Anderson and Edgar Johnson Goodspeed [New York: The Pilgrim Press, 1904], 100); for the critical edition see C. Datema, *Asterius of Amasea: Homilies I–XIV; Text, In-troduction and Notes* (Leiden: Brill, 1970), 35, l. 1–2. In the same sermon, "Against Covetousness," Aste-rius writes, "Such is the marked disparity in the conditions of life, between men created equal in worth, and the cause of this disordered and anomalous state of things is nothing else than covetousness. . . . Would it not be much more just that the poor man should feast to the full on the other's luxury, and that the support of the needy should be the decoration of the rich man's table?" (Καὶ τὸ ὁμότιμον ζῷον, ὁ ἄνθρωπος, τοσαύτην ἔχει τὴν διαφορὰν τῆς διαίτης πρὸς τὸ ὁμόφυλον· οὐκ ἄλλου τινὸς τὴν ἀταξίαν ταύτην καὶ τὴν ἀνωμαλίαν ἢ τῆς πλεονεξίας ἐπεισαγούσης . . . Καὶ πόσῳ δικαιώτερον ἦν τὸν μὲν ἐστιᾶσθαι ἀρκούμενον τῇ ἄλλῃ τρυφῇ, τῆς τραπέζης δὲ τὴν τιμὴν τῶν ἀπόρων εἶναι τρυφήν) (*Hom.* 3, "Against Covetousness," ch. 12.3, trans. Anderson and Goodspeed, 101; for the Greek see Datema, 35, l. 11–14, 18–19).

36. He continues to argue that if "the nature of things were such that our life was truly represented by the inequality (ἀνωμαλίᾳ τοῦ βίου) of [the beggar Lazarus's] career with that of the rich man, I should have cried aloud with indignation: that we who are created equal, live on such unequal terms with men of the same race!" (ἐφ᾽ οἷς οἱ κτισθέντες ὁμοτίμως οὕτως ἀνίσως μετὰ τῶν ὁμοφύλων διάγομεν) (*Hom.* 1, on the rich man and Lazarus, ch. 8.1, in Datema, 12, ll. 6–7); trans. Anderson and Goodspeed, 34. In another of his homilies, Asterius calls for justice, saying God loves "a philanthropic disposition and poverty (πενία) when it is paired with justice (δικαιοσύνη); "God loves "a kindly disposition and poverty when united to righteousness"(ἀγαπᾷν δὲ γνώμην φιλάνθρωπον καὶ τὴν μετὰ δικαιοσύνης πενίαν) (*Hom.* 1, on the rich man and Lazarus, ET 19, Datema, 7, l. 10–11).

37. *De misericordia et iudicio* (*CPG* 2929), PG 31.1705–1714, *Saint Basil: Ascetical Works,* Eng. trans. Sister M. Monica Wagner (New York: Fathers of the Church, 1950), 507–12. Wagner offers no commen-tary on the text but see Paul Jonathan Fedwick, *Bibliotheca Basiliana Vniversalis: A Study of the Manu-script Tradition, Translations and Editions of the Works of Basil of Caesarea* [= BBV], vol. 2.2, 1189–90. Κρίσις is a term that might be translated either "justice" or "judgement." This homily is, to my knowledge, the only Greek Christian sermon from antiquity with this title.

38. It survives in Greek and Coptic texts that are attributed variously to Basil, Athanasius, archbish-op of Rakote; Epiphanius of Salamis; and Athanasius of Alexandria (Fedwick, BBV II,2, 1189–90). Such a generic attribution suggests that it expressed popular Christian views.

cial justice with giving alms from one's own labor. Here the anonymous author makes an extended argument that true social beneficence is possible only when one practices *both* justice and mercy.[39] He too appeals to ἰσότης, "equality," although in context referring to that equality (or "fairness") that he says ought to characterize the justice (δίκαιος) one uses with slaves. The sermon describes justice with examples of trade, agricultural production, or manual labor, perhaps suggesting a village audience. It seems to speak of a situation in which people were providing so-called aid to the needy (εὐεργεσία πρὸς τὸν δεόμενον) that was "financed by unjust (ἀδικία) gains."[40] As we find in the *Didascalia*[41] and other early Christian texts, this author also suggests that injustice taints not just the donor and recipient, but also the exchanged objects.[42] "Exercise φιλανθρωπία to the one you have wronged," says the homilist, "and you will fulfill mercy with justice" (ἔλεον μετὰ κρίσεως)."[43] Among its appeals to community, we find a call for workers to become, through charity, both comrade (κοινωνός) and coworker (συνεργός) with Christ.[44]

These texts appeal to common good within a broad nonmonastic community, reminding us that ascetic virtues and communal sharing were viewed as part of the broad civic image of Christian social justice.[45] Yet we also know that not all patristic authors agreed on such concepts as political equality. Sis-

39. The sermon seems to use κρίσις interchangeably with δικαιοσύνη, "righteousness."

40. Wagner 507; PG 31.1708, l. 19.

41. "If [a widow] be nourished from (the proceeds) of iniquity, she cannot offer her ministry and her intercession with purity before God." *Didascalia* 18.4.6, trans. R. Hugh Connolly, *Didascalia Apostolorum* (Oxford: Clarendon Press, 1929), 158.

42. Have mercy on the results of your labors" (ἐκ πόνων ἐλέησον) "and do not commit injustice on the pretext of offering your mercy to God out of unrighteousness," trans. Wagner 509; PG 31.1709, ll. 26–28.

43. Trans. Wagner 509; PG 31.1709, ll. 15–17.

44. Trans. Wagner 512; PG 31.1713, ll. 3–4, 9.

45. I have focused here on examples applied to the broad, "secular" society of late antiquity, not "common good" as we find it in monastic rules and typica only because such texts generally did not present themselves as obvious examples. One suggestive exception may be found in a spurious ascetic sermon attributed to Basil, *Sermo* 13 (PG 31.869–81), where the author writes, "If any [monk] be found for any reason to have an inordinate affection for a fellow religious, be he brother or kinsman or anyone else, he should be chastised as one who works detriment to the common good; for an excess of affection for one individual bears a strong implication of defect with regard to the others." (Basil of Caesarea, *Ascetic Admonitions* 4/13 [= *CPG* 2891] ET Wagner, 213). However Wagner's "common good" is a translation of a compound concept, τὸ κοινὸν ἀδικῶν (PG 31.880, l.11), perhaps more literally "injustice to the community." Nonetheless, this text does support the general understanding of the common good as requiring equal justice to all members within the community, discussed in the third section of this essay.

ter Nonna Verna Harrison argues, for example, that Nyssen's views on social justice—seeing all of humanity as fundamentally equal—contrasts sharply with Chrysostom's view that true justice functions best within inherent and strict social hierarchies.[46] And though the anonymous homilist emphasizes that there is no conflict between social justice and mercy, one wonders if his very argument suggests an audience that held differing opinions.[47]

These texts show us that both patristic and modern responses seek to address similar problems of socially destructive human pain and deprivation rooted in behaviors that fail to reflect the justice and mercy seen in biblical and christological ideals about the nature of God and creation. *Both* patristic and modern Catholic social teaching documents define the beneficiaries as belonging to the broader society, though how they belong may be defined differently (as discussed further below). *Both* patristic and modern Catholic social teaching documents argue that Christian ideals affect harmonious political order, a theme seen already in the apologists.[48] The early arguments that

46. Nonna Verna Harrison, "Greek Patristic Perspectives on the Origins of Social Injustice," in *Evil and Suffering in the Patristic Period*, Papers from the Third Annual Conference of the Stephen and Catherine Pappas Patristic Institute, October 12–14, 2006, Brookline, Mass. (Grand Rapids, Mich.: Baker Academic, forthcoming).

47. Might he have had an imagined opponent, perhaps, who still held the once-Stoic position that regarded mercy as fundamentally opposed to ideally "dispassionate" justice? On the tension between philosophical ideals of dispassion and the popular practice of beneficent actions in Hellenistic culture before and outside of Christianity, see now Anneliese Parkin, "'You do him no service': An Exploration of Pagan Almsgiving," in *Poverty in the Roman World*, ed. Margaret Atkins and Robin Osborne (Cambridge: Cambridge University Press, 2006), 60–82; and Parkins, "Poverty in the Early Roman Empire: Ancient and Modern Conceptions and Constructs," Ph.D. diss., Cambridge, 1997.

48. In their arguments that Christianity was universally good for the global political order, that is, a positive force in civic justice and social harmony. Melito of Sardis's *Petition to Antoninus*, for example, claimed that "our way of thought . . . became to your empire especially a portent of good . . . an unmixed blessing. . . [since] from the reign of Augustus the Empire has suffered no damage" (Eusebius, *HE* 4.26, in *Eusebius: The History of the Church*, trans. G.A. Williamson [New York: Penguin Books, 1965], 188). Athenagoras's *Plea* argues that Christians are "of all men most religiously and rightly disposed toward God and your empire ("A Plea Regarding Christians by Athenagoras, the Athenian, a Philosopher and a Christian," chapter 1 in *Early Christian Fathers*, Library of Christian Classics 1, ed. and trans. Cyril C. Richardson, [New York: Collier, 1970], 301). Justin's first *Apology* claims that "we are in fact of all men your best helpers and allies in securing good order" (Justin Martyr, *Apol.* 1.12, trans. Richardson, *Early Christian Fathers,* 247). And the *Epistle to Diognetus*, addressing an unknown pagan reader, appeals to common ideals shared with Christians about community support: both pagans and Christians, he argues, teach that one admirably imitates God whenever he "takes up the burden of his neighbor," "wants to use his own abundance to help someone in need," and "provides for the destitute from the possessions he has received from God"; in fact, such benefactors "become a god to those who receive them" (*Epistle to Diognetus* 10.6, in *The Apostolic Fathers, Volume 2*, LCL, trans. Bart D. Ehrman; [Cambridge, Mass.: Harvard University Press, 2003], 152–53).

Christianity was good for the (non-Christian) state remind us of the modern concern that Christian ideals of common good might deliberately seek to coexist with, and mutually benefit, cultures marked by alternative ideologies. And *both* cultivate a right attitude to the common good by appealing to the dynamics of material distribution, the nature of the human person, and particular practices such as treating persons with dignity, discernment, and living in dispassionate piety and simplicity, although again we find diversity. Both patristic and modern Christian ethics seek to promote interdependent and harmonious community and support eschatological ideals.

## On Differences and Conclusions

But here we come to certain differences between early Christian texts and modern approaches, and that discussion brings us to the third and final part of this essay. A comparison of the terms in the top circles of Figures 6.1 and 6.2 demonstrates just a few of these differences. One of the most obvious differences is that of language. Early Christian texts, for example, define social good in terms that use such words as sacred, holy, image of god, patronage, mercy, charity, brother-and-kin, redemptive alms, and kingdom of heaven. Our modern approach, on the other hand, uses language that speaks of those issues we see in Hollenbach's top circle, in Figure 6.1: adequate housing, jobs, education, childcare, and healthcare. Such different word choices suggest different cultural images of how to measure the good of the human body as it affects the common good of society. As the vertical line across the bottom of Hollenbach's triangle shows, modern human rights language depends on democratic equality between individuals, and what he describes as value-for-value reciprocity in the social contract.[49] But patristic, and indeed Aristotelian, human rights imagery was formed within a society that assumed fundamental *in*equalities in social status. Christian authors used the concept of citizenship in pointing to the heavenly Jerusalem and the kingdom of God, and they often defined the relationship between persons in terms of their identity as *anthropoi* made in God's image, particularly when pointing to the destitute who suffer inhumane treatment. The currency by which one measures the valence of

49. I believe this particular phrase is my own but it is based on Hollenbach's discussion in *The Common Good and Christian Ethics*, 193.

ideals—what mercy and justice mean in a particular situation—varies across cultures. Alms, for example, were part of justice in patristic texts and ideal individual response to the common good were defined using terms of righteousness that share the broad meanings we find, for example, in Old Testament, Hebrew, and Syriac concepts of *tzedakah,* which meant both alms and righteousness.

We find other differences between the patristic authors themselves. For example, some are clear that one should give help and resources to the needy regardless of whether the recipient is Christian or not.[50] Others clearly limit distribution to members of the church community, or Orthodox believers.[51] These are genuine differences. Many patristic texts call for cautious discernment between the worthy and the unworthy supplicant,[52] while others call for a more indiscriminate generosity that leaves final judgement up to God alone.[53] Nor do authors seem necessarily to be consistent in their own position. Testing monasticism in Egypt as a young man, Basil argued in *Ep.* 42 that donors ought to give directly to the poor without seeking more "holy" (monastic) intermediaries to do it for them.[54] But later as a bishop he appears to change his tune and argues that the monastic bishop is the proper discerning intermediary (*Ep.* 150).[55] Some, like Anthony, practiced material divestment in a single act, after which they owned nothing. Others, like Melania and Pinian, seem to devote their entire monastic life to handling their personal wealth—as they keep giving it away. And Clement of Alexandria is the best known example of the advice to retain one's property and simply practice moderate divestment. This variety of views should perhaps encourage us to welcome salutary diversity within our shared modern commitments to justice and mercy.

50. E.g., Cyprian of Carthage (*Works and Alms* 25, as depicted by Pontius the Deacon in the *Life and Passion of Cyprian,* ch. 10), John Chrysostom (e.g., *Hom. on Hebr.* 10.8; PG 53.88), and many monastic desert sayings.

51. E.g., Leo of Rome and perhaps even Clement of Alexandria.

52. E.g., Basil.

53. E.g., John the Almsgiver and certain monastic stories from the desert tradition.

54. Basil, *Ep.* 42, "to Chilo his pupil," possibly from the 350s, speaking as a young man possibly in Palestine or Egypt, in ascetic training but with no role of church leadership. Deferrari says "as far as the style is concerned, it might well be Basil's," but notes that "some say it is the work of the holy Nilus [d. 430]"; Deferrari, *Letters of St. Basil,* 1.241.

55. Basil, *Ep.* 150 "To Amphilochius, as if from Heracleidas," in *Letters of St. Basil,* ed. and trans. Deferrari, 2.369; the whole is at 361–71.

But there is one issue that remains a special challenge. This is the issue of eschatology as it relates to heaven, hell, and redemptive almsgiving. Catholic social teaching tends to emphasize improving society and working for justice in this present life. This is quite clear in the top circle of Hollenbach's diagram, defining how common good is measured. Yet patristic constructions of the best community justice ultimately depend on redemptive almsgiving that is rooted in, and inseparable from an eschatologically eternal and other-world "kingdom of God." In a culture where life was short and medicine, travel, and other securities unreliable, mortality had a poignant immediacy. In such a setting there is comfort and logic in focusing on the material stuff of this present life as having real meaning only in relation to eschaton restoration of justice, physical bodies, heavenly mansions, and redeemed social relationships.[56] In Eastern Orthodox tradition there is an emphasis on redemptive reality as a continuum already present in the here and now, while modern Western Christian tradition tends to emphasize more the difference that physical death makes in one's experience of, and entry into, the eschaton. How one uses these patristic texts in modern discussion of civic or social identity may depend, I suggest, on how we and our audiences use and share—or differ from—these perspectives.

This issue especially challenges our application of these texts to Catholic social teaching respecting modern religious diversity on ideological issues. Both Jewish and Islamic ideas of almsgiving, for example, have similar visions of personal and global redemption mediated by divine engagement with human responses to physical stuff and the needs of the poor. But their rhetoric of philanthropy obviously does not see Jesus incarnate in street beggars, nor—as far as I know—a literal heavenly bank account or architectural mansion. And much of modern Western Europe denies any belief at all in the afterlife, or in omniscient divine justice and mercy. How relevant is patristic common good in this context, when its structure is built on an eschatological kingdom exchange that takes Matthew 25 rather literally? Can we use these arguments for beneficent divestment if we are engaging with an audience that does not share this exegesis? Indeed, if one cuts away patristic views on heaven and hell, is one in fact even talking about the same "common good"?

I leave this to other theologians and ethicists to answer. Yet it seems to

---

56. This is particularly emphatic, for example, in Salvian's *Ad Ecclesiam*.

me that patristic views on heavenly beneficence and justice cannot be entirely minimized in the attempt to apply them to modern ethics without collapsing the whole patristic argument for just social exchange. Ultimately for patristic authors, "the common good" has meaning only in the transfer of mutable, temporal reality to eternal social relationships—relationships with the divine and with one's fellow humans, relationships that will endure into eschatological perpetuity. This may be why we can state with some confidence that patristic Christian views on justice and human rights strongly affirmed and bolstered the *spiritual* status of the poor and needy in society (that is, the existential value that God had for them and therefore how their fellow human persons ought to regard them conceptually in terms of Christian identity and absolute value)—and yet at the same time the same views often seem to have had less of an effect (if any) on systematically improving their *social* status in late antique society itself by, for example, improving education, housing, and economic balance.[57] While the reasons for change, lack of change, and modern criticisms of early Christian efforts at change remain complex, Basil's appeal to "helping one another upwards" reminds us that the politics of interdependent social justice rests on the transitory nature of matter itself as even the poor and needy use earth to build heaven.

## Conclusion

In conclusion, I would like to offer for further discussion a discrete but provisional working definition of how patristic texts understood the common good. This is intentionally intended as a working definition to encourage further discussion. For patristic Greek texts that discuss social welfare issues, I suggest, the "common good" is the ideal of that which is best for all within the divinely-created order. It results from the divine absolute of eschatological justice. By it, all human persons benefit according to their place within the community network (or political civic order) and social relationships that reflect God's created order for the world as patristic authors understand it. The

---

57. For the argument that patristic responses to poverty were realized more as rhetoric than as social reality in ancient society, see Pauline Allen, Bronwen Neil, and Wendy Mayer, *Preaching Poverty in Late Antiquity: Perceptions and Realities*, Arbeiten zur Kirchen- und Theologiegeschichte 28 (Leipzig: Evangelische Verlagsanstalt, 2009); and Bronwen Neil, "Models of Gift Giving in the Preaching of Leo the Great," *Journal of Early Christian Studies* 18:2 (2010): 225–59.

"common good" is a natural characterization of divinely ordered social harmony and interdependence. It is inseparable from mercy, philanthropic divestment, and almsgiving, which are distinct activities subordinate to rightly ordered justice in present and future life. Common-good justice is actualized in the present life by—but not limited to—mercy with regard to such tangible substances or relational experiences as the acquisition, use, distribution, or divestment of material property; and social and liturgical harmony. These manifestations best emerge rightly from the individual, voluntary expression of personal virtues, such as "orthodox" Christian beliefs and "proper" piety; philosophical *sophrosune*; detachment, dispassion, and self-control as it relates to fleshly desires and material objects; and interdependence on God and others in the ordered community. For patristic authors, perfect attainment of the "common good" is founded on, presupposes, and ultimately realized in an eschatological reality that subordinates material survival in this world to the rightly ordered, relational substance of the next.

Despite the various challenges of these similarities and differences, it is clear that Greek patristic texts do offer a wealth of sources on the common good that overlap with our modern concerns sufficiently to be discussed respectfully and usefully in future research and practical religious ministry, humanitarian efforts, and international acts of social solidarity. The examples outlined here are only the beginning. We should not lose sight, for example, of the sermons on charity, beneficence, and social issues that lie neglected among the *dubia* and *spuria*.[58] While date and authorship of such sources may raise complex problems, at least for Eastern Orthodox Christians these too are patristic texts. They too represent that body of living tradition and difference that walks together with us in this opportunity to offer new shape to the ongoing formation of social thought in Christian tradition.

58. There are, for example, at least a dozen sermons appear among the many spuria in Migne's collection titled either *De eleemosyne* (in Chrysostom's spuria: PG 60:707–12; PG 60:747–52; PG 62:769–70; and his genuine sermon PG 52:261–72), *De jejunio et eleemosyne* (Chrysostom's spuria, PG 48:1059–62), *De charitate* (Eusebii, Alexandria, 5th C, PG 86a:323–28); *De eleemosyna, in divitem et Lazarum* (the same Eusebii, PG 86a:423–52), as well as numerous sermons on fasting that may be worth examining to see if they (as is true of Basil's on the same topic) are notably rich in language of social justice as it relates to the community (e.g., at least five under Chrysostom's spuria; Mark the fifth-century hermit [PG 65.1109–18]; and Eusebii [PG 86a:313–24]).

*Brenda Llewellyn Ihssen*

# 7. "That which has been wrung from tears"

*Usury, the Greek Fathers, and Catholic Social Teaching*

In the sixteenth year of the reign of Emperor Trajan, a woman who is described as "aged about 66 years, with a scar in the middle of her forehead," and who, being accompanied by her son—who also had "a scar in the middle of his forehead"—acknowledged in writing the recovery of a loan for the amount of 1,612 silver drachmae, as well as interest on the loan.[1] The debtor was one of the fortunate ones: she had taken a loan and managed to repay both the loan and the interest to her creditor. Sadly, evidence remains that many loans did not end with the same level of satisfaction. If they had, it is not likely that Christian bishops would have taken up verbal arms against the usurer.

In the early 1960s, Bernard J. Meislin and Morris L. Cohen wrote that the subject of usury is so low on the stimulation scale that only "the social and religious philosophers, historians and other scholars of the past are still excited by the moral implications of this prohibition."[2] Notwithstanding their esteemed list it is largely true that apart from scholars, until the very recent

I would like to thank Tim Ihssen and Dr. Alicia Batten of the University of Sudbury for reading an earlier version of this essay and providing helpful comments, and Dr. Rochelle E. Snee of Pacific Lutheran University for providing advice on the Greek translations, which are—unless noted otherwise—those of the author, who bears full responsibility for any errors.

1. *Select Papyri* 1, LCL, ed. and trans. A. S. Hunt and C. C. Edgar (Cambridge, Mass.: Harvard University Press, 1959), 213.

2. B. J. Meislin and M. L. Cohen, "Backgrounds of the Biblical Law against Usury," *Comparative Studies in Society and History: An International Quarterly* 6 (1963): 250.

subprime lending crisis of late 2008, no one's visage brightened at the mention of a discussion on interest or usury; in fact, the average citizen generally does not think much about usury or interest because interest on a loan—as they understand it—is not a troubling element of life, it is a *normal* element of life; we borrow money daily, multiple times over, and happily pay out (legal) interest to the banks without a second thought about the legitimacy of the situation (both the interest itself as well as endless purchases).[3] We are happy to pay 4 percent as long as we can get the holiday pillows that marketing experts tell us we need. But people who buy holiday pillows are not suffering from excessive interest rates, and so people with money to waste consider "interest" to be a nonissue. At the moment, millions across the globe suffer at the hands of others who would happily keep them in poverty through excessive and crushing interest rates. Currently the worst manifestation of unjust lending in the United States is the "payday" loan, which is specifically designed to keep people in debt; with interest rates up to 400 percent, these companies amass profits in the amount of approximately $4.2 billion annually, intentionally creating financially desperate circumstances for individuals and their families.[4] In a class that I recently taught titled "Wealth in the Ancient Church," one of my more jaded students asked: "Yeah, so people borrow $100 and they pay back $500; they are adults, they know what they are getting into . . . so what's the big deal?" Over the course of the semester this student learned that while the "big deal" for the twenty-first century might be grinding poverty, homelessness, starvation, and death for the borrower and their family, the "big deal" for the theologians of the early church was grinding poverty, homelessness, starvation, and death for the borrower and their family, *and* the salvation of

---

3. A few examples of outstanding scholarship on this topic include Robert Maloney's "Usury in Greek, Roman, and Rabbinic Thought," *Traditio* 27 (1971): 79–109; "Early Conciliar Legislation on Usury: A Contribution to the Study of Christian Moral Thought," *Recherches de théologie ancienne et médiévale* 39 (1972): 145–57; "Teaching of the Fathers on Usury: An Historical Study on the Development of Christian Thinking," *VC* 27 (1973): 241–65; "Usury and Restrictions on Interest-Taking in the Ancient Near East," *CBQ* 36 (1974): 1–20; Susan Holman, "You Speculate on the Misery of the Poor: Usury as Social Injustice in Basil of Caesarea's Second Homily on Psalm 14," in *Organized Crime in Antiquity,* ed. Keith Hopwood (Duckworth: Classical Press of Wales, 1999), 207–28; Craig L. Hanson, "Usury and the World of St. Augustine of Hippo," *Augustinian Studies* 19 (1988): 141–64; Hanson, Thomas Moser, *Die patristische Zinslehre und ihre Ursprünge: Vom Zinsgebot zum Wucherverbot* (Winterthur: Verlag Hans Schellenberg, 1997).

4. Center for Responsible Lending website available at http://www.responsiblelending.org/ issues/ payday (accessed 2010).

the usurer, whose economic ventures just might cut them off from the vision of God. Accordingly, our theologians had two concerns: one concern was for material conditions of the debtor, and the second concern was for the salvation of the lender. Indeed, the Fathers considered it their duty to reflect on the salvific implications of economic choices.[5]

While "usury" today refers to interest taken beyond legal limits, in antiquity usury was any interest charged for the use of money.[6] Though the practice of taking interest on a loan was condemned in Hebrew society,[7] under the Greek[8] and Roman[9] systems usury was a normal part of a lending transaction

5. Frances Young refers to this dual responsibility: "Put in historical terms, this struggle was about the call of the desert and the duty to society." Frances Young, "They Speak to Us across the Centuries," *The Expository Times* 109.2 (1997): 39.

6. Samuel Williston, in *Law of Contracts*, kindly lays out the modern understanding of, and contractual requirements for, usury: first, there must be a loan that is of money or that which circulates as money; second, it must be repaid; finally, some commodity or fee must be extracted for the use of the loan in excess and *in addition to* the amount allowed by law. Samuel Williston, *A Treatise on the Law of Contracts* (Rochester: Lawyers Co-operative Publishing, 1990), 22. In addition to Williston's definition, economist Franklin W. Ryan's statement on the dilemma of usury is worth noting: "Legal usury is not necessarily in all cases unsocial, but moral usury is always condemned by public opinion as unsocial. This condemnation is clearly indicated by such opprobrious epithets as loan shark, usurer, and "bleeding the wage-earner," all of which imply exploitation." Franklin W. Ryan, *Usury and Usury Laws: A Juristic-Economic Study of the Effects of State Statutory Maximums for Loan Chargers upon Lending Operations in the United States* (Boston: Houghton Mifflin, 1924), 14.

7. Exodus 22:25–27; Leviticus 25:35–37; Deuteronomy 15:7–11; 23:19–20. Neighbors extended interest-free loans to one another in times of agricultural difficulty; see Douglas Oakman, "The Ancient Economy," in *The Social Sciences and New Testament Interpretation*, ed. Richard L. Rohrbaugh (Peabody, Mass.: Hendrickson, 1996): 126–43. This is reminiscent of the method of loaning endorsed and encouraged by Hesiod in his *Works and Days*, in which he advocated fair lending practices without formal interest, but surely with motive: "Take good measure from a neighbour, and pay it back well, with the same measure, or better if you can, so that you may later find him reliable should you need him." Hesiod dedicated the text to his brother Perses who had lost his land because of too many debts. Hesiod, *Works and Days*, trans. David W. Tandy and Walter C. Neale (Berkeley: University of California Press, 1996), 349.

8. Interest on loans was never universally endorsed, but was a fact of life from the time of the maturing of the banking system in Greece in the seventh and sixth centuries BCE and the growth of trade and industry. Fritz M. Heichelheim, *Ancient Economic History: From the Palaeolithic Age to the Migrations of the Germanic, Slavic, and Arabic Nations* 1, trans. Joyce Stevens (Leyden: Sijthoff, 1965), 135–36.

9. The Romans banking system involved various financial transactions such as money-changing, mortgages on land, houses or slaves, or loans. Early commercial loans were high interest and high risk: the lender advanced money, gambling that the voyage would be successful. If it was, the lender got the money back plus interest; if it was not, the money was lost. Loans made to people who were short of funds or who found themselves in a financially awkward position were primarily from friends or family, and often carried no interest. A. H. M. Jones, *The Roman Economy: Studies in Ancient Economic and Administrative History* (Oxford: Basil Blackwell, 1974), 187. See also Jean Andreau, *Banking and Business in the Roman World,* trans. Janet Lloyd (Cambridge: Cambridge University Press, 1999), 90–99.

and was only questioned when usury was linked to scarcity.[10] This is not to imply that usury was appreciated, merely that it was present. So despite the low opinions of high minds on usury—Plato saw it as "vulgar"[11] and Aristotle as "unnatural"[12]—interest on a loan, even excessive interest, was considered to be

10. Rural debts were often contracted for consumption rather than production, and such debts mounted under the instability of crop production. Having lost land and entire families that were sold into slavery, peasants were left to farm land that was no longer theirs. This type of practice resulted in deep-seated misery and extreme hatred between the classes. Alfred French, *Growth of the Athenian Economy* (London: Routledge & Kegan Paul, 1964), 12. See also Gustave Glotz, *Ancient Greece at Work: An Economic History of Greece from the Homeric Period to the Roman Conquest,* trans. M. R. Dobie (New York: Norton, 1967), 80–81; Gustave Glotz, *The Greek City and Its Institutions* (New York: Barnes & Noble, 1965), 103–4. Solon, archon of Athens in 594 BCE, had as his priority the liberation of the "dark earth" from indebtedness. In one of the first acts of legislation against usury and other crimes against the poor, Solon annulled many rural debts and reduced others, forbade "loans on the person" and made this prescription retroactive: "As soon as Solon had been entrusted with full powers to act, he liberated the people by prohibiting loans on the person of the debtor, both for the present and the future. He made laws and enacted a cancellation of debts both of private and public, a measure which is commonly called *seisachtheia* [the shaking-off of burdens], since in this way they shook off their burdens." Aristotle, *Constitution of Athens and Related Texts,* trans. Kurt Von Fritz and Ernst Kapp (New York: Hafner, 1964), 73. See also Plutarch's *Solon,* in *The Rise and Fall of Athens: Nine Greek Lives by Plutarch,* trans. Ian Scott-Kilvert (London: Penguin, 1979), 43–76.

11. Plato believed that usury was an evil practice that must be eradicated for the following reasons: usury was a barrier to the happiness of the individual whose unjust lending practices made the lender unhappy (the happiness of the one in debt is not mentioned); as a result of the unhappiness engendered by usury, this foul practice disrupted the peace of the city-state; the advancement in the political system of men who engaged in usury resulted in civil unrest and not simply one, but two generations of incompetent leaders and citizens; the practice of such an evil must not continue, for it served only to undermine the moral order of society. See Plato, *The Republic,* trans. Paul Shorey (Cambridge, Mass.: Harvard University Press, 1978), 1.549e–550a, 742c, 8.555c–e; see also *The Laws of Plato,* trans. Thomas L. Prangle (New York: Basic Books, 1980), 684e, 915e. For a more developed explanation of usury and Plato, see "Usury in the Greek, Roman, Hebrew and Early Christian Worlds," in Brenda Llewellyn Ihssen, "They Who Give from Evil: The Response of the Eastern Church to Money-Lending in the Early Christian Era" (PhD diss., The University of St. Michael's College, 2004), 80–96.

12. Aristotle believed that usury was a hateful practice for the following reasons: First, the acquisition of interest was counterproductive to market equality; a seller should not expect to sell an object by expecting that over a period of time the buyer would have to keep paying for it. Aristotle saw usury in the same way; if one were to borrow one dollar, then one dollar should be returned, not two. To believe otherwise would go against his belief that money has a value independent of its fiscal function. Second, Aristotle did not share the ancient eastern idea that dead matter was capable of reproduction; money is not a living organism, and since an object that is not alive cannot be fertile, therefore money—which is neither alive nor fertile—cannot produce offspring. Third, usury was evidence of "meanness," which, in Aristotle's opinion, is not an effective way to lead an ethical life. Finally, Aristotle's writings contain the first attempts to unite the economic and the ethical; within this system, living and developing an ethical life is neither the pleasant contemplation of abstract notions of goodness and beauty nor selfish individualism, but is the acting out of one's own humanity within proper relationship to the other. Aristotle writes: "Of the two sorts of money-making one, as I have just said, is a part of household management,

a rightful compensation to the lender for time and risk; as the lender cannot use the money that has been loaned, interest is payment made to the lender "in gratitude" for the time it takes to return the money. Risk is involved when one considers that the lender has lent money to an individual *who might have none*, and whose potential for getting more of what they currently do not have is negligible. The lender is gambling that the money will return, rather than that the debtor will repudiate the loan. Because interest compensated for the risk the lender was willing to take, the greater the risk the higher the compensation.[13] For the Greek Fathers, however, time and risk were irrelevant; any degree of guarantee on money loaned was unconscionable, any percentage above and beyond the amount loaned was usury, and usury was equally foul regardless of the percentage of interest.[14] Be it three hundred percent, thirty or even three, the soul of the usurer hangs in balance; even a one percent desire for gain put salvation at risk.

## What Do Patristic Writers Have to Say about Social Ethics?

An analysis of eighteen passages from Greek patristic sources that include either reference to or are concerned specifically with the topic of usury reveals consistency with respect to how the theologians considered usury and usu-

---

the other is retail trade: the former necessary and honourable, the latter a kind of exchange which is justly censured; for it is unnatural, and a mode by which men gain from one another. The most hated sort, and with the greatest reason, is usury, which makes a gain out of money itself, and not from the natural use of it. For money was intended to be used in exchange, but not to increase at interest. And this term usury (τόκος), which means the birth of money from money, is applied to the breeding of money because the offspring resembles the parent. Wherefore of all modes of making money this is the most unnatural." Aristotle, *Politics,* trans. Benjamin Jowett (Oxford: Clarendon, 1920), 1258b. See also *The Nicomachean Ethics of Aristotle,* trans. Sir David Ross (London: Oxford University Press, 1961), 79–85. For more on Aristotle's theory of money, see "Graeco-Roman Economics," in *History of Economic Analysis,* Joseph A. Schumpeter (New York: Oxford University Press, 1954); see also Heichelheim, *An Ancient Economic History,* 104–5. For a more developed explanation of usury and Aristotle, see Ihssen, "They Who Give From Evil," 80–96.

13. Meir Tamari, *"With All Your Possessions"—Jewish Ethics and Economic Life* (New York: The Free Press, 1987), 36–28 and 178–9.

14. "Those who lent money at three percent were committing usury quite as really as those who lent it at forty percent." W. E. H. Lecky, *The History of the Rise and Influence of the Spirit of Rationalism in Europe* (London: Longmans, 1865), in Patrick Cleary, *The Church and Usury: An Essay on Some Historical and Theological Aspects of Money-Lending* (Dublin: M. H. Gill & Son, 1914), v.

rers fit—or did not fit—within Christian society.[15] This case study summarizes their position through three specific questions that I have been asked to address: What is the opinion of the Greek Fathers on usury? Who are the usurers? And finally, are there exceptions to lending?

## What Is the Opinion of the Greek Fathers on Usury?

Exceptions to patristic prohibitions against usury exist, but they are rare; thus it is fairly safe to say that *in general* none of the Greek Fathers considered usury beneficial.[16] The enigma for them was that charging interest on a loan

---

15. This study is not intended to be a comprehensive treatment of the Greek Fathers on usury. For a more thorough treatment of the various passages throughout their writings, please consult "Early Greek Fathers and Usury," in Ihssen, *They Who Give From Evil*, 135–74.

16. It is possible to conclude that some bishops suggest that usury rates set within legal limits were acceptable; examples to support this position include Clement of Alexandria, who may have suggested that the prohibition against interest applied only to loans to fellow believers; Clement of Alexandria, *Stromata*, PG 8.1023. Similar to Clement, St. Ambrose allows for the same distinction, but in much less ambiguous language; Ambrose, *De Tobia*, 15.51 (PL 14.779), in *St. Ambrosii, De Tobia: A Commentary with an Introduction and Translation,* Patristic Studies 35, trans. Lois Miles Zucker (Washington, D.C.: The Catholic University of America Press, 1933). Patrick Cleary notes that Bishop Sidonius Apollinaris of Clermont might have recognized the right of a cleric to demand usury, but I am not convinced that this is what the bishop is suggesting; Cleary, *The Church and Usury,* 57. Cleary also mentions St. Gregory of Tours, who relates the tale of Desideratus, Bishop of Verdun. The bishop asked for a loan from King Theudebert and promised to repay it with interest: "If in your compassion you have any money to spare, I beg you to lend it to me, so that I may relieve the distress of those in my diocese. As soon as the men who are in charge of the commercial affairs in my city have reorganized their business, as has been done in other cities, I will repay your loan with interest." Gregory of Tours, *History of the Franks,* trans. Lewis Thorpe (London: Penguin, 1974), 190–91. However, I disagree also here with Cleary, who states that this tale indicates that neither "his lordship nor Gregory thought it unreasonable that usury should be paid in the case." Cleary, *The Church and Usury,* 57. I would point out that Gregory's text does not suggest any such thing, as we have no indication about what any of the parties thought; the bishop recognizes that interest is a part of the lending process, and includes it in his request to someone who might very well not have lent to him otherwise. Worth noting, in the end King Theudebert repudiated not just the interest, but the principle as well, which indicates to me that the king realized that taking usury from a bishop who borrowed money to get an *entire community* out of poverty seems inappropriate. Gregory of Tours, *History of the Franks,* 191. Finally, a passage translated differently by both Cleary and McCambley places Gregory of Nyssa in the position of recognizing that usury might be employed amongst the wealthy, but not those of lesser means. The following, from his *Contra usurarios,* μηδὲ βιάζου πενίαν τὰ τῶν πλουτούντων ποιεῖν, is translated in Cleary as "Do not force poverty to give what pertains to the rich alone to give." Cleary, *The Church and Usury,* 51. From this, Cleary concludes, Gregory is recognizing that the wealthy might extract interest from *one another* but not the poor. McCambley, however, translates the passage to read: "[do not] force poverty upon those who are rich," which does not result in the same conclusion, if one considers that Gregory is, in this passage, soundly condemning the practice. McCambley, *Against Those Who Practice Usury,* 298. I am not of the opinion that Gregory allows for a distinction to be made when usury is involved between the wealthy or poor, at least with respect to this sermon. And

was legally acceptable at the same time that it was morally questionable. To deal with this conundrum, the condemnation of usury and the usurer falls under three overlapping themes: usury as prohibited by Christian scripture, the usurer as a menace to community, and the spiritual poverty of the usurer.

*Usury as Prohibited by Scripture*   Passages that fall under this category are usually straightforward treatments that place usury amongst a list of sins to avoid. The distinguished Clement of Alexandria wrote some of the first censures against usury in *Paedagogus*, his guide to the moral life of the Christian.[17] At the end of a chapter which expounds upon the way God encourages righteousness and discourages sinful behaviour, Clement quotes Ezekiel 18:4–9[18] and claims that this passage, in addition to other Hebrew Bible passages and Greek authors quoted,[19] contains "an outline of the daily life of Christians, a worthy exhortation to the blessed life, [which is] the gift of a righteous life—eternal life."[20] Simply put, salvation for the Christian can be attained by righteous living. The Ezekiel passage is quoted a second time in his *Stromata* where again he uses it to qualify that which the righteous person would not do.[21] Nestled between quotes from Plato, passages from Romans[22] and Isaiah,[23] the excerpt is utilised to press his point that by the integration of proper behaviour learned through the Mosaic code and the insight of the phi-

---

while some might conclude that bishops probably turned a blind eye to low rates extended among business partners, the explicit and consistent rejection of usury among the bishops are of such a tenor that it is more likely they would not have been shy to criticize the motives of anyone who thought even a small amount of interest would be appropriate.

17. Clement of Alexandria, *Paedagogus,* PG 8.247–684.

18. Ezekiel 18:4–9: "Know that all lives are mine; the life of the parent as well as the life of the child is mine; it is only the person who sins that shall die. If a man is righteous and does what is lawful and right—if he does not eat upon the mountains or lift up his eyes to the idols of the house of Israel, does not defile his neighbour's wife or approach a woman during her menstrual period, does not oppress anyone but restores to the debtor his pledge, commits no robbery, gives his bread to the hungry and covers the naked with a garment, does not take advance or accrued interest, withholds his hand from iniquity, executes true justice between contending parties, follows my statutes and is careful to observe my ordinances, acting faithfully—such a one is righteous; he shall surely live, says the Lord God."

19. Samian Pythagoras ("When you have done base things, rebuke *yourself*; but when you have done good things, be glad"), an aphorism that is not cited ("For virtue that is praised grows like a Tree"), Isaiah 48:22 and 57:21, and Proverbs 1:10–12. Clement of Alexandria, *Paed.*, PG 8.363.

20. Ταῦτα ὑποτύπωσιν Χριστιανῶν περιέχει πολιτείας, καὶ προτροπὴν ἀξιόλογον εἰς μακάριον βίον, γέρας εὐζωίας ζωὴν αἰώνιον. Clement of Alexandria, *Paed.*, PG 8.364.

21. Clement of Alexandria, *Stromata*, PG 8.685–9.602.

22. Romans 6:22.

23. Isaiah 55:6–9.

losophers into one's life, an individual can become righteous, living a life of wisdom and holiness.[24]

The most famous passage against usury—Deuteronomy 23:19–20—is also foundational in Clement's *Stromata* after his defence of the law and its usefulness.[25]

Concerning distribution and sharing, much might actually persuade, but it is sufficient [to say], that the law prohibits a brother from lending with usury; a brother not only in name, born from the same parents, but even one of the same community, and also who is of like mind in the same Word; for it is not right to take usury for money, but with open hands and mind to show favour to those in need. For God, the judge and dispenser of such grace, takes as sufficient usury things that are valued among men—kindness, mercy, magnanimity, reverence, and honour.[26]

As pointed out by Robert Maloney in "Teaching of the Fathers on Usury,"[27] a portion of this mimics Philo of Alexandria's *De virtutibus*.[28] In addition to confirming the influence of Philo, Clement turns from the defence of morality established by the Mosaic code to practical ways individuals might use biblical proscriptions to demonstrate Christian love and charity to one another out of gratitude and devotion to God. Clement provides no scripture as jus-

24. Clement of Alexandria, *Stromata*, PG 8.1085.

25. "You shall not charge interest on loans to another Israelite, interest on money, interest on provisions, interest on anything that is lent. On loans to a foreigner you may charge interest, but on loans to another Israelite you may not charge interest, so that the Lord your God may bless you in all your undertakings in the land that you are about to enter and possess" (Deut 23:19–20).

26. Περὶ τε τῆς μεταδόσεως καὶ κοινωνίας, πολλῶν ὄντων, ἀπόχρη μόνον τοῦτο εἰπεῖν, ὅτι νόμος ἀπαγορεύει ἀδελφῷ δανείζειν· ἀδελφὸν ὀνομάζων οὐ μόνον τὸν ἐκ τῶν αὐτῶν φύντα γονέων, ἀλλὰ καὶ ὅς ἂν ὁμόφυλος ᾖ, ὁμογνώμην τε καὶ τοῦ αὐτοῦ Λόγου κεκοινωνηκώς· οὐ δικαιῶν ἐκλέγειν τόκους ἐπὶ χρήμασιν, ἀλλὰ ἀνειμέναις χερσὶ καὶ γνώμαις χαρίζεσθαι τοῖς δεομένοις· Θεὸς γὰρ ὁ κτίστης τοιᾶσδε χάριτος, ἤδη δὲ ὁ μεταδοτικός, καὶ τόκους ἀξιολόγους λαμβάνει, τὰ τιμιώτατα τῶν ἐν ἀνθρώποις, ἡμερότητα, χρηστότητα, μεγαλόνοιαν, εὐφημίαν, εὔκλειαν. Clement of Alexandria, *Stromata*, PG 8.1024. The *ANF* has translated μεταδόσεως καὶ κοινωνίας as "imparting and sharing." While these are fine translations, I feel that "distribution and sharing" fits better in the context of what Clement is discussing, which is the sharing—or lending—of goods and/or money.

27. Maloney, "Teachings of the Fathers on Usury," 243.

28. "He forbids anyone to lend money on interest to a brother, meaning by this name not merely a child of the same parents, but anyone of the same citizenship or nation. For he does not think it just to amass money bred from money as their yeanlings are from cattle. And he bids them not to take this as a ground for holding back or showing unwillingness to contribute, but without restriction of hand and heart to give free gifts to those who need, reflecting that a free gift is in a sense a loan that will be repaid, by the recipient, when times are better, without compulsion, and with a willing heart." Philo, *On The Virtues*, from *Philo* 8, LCL, ed. G. P. Goold, trans. F. H. Colson (Cambridge, Mass.: Harvard University Press, 1999), 14.82–83.

tification for this ban against usury, but it is undeniable that he is drawing from Deuteronomy because of the mention of "the law" and because of the emphasis he puts on the injunction: first Clement restates the Deuteronomy passage not to charge interest "to another Israelite" by casting those involved as "brother(s)"; he then enlarges the circle by insisting that this definition applies not only to members of the same family or someone who shares the same racial background or even similar beliefs, but to a "participator in the same Word."[29] This enlarges the possibilities for Christians, or perhaps restricts them: those who might have been tempted to enter into business transactions with another based on a lack of shared culture would be forced to admit that as they share "the same Word" they are now expected to treat one another as family in the best sense. Any economic problems created by such an instruction are solved by the loophole that it provides: if one must treat those who participate in "the same Word" as family, then the logical conclusion is that those who do not participate in "the same Word" can be gouged financially.[30] It is an open invitation to fiscal favouritism.

Theologians will not rely solely on the Hebrew Bible as a defence against usury; late-second century Bishop Apollonius will use Jesus' instructions to the disciples as an ethical foundation for Christians in authority, with respect to money matters. Preserved in Eusebius's *History*, Bishop Apollonius addresses financially unscrupulous behaviour of prophets and prophetesses of a Phrygian sect led by Montanus:[31]

The Lord said, "Do not provide yourselves with gold or silver or two coats," but these people have done the exact opposite—they have transgressed by providing themselves with forbidden things.[32] I can prove that their so-called prophets and martyrs rake in the shekels not only from the rich but from poor people, orphans and widows. . . . All the fruits of a prophet must be submitted to examination. . . . Tell me, does a prophet dye his hair? Does a prophet paint his eyelids? Does a prophet love ornaments? Does a prophet visit the gaming tables and play dice? Does a prophet do business as a moneylender? Let them say plainly whether these things are permissible or not, and I will prove that they have been going on in their circles.[33]

29. Καὶ τοῦ αὐτοῦ Λόγου κεκοινωνηκώς, Clement of Alexandria, *Stromata*, PG 8.1024; emphasis mine in the English translation.

30. As mentioned previously, Ambrose treats usury in similar fashion; see *St. Ambrosii, De Tobia*.

31. Eusebius, *The History of the Church from Christ to Constantine*, trans. G. A. Williamson (London: Penguin, 1965), 5.18; see also Jerome, *De viris Illustribus* 40, PL 23.655.

32. "Take no gold, or silver, or copper in your belts, no bag for your journey, or two tunics, or sandals, or a staff; for laborers deserve their food" (Matt 10:9–10).

33. Apollonius, in Eusebius, *The History of the Church*, 5.18.

Apollonius does not censure usury itself, but he does not need to; people who are "money-lenders" make their profit by charging interest, a profession which is here included alongside a list of unsuitable behaviours, most especially for a prophet or prophetess. Like the Ezekiel passage they form a picture of an immoral person whose behaviours are rapacious.

John Chrysostom, in his *Homily* 18 on the book of Matthew, will also draw from the words of Jesus to speak against usury, and will implore his listeners to "'Give to everyone who begs from you, and do not refuse anyone who wants to borrow from you.'[34] . . . But by 'borrowing' here he does not say a contract with usury, but merely the loan [use]."[35] Chrysostom clarifies that Jesus is not referring to a contractual loan but a simple loan, perhaps even interest-free, between family and friends.[36] Ideally, the individual who is in a position to lend money would be in a position to give it, but at the very least it should be loaned without interest in the only type of loan not detested by the public, the ἔρανος loan,[37] an interest-free loan extend-

---

34. Matthew 5:42.

35. δάνεισμα δὲ ἐνταῦθα οὐ τὸ μετὰ τῶν τοκῶν λέγει συμβόλαιον, ἀλλὰ τὴν χρῆσιν ἁπλῶς. John Chrysostom, *Hom. in Mt.* 18, PG 57.268; Chrysostom will, additionally, refer also to Luke 6:34–35: "If you lend to those from whom you hope to receive, what credit is that to you? Even sinners lend to sinners, to receive as much again. But love your enemies, do good, and lend, expecting nothing in return."

36. Lack of a denunciation of lending does not mean that Chrysostom is allowing for it, though he is not explicitly connecting Jesus with a condemnation of lending.

37. The ἔρανος evolved into a loan from a social gathering among friends. Maloney, in "Usury in Greek, Roman and Rabbinic Thought," notes the evolution of the term from its mention in Homer's *Odyssey* as a communal banquet among friends, to a general gathering among friends, and finally to a gathering of friends who come together to help another friend with a loan. As he points out, the meal element eventually faded, but what remains central to the ἔρανος is the common base of friendship, to the extent that the ἔρανος can refer either to the loan itself, or to the group who have gathered in friendship. Information regarding any legal formalities of the ἔρανος is scant, and no evidence remains that provides a methodical explanation of the ἔρανος, but what can be uncovered is that the lender often received his money back through an installment plan, and the loan could be pressed for in court if necessary. The only interest paid was the gratitude of the debtor to the lender, and the lender hoped only to see a return of the capital. The risk involved in this type of loan was greater than simple interest, for in the ἔρανος loan both parties stood to loose a friendship as well as money if the debt was not repaid. The ἔρανος seems to anticipate how interest-free loans were supposed to take place among the Israelites, distinct from loans which they granted to those who lived removed from Hebrew communities. Glotz, *Ancient Greece at Work*, 240. See also Paul Millett, "The *Eranos* Relationship," in *Lending and Borrowing in Ancient Athens* (Cambridge: Cambridge University Press, 1991), 153–59. But to keep a check on people who might think that they were noble for engaging in the ἔρανος, Chrysostom raises the bar in *Homily* 37 from Matthew, where lending *and* borrowing comes under fire: καθάπερ γὰρ ῥύπος καὶ πηλὸς τὰ ὦτα τῆς σαρκός, οὕτω τὰ πορνικὰ ἄσματα, καὶ τὰ βιωτικὰ διηγήματα, καὶ τὰ χρέα, καὶ τὰ περὶ τόκων καὶ δανεισμάτων, ῥύπου παντὸς χαλεπώτερον ἐμφράττει τῆς διανοίαςι τὴν ἀκοήν (For as filth and mud closes the ears of our flesh, so [also] do lewd lyrics, and worldly stories, and debts, and the business of usury and loans; all grievous filth is a

ed among family and friends in a type of loan system known as "pooling."[38]

Almost all passages that one finds on usury in the Greek patristic writings are contained under the theme of usury as prohibited by scripture, but the passages to follow move theological reflection on usury, its socio-economic effects, and the effects on the soul of the lender beyond the self-evident.

*A Usurer as a Menace to Community (Evil, a Wild Beast, a Liar, even a Murderer!)*   For Gregory of Nazianzus, usury is a sign of disobedience that brings down God's wrath. In *Oration* 16[39] he faults the behaviour of the community for their troubles, including oppression of the poor, under which usury falls. [40] The passage is clearly inspired by the parable of the talents in Matthew 25:26, which he emulates in style and content,[41] writing that "[o]ne has defiled the earth with usury and interest, both amassing where he had not sowed

---

barrier to the ears of the mind). John Chrysostom, *Hom. in Mt.* 37, PG 57.425. Chrysostom distinguishes between "usury" and "loans," but both are filth. While these are harsh words for the usurer who is disobeying Jesus' injunction to "love your enemies, do good, and lend, expecting nothing in return" (Luke 6:34–35) they are harsher still, for the one who lends even *without* usury is equally as damnable as the one who attempts to profit off another's need; ultimately, both are eager for revenue: the one in principal, the other in principal and additional returns. Note that Chrysostom does not even let the borrower off the hook as the one with "debts" also is indicted. I think it is reasonable to believe that in this particular passage Chrysostom was not condemning the needy person who borrowed for consumption, but probably the individual who borrowed to maintain a certain lifestyle, a topic which emerges in other passages devoted to usury.

38. Marshall Sahlins, *Stone Age Economics* (Chicago: Aldine-Atherton, 1972), 188. "Pooling" is a type of lending that is primarily a distribution among equals. This type of lending among equals did not take place to assuage poverty but to provide an individual with a financial advantage. See Millett, *Lending and Borrowing in Ancient Athens*, 153. The ἔρανος did, however, sometimes cut across social boundaries, and a perfect example of this is found in Demosthenes, who writes of a prostitute who bought her freedom by raising ἔρανος contributions from her customers, including one Phrynion, who acted as an agent on her behalf: "When Phrynion came to her, she told him the proposal which Eucrates and Timanoridas [her Corinthian owners] had made to her, and gave him the money which she had collected from her other lovers as a contribution [ἔρανος] towards the price of her freedom, and added whatever she had gained for herself, and she begged him to advance the balance needed to make up the twenty *minae*, and to pay it to Eucrates and Timanoridas to secure her freedom. He listened gladly to these words of hers, and taking the money which had been paid in to her by her other lovers, added the balance himself and paid the twenty *minae* as the price of her freedom to Eucrates and Timanoridas on the condition that she should not ply her trade in Corinth." Demosthenes, *Private Orations,* trans. A.T. Murray (London: William Heinemann, 1988), 6.59.30–32.

39. Gregory Nazianzen, *Or.* 16, PG 35.933–64.

40. Similar to Basil's *Homilia dicta tempore famis et siccitatis*, PG 31.303–28; trans. Susan Holman, *The Hungry Are Dying: Beggars and Bishops in Roman Cappadocia* (Oxford: University Press, 2001), 183–92.

41. Concerning this method, Young claims that rewriting the Scriptures within their texts enabled the Christian authors to offer an alternative to the "stylistic inferiority" of the Bible. Frances M. Young, *Biblical Exegesis and the Formation of Christian Culture* (Cambridge: Cambridge University Press, 1997), 103.

and reaping where he had not strawed not farming the earth but the want of those in need."[42] According to Gregory, gathering interest is the work of the morally corrupt; they do nothing yet collect a wage. Gregory is here equating the one who has "defiled the land with usury and interest" with the wicked master—who also believed he was entitled to collect something for nothing.[43] Unlike other theologians who will write that the servant who fails to invest is the unfaithful Christian, Gregory writes that a proper understanding of the depravity of usury kept the servant from acting wickedly himself on behalf of his master.[44] Like those who oppress widows and children, manipulate property lines, rob God of the first-fruits of the harvest and build larger barns with their profits and for their profits rather than distributing the wealth, the usurer in Gregory's milieu prospers from the hardships of others like a wicked master. Gregory has set up the perimeters around which Christians must present themselves: there are those who obey the ordinances, whose behaviours result in beneficial spring showers, and there are those who stand outside the ordinances, whose behaviours bring about natural disasters.

No one put the usurer in worse company than Cyril of Jerusalem, who, perhaps modeling his list on the Ezekiel passage, includes usury within a catalogue of heinous crimes:

Shun every diabolical activity, and do not be mislead by the apostate Serpent . . . give attention neither to prophecies nor observations of the skies, nor omens, nor to the legendary oracles of the Greeks; do not accept hearing [about] poisons, and enchantments, and the unlaw-

---

42. ὁ δὲ τόκοις καὶ πλεονασμοῖς τὴν γῆν ἐμίανε, καὶ συνάγων δ᾽ ὅθεν οὐκ ἔσπειρε, καὶ θερίζων ὅπου μὴ διεσκόρπισε· γεωργῶν οὐ τήν γῆν, ἀλλὰ τὴν χρείαν τῶν δεομένων. Gregory Nazienzen, *Or.* 16, PG 35.957. Using Matthew 25:26 as his source, Gregory provides an "other" meaning at the same time that he interprets the passage. See David Dawson, "Allegorical Interpretation as Composition," in *Allegorical Readers and Cultural Revision in Ancient Alexandria* (Berkeley: University of California Press, 1992): 129–31. Gregory also lists additional sins connected with financial concerns: acquisition of a neighbor's land and encroaching landmarks, robbing God by denying offerings, oppressing the widows, orphans, the needy and the meek, and generally acting in a rapacious and miserly manner. Adding insult to injury, they praise God, saying Εὐλογητὸς Κύριος, εἰπὼν, ὅτι πεπλουτήκαμεν ("Blessed is the Lord, because we are rich"). Gregory Nazianzen, *Or.* 16, PG 35.960.

43. Recall that the wicked master/harsh man was told by his servant that the servant did nothing on behalf of his master because "I knew that you were a harsh man, reaping where you did not sow, and gathering where you did not scatter seed; so I was afraid and I went and hid your talent in the ground" (Matthew 25:24–25). This clearly falls under the first theme of usury as prohibited by scripture.

44. See Theodoret of Cyrrhus, *Eusebio episcopo Persicæ Armeniæ*, PG 83.1251–56. For Theodoret, the interest gained on one talent is the very least of one's obligations towards the master, who—for Theodoret—is God. See also John Chrysostom, *Hom. in Mt.* 78, PG 58.711–18.

ful business of necromancy; stand apart from all licentiousness, knowing neither gluttony nor hedonism, rising superior to all avarice and lending on interest.[45]

Usury is one amongst a most enticing list of depravity ranging from stargazing to necromancy, all of which cause harm to any community; but here the practices are not merely activities one should avoid, for Cyril has demonised the usurer in his list by association with practitioners of the dark arts and the appearance of the "the apostate Serpent"; naturally one who engages in these activities stand in conflict to Christian scripture, and therefore Christianity itself. Here, the usurer is not merely unjust; the usurer is evil, clearly lurking in the red-light district.[46]

According to Basil of Caesarea's *Homilia in psalmum* 14, the usurer is a liar; in fact, he writes, the seduction of the debtor begins with an elaborate performance:

Calling down curses on himself and swearing that he is entirely without money, and is looking around to see if he can find someone who lends money out with interest, he is believed in his lie because of his oaths, and incurs the guilt of perjury as the evil gains of his humanity. But, when he who is seeking the loan makes mention of interest and names his securities, then, pulling down his eyebrows, he smiles and remembers somewhere or other a family friendship, and calling him associate and friend, he says, "We shall see if we have any money at all reserved. There is a deposit of a dear friend who entrusted it to us for a matter of business. He has assigned a heavy interest for it, but we shall certainly remit some and give it at a lower rate of interest."[47]

Several layers of deceit happen in quick succession: the usurer claims that he has no money, he claims that the money he has belongs to someone else, and

---

45. φεῦγε δὲ πᾶσαν διαβολικὴν ἐνέργειαν, καὶ μὴ πείθου τῷ δράκοντι τῷ ἀποστάτῃ ... καὶ μήτε ἀστρολογίαις, μήτε ὀρνεοσκοπίαις, μήτε κληδόσι πρόσεχε, μηδὲ ταῖς μυθώδεσι τῶν Ἑλλήνων μαντείαις· φαρμακείαν, καὶ ἐπαοιδίαν, καὶ τὰ νεκυομαντειῶν παρανομώτατα πράγματα, μηδὲ μέχρις ἀκοῆς παραδέχου. ἀπόστηθι παντὸς ἀκολασίας εἴδους, μήτε γαστριμαργῶν, μήτε φιληδονῶν, ὑπεράνω τε φιλαργυρίας ἀπάσης, καὶ τοῦ τοκίζειν, γενόμενος. Cyril of Jerusalem, Lecture 4; On the Ten Points of Doctrine, Colossians, PG 33.501. N.B. I have chosen "poison" for *farmakeian* because of Gregory of Nyssa's comments that Cyril's see was morally corrupt and factious but doctrinally sound: "But as it is, there is no form of uncleanness that is not perpetrated among them; rascality, adultery, theft, idolatry, poisoning, quarrelling, murder are rife; and the last kind of evil is so excessively prevalent, that nowhere in the world are people so ready to kill each other as there." Gregory of Nyssa (*NPNF* 2:5.383). One must pity Cyril for what he was up against.

46. Chrysostom writes that he would rather live with thousands of demons than one covetous person, for they are "diseased" (ἢ μετὰ ἑνὸς ταύτην νοσοῦντος τὴν νόσον). John Chrysostom, *Hom. in Mt.* 28, PG 57.356.

47. Basil, *Hom. in Ps.* (PG 29:265–68); ed. Way, *On Psalm 14*, 182–83.

he claims that he is lowering the interest rate out of "kindness." The entire transaction from start to finish is a deception.

Moreover, the usurer is not merely a liar, but is like an animal. Basil describes the usurer as lower than a dog, unable to be satisfied once he receives what he wants,[48] and a "prolific wild beast"[49] to which the debtor has yoked himself; mirroring Plutarchs' *Moralia*,[50] he compares the rapid growth of interest to the fecundity of rabbits:

They say that hares bring forth and at the same time both rear young and become doubly pregnant. So also with moneylenders, the money is lent out and, at the same time, it reproduces from itself and is in a process of growth. You have not yet received it in your hands and you have been required to pay out the interest for the present month.[51]

While in other sermons Basil uses the hierarchy of the animal world as a superior paradigm, here it is a warning for the human world: what is natural in their world is immoral in ours.[52] As well, Gregory of Nyssa, in *Contra usurarios,* will liken the usurer to birds soon to be caught after greedily feasting on seed, or hunters who deplete each populated valley of wildlife, then move on with their nets to the next fertile valley.[53]

48. Basil, *Hom. in Ps.* (PG 29:273); ed. Way, *On Psalm 14*, 187.

49. Basil, *Hom. in Ps.* (PG 29:273); ed. Way, *On Psalm 14*, 187. Chrysostom's *Homily 13 on First Corinthians*, equates the rich and usurers with animals gorging themselves constantly: τὰ δὲ τῶν πλουτούντων ὁποῖα; χοίρων καὶ κυνῶν καὶ λύκων καὶ τῶν ἄλλων θηρίων. Οἱ μὲν γὰρ αὐτῶν περὶ τραπεζῶν καὶ ὄψων καὶ καρυκευμάτων καὶ οἴνου παντοδαποῦ καὶ μύρων καὶ ἱματίων καὶ τῆς ἄλλης διαπαντὸς διαλέγουνται ἀσωτίας; οἱ δὲ περὶ τόκων καὶ δανεισμάτων ("but of what kind are those who are rich? [They are] of swine and dogs and wolves, and all other wild beasts. For some of them concern [themselves] perpetually with what is on the table, and condiments and an abundance of wine and perfumes and garments and all the rest of the extravagances. And others about usury and lending money"). John Chrysostom, *Hom. in I Cor.* 13, PG 61.114.

50. "They say that hares at one and the same time give birth to one litter, suckle another, and conceive again; but the loans of these barbarous rascals give birth to interest before conception; for while they are giving they immediately demand payment, while they lay money down they take it up, and they lend what they receive for money lent." Plutarch, *De vitando aere alieno*, in *Moralia*, LCL, trans. Harold North Fowler (Cambridge, Mass.: Harvard University Press, 1936), 10.325.

51. Basil, *Hom. in Ps.* (PG 29:273); ed. Way, *On Psalm 14*, 187.

52. Basil's *Hex.* 7, PG 29.147–64.

53. Gregory of Nyssa, *Usur.* (PG 46:445; J 202); ed. McCambley, "Against Those Who Practice Usury," 299. Gregory does not dwell on this as much in *Contra usurarios* as he does in *Concerning Beneficence*, where he writes movingly about the rape of the natural world to gorge the maw of the self-indulgent: "Our gourmands do not, in fact, even spare the bottom of the sea, nor do they limit themselves to the fish that swim in the water, but they also bring up the crawling marine beasts from the ocean bed and drag them to shore. One pillages the oyster banks, one pursues the sea urchin, one captures the creeping cuttle fish, one plucks the octopus from the rock it grips, one eradicates the molluscs from their pedestal. All animal spe-

Worse than an animal, the usurer is a murderer; in his fourth homily from the *Commentary on Ecclesiastes* Gregory of Nyssa will question why society distinguishes between those who acquire through stealth and those who acquire by legal—yet immoral—means: "What is the difference between getting someone else's property by seizing it through covert housebreaking or taking possession of the goods of a passer-by by murdering him, and acquiring what is not one's own by extracting interest?"[54] In sum, the greed of an avaricious person has resulted in the birth [τόκος] of evil thoughts, the agent of subsequent sins: envy, robbery, usury, and murder.[55]

Within this theme we can see that the Greek Fathers used a variety of illustrations to demonstrate that they saw the usurer along a continuum of menacing behaviours, ranging from liars and beasts to thieves and murders; regardless, such behaviours bring down the wrath of God on the community.

*The Spiritual Poverty of the Usurer*    As stated above, it was not always the material poverty of the poor which was of importance to the bishops. John Chrysostom, in *Homily 43 on First Corinthians*, makes it clear that he is addressing the abuses of the wealthy because is he zealously concerned with "[their] salvation."[56] This concern for the salvation of the usurer comes out

---

cies, those that swim in the surface waters or live in the depths of the sea, all are brought up into the atmosphere. The artful skills of the hedonist cleverly devise traps appropriate to each." Gregory of Nyssa, *De beneficentia* (PG 46.465-68); ed. Holman, *The Hungry Are Dying*, 198.

54. Gregory of Nyssa, *Hom. 4*, from *Homiliae in Eccl.* (PG 44:615–754), *Gregorii Nysseni Opera, In Ecclesiasten homiliae* 5, ed. W. Jaeger (Leiden: Brill, 1986), 195–442, in *Commentary on Ecclesiastes,* trans. Stuart George Hall and Rachel Moriarty (Berlin: Walter de Gruyter: 1993), 79.

55. Although not writing directly about usury, in *Homily 11 on Romans*, Chrysostom writes that the one who inflicts financial oppression—in whatever form that might take—is indirectly a murderer: ἤ οὐ φόνος, εἰπέ μοι, καὶ φόνου χεῖρον, τὸ λιμῷ παραδοῦναι πένητα καὶ εἰς δεσμωτήριον ἐμβαλεῖν, καὶ μετὰ τοῦ λιμοῦ καὶ βασάνοις ἐκδοῦναι καὶ μυρίοις αἰκισμοῖς; κἄν γὰρ αὐτὸς ταῦτα μὴ ποιῇς, παρέχῃς δὲ τὴν αἰτίαν τοῦ γίγνεσθαι, τῶν διακονουμένων μᾶλλον αὐτὰ ἐργάζῃ. "Is it not murder—one might say even worse than murder—to hand a poor man over to famine, and to throw him into prison, and to enslave him not only to famine and tortures, but measureless sufferings? For even if (on the one hand) you do not do these to him, you (on the other hand) are responsible for them being done, even more than the attendants who do them." John Chrysostom, *Hom. in Rom.* 11, PG 60.491. See also John Chrysostom, *Hom. in Mt.* 5, PG 57.55–62. Basil demonstrates agreement with this assessment: "Starvation, the distress of the famished, is the supreme human calamity, a more miserable end than all other deaths. . . . But famine is a slow evil, always approaching, always holding off like a beast in its den. . . . Whoever had it in his power to alleviate this evil but deliberately opts instead for profit, should be condemned as a murderer." Basil, *Homilia dicta tempore famis et siccitatis,* in Holman, *The Hungry Are Dying*, 190; in Cicero's *Offices* he quotes Cato the elder who, after being asked "What do you think of lending at usury?" replied: "What do you think of killing a man?" Cicero, *Three Books of Offices, or Moral Duties,* trans. Cyrus R. Edmonds (London: G. Bell and Sons, 1916), 25.

56. σφόδρα γὰρ ἐρῶ τῆς σωτηρίας τῆς ὑμετέρας. John Chrysostom, *Hom. in 1 Cor.* 43, PG 61.369.

of the larger theme of the rich and poor existing together, one for the sake of the other.[57] Like Plato, Chrysostom is concerned for the spiritual and emotional state of the wealthy;[58] he assures them they should not be troubled when dealt blows to their material situations,[59] and invites them to offer alms before prayer and bedtime as a "shield against the devil," and to "give your prayers wings."[60] But nothing, he claims, is to be put into this coffer that comes from injustice[61] which includes usury: "For those who demand usury I have no promise, neither with soldiers who extort others, turning to their advantage the misfortunes of others. For God will accept nothing from that council."[62] Consider the interesting parallel: the soldier who engages in extortion—as opposed to the soldier who fights or abuses only the *enemy*—is like

57. See *The Shepherd of Hermas,* Clement of Alexandria, *Quis dives salvetur?* See also Mary Sheather, "Pronouncements of the Cappadocians on Issues of Poverty and Wealth," in *Prayer and Spirituality in the Early Church,* ed. Pauline Allen, Raymond Canning, and Lawrence Cross, with B. Janelle Caiger (Everton Park, Queensland: Center for Early Christian Studies, 1998), 383.

58. Plato is not concerned solely with the plight of the poor but also with the "happiness" of the wealthy, which might here be compared with Chrysostom's desire for the wealthy also to acquire salvation. Chrysostom notes that it is difficult for the wealthy to attain salvation because they focus their attention on worldly wealth rather than on Christian virtue, and because they do not understand the transient nature of material goods their riches become an impediment for them: ἀρετὴ μόνον οἶδεν ἡμῖν συναποδημεῖν, ἀρετὴ μόνη διαβαίνει πρὸς τὴν ζωὴν τὴν ἐκεῖ. ("Virtue alone is able to sojourn with us, virtue alone is able to pass over to the life in another world"). *Hom. in 1 Tim.* 11, PG 62.556. But for Chrysostom, wealth is an impediment to virtue because he believed that all wealth was at some point gained unjustly; in short: ἀλλ᾽ ἀνάγκη τὴν ἀρχὴν αὐτῆς καὶ τὴν ῥίζαν ἀπὸ ἀδικίας εἶναί τινος. πόθεν; ὅτι ὁ Θεὸς ἐξ ἀρχῆς οὐ τὸν μὲν πλούσιον ἐποίησε, τὸν δὲ πένητα ("but by necessity, the origin and the root of them must have been from injustice. Why? Because in the beginning, God did not make one wealthy and another poor"). John Chrysostom, *Hom. in 1 Tim.* 12, PG 62.563. Plato, too, believed that those who were wealthy only were so because of unjust means; because the wealthy were not able to be good, therefore they were not able to be happy. *The Laws of Plato,* trans. Thomas L. Prangle (New York: Basic Books, 1980), 742c–44a. To put this into Chrysostom's terms, because the wealthy are less likely to practice Christian charity they are less likely to attain salvation.

59. John Chrysostom, *Hom. in 1 Cor.* 43, PG 61.372.

60. τοῦτο δὲ ἔχων τὸ κιβώτιον, ὅπλον ἔχεις κατὰ τοῦ διαβόλου, τὴν εὐχὴν ὑπόπτερον ποιεῖς, ἁγίαν κατασχευάζεις τὴν οἰκίαν, τροφὰς ἔνδον ἔχων ἀποκειμένας τοῦ βασιλέως. John Chrysostom, *Hom. in 1 Cor.* 43, PG 61.373.

61. μόνον μηδὲν ἐξ ἀδικίας ἐκεῖ βαλλέσθω. John Chrysostom, *Hom. in 1 Cor.* 43, PG 61.373.

62. Πρὸς γὰρ τοὺς τόκους ἀπαιτοῦντας οὐδείς μοι λόγος, οὐδὲ πρὸς στρατιώτας διασείοντας ἄλλους, καὶ πραγματευομένους ἀλλοτρίας συμφοράς· οὐδὲν γὰρ ἐκεῖθεν βούλεται δέχεσθαι ὁ Θεός. John Chrysostom, *Hom. in 1 Cor.* 43, PG 61.374. Chrysostom's choice here—λόγος—is problematic for the translator, even as it is a simple word. There are so many possible options for this word that it is difficult to know precisely what he meant. The *NPNF* translation uses "concern," as in "For those who demand usury I have no concern." I am not fond of that choice, as it indicates a dismissal—rather like Chrysostom is swatting a fly—instead of condemnation. I decided to go with "promise," as in "I have no promise," because it seems he is saying to the usurer that he has no consolation for the one who inflicts violence on their neighbour.

the usurer, for they are both turning their neighbour's woe to their own advantage; they are both public enemies, menaces, serpents in the garden, eager for the downfall of the innocent for their own gain.[63] According to Chrysostom, God "will accept nothing"[64] from such an individual; the usurer and the unjust soldier might acquire material possessions, might have power and the fear of those around them, but they will be rejected by God. This sentiment will be echoed in the writings of other theologians, Greek and Latin, who will claim that God will accept neither the individual who profits from the misfortunes of others nor what the wicked offer; the most explicit example—from which this chapter draws its title—is found in the poetry of a mid-third century North African bishop Commodianus, who writes specifically about charities that come from usury: "Do you not believe that the Lord sees these things from heaven? . . . you wish to bestow charity that you may purge yourself as being evil, with that which is evil. The Almighty absolutely rejects such works as these. You have given *that which has been wrung from tears.* . . . O wicked one, you deceive yourself, but no one else."[65]

God will not accept "that which has been wrung from tears," that which has been acquired at the expense of another. So what will God accept? Proper investment. In Chrysostom's *Homily 3 on Second Corinthians*, he addresses usury and proper investment through the context of Abraham's willingness to sacrifice his son Isaac, who is understood in this context as "the principle": "On this account, he also received the principle with usury, and quite fairly . . . and whereas on account of God he gave of himself, because of this, God was beneficent to him with His own."[66] Here "usury" is not unjust but it is the inheritance Abraham will receive as a result of having placed, or "invested" his wealth—specifically his son's life—in the proper place, which is with God. Abraham invested Isaac at God's request, and as a result Abraham re-

63. This violates the injunction "You shall not revile the deaf, or place a stumbling block before the blind" (Leviticus 19:11–14). One is not to defraud another who does not understand, or is incapable of understanding; quite simply, not taking unfair advantage, or giving to someone something that will bring harm upon them. Meir Tamari, *"With All Your Possessions"—Jewish Ethics and Economic Life* (New York: The Free Press, 1987), 176.

64. οὐδὲν γὰρ ἐκεῖθεν βούλεται δέχεσθαι ὁ Θεός. John Chrysostom, *Hom. in 1 Cor.* 43, PG 61.374.

65. Commodianus, *The Instruction*, PL 59.163; *ANF* 4: 64. 216.

66. διὸ καὶ ἔλαβε μετὰ τόκου τὸ κεφάλαιον· καὶ μάλα εἰκότως . . . καὶ ἐπειδὴ ἀπέστη τῶν ἑαυτοῦ διὰ τὸν Θεὸν, διὰ τοῦτα καὶ ὁ Θεὸς μετὰ τούτων ἐχαρίσατο αὐτῷ καὶ τὰ αὐτοῦ. John Chrysostom, *Hom. in 2 Cor.* 3, PG 61.415.

ceived from God "with usury" (as in "'increase" or "more than was given") additional wealth in the form of family, through a promise made prior to the sacrificial event, and at a time when Abraham despaired of even having an heir.[67] Here God is the one returning "with usury, and quite fairly."[68] For Chrysostom, spiritual usury places the Christian in proper relationship with God, reinforcing the rarely believed appeal that "investing" in God brings a return, while refusing to do so is nothing short of plunder.[69] For Chrysostom, proper investment—and the only one from which a Christian might rightly expect to gain—is *with* God and the only gain worthwhile is eternal life *from* God, stated perhaps most explicitly in his *Homily 5 on Matthew:*

Do not engage in lending, for you do not know how to profit; but lend to Him who returns interest greater than the principle. Lend where [there is] no malice, where [there is] no accusation, no reason for fear. Lend to Him who has no want, but has need on account of you; [Lend] to Him who feeds all, yet hungers so that you may not know hunger; who is poor, so that you may be wealthy. Lend where your return will not be death, but life instead of death. For this usury is a witness of the kingdom; but that [usury] is of punishment; the one for those who love money, and the other for those who love wisdom, the one of cruelty, and the other of humanity. . . . For nothing, nothing is more shameful in this world than usury, nothing crueler.[70]

Chrysostom is suggesting a restructuring of how people understand investing or what it means to 'invest,' which means they have to restructure how they understand themselves, their role in society, and their role potentially in the afterlife. For emphasis, he differentiates between the results of the two types of usury: heavenly usury is a witness of the kingdom of God, of life, of wisdom, self-denial and humanity; usury of the world is the herald of cruelty, covetousness, death, and punishment.[71] Notice that what he highlights—wisdom and humanity—are "flesh" and "mind" affirming; these are qualities that benefit

67. Genesis 15:5–6; 22:16b–17a.

68. μετὰ τόκου . . . καὶ μάλα εἰκότως. John Chrysostom, *Hom. in 2 Cor.* 3, PG 61.415.

69. Malachi 3:8–10.

70. μὴ σὺ πραγματεύου· οὐδὲ γὰρ οἶσθα κερδαίνειν· ἀλλὰ δάνεισον τῷ πλείω τοῦ κεφαλαίου τὸν τόκον παρέχοντι. δάνεισον ἔνθα μηδεὶς φθόνος, ἔνθα μηδεμία κατηγορία μηδὲ ἐπιβουλὴ μηδὲ φόβος, δάνεισον τῷ μηδενὸς δεομένῳ, καὶ χρείαν ἔχοντι διὰ σέ· τῷ πάντας τρέφοντι, καὶ πεινῶτι, ἵνα σὺ μὴ λιμώξῃς· τῷ πενομένῳ, ἵνα σὺ πλουτήσῃς. δάνεισον ὅθεν οὐκ ἔστι θάνατον, ἀλλὰ ζωὴν ἀντὶ θανάτου καρπώσασθαι· οὗτοι μὲν γὰρ βασιλείαν, ἐκεῖνοι δὲ γέενναν προξενοῦσιν οἱ τόκοι· οἱ μὲν γὰρ φιλαργυρίας, οἱ δὲ φιλοσοφίας εἰσί· καὶ οἱ μὲν ὠμότητος, οἱ δὲ φιλανθρωπίας . . . οὐδὲν γὰρ, οὐδὲν τῶν ἐνταῦθα τόκων αἰσχρότερον, οὐδὲν ὠμότερον. John Chrysostom, *Hom. in Mt.* 5, PG 57.61–62.

71. John Chrysostom, *Hom. in Mt.* 5, PG 57.61–62.

the public, the community. To quell their anxieties, coupled with this urge to see them as lovers of humanity and wisdom, engaging in a life of at least appropriate self-denial, is an assurance to the lender that Chrysostom's intention is not for the lender to go without, but for ultimately greater gain: "[f]or instead of gold, I wish for you to receive heaven as usury."[72] Chrysostom is reversing the idea of usury, enlarging the scope of the discussion to include that which God gives in return for financial trust invested in God's people—"my people, the poor among you"[73]—and spiritual trust invested by the giver in God; God will not abandon the cause of the one who gives.[74]

Gregory of Nyssa also addresses the spiritual poverty of the usurer in *Contra usurarios*, in which he writes of God as the "Debtor," the Χρεώστης.[75] Not a financial "debtor," this debtor has control over the "entire world and its possessions," and will attend to the lender's needs if the lender will give abundantly rather than demand what is not theirs to secure.[76] Addressing the anxiety to which a usurer is enslaved, Gregory beseeches the lender to regard as a pledge the present bounty of the earth, and all which is inheritable from God: "Consider the sky's expanse, examine the boundless sea, learn from the earth's magnitude and count the living beings which it nourishes. . . . Do not demand gain but give bountifully and without corruption (Prov 191:7). Then you will

72. ἀντὶ γὰρ χρυσίου, τὸν οὐρανὸν βούλομαί σε τόκον λαβεῖν. John Chrysostom, *Hom. in Mt.* 5, PG 57.62.

73. Exodus 22:25.

74. This is seen in Basil's text: "Whenever you have the intention of providing for a poor man for the Lord's sake, the same thing is both a gift and a loan, a gift because of the expectation of no repayment, but a loan because of the great gift of the Master who pays in his place, and who, receiving trifling things through a poor man, will give great things in return for them. 'He who has mercy on the poor, lends to God.' Do you not wish to have the Lord of the universe answerable to you for payment?" Basil, *Hom. in Ps.* (PG 29:277); ed. Way, *On Psalm 14*, 190. This is seen also in Gregory's: "Make a pledge to him who is immortal and believe in his reliable bond which can never be sundered. Do not demand gain but give bountifully and without corruption (Prov 19:17)." Gregory of Nyssa, *Usur.* (PG 46:440; J 199); ed. McCambley, "Against Those Who Practice Usury," 297. Holman, in "'You speculate on the misery of the poor,'" writes that "God becomes, like the imperial treasury, a source of public assistance" (217).

75. Gregory of Nyssa, *Usur.* (PG 46:440; J 198); ed. McCambley, "Against Those Who Practice Usury," 296.

76. Gregory of Nyssa, *Usur.* (PG 46:440; J 198); ed. McCambley, "Against Those Who Practice Usury," 296. Gregory also uses this language in *Sermon 5* on the Lords Prayer: "For the forgiving of debts is the special prerogative of God, since it is said, *No man can forgive sins but God alone.*" Gregory of Nyssa, *Oratio 5* (PG 44:1178–94), in *Gregory of Nyssa: The Lord's Prayer; The Beatitudes,* ed. Philip Schaff and Henry Wace, in *Ancient Christian Writers: Works of the Fathers in Translation* 18; ed. Philip Schaff, trans. Hilda C. Graef (Washington D.C.: The Catholic University of America Press, 1954), 71.

see God who abundantly dispenses his grace."[77] Referencing Matthew, Gregory offers as insurance the promise Jesus makes to Peter, who wonders for what benefit have they left their homes and families behind: "Truly I say to you that everyone who has left houses or brothers or sisters or father or mother or wife or children or lands will receive a hundred-fold and will inherit eternal life."[78] Gregory's question to the lender—"Are you aware of his generosity and goodness?"[79]—is answered with a statement on the generosity of a God who gives freely to those who are obedient, which he then contrasts with the miserable condition of the money-lender who spends his days and nights agonising over the return: "Why do you harm yourself with anxiety by calculating days, months, the sum of money, dreaming of profit, and fearing the appointed day whose fruitful harvest brings hail?"[80] The cost of discipleship—though steep—yields a high return, and those whose hearts are not enslaved by the cares and anxieties of the earth but look heavenward instead are rewarded, Gregory assures, by a benevolent and charitable God who sees to the needs of those who are virtuous, such as Moses, Elizabeth, Hannah, and Mary.[81] Virtuous individuals honour God by petitioning God directly for their needs instead of looking for grain in a barren field, while the usurer—like Chrysostom's unjust soldier—humiliates their own nature and demonstrates their spiritual poverty by deigning to violent and corrupt actions.

While violent and corrupt actions are problematic, still they run a close second to an additional problem: the salvation of the lender. One gives away so that one might gain, and in doing so, the "poor" are the "proper" investment for the lender. Under those circumstances, the idea that the exchange between the lender and borrower is corrupt does not exist.

77. Gregory of Nyssa, *Usur.* (PG 46:440; J 199); ed. McCambley, "Against Those Who Practice Usury," 297.

78. Matt 19:29; See also Chrysostom's *Homily* 56 on Matthew, in which he urges the lender to give the money to the needy rather than to lend it, for then God would return that investment with a better deal: οὗτος μόλις ἑκατοστὴν ἀπόδιδσιν· ἐκεῖνος δὲ ἑκατονταπλασίονα, καὶ ζωὴν αἰώνιον ("While this scarcely gives back a hundred; this a hundred times as much, and eternal life"). John Chrysostom, *Hom. in Mt.* 56, PG 58.556. See also John Chrysostom's *Homily* 3 on Genesis, PG 53.33. Thanks to Brian Matz for alerting me to this passage.

79. Gregory of Nyssa, *Usur.* (PG 46:440; J 199); ed. McCambley, "Against Those Who Practice Usury," 297.

80. Gregory of Nyssa, *Usur.* (PG 46:440–41; J 199–200); ed. McCambley, "Against Those Who Practice Usury," 297.

81. Exodus 16:15b; 17.6b; Luke 1:3; 1 Sam. 1:20; Luke 2:7.

## *Who Are the Usurers?*

Now that we have some understanding of what the Greek Fathers had to say about usury, to whom were they addressing their comments? Who are the usurers? Based on our texts and the knowledge of the permeation of debts in late antiquity, usurers in the early church were probably known members of the Christian communities, and they were not happy to hear what the theologians had to say.

*Members of the Community*    While the usurer might very well be an unknown business person, analysis of the passages that include usury and the usurer have led me to conclude that the usurer of whom our theologians speak is likely an opportunistic "neighbor," someone within the Christian community. Only a member of a community would be privy to the information that leads to the shameful and shamefully public events as illustrated by Basil:

Dogs, when they have received something, are pacified, but the money-lender, on receiving something, is further provoked. He does not stop railing, but demands more. If you swear, he does not trust; he examines your family affairs; he meddles with your transactions. If you go forth from your chamber, he drags you along with him and carries you off; if you hide yourself inside, he stands before your house and knocks at the door. In the presence of your wife he puts you to shame; he insults you before your friends; in the market place he strangles you; he makes the occurrence of a feast an evil; he renders life insupportable for you.[82]

I am not suggesting that each loan transaction was an occasion for harassment and abuse, but it highlights an important point about the lending system: personality affected the system.[83] While most loan transactions were probably without the drama to which Basil refers, a significant amount of them surely involved the very public bullying maltreatment described above. The usurer Basil describes has done some homework, knowing where the debtors live, who their wives are, their friends, daily rituals, and even their social engagements. Further, the harassment that the lender is here forcing upon a debtor highlights an additional point: one person takes the loan, but many suffer for it. This is not a case of one person's debt affecting only that person because the

---

82. Basil, *Hom. in Ps.* (PG 29:269–72); ed. Way, *On Psalm 14*, 185.

83. "The rate of interest would vary, firstly, depending on the personality of the lender and that of the borrower." Andreau, *Banking and Business in the Roman World*, 95.

person is an "individual" as we in the western world understand it; but in late antique Mediterranean culture, where relationships are tied together by kinship and gender and the body is the microcosm of society, the entire family can be implicated.

An additional clue that indicates that the usurer is a member of the community is that Basil questions a specific portion of his audience—you "rich men"—as to why he even needs to be addressing those who "obey the Lord," as if it would be self-evident that one who considers oneself to be a Christian would not take usury: "Listen, you rich men, to what we advise the poor because of your inhumanity; rather to persevere in their terrible situations than to accept the misfortunes which come from the payment of interest. But, if you obey the Lord, what need is there of these words?"[84]

Gregory, who is addressing primarily the lender in *Contra usurarios*, provides us with some hint as to how it was received: his final statement to the usurer is a call to alter their pernicious ways, but he acknowledges those in his audience who are "murmuring under their lips"[85] about his words, and states that such persons are likely to "shut their doors to persons in need."[86] Faced with this threat, he advocates either the lending of money without interest or simple acts of charity, but his final bold words on the subject are a veiled threat that any who do otherwise act in a manner "hostile to God."[87]

We cannot know entirely the relationship between the usurer and the debtor, but these types of clues in the text can provide us with some indication that the parties know one another and are together listening to the words of their common bishops; but regardless of relationship between the usurer and the debtor, the lenders are charging interest to a degree that it is causing grave harm to individuals to whom money is being lent, and thus putting a strain on the community.[88] While this surely includes situations in which the bor-

---

84. Basil, *Hom. in Ps.* (PG 29:277); ed. Way, *On Psalm 14*, 190.

85. Gregory of Nyssa, *Usur.* (PG 46:452; J 206); ed. McCambley, "Against Those Who Practice Usury," 301.

86. Gregory of Nyssa, *Usur.* (PG 46:452; J 206); ed. McCambley, "Against Those Who Practice Usury," 301.

87. Gregory of Nyssa, *Usur.* (PG 46:452; J 206); ed. McCambley, "Against Those Who Practice Usury," 301.

88. Meislin and Cohen, in "Background of the Biblical Law against Usury," write about the destructive nature of interest in the case of need-based loans: "A loan to the needy at interest carring its

rower is merely borrowing so to continue to live in a style to which they have grown accustomed, it seems likely that the bishops are speaking out against usury because irreparable damage is being wrought upon households as a result of largely consumptive loans.

*Women* Passages in the *Apostolic Constitutions* reveal that women as well as men participated in usurious activity, and widows—specifically—supported by the Church were chastised for their concern with the cares of the world, and for being "not affixed to the altar of Christ."[89] According to the *Constitutions,* women living off of subsistence from the Church were investing what they had been given and were "heaping up to themselves plenty of money, and lend[ing] at bitter usury."[90] Such a woman who participated in such activities—though she may very well have been engaging in lending to gain for herself profit because the subsistence was not sufficient—was dealt with harshly at the discretion of her bishop: "But if without direction she does any one of these things, let her be punished with fasting, or else let her be separated on account of her rashness."[91]

*Clergy* Based on the amount of canons from ecumenical and local councils of the early church period, one can surmise that local clergy might have been among the usurers; consistent with our theologians, canons from various councils upheld the position that usury is not an activity befitting clergy. Canon 17 of the First Ecumenical Council of Nicaea in 325 states that if any clergy were to be found receiving usury that "he shall be deposed from the clergy and his name stricken from the list."[92] Canon 15 of "The Captions of the Arabic Canons" states "that clerics or religious who lend on usury should be cast from their grade,"[93] and Canon 52 states that "usury and the base seeking of worldly gain is forbidden to the clergy."[94] The Council of Carthage in 348

---

threat of forfeiture was a challenge to the cohesive community since it would tend to fragment the group into conflicting individual interests" (266).

89. *The Apostolic Constitutions* 3.7 (*ANF* 7), 428.

90. Ibid.

91. Ibid., 429.

92. *Canons of the 318 Holy Fathers Assembled in the City of Nice, in Bithynia* (*NPNF* 2:14), 36.

93. *The Captions of the Arabic Canons Attributed to the Council of Nice*, in *Seven Ecumenical Councils* (*NPNF* 2:14), 46.

94. Ibid., 49.

reinforced this position, citing the Hebrew Bible and New Testaments as authority.[95] Canon 4 of the Synod of Laodicea states that "a priest is not to receive usury nor *hemiolioe*,"[96] and Canon 5 of the African Code—or Council of Carthage—of 419 states that "as the taking of any kind of usury is condemned in laymen, much more it is condemned in clergymen."[97]

While I recognize that have not answered the question "Who are the usurers?" *definitively*, we have some sense of the individuals who were addressed by the Greek Fathers. To summarize: evidence suggests that they are most likely local people in the Christian community, they might be female as well as male, they might be in the employ of the Church, and they are not happy to be chastised. A secondary—but no less important question—is who is the debtor? It is not so simple to say that the debtor is just a poor person, as Basil's sermon against usury suggests that some borrowed either to maintain a "lifestyle" or because they were not interested in economizing, rather than because they were in desperate circumstances.[98] Interestingly, Basil begins his sermon on usury by stating that although he had run out of time preaching on the Psalm

95. *The Council of Carthage*, in *Seven Ecumenical Councils* (*NPNF* 2:14), 37.

96. *The Synod of Laodicea*, in *Seven Ecumenical Councils of the Undivided Church* (*NPNF* 2:14), 126. *Hemiolioe* is a form of the Latin *hemiolios* (Gk. ἡμιόλιος), which means "consisting of one-and-a-half times as much." *Oxford Latin Dictionary*, ed. P. G. W. Glare (Oxford: Clarendon, 1994), 790.

97. *The Council of Carthage*, in *Seven Ecumenical Councils of the Undivided Church* (*NPNF* 2:14), 445. The practice of usury among the clergy continues to be denounced well beyond the era of the early Church: Canon 44 from the *Apostolical Canons* in Trullo reads: "Let a bishop, presbyter, or deacon, who takes usury from those who borrow of him, give up doing so, or be deposed." *Seven Ecumenical Councils of the Undivided Church* (*NPNF* 2:14), 597. For an excellent article on usury and councils see Maloney, "Early Conciliar Legislation on Usury"; see also Moser, 189–90, and 204–5.

98. "He who has received the money is at first bright and cheerful, gladdened by another's prosperity and showing it by the change in his life. His table is lavish, his clothing more costly, his servants are changed in dress to something more brilliant; there are flatterers, boon companions, innumerable dining-hall drones. But, as the money slips away, and the advancing time increases the interest due, the nights bring him no rest, the day is not bright, nor is the sun pleasant, but he is disgusted with life, he hates the days which hasten on towards the appointed time, he fears the months, the parents, as it were, of his interest." Basil, *Hom. in Ps.* (PG 29.268); ed. Way, *On Psalm 14*, 183–84. While Basil's suggestion that individuals divest themselves of everything save their own freedom rather than owe money to a usurer seems perhaps naive, Holman writes that individuals in these circumstances might very well have been avoiding selling off their patrimony. "In this society the loss of one's patrimony is social death: the end of family land, the end of stable civic identity, the end of all political rights which may be tied to land ownership." Holman, "'You speculate on the misery of the poor,'" 214. For additional study on the debtor, see also Susan Holman, "Everyday Life in the Poor in 4th C. Cappadocia," in *Social and Political Life in Late Antiquity*, vol. 3.1 of *Late Antique Archaeology*, ed. William Bowden, Adam Gutteridge, and Carlos Machado (Brill, 2006), 441–64.

the previous day, he dared not neglect finishing it for the sake of his audience because he understands the "great power in the affairs of life."[99] A statement such as this suggests that debt is a pressing problem in his community, and far too important for him to dismiss. Further, his statement that "probably, it escaped the notice of most of you,"—referring specifically to the neglected line from the Psalm—suggests that as in our current circumstances, Basil's community considers usury to be a normal part of life, and therefore not worthy of special treatment or comment. [100]

### Are There Exceptions to Lending?

The most overt exception to usury is provided by a bishop outside of the scope of this study, Bishop Ambrose of Milan; therefore, I will only briefly mention his *De Tobia*, in which he conveniently defines "brother" as "every people which, first, is in the faith, then under Roman law, is your brother."[101] As a result, Ambrose claims, usury is acceptable under hostile circumstances:

Upon him whom you rightly desire to harm, against whom weapons are lawfully carried, upon him usury is legally imposed. On him whom you cannot easily conquer in war, you can quickly take vengeance with the hundredth. From him extract usury whom it would not be a crime to kill. He fights without a weapon who demands usury; without a sword he revenges himself upon an enemy, who is an interest collector from his foe. Therefore, where there is the right of war, there is also the right of usury.[102]

The closest among the Greek Fathers is the aforementioned Clement of Alexandria's loophole, very similar to that provided by Philo of Alexandria.[103] To restate, Clement writes that "the law prohibits a brother from lending with usury; a brother not only in name, born from the same parents, but even one of the same community, and also who is of like mind in the same Word."[104] This implies—like the Deuteronomy passage—that one might charge interest from a foreigner, but not from one of the same religious or national identities.

---

99. Basil, *Hom. in Ps.* (PG 29:264); ed. Way, *On Psalm 14*, 181.
100. Ibid.
101. Ambrose, *De Tobia*, 15.51 (PL 14.779); ed. L. Zucker, *St. Ambrosii, De Tobia*, 67.
102. Ibid.
103. See n. 28.
104. Clement of Alexandria, *Stromata*, PG 8.1024–25.

## What Are the Important Questions to Ask and of Which a Scholar Ought to Be Aware when Approaching a Patristic Socio-Ethical Text?

Are the Greek Fathers relevant? Do they care about being relevant? And what Graeco-Roman themes emerge in their theology?

### Are They Relevant?

The portions of the texts that indicate that our theologians are addressing known people in the communities lead to the conclusion that they are addressing a problem that is *quite* relevant in their own era. With respect to our own era, they remain relevant for the following reason: each and every community still contains people who are willing to profit at the expense of others, thus we can learn from what these authors had to say to their communities about what that type of behaviour can mean and what the results of greed *look like* within a given community.[105] These writings on usury are mostly small portions of texts that deal with larger issues; while they can be viewed as social admonitions to the wealthy and to the poor that emerge out of analysis of biblical passages, still, they also are reflections of the ascetic ideals of theologians for whom the primary importance of these texts was the extraction of moral meaning for application to present circumstances.[106] Using language from Christian scripture to explain the fundamental problems with the behaviour of those within their own communities, the theologians invite the listeners to participate in the narrative in such a way that transcends the particulars of the passages, whether the passage is about righteous living, a wicked master, or lending without hoping for return.[107] Ultimately, all of our theologians seem to hold to the position that money—whether one has it or not, and whether one lends it or gives it—is a barrier to an effective relationship with one another and with God. They communicate this message in different ways, but they all approach it with incredible passion and sincerity. Basil, a man of ac-

---

105. See Nehemiah 5:1–13 as an example of how usury can tear apart a community.

106. "Chrysostom constantly oscillates between the world of the text and the world of his hearers. For, in his eyes, as in the schools of antiquity, the really important thing, is the moral meaning which can be extracted from the text." Young, "They Speak to Us across the Centuries," 38.

107. Young, "They Speak to Us across the Centuries," 38.

tion who never hesitated to shame the wealthy into aiding the poor,[108] appealed to the poor to sell everything before relying on the creditor.[109] Gregory, a mystical theologian, saw usury as a distortion of creation, and appealed to the lender to alleviate poverty, writing that a proper understanding of shared humanity can result in a goodness which clothes one with Christ while acts of benevolence towards the needy clarify the divine image.[110] John Chrysostom, patriarch, preacher and trouble maker, was not above all but denying the usurer access to heaven.

## Do They Care about Being Relevant?

Yes, they care about being relevant. Usury is an ethical as well as an economic issue; when interest is excessive, it is universally condemned. Our theologians were addressing a concern that had long plagued society, a problem that transcended a Christian ideology. Laws had not curbed the problem, nor did public shame,[111] and while I am not suggesting that they consciously thought, "What can I tell these people to get them to stop lending with usury? Deny them access to heaven!" still they would have thought there was something wrong with a heaven than would admit someone who stood so publicly against both the Hebrew prohibitions and the message of Jesus; the usurer brings about immediate and visible suffering to the poor, and natural

108. Basil, *Hom. in divites 4*, in *Faith and Wealth: A History of Early Christian Ideas on the Origin, Significance, and Use of Money*, Justo González (San Francisco: Harper & Row, 1990), 178.

109. "'Drink water out of thy own cistern,' that is, examine your own resources, do not go to the springs belonging to others, but from your own streams gather for yourself the consolations of life. Do you have metal plates; clothing, beasts of burden, utensils of every kind? Sell them; permit all things to go except your liberty." Basil, *Hom. in Ps.* (PG 29.268-70); ed. Way, *On Psalm 14*, 184.

110. Gregory of Nyssa, *In verba "faciamus hom,"* 1; in Gonzalez, *Faith and Wealth*, 180.

111. Aristotle lists those "who ply sordid trades, pimps and all such people, and those who lend small sums and at high rates" as those who have caused damage by oppressing when they should be benevolent. Aristotle, *The Nicomachean Ethics of Aristotle*, trans. Sir David Ross (London: Oxford University Press, 1961), 84. Cicero, who slanders close to all available professions except for the ones in which he engaged, begins his list of infamy with the two most well known and despised: "Now with regard to what arts and means of acquiring wealth are to be regarded as worthy and what disreputable, we have been taught as follows. In the first place, those sources of emolument are condemned that incur the public hatred; such as those of tax-gatherers and usurers." Cicero, *Three Books of Offices, or Moral Duties*, trans. Cyrus R. Edmonds (London: G. Bell and Sons, 1916), 1.8. An interesting law appears in the reign of Diocletian (284-305 CE), who struck at usurers not with legal restrictions, but with a shameful identity and an ethical stigma; in 284 CE he called for the fine of "infamy" on lenders who accepted illegal interest. *Codex Justinianus*, in S. P. Scott, *The Civil Law*, 17 vols. (Cincinnati: The Central Trust Company, 1932), 16.2.12.20.

disasters will befall a community that allows usury to flourish. Debt is clearly a part of the social context of these theologians, and they understood the scarcity that exists in any community as usually a human—not a natural—problem, meaning that the rich bring it on themselves by hoarding and the poor have it placed upon them;[112] but they understood poverty and scarcity as problems that would be solved if people would only commit themselves to solving them, which tended to manifest itself in sometimes simplistic terms.[113] Part of that solution had to be provided by the church, whether through the alleviation of the actual debt itself, or the elimination of unjust lending practices within their communities, or both.[114] Either way, our bishops were responsible—and believed that they would be held accountable—for the usurer and the scarcity that usury engendered.

### What Graeco-Roman Themes Emerge in Their Theology?

The presence of Graeco-Roman themes in the writings on usury in the early church is undeniable; the education of the theologians alone would account for the presence of philosophical positions that transcend cultural and religious identity. However, the influence of the philosophers on the early church is debated by scholars Robert Maloney and Thomas Moser. While Maloney wrote that primary motivation against usury was the Christian concern for "practical charity among the brethren,"[115] Moser claims that the usury pro-

---

112. Barry Gordon, "The Problem of Scarcity and the Christian Fathers: John Chrysostom and Some Contemporaries," *Studia Patristica* 22 (1989): 113.

113. E.g., Wendy Mayer will highlight John Chrysostom's claim that if each Christian gave a loaf of bread to one in need, then poverty would be eliminated; "Poverty and Society in the World of John Chrysostom," *Society and Political Life in Late Antiquity* 3.1 of *Late Antique Archaeology*, ed. William Bowden, Adam Gutteridge, and Carlos Machado (Leiden: Brill, 2006), 468.

114. See Holman, "'You speculated on the Misery of the Poor,'" 207.

115. Maloney, *The Background for the Early Christian Teaching on Usury* (Ann Arbor, Mich.: University Microfilms, 1969), 4. That being said, continuously the Greek Fathers will refer to Jesus' statement to "lend, expecting nothing in return," which is, actually, a radically new way of understanding lending, for it is not *lending*, it is *giving*. Paul Mills claims that "lend, expecting nothing in return" could be better translated as "lend, *hoping* nothing in return," which he notes is a common fourth-century idiom. The result of this interpretation, he maintains, is that the individual was to loan without hope that the principal would be returned, which turns the loan into a gift. Paul Mills, "Interest in Interest: The Old Testament Ban in Interest and Its Implications for Today" (*Jubilee Centre Publications*, 1993). Mills cites in his article the contrary opinion of I. H. Marshall, who asserts that "lend, expecting nothing in return" did not mean that the lender was to consider the loan as a "gift," but that the lender was not to expect that he could gain by way of "loan" from the same—or another—individual. H. Marshall, *The Gospel of Luke* (Exeter: Paternoster Press, 1978), quoted in Mills, "Interest in Interest," 7. Regardless, Jesus is exhorting his commu-

hibition adopted by the patristic authors is not dependent solely on Christian scripture but comes to be formed by the equal influences of scripture, Hellenistic philosophy and Roman legislation hostile to interest taking.[116] Because of the amount of themes that one can trace between philosophers and historians including Plutarch, Aristotle, Cicero, and Philo and our theologians, Moser's position is convincing; themes that cross the boundaries from philosophy and legislation to theology include animal metaphors,[117] the analysis of and play on the word τόκος[118] the notion of taking interest as tantamount to murder,[119] and the anxiety of either lender or the debtor.[120]

## Under What Conditions or to Which Limits May Patristic Sources Be Considered as Contributors to the Construction of Catholic Social Teaching?

First, of course, we have to qualify that we understand "economy" and "economics" differently than our theologians did, because it is important that

---

nity to change their attitudes about the departure of money from one's own purse. Whether the money is considered by them to be a free loan or as a gift, or even as a possibility of future credit, Jesus counsels his listeners to detach themselves from concern over the money once it has left their hands. This method suggests a shift in behaviour *and* thinking which has at its core love for neighbour and trust in God rather than justice. Eric Roll, *A History of Economic Thought* (New York: Prentice-Hall, 1952), 32. While loans are mentioned few times in the New Testament, characteristically Jesus proposes a radical shift in economic understanding which can be reduced to the simple injunction to "Forgive us our debts, as we also have forgiven our debtors (καὶ ἄφες ἡμῖν τὰ ὀφειλήματα ἡμῶν ὡς καὶ ἡμεῖς ἀφήκαμεν τοῖς ὀφειλέταις ἡμῶν)." Matt 6:12; literally, "as also we *forgave*—[the assumption being made that the forgiveness to the debtors has already happened]—our debtors."

116. Moser, *Die patristische Zinslehre und ihre Ursprünge*, 5.

117. The imbalance in the human world contrasted with the natural balance in the wild kingdom is a theme adopted from the Greek philosophers, who would hold the two domains up against one another for unfavourable comparisons. Philo employs similar rhetorical devices when writing about usury and usurers, such as casting the lender in the role of one who has been overtaken by his savage nature, taking on the "nature of wild beasts." Philo, *On The Virtues*, 14.87. See also n. 50 for Plutarch's statement on the accumulation of interest and hares compared with that of Basil's; additional examples exist, as usurers will be referred to in both patristic and the texts of philosophers as beasts or vultures.

118. The idea of money being either fertile or infertile comes up many times in the discussion of usury; essentially, the question is: Can money breed? According to Aristotle, the answer is no, money cannot breed, and to attempt to do so is perverse, for "of all modes of making money this is the most unnatural." Aristotle, *Politics*, trans. Benjamin Jowett (Oxford: Clarendon, 1920), 1258b.

119. See n. 55 for Cato the elder's statement on usury as murder in Cicero's *Offices*. The conception that one can murder through financial snares is also found in the Hebrew Bible, as well as in the writings of the early Church authors.

120. See Brenda Llewellyn Ihssen, "Basil and Gregory's Sermons on Usury: Credit Where Credit

we not hold the Fathers hostage to modern ideas about money and economy. One would need to describe, or at least account for a number of the theoretical and contextual differences between economics in antiquity and economics today before addressing how patristic texts might be relevant. It is sufficient to point out at this beginning stage that as the patristic authors were not always in agreement within one another with respect to matters of wealth—including sometimes seeming to contradicting themselves—they were also not concerned with economic growth or development the way we understand it, but first and foremost with the possibility that all might live a decent existence (decent meaning, "not starving").[121] It is also sufficient point out at this stage that though the discussion on usury by theologians and moralists would change over the centuries, the Church has not changed its mind about the moral issue of usury; what the Church did recognize in later centuries with the rise of nation states, changes in transportation, trade and banking, is that not all circumstances of lending that involved interest were 'usurious,' which now meant precisely "exploitative."[122]

Second, we must keep in mind that the Fathers largely spoke from a monastic position. However, I caution against using their ascetic religious vocation as an excuse to dismiss their bold and sometimes simple solutions; just because they wrote in such stark terms about the human body and the desires and passions to which one can fall prey, using language that is rich in social

---

Is Due," *JECS* 16.3 (2008), for comparisons between Gregory of Nyssa's suggestion that the usurer loses his own personal freedom through his occupation echoes that of Seneca, who wrote: "He who craves riches feels fear on their account. No man, however, enjoys a blessing that brings anxiety; he is always trying to add a little more. While he puzzles over increasing his wealth, he forgets how to use it. He collects his accounts, he wears out the pavement in the forum, he turns over his ledger,—in short, he ceases to be a master and becomes a steward." Seneca, *Ad Lucilium Epistulae Morales,* trans. Richard A. Gummere (London: Heinmann, 1967), 3.110. Finally, Sheather, touches on additional Graeco-Roman influences and themes that emerge in their theology: the notion of God as the benefactor is present in Epictetus' *Discourses I.7,* and that of Diogenes Laertius's *Lives of the Eminent Philosophers,* in which he muses on the distinctions between the person who is rich by the world's standards and the "true" rich person. Sheather, "Pronouncements of the Cappadocians on Issues of Wealth and Poverty," 379 and 385.

121. Gordon, "The Problem of Scarcity and the Christian Fathers," 118. For the Greek Fathers, the purpose of money was to meet the needs of one's household; beyond that there was little need for it. Peter Brown writes that there were a variety of motivating factors for the poverty relief that developed in the fourth century, and that prominent bishops of the late fourth and fifth centuries will use privileges granted them by the growing Christian empire to organize relief for the poor, ill, and destitute. Peter Brown, *Poverty and Leadership in the Later Roman Empire* (Brandeis University Press, 2002).

122. Albert R. Jonson and Stephen Toulmin, *The Abuse of Casuistry: A History of Moral Reasoning* (Berkeley: University of California Press, 1990), 310.

contrasts that may not have been so self-evident (if such stark social contrasts existed at all),[123] this does not mean that they did not understand the possibilities or alternatives in living out a Christian life. So although our bishops were ascetics, they were born *neither* ascetics *nor* bishops; they knew as well as anyone that the environments of the secular and of the professional religious both give rise to distinct and sometimes common tensions and trials. It is important here to point out that both of those tensions and trials are being worked out in economies that are largely if not entirely subsistence, and will continue to be so up until early Middle Ages. What we learn from the discussion on usury that will emerge in the ensuing centuries is that when the economy changes, it is appropriate and perhaps even entirely necessary for the thinking about the role of the individual within that economy to change as well. Thus, the paradigm presented by our theologians presents significant challenges.

Third, our theologians are not saying anything *new* about usury itself, in that it is largely a universally despised profession and problem, even as the Greeks made use of it and learned to live with it, and the Romans despised it and profited greatly. What they do add to the conversation about usury is coupled with what they have to say about wealth, which is that it is often a barrier to God, and that someone who lends money with usury is in danger of losing their salvation: "Lend," said John Chrysostom, "where [there is] no malice, where [there is] no accusation, no reason for fear. . . . Lend where your return will not be death, but life instead of death."[124] Knowing that the Greek Fathers continued in this tradition of denunciation, and knowing that they borrowed heavily from biblical, philosophical and legal precedents, what can they add to dialogue with Catholic social teaching? Primarily this: they reinforced that legal status does not justify or sanction behaviour. Rather than argue against the legal protection conceded to usury, they focused on the behaviour of those who lived under a system that offered legal protection for actions that should have been considered unlawful, just as we do today. It was not so much the system under which usury and the usurer flourished that was the object of their concern, as the individual who engaged in and profited by usury and the one who suffered because of it.[125]

---

123. See "Governor of the Poor: The Bishops and Their Cities," in Brown, *Poverty and Leadership in the Later Roman Empire*, 45–73.

124. John Chrysostom, *Hom. in Mt.* 5, PG 57.61–62.

125. Sheather, "Pronouncements of the Cappadocians on Issues of Poverty and Wealth," 377.

How can Catholic social teaching statements on usury benefit from the Fathers? Catholic social teaching and the Greek Fathers share three common links. First, both believe that wealth exists to be shared.[126] Consistently throughout passages on usury the Greek Fathers will urge the usurer to give, rather than lend money to those in need. At the very minimum, Basil writes, do not turn someone away who wishes to borrow, and be content to receive the interest "from the Lord."[127] It is in this portion of Catholic social teaching that the words of the Fathers—Clement of Alexandria, John Chrysostom, and Gregory the Great—will be invoked, and in like mind Catholic social teaching will insist that "economic activity and material progress must be placed at the service of man and society,"[128] and that "Goods, even when legitimately owned, always have a universal destination; any type of improper accumulation is immoral, because it openly contradicts the universal destination assigned to all goods by the Creator."[129]

Second, both believe that there is an intrinsic connection between economic and moral activities.[130] Appeals to righteous behaviour are characteristic of dealing with usury or other social diseases associated with poverty. But unlike theological stumbling-blocks, usury is a different kind of dilemma for two reasons: First, engaging in usury is not an act of heresy. To be a usurer does not preclude the usurer's system of belief; that is, one can be both a Christian and a usurer at the same time, just as one can be a heroin addict and a Christian at the same time. Second, usury was legal, so any one who engaged in usury was not breaking the law. Murdering someone is, however, against the law, and the *Catechism of the Catholic Church* states that "Those whose usurious and avaricious dealings lead to the hunger and death of their brethren in the human family indirectly commit homicide, which is imputable to them."[131] This is clearly in line with what Basil, Gregory of Nyssa, and John Chrysostom believed about the lines of accountability that connect one human to anoth-

---

126. Pontifical Council for Justice and Peace, *Compendium of the Social Doctrine of the Church*, United States Conference of Catholic Bishops (Washington D.C.: Libreria Editrice Vaticana), 328; 143.

127. Basil, *Hom. in Ps.* (PG 29:280); ed. Way, *On Psalm 14*, 190. This is similar to Philo, who writes that giving "is the best course, but, if they are unwilling to give, they should at least lend with all readiness and alacrity, not with the prospect of receiving anything back except the principal." Philo, *On the Virtues*, 14.83.

128. *Compendium of the Social Doctrine of the Church*, 326, 142.

129. Ibid., 328, 143.                               130. Ibid., 330–35, 144–46.

131. Ibid., 341, 149, n. 714.

er; not allowing the rich abuser to avoid responsibility, Chrysostom will write that though "you do not do these to him, you are responsible for them being done [to him], even more than the attendants who do them."[132] Even Emperor Justinian would write this into his *Novellae*.[133] With respect to the treatment of the body of the poor, our Greek Fathers seem quite firm that to wound the individual who stands before one in need is to continue to wound the body of Christ; the degree to which Catholic social teaching accepts this—and agrees with it—is the degree to which a conversation will take place between the two.

Third, both Catholic social teaching and the Greek Fathers reflect on the emotional state of one who seeks wealth or who is unable to reconcile their reduced economic circumstances and requires consolation through the accumulation of goods and services. Commenting on the way in which contemporary consumerism orients an individual towards "having" rather than "being," Pope John Paul II, in his Encyclical Letter *Centesimus Annus*, writes that this orientation blurs the "criteria for correctly distinguishing new and higher forms of satisfying human needs from artificial new needs which hinder the formation of a mature personality."[134] While we tend to think that consumerism is unique to our culture—and I agree that our century and our social context does present some unique challenges with respect to the ills of consumerism—still, even Basil in fourth century Cappadocia (a society that managed to function without Starbucks, iPods, or Amazon.com) addressed the emotional state that manifested itself in a need to "acquire." He will write: "Let us not in addition to our involuntary evils bring on through our folly a self-chosen evil. It is the act of a childish mind (νηπίας φρενός) not to adapt oneself according to present circumstances."[135]

One notable difference between Catholic social teaching and the Greek Fathers is the degree of autonomy granted by the Catholic social teaching to

---

132. κἂν γὰρ αὐτὸς ταῦτα μὴ ποιῇς, παρέχῃς δὲ τὴν αἰτίαν τοῦ γίγνεσθαι, τῶν διακονουμένων μᾶλλον αὐτὰ ἐργάζῃ. John Chrysostom, *Hom. in Rom. 11*, PG 60.491. See n. 55.

133. "[F]or it has come to Our ears that certain persons, in the province which you govern, being induced by avarice to take advantage of the pubic distress, and, having drawn up agreements by interest, by which they loaned a small amount of grain, have seized the lands of the debtors, and that, for this reason, some farmers have fled and concealed themselves, others have died of starvation, and pestilence, not less terrible than a barbarian invasion, has, in consequence of the failure of the crops, afflicted the people." *Nov. Just.* 32, Scott, *The Civil Law* 16, 185.

134. *Compendium of the Social Doctrine of the Church*; 360, 155, n. 746.

135. Basil, *Hom. in Ps.* (PG 29:271); ed. Way, *On Psalm 14*, 186.

the consumer with respect to economic choice, specifically investing. In *Centesimus Annus*, Pope John Paul II writes that "the decision to invest in one place rather than another, in one productive sector rather than another, is always a moral and cultural choice."[136] I believe that our theologians might disagree, and would claim that the only choice is to invest in heaven. This of course, might take one of two forms: giving to the person in need or giving to the bishops who care for the poor. The notion of investing in order to gain so that one might have more to give is not an argument that goes very far with the Fathers, and Chrysostom will outright reject the complaint of the usurer who turns the interest over to the church: "But what is the account of many? "When I have taken the interest," he says, "I give it to the poor." Speak honorably, O man; God does not want these offerings."[137] These are unyielding words, and hard to reconcile in our age, which allows for so many degrees and shades of morality and compromise.

## Conclusion

The virtue of giving, like detachment, is an ongoing process, it is rarely "perfected"; but according to our theologians, by working to detach oneself from money and goods, by giving and meeting the basic needs of the vulnerable body, the individual who gives their money rather than lending it removes boundaries created by sin, boundaries that prevent humans from engaging in healthy and sustainable relationships with one another and with God.[138] This is true φιλανθρωπία, this is true loving kindness. True loving kindness desires to share itself, while true greed desires only its own advantage. The one who loves with a pure love thinks little to nothing of the self, but wishes to give to others what they themselves possess, wishes for others to know what they themselves know, and wishes for others to believe what they themselves believe, for the direct welfare of the beloved. Usury functions in such a way that it can only represent the exact opposite of love, for while it appears that one

---

136. *Compendium of the Social Doctrine of the Church*, 358; 154, n. 744.

137. ἀλλὰ τίς τῶν πολλῶν ὁ λόγος; λαβὼν τὸν τόκον, πένητι δίδωμι, φησίν. εὐφήμει, ἄνθρωπε· οὐ βούλεται τοιαύτας θυσίας ὁ Θεός. John Chrysostom, *Hom. in Mt.* 56, PG 58.557.

138. John Chryssavgis, "The Power of Detachment in Early Monastic Literature," in *Good and Faithful Servant: Stewardship in the Orthodox Church,* ed. Anthony Scott (Crestwood, N.Y.: St. Vladimir's Seminary Press, 2003), 87–103.

is performing a beneficial and life-sustaining action, in fact the actions of the usurer hide a murderous intent which is even *worse* than actually being murderous for it is masked with the appearance of benevolence. Usury is both a premeditated and predatory action; there is no "accidental" sinning, it is an action that is fuelled solely by a self-interest that too often motivates the moral centre, including the moral centre of the Christian who—conveniently separating the theological from the secular—would claim that "business is business" regardless of circumstances. A Christian powered by self-interest would assert that an individual has a right to take interest on a loan—even excessive interest—first of all because it is legal to do so, and second, because the Christian has been released from the law. This is the same logic Paul encountered in Corinth, and his response to the rhetorical statement that "All things are lawful for me"[139] was a reminder that despite this freedom, "not all things are beneficial."[140]

To return to the generalization by which I began, none of the Greek Fathers considered usury beneficial, and addressed usury and the usurer either by outright denunciations of the practice based on Christian scripture, by casting the usurer as a menace to communities, or by assuring the usurer that what they had to offer would be rejected by God, even down to their very soul. Despite the rare occasion when interest gained on a loan might be turned to the advantage of the faithful,[141] when eviction, starvation, enslavement and even salvation hang in the balance, the risks taken far outweigh the probability of success.[142] From this, one can safely conclude that the Greek Fathers did not consider usury to be either a moral, justifiable, or advantageous action, but consistently argued against the practice.

Bishops clearly employed the sermon as a vehicle to address economic injustices; it is right to question the effectiveness of such measures. At the risk of

---

139. 1 Corinthians 6:12a.

140. 1 Corinthians 6:12b.

141. Bishop Desideratus, as mentioned above, secured a loan through the charity of King Theudebert and carefully managed the loan to the benefit of his community. Gregory of Tours, *History of the Franks*, 190–91.

142. "How many men, after building castles in the air, have as their only benefit, a loss beyond measure? 'But many,' he says, 'grow rich from loans.' But more, I think, fasten themselves to halters. You see those who have become rich, but you do not count those who have been strangled, who, not enduring the shame incurred by their begging, preferred death through strangling to a shameful life. I have seen a piteous sight, free sons dragged to the market place to be sold because of the paternal debt." Basil, *Hom. in Ps.* (PG 29:277); ed. Way, *On Psalm 14*, 189–90.

sounding cynical, it did Greek and Roman philosophers, emperors, historians and our theologians little good to write, draft laws, or preach against usury, as the practice continued to prevail. Greed will always be stronger than the desire to help the poor. But despite the continued presence of usury, enduring denunciations against the practice has led to the inability of the usurer ever to gain a reputation as being anything other than completely foul.[143] The usurer might well escape legal retribution, but that will be sorry consolation when their salvation is placed on the scales.

Just prior to and around the same time as the arrival of subprime lending in the early 1990s, scholars habitually wrote that usury in our day was a dead issue,[144] that Christians repeatedly paid out interest without thinking twice,[145] and that society was numb to both the idea of moderate interest and dialogue on the subject altogether.[146] But I would argue that the world poverty situation is such that usury remains an important topic for those who choose to reflect upon the contemporary economic disasters brought about by unjust lending practices; we need look no further back than the mortgage crisis of late 2008 for evidence that it is time for reevaluation of the role of debt in our lives and its effects on local and global communities. The distortion of the "American Dream" of a home and two cars financed by debt has instigat-

143. Perhaps the most well-known and most-imitated usurer is Charles Dickens's Ebenezer Scrooge from *A Christmas Carol* (originally published in 1843). It is not by accident that Dante places the usurers in the third round of the seventh level of Hell; he classifies usury as a sin of violence rather than fraud, and includes usurers among the company of blasphemers and perverts. Dante, "Canto 11," *Dante's Inferno: The Indiana Critical Edition*, trans. and ed. Mark Musa (Bloomington: Indiana University Press, 1995): 89–94. If the modern, post-Holocaust reader is able to look beyond the stereotypical negative traits so long and so unfortunately attributed to Jewish persons, Shakespeare's *The Merchant of Venice* delivers a brilliantly vengeful and greedy creditor in his character Shylock (written c.1596–98). Another fine example of a usurer devoid of a soul is Edward Lewis Wallant's Sol Nazerman, from *The Pawnbroker* (New York: Harcourt, Brace and World, 1961). As recently as 2000, award-winning writer Lynn Hightower published a murder mystery in which an entire family is brutally murdered as revenge for a defaulted debt. Lynn Hightower, *The Debt Collector* (New York: Dell, 2000).

144. Bruce Ballard, "On the Sin of Usury: A Biblical Economic Ethic," *Christian-Scholar's Review* 24.2 (1994): 210; John R. Sutherland, "The Debate Concerning Usury in the Christian Church," *Crux* 22 (1986): 3.

145. Maloney, "Early Conciliar Legislation on Usury," 145, and "Teaching of the Fathers on Usury," 241; see also McCambley, "Against Those Who Practice Usury by Gregory of Nyssa," 287.

146. Sutherland, "The Debate Concerning Usury in the Christian Church," 3; see also John R. Sutherland, "Usury: God's forgotten doctrine [Ex 22:25–27; Lev 25:35–37; Deut 23:19–20]," *Crux* 18 (1982): 14; see also Paul Mills, "The Ban on Interest: Dead letter or Radical Solution?" *Cambridge Papers*, 2.1 (1993): 1; see also Paul Mills, "Interest in Interest: The Old Testament Ban in Interest and its Implications for Today" (Cambridge: Jubilee Centre Publications, 1993): Summary.

ed new academic conversation[147] on this topic, and new legislation as well.[148] Usury, credit, debt—however you want to name it—has for too long subordinated human health and dignity to economic ends[149] and despite the advances of science and technology, people yet live in the same circumstances as the original recipients of laws against it.[150] As a topic, usury might not be provocative, but the circumstances of dire poverty are; we should be deeply troubled by the damage that interest on loans does to individuals, families, communities, countries and even—if our theologians are correct—one's own salvation.

147. Charles R. Geist, *Collateral Damaged: The Marketing of Consumer Debt to America* (Hoboken, N.J.: Wiley, 2009). See also Jesse James Deconto, "A new battle against usury: The people's interest," *Christian Century,* January 2010.

148. H. R. 627, titled "Credit Card Accountability Responsibility and Disclosure Act of 2009," on the Library of Congress website, available at http://thomas.loc.gov/cgi-bin/thomas (accessed 2010).

149. Arthur Jones, *Capitalism and Christians: Tough Gospel Challenges in a Troubled World Economy* (New York: Paulist Press, 1992), 8.

150. Sutherland, "Usury: God's Forgotten Doctrine," 14.

# 8. The Principle of Detachment from Private Property in Basil of Caesarea's *Homily* 6 and Its Context

I have two sons. The older of my boys, now age four, enjoys building elaborate sets with his wooden train tracks. The younger of my boys, now age one, enjoys "playing" with his older brother by tearing apart the train set as it is being built. The four-year-old is understandably upset, and some sort of physical behavior is displayed to retrieve the tracks from his younger brother. What is a parent to do in this situation? I suggest the problem is not simple. The older boy has applied his time, energy, and talents into constructing something new from which he now draws some sense of personal dignity. He has put his labor to good use to fashion some sort of property, and he believes he has earned the right to enjoy what he has made. The younger boy believes that this new property should not be treated as private, but should be for all to share and to play. As a parent, I would like to find some middle ground between asking the older boy to share his property and trying to occupy the younger boy with some other activity. Yet, if pressed on the matter, ought I to lean towards protecting the right to private property or towards ensuring all property is made common? In addition, how much does the application of a child's own labor in the production of property figure into the calculation?

These types of questions have long been a part of Christian ethical reflection on the merits of private property. This includes studies of the early Church's teachings with respect to private property. In fact, a debate over whether or not the early Church was proto-communist in its views of property dominated scholarly discussion from the mid-nineteenth to the mid-twentieth century, and continues even today in some quarters.[1] More recently, scholarship turned its attention to the socio-cultural and economic backdrop of late antiquity in order to better understand the context to which the Fathers addressed their concerns about property.[2] Most recently, questions about early

1. The tendency within this body of literature is to conclude that they were, although it is understood that early Christians shared their goods voluntarily. L. William Countryman, *The Rich Christian in the Church of the Early Empire: Contradictions and Accomodations*, Texts and Studies in Religion 7 (New York: Edwin Mellen Press, 1980), 1–18, rather capably summarized this body of literature up to the mid-1970s insisting, at the end, that contemporary political questions are ultimately unhelpful when approaching early Christian texts. Countryman suggested limiting the scope of any inquiry to the few Christian texts that can be reliably dated and whose authorship is in little doubt. For his part, he focused on Clement of Alexandria's *Quis dives salvetur?* and related texts from Clement that shed light on his understanding of private property. For an earlier summary of the debate, see Franz Meffert, *Der "Kommunismus" Jesu und der Kirchenväter* (München-Gladbach: Volksvereinverlag, 1922).

The secondary literature affirming the voluntary nature of early Christian poverty and wealth-sharing includes, among many others, Ephrem Baumgartner, "Der Kommunismus im Urchristentum," *Zeitschrift für katholische Theologie* 33 (1909): 625–45; Etienne Chastel, *Études historiques sur l'influence de la charité durant les premiers siècles chrétiens, et considérations sur son rôle dans les sociétés modernes* (Paris: Capelle, 1853); Eng. trans. George-Auguste Matile, *The charity of the primitive churches: Historical studies upon the influence of Christian charity during the first centuries of our era, with some considerations touching its bearings upon modern society* (Philadelphia: Lippincott, 1857); F. X. Funk, "Über Reichtum und Handel im christlichen Altertum," *Historisch-politische Blätter* 130 (1902): 888–99; Stanislas Giet, "La doctrine de l'appropriation des biens chez quelques-uns des Pères," *Recherches de science religieuse* 35 (1948): 55–91; Edmond Le Blant, "La richesse et las christianisme à l'age des persécutions," *Revue archéologique*, Series 2 (1880): 39: 220–30; Shailer Matthews, *The Social Teachings of Jesus: An Essay in Christian Sociology* (New York: Macmillan, 1897); Ernst Troeltsch, *Die Soziallehren der christlichen Kirchen und Gruppen, Gesammelte Schriften* 1 (Tübingen: Mohr [Paul Siebeck], 1912); Eng. trans. Olive Wyon, *The Social Teaching of the Christian Churches*, 2 vols.(London: Allen and Unwin, 1931), esp. 89–161; Gerhard Uhlhorn, *Die christliche Liebestätigkeit. Vol. 1: In der alten Kirche* (Stuttgart: Gundert, 1882).

Among those who find in the early Christian literature a less voluntary and more controlled system of property redistribution include Lujo Brentano, "Die wirtschaftlichen Lehren des christlichen Altertums," in *Sitzungsberichte der philosophische-philologischen und der historischen Klasse der kgl. Akademie der Wissenschaften* (Munich, 1902), 141–93; W. Haller, "Die Eigentum im Glauben und Leben der nachapostolischen Kirche," *Theologische Studien und Kritiken* 64 (1891): 478–563; Karl Kautzsy, *Der Ursprung des Christentums, eine historische Untersuchung* (Stuttgart: J. H. W. Dietz Nachf., 1908), of which there were many subsequent editions; Gérard Walter, *Les origines du communisme, judaiques, chrétiennes, grecques, latines* (Paris: Bibliothéque historique, 1931). A more recent collection of texts and commentary by Charles Avila, *Ownership: Early Christian Teaching* (Maryknoll, N.Y.: Orbis Books, 1983) summarizes the views of four authors (Clement of Alexandria, Ambrose of Milan, John Chrysostom, and Augustine of Hippo). It concludes the Fathers largely condemned the prevailing view of their contemporaries that the holding of private property was an inviolate right and should be passed down from one generation to the next within one's family.

2. Santiago Guijarro, "The Family in First-Century Galilee," in *Constructing Early Christian Fami-*

Christian teaching on private property fall under a broader category of *wealth* and of the response of the rich to the poor. Even the words "rich" and "poor" have become the objects of greater scrutiny; now we speak both of "poor" people and of "shallow poor" people (to which I would add also "shallow wealthy" people).[3]

---

*lies: Family as Social Reality and Metaphor*, ed. Halvor Moxnes (London: Routledge, 1997), explores how the scarcity of goods created unstable family structures in the first through third centuries.

Evelyne Patlagean, *Pauvreté économique et pauvreté sociale á Byzance 4e—7e siècles*, Civilisations et Sociétés 48 (Paris: Mouton, 1977) is a ground-breaking study of economic poverty in Byzantium between the fourth and seventh centuries. Patlagean made careful distinctions both between types of poverty and the impact of poverty on different communities of persons both within cities and rural areas. Patlagean laid the groundwork for later studies of the interchange between Christian teaching about social ethics and the real life impact on social policies and mentalities. See also Patlagean, "The Poor," in *The Byzantines*, ed. Guglielmo Cavallo (Chicago: University of Chicago Press, 1997), 15–42, although only the first few pages overlap with the period of the Fathers considered here.

Blake Leyerle, "John Chrysostom on Almsgiving and the Use of Money," *Harvard Theological Review* 87 (1994): 29–47, surveyed Chrysostom's homilies with respect to his teaching about the correct use of wealth by those otherwise prone to lavish displays of it in the marketplace. See also Roger Bagnall, "Monk and Property: Rhetoric, Law, and Patronage in the *Apophthegmata Patrum* and the Papyri," *Greek, Roman, and Byzantine Studies* 42 (2001): 7–24; Andrew T. Crislip, *From Monastery to Hospital: Christian Monasticism and the Transformation of Health Care in Late Antiquity* (Ann Arbor, Mich.: University of Michigan, 2005). Richard Finn, *Almsgiving in the Later Roman Empire: Christian Promotion and Practice, 313–450*, Oxford Classical Monographs (Oxford: Oxford University Press, 2006); Susan Holman, *The Hungry Are Dying: Beggars and Bishops in Roman Cappadocia*, Oxford Studies in Historical Theology (Oxford: Oxford University Press, 2001).

A modern economist would argue the Fathers did not appreciate the value of entrepreneurship, which is what could develop out of excess land and possessions among the wealthy, in addition to the gainful employment such entrepreneurship would provide. Barry Gordon suggests the empire was not set up to accommodate such entrepreneurship and thus it did not enter the Fathers' minds. See B. Gordon, "The Problem of Scarcity and the Christian Fathers: John Chrysostom and Some Contemporaries," *Studia Patristica* 22 (1989): 108–20; Gordan, *The Economic Problem in Biblical and Patristic Thought*, Supplements to Vigiliae Christianae, Texts and Studies of Early Christian Life and Language IX (Leiden: Brill, 1989).

3. Christel Freu, *Les figures du pauvre dans les sources italiennes de l'antiquité tardive* (Paris: De Boccard, 2007), is a detailed study both of the different words used for the poor and the rich and of the differences in meaning even for the same word depending on literary genre in texts by several Latin Fathers of late antiquity. See also Peter Brown, *Poverty and Leadership in the Later Roman Empire* (Hanover, N.H.: University Press of New England, 2002), 14–16. There he explains that we should no longer think of late antique societies as being comprised of "the poor" and "the rich," but that there was a broad middle class—likely 80 percent or more of the total population—that forever lived in "shallow poverty," meaning that any one bad economic year could thrust even skilled craftspeople or farmers into destitution. My own research suggests that we can not only speak about "shallow poverty" but also "shallow wealth," for during the good economic years, those same groups of people were prone to take advantage of the destitute. See Gregory of Nyssa's homily, *Against the Usurers* (GK: "Contra Usurarios," in *Gregorii Nysseni Opera* IX, ed. Ernest Gebhardt [Leiden: Brill, 1967], 195–207; Eng. trans. Casimir McCambley, "Against Those Who Practice Usury by Gregory of Nyssa," *Greek Orthodox Theological Review* 36 [1991]:

Basil's writings are among those that have received some of the greatest scrutiny, for he has addressed concerns about private property in several homilies, including *Homily 6*. In this paper I argue that in *Hom. 6* we discover both that Basil co-opted the Stoic teaching of ἀπάθεια with respect to property and that, in the process of doing so, he taught his audience important, theological concepts that both transcend the issue of property and are distinctive of the Christian, rather than the Stoic, tradition.[4] Consideration of these theological arguments moves us rather away from the Marxist political concerns of earlier studies. It builds on the socio-cultural and economic context studies and provides what may be a more helpful contribution to modern, Christian ethical reflection about private property. Indeed, although Basil's theological arguments are very much a product of his time, they nevertheless reconfigure well-trodden biblical texts and themes for an audience removed from the first century context. They open to us a Ricoeurian, "world in front of the text" that we may appreciate today. For this reason, contemporary Christian ethics owes a debt of gratitude to this forebearer of the Christian message.

Having said all of this, before we turn to Basil's text, it should be borne in mind that Basil was doubtless aware that the topic of private property concerned classical writers dating back at least to the fifth century BCE Thus, this paper begins with a rehearsal of some of that history in classical and Christian authors up to the time of Basil. Towards the conclusion, this paper suggests some of the trajectory of these ideas in Catholic social teaching with an acknowledgment that detachment language has now been surpassed by a concern for the universal destination of the world's goods.

## Private Property before Basil

Even a cursory review of the ideas about private property in the Graeco-Roman and Christian milieu reveals the difficulty everyone felt about the

---

287–302), in which he does not address himself to "the rich" so much but to all who take advantage of the needy during times of want. It seems that "shallow wealth" could be a spiritual problem as much as shallow poverty was a social and economic problem.

4. According to Michel Spanneut, *Le stoïcisme des pères de l'église, de Clément de Rome a Clément d'Alexandrie* (Paris: Éditions du Seuil, 1957), 72–77, a better way to understand the relationship between Stoicism and early Christianity is one of "influence" by the former on the latter. This means the early Christian homilists ended up being really neither properly Stoic nor properly Christian, if we take Christian to mean life in accordance with a literal reading of the Gospel teachings.

topic. Private property was understood to be a social problem, but forcibly redistributing property had few, if any, supporters. With respect to the classical writers, some suggestions for how to solve the private property dilemma emerged. In the fourth century BCE there were calls for the creation of a common stock of property from which all citizens could draw in order to satisfy their needs. The playwright Aristophanes suggested women would be the best managers of such a common stock, which would include land, money, and most goods.[5] Plato's teaching on the role of Guardians is strikingly similar to Aristophanes's promotion of women as better managers of civic affairs.[6] In the wrong hands, according to Plato, property undermines social unity.[7] Consequently, Guardians will oversee a common stock of property and, in so doing, preserve the good of the city.[8] Yet, neither Aristophanes nor Plato denounced the right of people to different levels of private property. Plato suggested the goal is not for everyone to be happy in the sense of possessing many things: everyone is to be happy with the goods appropriate to their position within the city (421b–d).[9] In another of Aristophanes' plays, *Ploutos* (388), the character Chremylus sets off to heal the sight of Ploutos, the god of wealth, in order that

5. Aristophanes, *Ecclesiazousae*, The Comedies of Aristophanes, vol. 10 (Warminster: Aris and Phillips, 1998), esp. ll. 590–710. Aristophanes's play is set within the time of war in which the poor of Athens experienced continually degrading conditions. Praxagora, a woman, dresses up as a man to participate in a city council debate. She convinces the other council members that they delegate to women the task of managing a common stock of civic resources in order to alleviate suffering of all, including the poor.

6. See Plato, "Republic" in *Plato: Complete Works*, trans. G. M. A. Grube, trans. rev. C. D. C. Reeve (Indianapolis: Hackett Publishing, 1997), books III and V. On the comparison between Plato's Guardians and Aristophanes's women, see Alan Sommerstein, ed. and trans., *Ecclesiazousae*, 13–18. Sommerstein dismisses as unlikely two other arguments put forward for this comparison, either that Plato surmised his ideas before Aristophanes wrote or that both Plato and Aristophanes relied on an earlier, common source. Both of these arguments are based on silence in the historical record and, what is worse, they seem to Sommerstein to be an attempt to protect Plato from being thought of as influenced by a comedic play.

7. Plato, "Republic," 971–1223. In his *Republic* Plato exposited a vision for justice and for its preservation in the context of a Greek *polis*.

8. Plato, *Republic*, book III, argued Guardians must be housed and cared for at the expense of the city (416c–17b). This was to protect the integrity of the Guardians, insofar as this arrangement preserved as the source of the Guardians' happiness the good of the city rather than the acquisition of property, land or power for personal gain. In book IV, a challenger to this argument puts forward the claim that Guardians will be disposed towards unhappiness in this arrangement since they can enjoy none of the goods that a city offers its citizens (419). Plato, through the voice of Socrates, rejoins that the goal

9. Plato suggests both wealth and poverty can corrupt a person, for a wealthy craftsperson will no longer want to work at his craft, and a poor craftsperson will not have the resources to do so. The same is true for farmers and for Guardians. Wealth and poverty equally distract a person from the work to be done.

wealth might begin to come only to those who are virtuous.[10] Along the way, Chremylus meets Poverty, who informs Chremylus that he is embarking on an ill-concieved plan, for, once everyone becomes rich, no one will have anything. This is because no one will be willing to work long hours at trades; there will be no bakers or harvesters. Everyone will want someone else to do it, and no one will agree to do it. Poverty, she argues, alone fosters a productive society. Some deprivation of wealth actually is good for the soul (ll. 507–589).[11]

A different approach to the problem of private property is that of Xenophon and, later, of Aristotle. They advocated a distinction between "use" and "ownership" of property, a distinction which meant that laws that protect private property ownership may continue to exist, but the better instincts of people should draw them to a sharing of property based on use. Xenophon (c. 429–c.357 BCE), in his *Education of Cyrus*, writes of a particular episode of Cyrus' schooling in which Cyrus was asked to judge between two boys of different heights who each owned coats that were better suited to the height of the other boy.[12] Cyrus judged that use, rather than ownership, of property was a better arbiter for the distribution of goods. Consequently, he ordered the boys to switch coats. Yet, for this he was severely reprimanded by his teachers. To keep the application of justice simple and fair, Cyrus' teachers said, ownership is the more just means of deciding who should possess what. Aristotle seems to be in agreement with Cyrus' first instincts, but he too comes down on the side of maintaining property rights based on current ownership.[13] To his

10. Aristophanes, *Wealth* in *The Comedies of Aristophanes*, vol. 11, ed. and trans. Alan H. Sommerstein (Warminster: Aris and Phillips, 2001).

11. Importantly, Aristophanes distinguishes between people who are poor (πτωχοί) and people who are destitute (πένητες). The Church Fathers also seemed to accept some social stratification as a necessary part of a functioning society. See Susan Holman, *The Hungry Are Dying*, 32; Mary Sheather, "Pronouncements of the Cappadocians on Issues of Poverty and Wealth," in *Prayer and Spirituality in the Early Church* 1, ed. Pauline Allen, Raymond Canning, and Lawrence Cross (Everton Park, Australia: Centre for Early Christian Studies 1998), 375–92, here 376.

12. Xenophon, *The Education of Cyrus*, Agora Editions, trans. Wayne Amber (Ithaca, N.Y.: Cornell University Press, 2001), here 32–33. Xenophon's *Education of Cyrus* is important to social ethicists for a variety of reasons, not the least of which is its significant contribution to Machiavelli's understanding of the common good. Indeed, Xenophon's text is the only classical source to which Machiavelli referred in *Prince* and it was the classical text most frequently cited in his *Discourses*. See Christopher Nadon, "From Republic to Empire: Political Revolution and the Common Good in Xenophon's *Education of Cyrus*," *American Political Science Review* 90 (1996): 361–74, see esp. 373–74 on comparisons to Machiavelli.

13. Aristotle, *Politics*, trans. Carnes Lord (Chicago: University of Chicago Press, 1984), here 2.1263a–b.I at 60–62. One must read all of books I and II to appreciate the argument at stake, for in them is a long discussion of how it is inappropriate to look to the man successful either in business or in

mind, human depravity would never allow the lifelong sharing of goods from a common stock, no matter how useful a particular piece of property was to a person at any given time.[14] Thus, despite their misgivings, Xenophon and Aristotle accepted the status quo as that which would cause the least amount of injustice. This basic understanding is behind Cicero's later insistence that the taking of the goods of another—whether by force of law or of banditry—is an injustice. In agreement with the Stoics, he argued that the goods of the earth belong to all and exist for the benefit of all persons.[15] Private property, then, is an aberration of nature and so the ideal is for all things to be held in common. Yet, private property exists and so it is a matter of *justice* that humans respect existing private property rights. Justice in the present trumps a reordering of society in accordance with nature for the future.[16]

Somewhat in contrast to Xenophon and Aristotle (also Cicero, though an anachronism) are the ideas articulated by their contemporary Menander in his play, *Dyskolos*.[17] On the one hand, Menander agreed with their discontent that laws protect property rights based on ownership rather than use. On

---

overseeing slaves or in managing a household for the care and administration of a city. The three realms of business, slave, and household management do share things in common with civic rule, but none fully prepare a person or persons for the just rule of free citizens. On that note, *Politics* is a training manual for just such an aspiring civic ruler or rulers, and one of the first questions tackled is that of how to administer property.

14. To be clear, Aristotle distinguishes between the *care* of possessions and the *use* of them. Care of possessions ought to be private, but the use of possessions ought to be common. This distinction between care and use preserves a sense of dignity for each property owner insofar as both pleasure is derived from calling something one's own and greed is restrained. What is more, Aristotle asserts that the distinction between care and use instills two important virtues: moderation and liberality. With respect to the former, this distinction preserves an awareness that some goods are not properly shareable (e.g., wives, women); for the latter, it recognizes that sharing is only possible when goods are held privately (2.1263b).

15. Cicero, *De officiis*, LCL, ed. and trans. Walter Miller (Cambridge, Mass.: Harvard University Press, 1913), here I.7, 21. Cicero writes, "There is, however, no such thing as private ownership established by nature, but property becomes private either through long occupancy (as in the case of those who long ago settled in unoccupied territory) or through conquest (is in the case of those who took it in war) or by due process of law, bargain, or purchase, or by allotment. . . .Therefore, inasmuch as in each case some of those things which by nature had been common property became the property of individuals, each one should retain possession of that which has fallen to his lot; and if anyone appropriates to himself anything beyond that, he will be violating the laws of human society."

16. Even so, Cicero, *De officiis* III.5, argued one should not take the goods of one's neighbor even if it means bringing upon oneself pain, poverty, or even death! The taking of the goods of another is itself a violation of nature, an injustice. Cicero argues, "[H]e is mistaken in thinking that any ills affecting either his person or his property are more serious than those affecting his soul."

17. Menander, *The Bad-Tempered Man (Dyskolos)*, trans. Stanley Ireland (Warminster, U.K.: Aris & Phillips, 1995).

the other hand, he believed there was a solution: distinguish between needs and superfluities with respect to private property. Laws may then protect a person's right to own needed, or useful, property, but not property that is superfluous to needs. He based this distinction on the fact that property is temporary, and so people may safely detach themselves from it. If nothing else, the short span of human life will mark out the limits of one's ability to "own" property.[18] This detachment view of private property will later find an articulate proponent in Seneca who, a substantially wealthy court official himself, in the mid-first century CE composed the treatise *De vita beata*, in which it is argued that the man who possesses virtue possesses the only thing that is truly good.[19] Consequently, the accumulation of goods, land, money and the frivolous spending subsequent to it are no adequate measure of pleasure.[20] Moreover, property and wealth are fleeting, so any virtue tied to things temporary will always put true happiness in jeopardy. Far better, in Seneca's view, to hold property and wealth at a distance. One may possess wealth and property, but their acquistion should be by just means.[21] In the end, *indifferentia* (equivalent to the Stoic ἀδιάφορα) is the goal (xxii.4), and thus riches may be despised

18. Menander, *The Bad-Tempered Man*, 85. Sostratos, a character in Menander's play, asks his father for his blessing for Sostratos's planned wedding. Sostratos's father hesitates, for the family of the woman his son wants to marry is poor and he is afraid of becoming responsible for the care of a poorer family. Sostratos counters (see ll. 797–812) with two points that convert his father, and the wedding is able to proceed. The first point was that the money or property of a hoarder may very well end up in the hands of those thought to be undeserving by a hoarder at the hoarder's death. The second point was that it is okay to have wealth so long as it is shared liberally with those who have needs.

19. Seneca, "De vita beata," in *Seneca: Moral Essays, Vol. II*, LCL, ed. and trans. John W. Basore, (Cambridge, Mass.: Harvard University Press, 1965). As the tutor of the young Nero, Seneca's political and financial fortunes swung like a pendulum largely in sync with those of Nero's mother and, then, Nero himself. Seneca's position gave him ample opportunities not only to acquire substantial wealth but also to write, and much of his corpus is devoted to ethics and the promotion of a life of philosophy. For an appreciation of Seneca's views about private property and, more generally, wealth, one could turn either to his *Ep.* 20 or *Ep.* 90 or to one of his other ethical treatises, *De brevitate vitae*. The writing of *De vita beata* may date to 58, following the exile of Sullius, who had criticized Seneca for the seeming contradiction of his life: on the one hand great wealth and, on the other hand, claims to Stoic *indifferentia*. This would also coincide with the time during which Nero's own decisions were growing increasingly, ethically questionable. See Paul Veyne, *Seneca: The Life of a Stoic*, trans. David Sullivan (New York: Routledge, 2003), esp. 20–22, 191.

20. Here one may also look to Seneca's exposée on the pitiable life of the wealthy and politically powerful found in his *De brevitate vitae*. No sooner do they acquire wealth or power, they are looking to give it away because of the burdens such things bring upon them.

21. Seneca, *De vita beata* xxiii.3, in *Seneca: Moral Essays*, ed. and trans. Basore, 158: *Sapiens nullum denarium intra limen suum admittet male intrantem.*

whether one has them or not. It is the ideas of Menander and of Seneca that will aquire great currency in the later teachings of the Fathers, particularly those in Basil's milieu.

We may, at this point, turn our attention to the Christian context from which Basil's text emerged. Jesus, in Mark 10:21, taught the rich young ruler to "sell all that you have and give the proceeds to the poor." This suggests Jesus called for a lifestyle of renunciation, and, in the second century, some Christian writings taught as much with respect to private property. The *Epistle of Barnabas* 19, for example, exhorted its readers, "Treat as common all things with your neighbor, and do not say things are 'one's own,' for if you are sharers in incorruptible things, how much more ought you to be sharers in corruptible things!"[22] The command not to call things "one's own" is also found in *Didache* 4.8, a late first- or second-century document, although it is less clear in *Didache* that the author held strictly to a renunciation view.[23] In any case, the dream of a community that continued the type of sharing of goods recorded in Acts 2 did not go away quickly.

At least two works in the second century signaled a definite shift away from renunciation: Irenaeus's *Against Heresies* IV.30.1–3 and Shepherd of Hermas, especially *Parables* (or, *Similitudes*) 1–2.[24] Irenaeus accepted property's

22. *Epistle of Barnabas,* 19.8a, in *The Apostolic Fathers I,* LCL, 2 vols., ed. Bart Ehrman (Cambridge, Mass.: Harvard University Press, 2003], II.78, translation mine: κοινωνήσεις ἐν πᾶσιν τῷ πλησίον σου καὶ οὐκ ἐρεῖς ἴδια εἶναι· εἰ γὰρ ἐν τῷ ἀφθάρτῳ κοινωνοί ἐστε, πόσῳ μᾶλλον ἐν τοῖς φθαρτοῖς. Even so, it is possible the author of the epistle harbored some allowance for private property. At §10, the author reads Leviticus 17:11 and Deuteronomy 14:8 in a spiritual way—"don't eat the pig" means "don't cling to those who act like pigs." This is in support of the larger point by the author that labor, rather than thievery, is the way to acquire food. May we read into this the author's appreciation for the acquisition of some private property following the application of personal labor? I suspect so, but this is by no means conclusive.

23. See *Didache* 13, in *The Apostolic Fathers I,* 438, at which place the author asks that the firstfruits of one's food, money, clothing and everything else(!) be given to support the teaching ministry of a local prophet or pastor. In the absence of such a person, then the firstfruits are to be given to the poor. Presumably, what remains beyond the firstfruits belongs to each person. So, the command in §4.8 to claim nothing is one's own may suggest a life of detachment from goods; offering the firstfruits of one's goods to a prophet or to a poor person would serve as a regular reminder of this call to detachment. In this case, early readers of *Didache* would accept that its theological instruction cannot be separated from the practices of daily life.

24. Irenaeus of Lyon, *Adversus haereses* IV.30.1–2, in *Contre les hérésies, Livre 4,* SC 100, ed. Adelin Rousseau (Paris: Les Éditions du Cerf, 1965), 770–79; Norbert Brox, ed., *Adversus haereses,* Fontes Christianae 8 (Freiburg: Herder Press, 1997), part 4, 236–41; Eng. trans. Alexander Roberts and James Donaldson, "Against Heresies," in *The Apostolic Fathers with Justin Martyr and Irenaeus, ANF* 1 (Edinburgh: T. & T. Clark, 1867), 503. Hermas, Shepherd (*Parables/Similitudes* 1 and 2), in *The Apostolic Fathers II,* 304–14; Eng. trans. Ehrman, LCL, II.305–15.

inherent, moral neutrality. Echoing Xenophon and Aristotle, property itself was not to blame; rather, one's use of property was to be the subject of any scrutiny. To Irenaeus, the possession of property was not a right following upon the expension of one's own labor to acquire it. This is because all property is the result of someone else's earlier labor. Thus, property could never really be considered "private" because no one person could ever claim to have produced it.[25] For his part, Hermas framed the need for detachment in terms of a need for Christians to be aware that earth is not their home.[26] Yearning for earthly goods is an affront to God.

---

John A. McGuckin, "The Vine and the Elm Tree: The Patristic Interpretation of Jesus' Teaching on Wealth," in *The Church and Wealth: Papers Read at the 1986 Summer Meeting and the 1987 Winter Meeting of the Ecclesiastical History Society*, ed. W. J. Shiels and Diana Wood (Oxford: Basil Blackwell, 1987), 1–14. McGuckin suggests this tension over renunciation versus detachment may be due not simply to shifting cultural forces in late antiquity but perhaps even more to a tension in how the *logia* of Jesus were brought together into the canonical gospels themselves. McGuckin argues, *contra* those who think passages like Mark 10:21 are apocalyptic teaching—that Jesus is concerned with the prophetic and missionary role his disciples must assume. By the time the *logia* of Jesus are incorporated into the canonical gospels the community had settled into an early pattern of doing church, and thus *logia* such as Mark 10:21 were recalled in order to encourage some in the Church to pursue a lifestyle of living lightly and traveling broadly for the sake of missions. See also Howard Clark Kee, "Rich and Poor in the New Testament and Early Christianity," in *Through the Eye of a Needle: Judeo-Christian Roots of Social Welfare*, ed. Emly A. Hanawalt and Carter Lindberg (Kirksville, Mo.: Thomas Jefferson University Press, 1994), 29–42.

For a different perspective on the question, one may turn to G. E. M. de Ste. Croix, "Early Christian Attitudes to Property and Slavery," in *Church, Society and Politics: Papers Read at the Thirteenth Summer Meeting and the Fourteenth Winter Meeting of the Ecclesiastical History Society*, Studies in Church History 12 (Oxford: Basil Blackwell, 1975), 1–38. He argued the Church Fathers were interested more in man-to-man or man-to-God relationships and not in the men-to-men relationship (the latter of which would have concerned conflicts of class, social status, economic condition, political rights, etc.). This meant the Fathers were able to talk about the dangers of riches and property without demanding that Christians renounce all riches and property. So long as a person's use of his or her riches was honoring to God and to other people, the economic and social class realities could remain in place—they were no hindrance to personal relationships with God.

25. Inherited wealth would be a particular evil in such a scheme, for not only did it require no labor from the beneficiary, but also its own origins likely are stained with injustice. The only way to redeem for God's glory such tainted goods would be to put them at the disposal of the poor. See Irenaeus, *A.H.* IV.30.3. He compared the offering up to God of inherited property to the redeeming use of building the Temple with goods the Israelites took from the Egyptians. Two centuries later, Epiphanius, in his *Panarion* 61.3–4 (PG 41.1040); Eng. trans. Frank Williams, *The Panarion of Epiphanius of Salamis, Books II and III*, Nag Hammadi and Manichaean Studies 36 (Leiden: Brill, 1994), 116, argued the true Church does not despise those who have inherited wealth if such individuals use that wealth to meet the needs both of their family and of others. Chrysostom would agree, for he wrote in *Homilies on Matthew* 77.5 that goods possessed either by inheritance or by honest labor all belong to the poor.

26. Hermas, Shepherd (*Similitudes* 2), suggested the rich aid the poor by their wealth in exchange for the poor aiding the rich by their prayer. This argument will surface many times in later centuries. See, e.g., Theodoret of Cyrus, *On Providence* 6.31, who says that the rich have been blessed by God with mon-

In the third century this detachment view was picked up by Clement of Alexandria in his *Quis dives salvetur?* Clement applied a spiritual style of exegesis to his reading of Mark 10 that had gained some currency by that time. Clement argued Jesus could not have meant for every person to be without property, for such a situation would mean that no one would have anything to give to the poor.[27] From this starting point, Clement articulates a different vision for private property, one in which a person may freely possess what he or she needs or is useful to him or her, but all that is superfluous must be given to the poor or otherwise needy.[28] This recalls the necessities and superfluities distinction of Menander. Thus, with Clement, a more fruitful course of inquiry about private property has been opened: how much is *enough*?

From that point, it seems that the Greek Fathers were in agreement with a detachment, as opposed to a renunciation, view of property.[29] This is not to say the renunciation view had disappeared,[30] for Epiphanius, in the mid-

---

ey and the poor have been blessed by God with skills in trades and crafts. In such a situation it is the rich, he argues, who are compelled to come begging at the door of the poor person. I find this to be an interesting point, and perhaps what Theodoret says was true regarding the mobility of goods in the economic context of Cyrus in the early fifth century. However, our modern economic context no longer limits the choices of from which poor the rich are obliged to beg. The global marketplace allows the rich regularly to move from one poor person to another until they find a satisfactorily low enough price for the crafts they desire. The poor are not in an advantageous position in such a market.

27. Clement of Alexandria, *Quis dives salvetur* 4–5, in *Stromata: Buch VII und VIII; Excerpta ex Theodoto; Eclogae propheticae; Quis dives salvetur; Fragmente*, GCS 17, ed. Otto Stählin, Ludwig Früchtel, and Ursula Treu (Berlin: Akademie Verlag, 1970), 162–63; Eng. trans. G. W. Butterworth, *Clement of Alexandria: The Exhortation to the Greeks, The Rich Man's Salvation, and the fragment of an address entitled To the Newly Baptized*, LCL (Cambridge, Mass.: Harvard University Press, 1919, repr. 1982), 279–83. Clement made a similar point in another of his works, *Stromata* 4.13. There, he affirmed that goods and possessions are not, in themselves, bad lest they be not a creation of God.

28. Clement, *Quis dives salvetur* 13, in *Quis dives salvetur*, GCS 17, ed. Stählin, Früchtel, and Treu, 167–68. Eng. trans. Butterworth, *Clement of Alexandria*, LCL, 295–97. See also Clement, *Paedogogus* 2.3 and *Stromata* 6.12. In these passages he argued we ought to acquire only such objects as are useful for completing more than one task. Clement even identifies the types of "superfluities" he has in mind, including makeup, jewelry, silver dishware, and other such decorous goods. True adornment is the pursuit of Christ and spiritual life rather than the wearing of jewelry. Clement, *Quis dives salvetur* 3. See also Clement, *Paedogogus* 2.12, 3.7.

29. Wolf-Dieter von Hauschild, "Christentum und Eigentum: Zum Problem eines altkirchlichen 'Sozialismus,'" *Zeitschrift für Evangelische Ethik* 16 (1972): 34–49, argues that, while Jesus' teachings and the second-century Christians had laid the groundwork for a socialist, or proto-communist, trajectory, the views of Clement of Alexandria were so quickly accepted and disseminated that the earlier momentum was derailed. The teachings of Basil and John Chrysostom served to cement Clement's view for the late fourth and into the fifth centuries.

30. Rainer Kampling, "'Have We Not Then Made a Heaven of Earth?' Rich and Poor in the Early Church," *Concilium* 22 (1986): 51–62, here 58–59.

fourth century still found adherents to a renunciation view deserving of condemnation in his *Panarion*[31] and a fifth-century text (in the West) by an adherent to Pelagius's views argued for renunciation as well.[32] The Pelagian text
insisted that only renunciation of property and wealth would ensure elimination of poverty for others. Yet, the detachment view was articulated by more
and more of the ecclesiastical elite. One of Clement's early successors in the
Alexandrian see, Peter, also preached on the need for detachment from property in his sermon *On Riches*.[33] Peter argued God makes a separation between
the rich person and the *merciless* rich person (§§14–15). The former gives little
thought to his wealth and shares it liberally with the poor; the latter is consumed with thoughts of wealth and despises the needs of the poor. Gregory Nazianzen preached a homily encouraging love for the poor, particularly
those with serious health problems. He observed in this homily that disordered affection for property was responsible for the strife between persons
and between nations.[34] Love for the poor begins, in part, with a recognition

31. Epiphanius, *Panarion* 80.4 (PG 42.761), 764; Eng. trans. Williams, *The Panarion of Epiphanius*, 631–32. A sign that Clement's arguments held sway well into the late fourth century, Epiphanius at
*Panarion* 60.1 (Her. 64), suggested that, were it not for the serpent's infusion of envy into human desires
(see Gn 3), humans would be able to keep their material desires in check in accordance with their need.
Furthermore, Epiphanius, at *Panarion* 61.3–4, argued the acquisition of property through labor or other
honest means is appropriate in so far as such behavior makes possible fulfilling the command of Christ to
feed and care for the needy.

32. The Pelagian tract is entitled, *On Wealth,* in *Reichtumskritik und Pelagianismus: die pelagianische
Diatribe de divitiis: Situierung, Lesetext, Übersetzung, Kommentar*, Paradosis 43, ed. Andreas Kessler
(Freiburg: Universitätsverlag, 1999); Eng. trans. B. R. Rees, *The Letters of Pelagius and his Followers* (Suffolk, U.K.: Boydell Press, 1991), 171–211. However, Richard Newhauser, *The Early History of Greed: The Sin
of Avarice in Early Medieval Thought and Literature* (Cambridge: Cambridge University Press, 2000), 89–
90, suggests that the text is not so much about renunciation as about sufficiency of property, that readers
since Augustine have been too influenced by his exaggerated reaction in his correspondence with Hilary of
Syracuse. Perhaps Newhauser is right and the critique of avarice masks an accpetance of owning sufficient
property, but one would be hardpressed to find in this Pelagian treatise a particular passage that supports
this view. The author yields no ground to those who would support some ownership of private property.

The renunciation view was not only that of some divisive Christians, but may already be found in
Philo. In one of the collected essays by Valentin Nikiprowetzky included in his *Études Philoniennes*, Patrimoines Judaisme (Paris: Les Éditions du Cerf, 1996), 243–91, it is argued that Philo was like the Essenes
insofar as he believed riches were useless and were very often the fruit of injustice. Philo believed the scrip-
tural ideal is poverty and opulence is an affront to one's claims of love for men and love for the Torah.

33. Birger Pearson and Tim Vivian, eds., *Two Coptic Homilies Attributed to Saint Peter of Alexandria: On Riches, On the Epiphany* (Rome: C.I.M., 1993). On the original "core homily" and its author, Peter, see 26–31. See also Tim Vivian, *St. Peter of Alexandria: Bishop and Martyr*, Studies in Antiquity and
Christianity (Philadelphia: Fortress Press, 1988).

34. Gregory of Nazianzus, *Oration* 14.25. This argument is found in other Greek Fathers, includ-

that property truly belongs only to God.[35] Similarly, Asterius of Amasea, in his homily *The Unjust Steward*, balanced a concern for the temporariness of property with each person's responsibility towards God for his or her use of property.[36] Everyone will be obliged one day to give an account of his or her use of property before God.[37]

At this point we may step back and paint in broader strokes the depiction of private property across these texts from both the classical writers and the Fathers in the Greek milieu to the time of Basil. First, there is a general unease about the existence of private property. Yet, none of the writers—with the possible exception of Menander, although he was not addressing the legal context—propose changes to the legal situation that protected property rights, for, in the near term, they surmised such changes would create more problems than they would solve. A second, equally important point is the gradual shift, beginning with Seneca and continuing with the Christian writers, away from arguments about reordering property rights and towards reordering the interior disposition of the rich and poor. Property is temporary and so can never bring more than temporary pleasure. True happiness comes with the cultuva-tion of virtue or, more Christianly, with the cultivation of a proper orientation of one's life towards God. In concrete terms, this begins with a detachment from property. In any case, the church increasingly found itself responsible during the fourth century for the care and financial maintenance of a greater percentage of the population. One way both of managing the expectations of the "shallow poor" and of playing to the self-interest of the "rich" was to pro-mote a vision for detachment from private property.

## Basil of Caesarea's *Homily 6*

Our consideration of this text by Basil reveals how this detachment view of private property functioned within the context of a homily, for the call to

---

ing Clement of Alexandria, *Quis dives salvetur* 15; Asterius of Amasea, *The Unjust Steward*; Chrysostom, *Homilies on John* 19.3; Basil of Caesarea, *Hom.* 8.2 and 4, especially the former on account of the fact that Basil suggests God has brought the drought on the land in order to punish the people for their hoard-ing of goods.

35. Gregory Nazianzen, *Oration* 14.29. See John Chrysostom, *Homilies on I Corinthians* 10.3–4.

36. Asterius of Amasea, *Hom.* 2 (*The Unjust Steward*).

37. Asterius, *Hom.* 2.

be detached from property is precisely this homily's purpose.[38] Specifically, we shall consider the *hermeneutical function* of this principle of detachment. For example, how did the principle apply to concrete situations, and, once applied, what applications for Christian living did it suggest? The objectification of the hermeneutical function of the principle of detachment may very well open a space for dialogue between the world of the Fathers and that of Catholic social thought.

The context for Basil's *Hom. 6* is unclear. The latter half of the homily confronts problems resulting from a famine, so it may be that the homily was delivered at Caesarea following the particularly devastating famine that began in Cappadocia in 368.[39] It was during this time that Basil made plans for a

38. Basil of Caesarea, *Hom. 6* (*On the Saying "I will tear down my barns . . ."*). The critical edition is Basil of Caesarea, *Homélies sur la richesse*, Collection d'études anciennes, ed. Yves Courtonne (Paris: Firm-Didot, 1935), 15–37. Eng. trans. Hieroschemamonk Janis (Berzins), "Homily on the Words of St. Luke's Gospel: 'I will pull down my barns and build larger ones' and on Avarice," *Orthodox Life* 42 (1992): 10–17; M. F. Toal, *The Sunday Sermons of the Great Fathers* 3 (Chicago: Henry Regnery, 1959), 325–32; Walter Shewring, *Rich and Poor in Christian Tradition* (London: Burns and Oats, 1948), 51–62. See especially 6.5, "Let the example of the condemned rich man be before you continually: how he guards what he has and strives for what he hopes to gain, not knowing whether he will live until tomorrow, today already sinning for tomorrow." πανταχοῦ σοι τὸ ὑπόδειγμα τοῦ κατηγορουμένου πλουσίου προσαπαντάτω· ὃς, τὰ μὲν ἤδη παρόντα φυλάσσων, περὶ δὲ τῶν ἐλπιζομένων ἀγωνιῶν, καὶ ἄδηλον ἔχων εἰ βιώσεται τὴν αὔριον, τὸ αὔριον σήμερον προημάτανεν.

Paying special attention to Basil's *Hom. 6* may surprise some, for he has another homily entitled "On Detachment from Wealth" (*Hom. 21*; see PG 31.625–648; Eng. trans. M. Monica Wagner: *Saint Basil: Ascetical Works*, FOTC 9 [Washington D.C.: The Catholic University of America Press, 1950], 487–506). *Hom. 21* situates detachment in the wider context of one's need for a light burden while traveling the road known as the Christian life. (Basil connects this notion of the spiritual life as a road or way to Psalm 118:1, yet one perhaps also ought to have in mind the "two ways" teaching of the *Didache*, the *Epistle of Barnabas*, Irenaeus *A.H.* V.28.1, and other Christian literature.) Basil also gave careful thought to private property in his *Hom. 8* ("In the Time of Famine and Drought"). In *Hom. 8.2* Basil suggested what is enough is often far less than people presume; for example, he said that, at any one time, it is enough to possess only one tunic and to have in the kitchen only one loaf of bread. Incidentally, an echo of this point may be found in Cyril of Alexandria, *Paschal Homilies* 11.3. See also Basil's *Shorter Rules* Q. 92, in which text Basil affirmed that property cannot in itself be bad lest it be not a creation of God. Although restricting this study to *Hom. 6* removes from our study some of this larger perspective about property, one gains instead the ability to perceive the hermeneutical function of detachment both in regards to Basil's reading of a particular, biblical text and in his reading of a concrete, social problem (here, famine) that he constructs for his audience.

39. I find no speculation as to an exact date for this homily among any of several scholars who have evaluated it. Susan Holman, *The Hungry Are Dying*, seems to assume that it is post-368, but without explicitly saying so (see 107–9). The editor of the homily, Yves Courtonne, nowhere speculates on a possible date, but only accepts as likely the suggestion of A. Puech, *Histoire de la littérature grecque chrétienne*, 3 vols. (Paris: Société d'édition "Les belles lettres," 1928–1930), III.266, in Courtonne on 7, that it seems to agree with the famine situation that is explicitly the subject of Basil's *Hom. 8*.

hospice and pilgrimage center to be constructed just outside the city's walls. The homily was clearly directed towards those with some financial means in the midst of this time of famine for, in view of its consideration of rewards and punishments in the afterlife, Basil preaches here a redemptive understanding of almsgiving. In this sense, the detachment view of property functions as a pastoral tool for helping the congregation apply redemptive almsgiving in their own lives.

The content of the homily centers around a consideration of Jesus' parable about the rich man who, upon discovering an unusually bountiful harvest among his crops, decided to build bigger barns to store the harvest for himself (see Lk 12:16–18). Basil accepted that Jesus left little doubt his own wish was that the rich man distribute the excess harvest to the poor rather than storing it up for himself. Thus, the homily challenged the appropriateness of superfluous property, and this was not an unimportant matter to Basil. As bishop of Caesarea, he oversaw a wealthy, if not particularly prominent, ecclesiastical see during a time in which imperial legislation compelled his office to distribute this wealth to the poor. It is understandable that he would preach what he was practicing, and the sermon is a remarkably versatile tool in the hands of Basil. In this case, the biblical passage itself makes a compelling case for social action, but Basil added to the biblical text the experience of his own relief work on behalf of the poor and sick in Caesarea. He also painted word-pictures that critique the character flaws he saw in his own congregants. In short, Basil was forming the moral imagination of his audience. His congregants could enter briefly into worlds of the poor or of the rich that they might not otherwise know. Even reading the homily today, one can feel, taste, and see the problems of the world as Basil wanted us to see them, inasmuch as one can feel, taste, and see the joys of heaven that await those who detach themselves from property.[40]

Turning now to a more detailed consideration of the principle of detachment in this homily, one discovers no less than four hermeneutical functions for the principle, four ways in which the principle of detachment interprets either human life or the Christian life or the surrounding culture or some com-

40. My acquaintance with Basil's text made me rather alert to an NPR news story I encountered in late December 2006. It surveyed current research by neuroscientists on how mechanisms within the brain cause us to feel as though we've participated in something just by thinking about it (e.g., I can experience the taste of salsa in my mouth just by thinking about salsa or seeing it set before me on a table). It will be interesting to find out where this research goes.

bination of the three. To begin with, and perhaps most important, the principle reveals that avarice, not property, is the rich person's problem. In the homily's opening paragraph, Basil lets the biblical text do most of the speaking, but he situates our reading of the parable in terms of the testing of souls. Some souls are tested by poverty, he suggests, but others are tested with respect to their propensity towards arrogance. The story of Job in the Hebrew Bible is the story of one who was tested by poverty—and passed; Jesus' parable of the rich man with a bountiful harvest is the latter test, and he failed. Thus, Basil wants his hearers to read Jesus' parable with the story of Job in the back of their minds. Basil writes of the rich man, "His greed would not allow him to part with what he already possessed, but he was unable to put away anything new because of space."[41] The rich man had what we oxymoronically refer to today as "a good problem." Yet, to solve this good problem, the rich man made all the wrong decisions. To Basil, the man's inability to detach himself from property revealed an arrogant, avaricious spirit. Attachment to property, then, is merely a symptom of a more damning problem. Thus, the detachment principle is a tool that cuts to the heart of a person's character.

Second, the principle of detachment deepens one's awareness of God's providence. In *Hom.* 6.2, Basil writes, "Think, O man, of who it is that has given to you. Remember yourself, who you are, what your duty is, from whom you have received it, why you have been preferred to others. You have become an agent of the good God, a steward for your fellow servants."[42] The person attached to property does not want to believe that anyone but himself or herself is responsible for his or her acquisition of property. Consequently, such a person could not imagine that his or her ownership of property comes with a responsibility to others. Yet, to Basil, for whatever reason God has seen fit to distribute goods to all via the labor of a few. The result is a new way of thinking about one's place in the world. Basil invites his hearers to "imitate the earth"; much as the earth brings forth fruit for the enjoyment of others, so, too, the rich person ought to imitate the earth by laboring for the enjoyment of the needy. This is God's providential care for the world. People with

41. Basil, *Hom.* 6.1, in *Homélies sur la richesse*, ed. Y. Courtonne, 15. Eng. trans. H. Janis, "Homily on the Words of St. Luke's Gospel," *Orthodox Life* 42 (1992):10: ὑποχωρεῖν μὲν τοῖς παλαιοῖς διὰ τὴν πλεονεξίαν μὴ συγχωρῶν, ὑποδέχεσθαι δὲ τὰ νέα διὰ τὸ πλῆθος μὴ ἐξαρκῶν.

42. Ibid., 11: σύνες, ἄνθρωπε, τοῦ δεδωκότος. μνήσθητι σεαυτοῦ, τίς εἶ, τί οἰκονομεῖς, παρὰ τίνος ἔλαβες, διὰ τί τῶν πολλῶν προεκρίθεις. ἀγαθοῦ Θεοῦ γέγονας ὑπηρέτης, οἰκονόμος τῶν ὁμοδούλων.

financial means and the ability to labor are to transfer their wealth, that is, the property that comes as a result of their labor, to those who are unemployed or underemployed. To be detached from property, then, is to be attached to a particular view about God, about God's providence.

Third, the principle of detachment reveals a Christian anthropology in which the commonness of humanity serves as the basis for detachment. At the midpoint of the homily Basil departs from the biblical parable and tells a parable of his own.[43] He describes a poor father who has finally reached the point at which he is completely out of resources. The family has no more grain, and so the father has gone to the market in search of a vendor willing to give to him some for free (incidentally, Basil's use of grain ties his own parable to the biblical one). Finding no such vendor, the father must now decide which of his sons he must sell in order to buy more grain for the family. Basil's audience is then treated to a delightful word picture. Basil describes the groans of the father, the fear of his children, the tension in the family, the pangs of hunger. Then from out of the picture's background emerges the sinister rich man with grain to spare but who will neither share it with the poor man nor sell it at a discount to him. Basil writes, "With a myriad of tears he [i.e., the poor father] goes to sell his dearest child, but his suffering does not move you [i.e., the rich man], you take no account of nature. . . . His tears do not arouse your pity, his groans do not soften your heart."[44] The experience of the father in this parable is quite similar to what nutritionists understand today to be the third and final stage of the human experience of famine: exhaustion, which "is marked by the collapse of all cooperative effort, including maintenance of the family unit."[45] Basil has taken his audience through a rollercoaster of emotions with this parable. First, the audience groaned with the poor father. Then, it seethed with anger at the vendor. Finally, it joined Basil in jeering the vendor for his avarice. The consequence of all this is that detachment from private property breeds a certain amount of solidarity with the poor, but this is a

43. Although this is probably not a story of an actual event witnessed by Basil, in his *Homily on Psalm 14,* 4, he relates a similar event and says explicitly it was something he had seen. See Agnes C. Way, *Saint Basil: Exegetic Homilies*, FOTC 146 (Washington D.C.: The Catholic University of America Press, 1963), 189.

44. Basil, *Hom.* 6.4; ed. Courtonne, *Homélies sur la richesse*, 13: καὶ ὁ μὲν μετὰ μυρίων δακρύων τὸν φίλτατον τῶν παίδων ἀπεμπολήσων ἔρχεται· σὲ δὲ οὐ κάμπτει τὸ πάθος, οὐ λογισμὸν λανβάνεις τῆς φύσεως . . . οὐ δάκρυόν σοι ἐλεεινὸν, οὐ στεναγμὸς καρδίαν μαλάσσει.

45. Holman, *The Hungry Are Dying*, 91–92.

double-edged sword. From a pastoral perspective, if one person can do it (i.e., be detached from property), so everyone else ought to do it as well, and those that do not rightly deserve criticism. Yet, this perspective actually obscures the poor, as such.[46] Although Basil's audience will, after hearing this homily, incline towards the poor rather than the rich, the poor father here is little more than a tool to move the sympathies of those with property towards an attitude of detachment. The poor are not Basil's ultimate concern here; for that matter, and perhaps as one explanation for Basil's own treatment, the poor were not mentioned at all in the biblical parable.

Fourth, the principle of detachment elucidates an alternative economic system used by God to measure wealth and poverty. Much as in the world's economy a single currency—wealth, or at least one's access to wealth—is the measure of each person, so in God's alternative system is there a single currency: treasure in heaven, or at least one's pursuit of that treasure. On this score, Jesus' words in Matthew 25, "Come, O blessed of my Father, inherit the kingdom" are particularly poignant. Basil recalls these words of Jesus to explain that God pays with heavenly currency for the clothing, food, and shelter needs of the poor.[47] The possessor of private property, then, must both appreciate the value of heavenly currency and be willing to sell his or her goods to God in exchange for it. For this reason, the principle of detachment defines what happens to each person in the next age, in the life to come. There is a Judgment Day, a day in the future at which God will settle his account with every person. Those who are detached from property neither worry about that day nor when it will come. They are prepared to enter the next age at every moment. There is no "tomorrow" to such a person; tomorrow is always today.[48]

What all of this leads to, in fact and rather surprisingly, is a denouncement of *private* property in favor of *common* property. Near the end of the homily Basil writes that the rich, "[Grab] what is common property, they make it their own on account of their priority. If only each were to take enough to

---

46. For a different reason—from the perspective of redemptive almsgiving—Holman, *The Hungry Are Dying*, 54–55, 103, 107–9, seems to agree that the poor, as such, are not the main concern of Basil here.

47. On the matter of divine compensation for rejecting earthly goods, see Cyprian of Carthage, *On the Lapsed*, 12.

48. Basil, *Hom.* 6.6. Basil invites his hearers to recall the words of Solomon in Proverbs 3:28 ("Do not say to your neighbor, 'Go, and come again, tomorrow I will give it'") and Proverbs 27:1 ("Do not boast about tomorrow").

meet his own requirements and the rest leave to those in need, no one would
be rich, no one poor, no one needy" (*Hom.* 6.7). This is an echo of Aristophanes and Plato, but I do not think we should confuse Basil's understanding of *common* with *communistic*. Basil is very much in the line of Clement of
Alexandria in arguing for sufficiency in private property, for in the very same
part of the homily he writes, "What is a miser? One who does not keep within
the bounds of sufficiency."[49] To Basil, everyone should possess what he or she
*needs*, which is not necessarily the same as what he or she *wants*. Thus, it seems
that Basil is wrestling with two emotions at the same time, and this would not
be out of character for a good pastor. On the one hand, he recognizes there is
an ideal of common property. On the other hand, as a pastor, he will be happy
if his congregants agree at least to detachment.

To summarize, the hermeneutical function of the principle of detachment
reveals that the principle is as much a multi-faceted tool in Basil's workshop
as the homily itself in terms of forming the moral imagination of his congregants. The principle correctly interprets the character of a person with superfluous property. It corrects misunderstandings of God's providence. It evaluates the extent to which we are in solidarity with the needy. Finally, it pulls
back the curtain on how the divine economy works and defends the wealth in
that economy over and against the wealth in the earthly economies. The hermeneutical function of the principle is another pastoral tool. In Basil's hands,
it is used to proclaim the ideal of common property while accepting detachment as a sufficient enough change in behavior.

## Private Property in Catholic Social Teaching

We pass over some fifteen centuries now to consider the teachings of the
modern Catholic Church on private property. In doing so, we may ask to
what extent it may be a dialogue partner with the patristic world. In 2004, the
Pontifical Council for Justice and Peace published an "authoritative synthesis" of Catholic social teaching.[50] It brought together the major themes and

---

49. Basil, *Hom.* 6.7.

50. Pontifical Council for Justice and Peace, *Compendium of the Social Doctrine of the Church*
(Rome: Libreria Editrice Vaticana, 2004). English and Italian editions were prepared first; subsequent
translations were prepared from the Italian. This was not the first such compendium from the PCJP; indeed, they had in 2000 approved a work prepared by the staff of the Acton Institute based in the Unit-

particular teachings of the Catholic Church on social ethics since *Rerum no-varum* (1891). Private property is taken up in the compendium's fourth chapter. Though tempting simply to take up our review of Catholic social teaching with this text, it would be a disservice to the *Compendium* if we did not first understand the instructional trajectory regarding private property teaching it summarized.[51]

*Rerum novarum* identified private property as a natural right, and, at the time, this was an important claim in support of workers with few avenues for improving their situation.[52] The encyclical challenged employers to pay workers a just wage, which was expected to facilitate their acquisition of land and property for personal use. Property was deemed a constitutive expression of human dignity. In 1931, Pope Pius XI issued *Quadragessimo anno*. Although the encyclical explicitly affirmed the teaching of *Rerum novarum*, its teaching on private property moved decisely away from legal and natural law arguments. Instead, it emphasized the communal responsibility each person has toward the use of his or her private property. It further claimed that superfluous income and property was *not* at the discretion of the owner; rather, what is superfluous belongs to the needy.[53] This introduced into Catholic social

---

ed States. Robert A. Sirico and Maciej Zieba, eds., *The Social Agenda: A Collection of Magisterial Texts* (Rome: Libreria Editrice Vaticana, 2000). The 2004 compendium, however, is substantially more broad; in the preface to the 2000 book, the president of the PCJP, François-Xavier Nguyen Van Thuan, mentioned that the later book was then in development and that it would be the "authoritative synthesis of the social teaching of the Church" (vii).

51. For lengthier studies of this topic, see I. G. Gabriel, "Eigentum im Dienste des Menschen. Die Lhre zum Eigentum in den päpistlichen Enzykliken von Rerum novarum bis Centesimus annus und die Entwicklung in Oesterreich im Ueberblick," in *Der Mensch is der Weg der Kirche. Festschrift für Johannes Schasching*, ed. H. Schambeck and R. Weiler (Berlin: Dunker and Humblot, 1992), 17–33; Johan Verstraeten, "Eigendomsrecht herdacht. Het recht van de mens op een rechtmatig deel van de goederen," *Communio* 23 (1998): 1, 29–47.

52. It made this claim by balancing seemingly incompatible approaches to defending a person's right to private property. In an important article on this topic, Ernest Fortin, "'Sacred and Inviolable': *Rerum Novarum* and Natural Rights," *Theological Studies* 53 (1992): 203–33, critiqued *Rerum novarum* (mostly, *Quadragessimo anno* and later Catholic social teaching more briefly) for its claim to being Thomistic but adopting the language of Locke and doing justice to neither in the process. Fortin pointed out that *Rerum novarum* enshrined a person's right to private property both in civil law (i.e., it is a matter of law that man is able to hold private property, à la Aquinas, in *RN* 22) and in natural law (i.e., property is a *sacred* and *inviolable* right, à la Locke and, later, Adam Smith, in *RN* 9 and 46) at the same time. Such a synthesis, according to Fortin, fostered a rights-oriented culture within and without the Church. Moreover, it continues to make it difficult for the Church to support actions by civil authorities who might wish to restrict property rights when presented with injustice.

53. QA 50–52. This teaching would continue in *Gaudium et spes* (1965) and *Populorum progressio* (1967).

teaching discourse a concept that Pius XI would himself recall in later documents (e.g., *Sertum Laetitiae*), that of the universal destination of the world's goods.

Three decades later Pope John XXIII issued *Mater et magistra* (1961). In the balance of communitarian versus individual rights to private property, the balance in this encyclical continued to tip slightly towards the former, for John XXIII emphasized the universal destination of the earth's goods, paying particular attention to the needs of poor, rural farmers oppressed by ever-decreasing prices in the face of increasing, global competition. Only with *Gaudium et spes* (1965) was a link drawn between the right of all to the earth's goods and the right of poor people to take from wealthy people what they need for survival (see *GS* 69). Then, in 1981, the various threads of private property teaching are drawn together when Pope John Paul II, in his encyclical *Laborem exercens*, returned to an earlier theme that the right to private property is to be subordinated to common use. Work is the source of property, this encyclical argued, and property is to be used to serve the furthering needs of labor. Thus, corporations that pursue capital (i.e., possessions, property) in order to diminish labor transgress the nature of capital and so deny the common use of goods. John Paul II extended this argument even further in his encyclical *Centesimus annus* (1991). In it, he argued the ethical criterion for owning the means of production (in the agrarian as well as in the business sector, including the ownership of corporate stocks) is the creation of meaningful work (see §43). Thus, governments, corporations, and trans-national institutions are obliged to ensure human persons have access to meaningful work through the common use of property, a means of production.

Though brief, this survey provides some sense of the history the 2004 *Compendium* sought to capture. At least three elements of the Church's understanding of private property are summarized within it. First, the compendium reminds its readers that Catholic social teaching has situated private property's origin in the teaching of Genesis 1:28 that humans multiply, fill the earth, and subdue it. "By means of work and making use of the gift of intelligence, people . . . 'make part of the earth [their] own.'"[54] Consequently, the acquisition of private property is not, from the beginning, an expression of

---

54. Pontifical Council, *Compendium*, 99, drawing, as the compendium does, on a citation from John Paul II's encyclical *Centesimus annus* 6.

sin but an expression of human freedom to fulfill the command of God. As discussed earlier, this was not the teaching of the Fathers, for they were unequivocal in their understanding that private property had its origins in avarice, and avarice began with the sin of Adam and Eve. However, a second point made in the compendium counter-balances its seeming praise for private property. The compendium teaches that the opportunity to acquire private property ought to be made accessible to all, for only in such an environment may authentic "social and democratic economic policy" thrive. [55] Thus, private property is not an absolute right in Catholic social teaching. Rather, "the right to private property is subordinated to the right to common use."[56] In other words, corresponding to a celebration of private property is a celebration that the earth's goods were created by God for the enjoyment of all. Every person must be willing to distribute his or her private property to others in accordance with the need(s) of others. The third component to private property in Catholic social teaching, which corresponds to the second, is its social function. Whereas the second component emphasized each person's responsibility to share what he or she has with others, this third component considers the responsibility had by private property's owner to consider what might be the social effects associated with possessing that property. According to the compendium, the owners of private property must always bear in mind the common good. "From this there arises the duty on the part of owners not to let the goods in their possession go idle and to channel them to productive activity, even entrusting them to others who are desirous and capable of putting them to use in production."[57] Moreover, this is not to be limited to the agrarian sphere of developing nations but also to include the knowledge economy of more developed nations. Indeed, Catholic social teaching is clear that it is incumbent upon those who possess knowledge and technical skills to share such "property" with the poor in order that the poor may have access to the same benefits as are obtainable in the more developed economies.[58]

55. Pontifical Council, *Compendium*, 99.

56. Ibid. This goes back to Thomas Aquinas, according to whom only the *usus communis rerum* is natural law. Private property is subordinate to the *usus communitarium*. Private property, then, is only a "good idea" to Aquinas, which he has taken over from Aristotle et al. (see Aquinas, *ST* II.2.Q.66., art. 1 and 2; Aristotle, *Politics*, book II, v, 1263a).

57. Pontifical Council, *Compendium*, 100.

58. Ibid., 101–2.

These things having been said, it is clear that Catholic social teaching has grown in its appreciation for the difficulties of private property. Certainly, one is able to appreciate the influence of historical context on the particular arguments of each Catholic social teaching document. Oppression of workers in the late 1800s was as much an influence on *RN* as, for example, was globalization of trade and agriculture on *Mater et magistra* and was the burgeoning "knowledge economy" on *Laborem exercens*. By 2004, it is clear that Catholic social teaching has recognized the "problem" with private property can only be solved with an appeal to the common good. It argued private property is, by nature, good, but that every person must subordinate his or her demand to own property to the needs of others. This, of course, will require that every person make some determination about the real needs of others, and this decision is either helped or hurt by one's ability to accurately apply the somewhat elusive criteria of the "common good."

## Conclusion

Early Christian teaching on detachment from private property took its cues from the classical and philosophical context that preceded it, in which it was shown there existed a tension between the ideal of common property and the judicial reality of protecting private property rights. The Church Fathers, including Basil, could not avoid holding in tension the same things. Yet, the Fathers paid greater attention than did the classical authors to the injustices created by unmitigated accumulation of wealth and property. They advocated for a "sufficiency" test; to pass the test, a person needed to detach him or herself from private property. Basil's use of the detachment principle revealed that attitudes towards property are a barometer of one's Christian faith. This is why the principle could function hermeneutically in so many ways—economically, anthropologically, theologically, and eschatologically. It was an extremely versatile, pastoral tool.

Towards the beginning of this paper I suggested that Basil's homily is helpful for purposes of constructing a dialogue between patristic and modern Catholic social thought because its theological ideas in relation to detachment open up for us a Ricoeurian "world in front of the text." Catholic social thought today nowhere advocates for detachment from private property in the sense that we have seen from Basil and other Fathers. Its liberationist periphery aims at a reversal of property fortunes rather than a change in attitude, and official church documents uphold private property as a constitutive expression of human dignity and freedom. The patristic world's wide concern with detachment has been lost. A recovery of the world in front of Basil's homily for Catholic social thought today may include, among other things, a repudiation of specific manifestations of avarice, a renewal of teaching about God's providential care of the world (that may not include material prosperity), and a reengagement with eschatology in the biblical texts. Catholic social thought today likes to think of itself as concerned with charity rather than justice, for only the former is within the scope of its expertise; yet, putting a human face on avarice and on destitution—which Basil does in his homily—may open further doors of justice via charity.

*Thomas Hughson, S.J.*

# 9. Social Justice in Lactantius's *Divine Institutes*

## An Exploration

This inquiry interprets a fourth-century Church Father's main work in reference to social justice, a characteristic theme in Catholic social thought and Catholic social teaching.[1] The overall perspective is postcritical in the sense of probing for a relation between an ancient text and a modern or post-modern context in Church and world. That approach does not derogate from critical study, on which it relies, though a postcritical purpose inherently assumes that readers from later contexts can bring new questions to the text as well as submit to its otherness. Moving from critical exegesis of a biblical passage to preaching an application would be parallel to this.[2] Because of different starting-points, the former ready to distance itself from the modern context, the latter not, different habits of mind are operative in critical and postcritical study of an ancient text.[3] The tension between them is inevitable

1. "Catholic social thought" is roughly equivalent to another concept, "social Catholicism." They both encompass local, pastoral, grass-roots initiatives, and thinking throughout the Church in reciprocity with official Catholic social teaching. Catholic social thought and social Catholicism go beyond a purely top-down idea of Catholic social teaching.

2. Brian Daley upholds both historical-critical study of the Bible and the Church Fathers' theological, figural mode of biblical exegesis oriented to preaching, worship, and prayer. "Is Patristic Exegesis Still Usable? Some Reflections on Early Christian Interpretation of the Psalms," in *The Art of Reading Scripture,* ed. Ellen F. Davis and Richard B. Hays (Grand Rapids, Mich.: Eerdmans Publishing, 2003), 69–88.

3. This is clear in Hans-Georg Gadamer's distinction between a legal historian and a judge as they

and understandable. Critical analysis may have reason to correct or challenge factual matters in a postcritical interpretation. Postcritical application completes critical study by integrating application into interpretation—respect for each task is appropriate.

Admittedly, while hermeneutics shows the legitimacy of postcritical questions and offers some main orientations in seeking answers, neither questions nor answers have a controlled precision comparable to critical investigation into, for example, paleography or the date and authenticity of a text. So it may be most forthright to treat postcritical application as a hypothesis on an ancient text's meaningfulness today. But then, arguing for a hypothesis rather than establishing certainty after certainty belongs to critical study too.

The textual point of departure here is *From Irenaeus to Grotius: A Sourcebook of Christian Political Thought 100–1626*.[4] Readers of this valuable anthology come across excerpts from books V and VI of Lacantius's *Divine Institutes* likely to intrigue anyone interested in Catholic social thought and social justice. The editors point out that Lactantius (ca. 250–325 CE) was "the first Christian thinker to subject the idea of *justice* to serious analysis."[5] More to the point, passages seem to present a Christian critique of the structure of imperial society, not just the vices, errors, and follies of individuals.

For instance, in the following excerpt Lactantius criticizes the greed of a whole sector of Roman society, the prosperous who multiply their possessions at the expense of others left poorer by this rapacity. And he situates this tendency within an overall picture of societal decline from the Golden Age of King Saturn to the more acquisitive Age of Jupiter reflected in Virgil's *Aeniad*, still a potent epic of Roman identity in late antiquity.

---

pore over legal history. The judge has an eye toward application and an exercise of *phronesis*, prudence, in making a legal decision on a case before him or her. For Gadamer and hermeneutics the judge represents the situation of all knowers while the legal historian prescinds from application. Gadamer does not rule that out altogether but does not see it as exemplary, universal, and complete either. Hans-Georg Gadamer, *Truth and Method*, 2nd rev. ed., trans. Joel Weinsheimer and Donald G.Marshall (New York: Continuum Books, 1999), especially the section on "The Recovery of the Fundamental Hermeneutical Problem," 307–41. This English edition is based on the revised, expanded 5th German edition of *Wahrheit und Methode*, in *Gesammelte Werken* 1 (Tübingen: Mohr, 1986); Mohr published the first German edition at Tübingen in 1960.

4. Oliver O'Donovan and Joan Lockwood O'Donovan, eds., *From Irenaeus to Grotius: A Sourcebook in Christian Political Thought 100–1626* (Grand Rapids, Mich.: Eerdmans, 1999), 46–55. The editors translated excerpts from the *Divini Institutiones* in CSEL 19.

5. Ibid., 46–47.

The source of all these evils is greed and greed presumably erupted out of contempt for the true superior power [God]. Not merely did people of any prosperity fail to share with others but they also seized the property of others, diverting everything to private gain, and what had previously been worked even by individuals for the benefit of everyone was now piled up in the houses of a few.[6]

This study asks, Does further analysis tend to substantiate, modify, or negate thinking about the *Divine Institutes* in reference to social justice and Catholic social thought? Or, to the contrary when it came to matters of social existence in late antiquity did Lactantius focus on justice as a practical matter of legitimate Christian self-interest seeking exemption from imperial coercion, so that as Peter Garnsey comments, "a good Emperor for Lactantius is above all one who leaves Christians undisturbed"?[7] If the *Divine Institutes* have a broader interest in justice than this, did the *Divine Institutes* also carry a prospect of social change toward social justice?

## Ancient and Modern Otherness

A complication immediately arises from the larger, contextual issue of whether Church Fathers in general had any idea of and interest in changing the imperial status quo. Both G. E. M. de Ste. Croix[8] and Pauline Allen[9] say in variant ways that the Church Fathers accepted the societal status quo as a given. Just the opposite has been the case, indeed the very purpose, for Cath-

6. Lactantius, *Divini Institutiones*, book V, 6.1, in *Lactantius: Divine Institutes*, Translated Texts for Historians 40, trans. Anthony Bowen and Peter Garnsey (Liverpool: Liverpool University Press, 2003), 292. In the Bowen and Garnsey translation book V follows the Latin text in Pierre Monat, *Sources Chrétiennes, Lactance: Institutions Divines, Livre V, Tome I*, Introduction, Texte critique, traduction par Pierre Monat (Paris: Éditons du Cerf, 1973). The translation of book VI follows the Latin text in *Opera Omnia*, L. Caeli Firminani Lactanti, in *Pars I, Sectio I Divine Institutiones et Epitome Divinarum Institutionum*, ed. Samuel Brandt (Vienna: F. Tempsky, 1890).

7. Peter Garnsey, whom the Preface identifies as primary author of the Introduction to *Lactantius: Divine Institutes*, 43. This view of Lactantius's good emperor is more circumscribed than that of Elizabeth DePalma Digeser, in *The Making of a Christian Empire: Lactantius and Rome* (Ithaca, N.Y.: Cornell University Press, 2000). She argues convincingly that book V, 19–23, makes a case for religious toleration and/or concord as imperial policy.

8. G. E. M. de Ste. Croix, "Early Christian Attitudes to Property and Slavery," in *Church, Society, and Politics*, Papers Read at the Thirteenth Summer Meeting and the Fourteenth Winter Meeting of the Ecclesiastical History Society, ed. Derek Baker (Oxford: Blackwell, 1975), 1–38.

9. Pauline Allen, "Reading Patristic Socio-Ethical Texts," printed paper presented at the Catholic University of Leuven Expert Seminar on Patristics and Catholic Social Teaching, September 1–3, 2007, 1–8.

olic social thought and Catholic social teaching. The explanation of patristic indifference from de Ste. Croix is that, "precisely the exclusive concentration of the early Christians upon the personal relations between man and man, or man and God, and their complete indifference, as Christians, to the institutions of the world in which they lived, that prevented Christianity from even having much effect for good upon the relations between man and man."[10] This individualism contrasted with Israel's prophets, with Plato and Aristotle too. They all, according to de Ste. Croix, held that a society had to "have good institutions" before people "could live the good life within it."[11] But the early Church, in this view, gave up on creating a good society with good institutions.

The early Christians settled instead for discovering how individuals can convert to the gospel and become holy in an indifferent or hostile society with rotten institutions they did not try to change. In a more nuanced way referring to patristic homilies and cautioning against "the anachronistic treatment of patristic social-ethical texts," Allen takes a position similar to de Ste. Croix's, stating outright that, "the Fathers . . . had no intention of changing the status quo."[12]

Before I support Allen's insistence on avoiding anachronism, I feel obliged to mention in a preliminary way why I cannot give unqualified assent to statement that "the Fathers . . . had no intention of changing the status quo" or to de Ste. Croix's conclusion that the early Church and by implication the Church Fathers had no interest in changing imperial institutions. To whatever extent that general position may be valid, it does not apply with completeness to Lacantius's *Divine Institutes*. It does not apply completely because this text is all about proposed change in the (declining unless reversed) status quo of the empire. The *Divine Institutes* advocated new knowledge of God, new practice of virtue, and new public law and policy touching religious tolerance.[13]

Still, patristic acceptance of the imperial status quo applies to some extent because in the *Divine Institutes*, Peter Garnsey remarks, "there is no programme of political and legal reforms put together for the benefit of Con-

---

10. Ibid., 36.                                    11. Ibid., 37.
12. Allen, 3–4.
13. Digeser also argues in her first chapter that the *Divine Institutes* proposed an end to the Diocletian "Dominate" (emperor as *deus et dominus*) by a return under Constantine to the principate (emperor as human *princeps* in the Senate) modeled on Augustus.

stantine."[14] I will submit an argument for thinking that the *Divine Institutes* contained a definite plan if not a programme for implementing what Lactantius propounded. And in that light the theme of *aequitas* in Lacantius's text becomes a point of affinity and continuity with Catholic social thought on social justice.

Modern readers interested in Catholic social thought and social justice might be thought likely to be guilty of anachronistic treatment of patristic social-ethical texts. So, I wish to acknowledge at the outset the essential role for otherness and critical study. Emphasis on difference or otherness corrects a naïve impression of seamless sameness between a reader's reality and the era, culture, language, mentality, place in the course of history, social structures, and frame of reference in a text and the world behind the text. A leaving behind of preconceptions and expectations has to occur. That denial of universality in a reader's outlook opens the door to discovery of others in a past to which a text brings the reader. But the past doesn't fit into the personal and institutional patterns of the present.

This is true for Lactantius and the *Divine Institutes*. His was a very different era in which Christianity underwent a sudden reversal from persecution to excellent public standing and a new condition of power and responsibility. Originally from North Africa, he studied with fellow North African Arnobius, converted from paganism to Christian faith as an adult, gained renown as the premier rhetorician in the Roman empire of his time, and was appointed to a prestigious academic post in Nicomedia. During Diocletian's Great Persecution (303–305 CE) he lost the position. Soon after, Lactantius composed the *Divine Institutes* to rebut ideas that had justified a policy of torture and death for professing Christians on behalf of imperial polytheism, which was supposed to insure imperial unity and security. With Constantine's accession he reascended to the upper echelon of imperial society, arriving at the western court in Trier where he instructed Crispus, the ill-fated son of Constantine, possibly starting in 310 CE.[15] The *Divine Institutes* may have been published as early as 310 CE, with a second edition coming later. The exact dates of both are not certain to the year. The date of the second edition remains a matter of controversy.[16]

14. Garnsey and Bowen, *Divine Institutes*, 36.
15. Constantine had Crispus executed in 326 CE for reasons unknown.
16. This is the dating given by Digeser, 12, based on the work of Eberhard Heck that Digeser foot-

Catholic social thought and Catholic social teaching never have tolerated slavery. Lacantius's text did not support slavery but abolishing it was not its chief objective either. Slavery, despite Christian misgivings and some measures by a few bishops, was an institution accepted in practice within a Roman empire absorbing the influence of Christianity very slowly. Disciplinary killing of a slave was legally permissible if it did not follow a long train of cruelty and abuse.[17] A Constantinian innovation in law granted legal status to the practice of an owner emancipating a slave within the walls of a church.[18] However, "slavery remained a structural element in the Roman economy throughout late antiquity," although "it seems to have lost the role it had played in early imperial Italy as a dominant mode of production."[19] The Church became a landholder and so had slaves working on its properties. Constantine did outlaw tattooing the face of a slave, because the face reflected the image of God.[20] It is fair to say that Paul's Letter to Philemon rather than abolition of slavery represented a common Christian view.

De Ste. Croix concludes that Christian thinking did not place the institution of slavery in doubt, because it was an "absolute necessity for the dominant classes of the greco-roman world to maintain those social institutions upon which their whole privileged position depended, and which they were not willing, or even able, to forego."[21] Asking why Christianity produced no important change for the better in Graeco-Roman society, de Ste. Croix discounts the completeness of a standard answer that Jesus and the early Church had no interest in "social, economic, or political institutions" but only in relations between humans and God and interpersonal relations among human beings.[22] De Ste. Croix notes that Paul in Romans 13:1–10 advised compliance with imperial authorities and this sufficed for New Testament advice on how Christians should relate to political institutions.[23]

---

notes as 21, on 147. The outside parameters for composition have to be the end of the Great Persecution in 305 CE and 324 CE, when Constantine's letter to the eastern provinces contained ideas from the *Divine Institutes*. For the second edition, 307 CE–ca. 312 CE seems the likeliest period.

17. Caroline Humfress, "Civil Law and Social Life," in *The Cambridge Companion to the Age of Constantine,* ed. Noel Lenski (Cambridge University Press, 2006), 205–23.

18. Ibid., 220.

19. George Depeyrot, "Economy and Society," trans. Noel Lanski, in *The Cambridge Companion to the Age of Constantine,* ed., Noel Lenski, 226–52, at 231.

20. Ibid.                                                     21. De Ste. Croix, 24.

22. Ibid., 36.

23. Romans 13 by itself is not the key to how Paul or the early Church saw the relation between

So I do want to agree with de Ste. Croix and Allen as well as others who insist on not reading the Church Fathers as if they proceeded from the same context and framework of assumptions as do modern readers concerned about social justice. Mountainous differences in context and content divide the *Divine Institutes* from modern Catholic social thought. Critical study remains a sine qua non. Precritical incorporation of patristic quotations into Catholic social teaching is regrettable.[24] At the same time there are reasons to open up space for postcritical application of patristic texts in contemporary Church life and thought. The hermeneutical essay by Reimund Bieringer is a premise for exploring whether or not anything with an affinity to social justice can be found in the *Divine Institutes*.[25]

## Social Change and Social Justice in a Patristic Text?

What is social justice in Catholic social thought and Catholic social teaching? Social justice is about the common good of a society. What is the common good? According to *Gaudium et spes*, the common good "embraces the sum of those conditions of social life by which individuals, families, and groups can achieve their own fulfillment in a relatively thorough and ready way."[26] In more detail, the common good includes the major institutions (political, economic, social, cultural, religious) of the society, and the basic structure of the society.

Christianity and the empire. See Walter Pilgrim, *Uneasy Neighbors: Church and State in the New Testament* (Minneapolis: Fortress, 1999).

24. Brian Matz with Johan Leemans and Johan Verstraeten, "Position Paper: The Church Fathers and Catholic Social Thought," printed paper read at the Seminar on the Church Fathers and Catholic Social Thought, Catholic University of Leuven, September 1–3, 2007, 1–28. See also Brian Matz, "Problematic Uses of Patristic Sources in the Documents of Catholic Social Thought," *Journal of Catholic Social Thought* 4 (2007): 2:459–85.

25. Reimund Bieringer, "Texts That Create a Future: The Function of Ancient Texts for Theology Today," printed paper read during the Seminar on Church Fathers and Catholic Social Thought, 1–16 at 2–9; Francois X. Amherdt, "The Utility of Paul Ricouer's Hermeneutical Theory for Reading Theological and Patristic Texts: Distanciation of a Text and Hermeneutical Arc," printed paper read during the Seminar on Church Fathers and Catholic Social Thought, September 3–5, 2007, 1–15.

26. Vatican Council II, *The Pastoral Constitution on the Church in the Modern World (Gaudium et spes)*, in *The Documents of Vatican II*, ed. Walter M. Abbott, S.J., trans. ed. Joseph Gallagher (New York: Guild Press, 1966), 199–316 at 284. The *Compendium of the Social Doctrine of the Church* states that, "Social justice concerns . . . the social, political, and economic aspects and, above all, the structural dimensions of problems and their respective solutions," Pontifical Council on Justice and Peace; English trans. Libreria Editrice Vaticana (2005), 201, nn 89–90.

Major institutions are the specific mode of governance (monarchy, parliamentary democracy, democratic republic, democracy, or dictatorship), the type of economy (minimally regulated free market, highly regulated free market, state-run, centralized economy, or state capitalism), family structure (primacy of extended family, or of the nuclear family), common cultural meanings, and whatever religion(s) animates the culture. The basic structure is the overall, combined, net effect of the operations of the major institutions.[27] Commitment to social justice involves comparing these structural aspects and their effects with requirements of human dignity, human rights, and the common good.[28]

Social justice, as part of the virtue of justice, is other-directed.[29] Social justice is the successor to general justice. Orientation beyond an individual, family, or group to the common good can be immanent in all manner of virtuous acts, including distributive and commutative justice.[30] "The virtue of a good citizen is general justice, whereby the person is directed to the common good."[31] Social justice has a first and defining aspect of as a person's and a group's active contribution to the common good of society. A second aspect is a responsibility on the part of society to put conditions in place, as far as possible, that enable people to fulfill their duty to the common good.[32] This

27. John Rawls's influential *A Theory of Justice* (Cambridge, Mass.: Harvard University Press, 1971, rev. ed. 1999) conceives social justice as an attribute of what he calls a society's "basic structure." The basic structure is the combined, operational effects of the major political, economic, cultural, and social institutions as potential for people's life-opportunities. I am taking from Rawls his analytic distinction between major institutions and basic structure, but not his arguments or whole position.

28. In Duane Alwin's analysis, "Justice sentiments derive from a comparison . . . of the real with the ideal in a particular context," "Social Justice," in *Encyclopedia of Sociology* 4, ed. Edgar F. Borgatta and Rhonda J. V. Montgomery (New York: Macmillan, 2000), 2695–711 at 2696.

29. Aquinas remarks that, "the rightness of other moral virtues is not determined apart from the frame of mind of the person acting," adding that justice has its rightness "even abstracting from the temper in which it is done" *(qualiter ab agente fiat)*, *Summa Theologiae* 37, 2a2ae, Q. 57, art. 1.

30. Jean-Yves Calvez, S.J., "Social Justice," in *The New Catholic Encyclopedia* 13 (Palatine, Ill.: Jack Heraghty, repr.1981), 318–21 at 319.

31. Thomas Aquinas translated and quoted by David Hollenbach in *The Common Good and Christian Ethics* (Cambridge: Cambridge University Press, 2002), 195. See the translation, introduction, notes, and glossary by Thomas Gilby, O.P., *Justice,* vol. 37, in the Blackfriars' *Summa Theologiae* (2a2ae. 57–62) (New York: McGraw Hill, 1975), Q. 58, art. 6. Hollenbach's translation is clearer than Gilby's ("this last [virtue . . . of a good citizen] is general justice, which governs our acts for the common good"), 35.

32. Hollenbach explains and applies general or social justice to the split between affluent American suburbs and struggling inner cities in "Poverty, Justice, and the Good of the City," in *The Common Good and Christian Ethics,* 173–211, esp. 190–200.

does not put entitlements into first place but demands certain kinds in second place if they would be necessary means to factual conditions enabling all to contribute to and participate in the major institutions of society.

Consequently, an interest in social justice leads immediately to seeking to analyze how in fact the basic structure affects people, how it succeeds or not in enabling people, especially the poor, vulnerable, and marginalized, to participate in the basic institutions.

Bryan Hehir observes that social justice continues the classic focus on the common good but also incorporates new insight into "the structured organization of society" with emphasis on "the need to shape the institutional patterns of social life in accord with the demands of justice so that commutative and distributive justice may be more easily fulfilled."[33] Social justice in Catholic social thought and Catholic social teaching implies readiness to reshape the institutional patterns of social life in accord with justice, especially for the poor and marginalized. If readiness for social change were altogether missing from the *Divine Institutes*, there would be less continuity with Catholic social thought and Catholic social teaching. Did the *Divine Institutes*, then, instantiate a general patristic indifference to changing the status quo? The following section explains why the answer is no.

## The Emperor as Agent of Transformation

Book V of the *Divine Institutes* proposes *aequitas* (equity) as a basic form of justice in human relationships that is due to God creating all human beings as *imago Dei* equal in humanity. The opposite of *aequitas*, varying types of inequity, were rife throughout the empire, dividing rich from poor, elite from the hoi polloi, citizens from noncitizens, slaves from owners, powerful from powerless. Book V presents a manifesto for reform of the empire under the law of God now clearly known from Christian sources. It drew, Monat says, "*de la sagesse classique et de la révélation chrétienne*," on the topic of justice.[34] I think it accurate to conceive these two sources not only as a confluence but as in an ordered relationship in which the biblical revelation *(révélation chretienne)* is pri-

33. Bryan Hehir, "Social Justice," in *HarperCollins Encyclopedia of Catholicism*, ed. Richard McBein (San Francisco: HarperSanFrancisco, 1995), 1203–4 at 1204.

34. Monat, *Institutions Divines, Livre V, Tome I*, 19.

mary yet mediated through the classical heritage *(sagesse classique)*. Christian revelation including the whole Bible was that in whose light Lactantius interpreted, corrected, criticized, and also appreciated the classical heritage.

The most influential classical source, according to Monat, was the work of Cicero, above all *De republica*, *De legibus*, and *De officiis*.[35] In the *Divine Institutes*, justice was the chief virtue and comprised piety *(pietas)* as duties in relation to God, and equality or equity *(aequitas)* as duties in human relationships. Book V concentrated on *aequitas*, equity, applying it across a broad range of meaning, relations, and conduct. Book V proposed a change in imperial mores in the direction of respect for human dignity *(imago Dei)* and consequent justice as equity *(aequitas)*.

The *Divine Institutes* did not lack a plan for the transformation of imperial society toward equity by political means. The plan was the formation of a Christian conscience in Emperor Constantine, whom the additions made the first and most important auditor and reader of Lacantius's *Divine Institutes*. The essential political means for transformation was first of all the thinking, deciding, and acting of the emperor. After Constantine defeated Licinius in 324 CE he had supreme civil power in the empire and was the one who could bring about change. The emperor was the law in person, not under the law. Constantine was in a position to make and enforce laws better respecting the law of God, starting with *aequitas*, known in Christianity. Without a changed emperor there could be little expectation of a changed empire.

A Constantine educated by the *Divine Institutes* in the political implications of Christian faith would be in a position to set about some steps to reform the major institutions of the empire. The Senate was a weakened institution. The army was not capable of a spiritually based reform of imperial policies. Ordinary citizens and the many noncitizens, not to mention slaves, were not a force to be reckoned with politically. True, this was not a set of measures and a programme of reforms, as Garnsey rightly notes, but it was a plan to make reform effective and in that sense was intended as a source of change in the status quo by the indispensable means of imperial authority and policy.

The validity of this proposal depends on according a high level of significance to dedicatory additions to the text of the *Divine Institutes*, originally

35. Ibid., 21–24.

composed without the prospect of a Christian emperor and so without the goal of forming an emperor in his conscience. Lactantius did not revise the text in a wholesale way after Constantine's conversion, usually dated to 312 CE. He introduced minor additions that changed large sections from indirect to discourse directed to Constantine.[36] This can only mean that the modified text had the emperor as first, in the sense of most important, reader. Lactantius did not adjust the arguments or content. The advent of a Christian emperor apparently did not so reconstitute the empire as to make Lacantius's criticisms and proposals inapplicable. He did not forbear bringing the text's socio-religious critique to bear upon polytheistic worship, on pervasive injustice, on greed, and on error about the meaning of life just because Constantine's rule replaced that of Diocletian and the tetrarchs.

Lacantius's quantitatively minor additions (e.g., bk I 1.13–14, bk. II 1.2, bk. III 1.1, bk. IV 1.1, bk. V 1.1, bk. VI 3.1, bk. VII 26.10–16) can be understood not as honorific and obsequious platitudes but as an implied charge of responsibility. Positioned at or near the heads of six chapters and near the end of the work, they frame the whole *Divine Institutes* as a dialogue between Lacantius's text and a "you."[37] Constantine is the identified singular "you" to whom Lactantius dedicates the work as a whole. Sometimes, when the text uses a plural "you," not a singular in reference to the emperor as a definite, named, anticipated auditor,[38] that plural "you" (e.g., book II 18 "*ad cuius spectaculum vos excitiavit ille artifex vester deus*") addresses a generic, indefinite plurality of readers and hearers.[39] They are the usual suspects identified as the original audience for the *Divine Institutes*: educated non-Christian monotheists and educated Christians irresolute under government pressure.

Adding direct discourse to Constantine and appealing to his sense of Christian duty alters that original readership. It becomes as if Constantine was the very one for whom and to whom the *Divine Institutes*, with book V's heavy emphasis on equity, was written. Most of it was composed before his conversion, so he could not have been the original audience. Constantine be-

36. See Bowen, *Lactantius: Divine Institutes*, xi.

37. This excludes use of the figure of speech, apostrophe, that conducts a dialogue with a figure in the text as a singular "you," as happens with Cicero in book II 3.4; Bowen and Garnsey, 123; Brandt, 104.

38. Digeser, 12–13, refers to Constantine as among the "first auditors" of the *Divine Institutes* delivered as a series of lectures by Lactantius between 310 and 313 CE.

39. Brandt, 102.

came the primary audience or readership by means of the revisions that added direct address to him. A dialogical linguistic structure organizes the whole final text, which returns again and again to first person discourse, sometimes in the singular number, I, and sometimes as the plural, "we." The grammatical structure of first person discourse necessarily involves a "you," singular or plural. The grammar of speech and writing allows no alternative to an implied or explicit "you" when words come from an "I" or "we." Even a soliloquy has an imaginary audience, and the *Divine Institutes* is no soliloquy. Constantine was the privileged hearer and reader, though not by that fact the only one. The dialogical structure already directed the text to the plural, anonymous "you" of readers or hearers. The additions focused the dialogical structure on Constantine.

Dedicating and directing it to Constantine did not turn the work into a meditation for Constantine's private spirituality. The revised text spoke to Constantine precisely as emperor uniquely under God and with God. The vista opened by the seven books is empire-wide not local, and was not restricted to Christians. Book VII 26.10b tells the emperor that "The providence of the most high godhead has promoted you to supreme power so that you can in the trueness of your piety rescind the wicked decrees of others, correct error, provide for the safety of men in your fatherly kindness, and finally remove from public life such evil men."[40] The "wicked decrees of others" probably referred to previous policies by Diocletian and other emperors, along with lesser civil authorities complying with and carrying out imperial commands.

The dialogical structure and the imperial focus in the text substantiate the idea that Constantine was not only the most highly placed, most august reader but the principal agent, providentially raised up, for the imperial transformation put forward by the *Divine Institutes*. Now, because the substance of Lacantius's text antedated Constantine's accession, it could be objected that the content was originally an idealistic utopia without too much chance of practical implementation. In regard to the unrevised text Allen, Garnsey, and to some extent Young are correct in doubting or denying that it had anything like a practical plan for implementation. The argument here, however, is about

---

40. Bowen and Garnsey, book VII 26.10b. This belongs to one (10a–10g) of several passages in MSS S and G that Brandt did not incorporate into the Latin text, putting it into a footnote instead, 668.

the text after its quantitatively minor but qualitatively major revisions once Constantine has become emperor.

The education of Constantine in the duties of a Christian emperor was the plan for the transformation of imperial society.[41] How well that plan worked is another matter. The proposal here is only that the *Divine Institutes* had a practical plan by which, especially, *aequitas* could be put in place in imperial society. The emperor had a unique capacity, and as Lactantius saw it, a singular responsibility to transform the empire according to the law of God and *aequitas* was a large part of that. Constantine's conversion was a golden, providential opportunity for Lactantius.

Garnsey comments that Lactantius did not present Constantine with a series of detailed public policy measures and legal reforms. This is true. And yet a plausible reason was that Constantine as emperor was himself source of policy. Others might be deputed to draft the legal formulae but the emperor's authority and power were the principal means for initiating and effectively installing reformed policies. In the imperial court there were those who devised legal measures for presentation to the emperor but Lactantius was not among them.

Likewise, considering the emperor as agent of transformation answers a question raised by Frances Young about *aequitas* in book V.[42] Young first observes that Lacantius's claim that Christians, rich and poor, slave and master, think of themselves as equal "might seem to have political implications, but it turns out that Christians measure things 'not by the body but by the spirit'—in lowliness of mind, in humility, Christians are on an equality (V 15)." Equity among Christians in possessing virtues would not be public equity in society. So she puts a question, "Is equity merely spiritual then?"[43]

Answering in the negative, she finds evidence for equity in concrete action in book VI's description of Christian virtue practiced in almsgiving, care for widows and orphans, and hospitality to strangers. Moreover, equity is a

41. In this, perhaps the *Divine Institutes* anticipated medieval and early modern treatises designed for the education of kings and princes in their duties in light of Christian faith and justice, in hopes of enlightening and influencing their decisions away from tyranny (rule for the benefit of the ruler) and toward just governance (rule for the sake of the ruled).

42. Frances Young, "Christianity," in *The Cambridge History of Greek and Roman Political Thought*, ed. Christopher Rowe and Malcolm Schofield (Cambridge: Cambridge University Press, 2000), 636–60 at 657.

43. Ibid.

chief part or stream of justice that comes to perfection in actions such as generosity to the blind, lame, and destitute (VI 11). So equity in the *Divine Institutes* is not "merely spiritual" because it becomes active, visible, and concrete in practice.

Young's question springs from wondering whether or not equity has "political implications." She refers to visible Christian conduct governed by the universal divine law in contrast to following a multitude of civil laws designed out of utility in various countries. Can anything else be said to clarify the positive content of the political implications of the *Divine Institutes* on equity? Yes, there is Young's other idea, that the *Divine Institutes* offers a vision for the transformation of imperial society. This is true. But she leaves the kind of transformation undefined. It could be that this transformation was to be a moral conversion of individuals one by one. That would not be political in the strong sense of involving governance and law but eventually could become political in the weak sense of morally reformed individuals entering civil service and influencing the administration of law. Does equity have political implications in the strong sense of involving governance and public policy? Lactantius' plan for implementation by means of a reformed emperor educated in the duties of Christian faith was political in that sense. And that makes the *Divine Institutes* an exception to patristic indifference toward changing the social status quo.

## The *Divine Institutes* and Catholic Social Thought

The public scope in the exercise of Christian virtue adverted to by Young, together with the public nature of justice drawn from Cicero and Scripture pointed out by Monat, and the dedicating of the *Divine Institutes* to Emperor Constantine permit a conclusion contrary to de Ste. Croix's and Allen's idea of an early Church indifferent to imperial society in its structural aspects. To the contrary, in the *Divine Institutes* a Church Father presented the vision of a revised basic structure of early fourth-century imperial society as well as of its major political institution, the emperor, with special attention to the plight of the poor and powerless.[44] Lactantius, that is, had done social analysis, pre-

---

44. On reforming the major institution that is mode of governance, see also Digeser's discussion of Lactantius's influence on Constantine's religious policy, 121–43.

sented contrary monotheistic and Christian ideals for a more just social order, and aimed this at the number one reader and most powerful-decision-maker, Emperor Constantine. That allows a conclusion that the *Divine Institutes* has some affinity with social justice in Catholic social thought.

Book V presents equity as a norm and virtue with a political dimension in its exercise, in the sense that equity challenged Constantine and imperial government to move in the direction of protecting the poor from exploitation by the wealthy and powerful. Equity, like social justice, was not only a virtue in persons but also a desired societal goal. It must be conceded to de Ste. Croix, Allen, and Garnsey that book V treats equity less as a restructuring of society law by law and more as a matter of an instruction in a value that can change consciences. The key conscience, nonetheless, was Constantine's. Identifying the primary decision-makers has been a cardinal principle in modern community organizing that has enjoyed the support of regional Catholic social thought in the Campaign for Human Development under the auspices of the United States Conference of Catholic Bishops. Lactantius certainly had no difficulty pinpointing who had the capacity to make binding decisions for the Roman empire.

Book V taught what approximates the principle of equality in dignity due to all humans being created by God. Although fiercely opposed to the rich or poor division that results from greed and pride, the text does not present a contrary ideal of uniformity in concrete circumstances and power. In fact book III rejected a Platonic ideal of common property,[45] while book V decries not private property but unbridled greed in acquiring and using it.[46] Lactantius distinguished between private property as an absolute, and private property subordinate to the Creator's purpose that the goods of the earth benefit all people. Later, in Aquinas, and then in Catholic social thought this is called the universal destination of goods that should govern the use of private property. But like the later Catholic social thought, the *Divine Institutes* opposed a solution to exploitation of the poor by the rich by means of collectivism that eliminated personal decision and dignity.

Equality in dignity, a meaning of *aequitas* in book V, became the practical and theoretical ground on which modern Catholic social thought has taught

---

45. Bowen and Garnsey, book III 21.1–22.1, 209–11; Brandt, 248–52.
46. Bowen and Garnsey, book V 5.1–6.1, 290–94; Monat, 150–60.

an inclusive participation in the major institutions of a society and on which it espouses human rights.[47] Affirmation of universal equality in human dignity is a significant point of continuity between the *Divine Institutes* and Catholic social thought. So is the general danger of a certain lack of practical efficacy and historical success with a social vision consonant with if not derived from Christian faith.

## The *Divine Institutes* and Two Orientations in Political Theology

The *Divine Institutes*, despite firmly embracing the Roman empire and notwithstanding theological critiques of all manner of empire, can be put in (postcritical) reference to two orientations in political theology. Political theology is a broad genre that encompasses continental European political theology, Latin American, and other liberation theologies, and public theology developing in the U.S. and U.K. The two orientations are roughly speaking Augustinian and Thomist, or in biblical concepts, the prophetic and the kingly. The former concentrates on being socially critical on behalf of human emancipation and excels in a critique of the status quo. The latter, on the basis of a more definite acceptance of liberal democracy and a humanized capitalism, devotes more attention to practical improvement in these major institutions.

Both orientations run through all three types of theology mentioned above but European political with Latin American and other liberation theologies tend more toward the prophetic while public theology tends more toward the kingly. Black liberation theology often accepts both liberal democracy and a humane capitalism while promoting emancipation from exclusion from just and respectful participation in them.

In line with the prophetic orientation, a significant aspect in the *Divine Institutes* to consider in relation to a way-of-being-in-the-world open to commitment to social justice is Lacantius's systematic placing of the basic structure and fundamental cultural themes of imperial society on trial before the Christian faith, the classical heritage, and human reason. This is an analytic and pro-

---

47. See George Newlands, *Christ and Human Rights: The Transformative Engagement* (Aldershot, England: Ashgate, 2006), for human rights in reference to the center of Christian faith, Jesus the Christ.

phetic orientation in the *Divine Institutes* that encourages a similarly prophetic way-of-being-social today. On this point, despite condoning the Roman empire, Lacantius's text could be put into dialogue with continental European political theology and public theology. Nor need public theology assume that contemporary liberal democracy is either an absolutely perfect product of political reason or the "end of history." In its actual operations and deeds, it too stands accountable before the bar of human hope and divine judgment. Unlike liberation theology the central emancipation in the *Divine Institutes* is primarily from false religion, false wisdom, and false worship that caused persecution of true religion, wisdom and worship, not primarily from a type of Christianity accommodated to socio-economic oppression.

In addition, Lacantius's honoring of the reality and memory of victims of Diocletian's persecution could be put in reference to political and liberation theology's lifting up of the oppressive underside of modernity. However, in the *Divine Institutes* the victims are not the poor of many religions in poorer parts of the world run over by the economic engines of wealthy nations, many of them populated by Christians, but Christians who suffered cruel physical torments at the hands of pagan authorities. Lacantius's work, nonetheless, supports a posture in Catholic social thought tilted toward learning from European political theology on listening to victims, from liberation theologies on their well-known hermeneutical privilege of the poor, and from the lesser-known theme of marginalization in public theology.[48] The *Divine Institutes*, that is, preserves a memory of Christianity as a persecuted minority from an era before the Wars of Religion with their Christian victims of other Christians. Such memories support Catholic social thought in unequivocally opposing Christian tolerance for the abuse of law and torture by anyone or any state.

Consequently, in criticizing the mores and laws of the empire the *Divine Institutes* represents a prophetic exercise of theoretical and practical reason. Prophetic, because it interprets the Roman empire in light of God's existence, unity, plan, and judgment, instructed both by the Bible and by the heritage of classical wisdom and philosophical reason. Theoretical, because works in the genre of "Institutes" expound the basic principles and full substance of a topic. The "Institutes" of civil law by Gaius, Ulpian, and Julius Paulus "set

---

48. See John Atherton, *Marginalization* (London: SCM Press, 2003).

out systematic, theoretical expositions of legal principles."[49] Garnsey advises, "The work is nothing less than the first attempt at a summary of Christian thought."[50] Public, because it addresses the practice of witness unto public death for not performing the public deed of venerating Diocletian and other Roman gods. And reason, because there is consistent appeal to arguments, reasoning, and substantiation of conclusions. As prophetic the *Divine Institutes* stands in a line of Christian social critique later evident in Augustine's *City of God*, and more recently in political and liberation theologies.

There are contextual applications. In the United States prophetic engagement with "American exceptionalism" by political theology, liberation theology, Black liberation theology, and public theology is crucial. American exceptionalism takes for granted that the original colonists on the shores of what became the United States were "an almost chosen people," that "God is on our side," that in God's providence the U.S. has a national purpose beyond its borders, almost has received a divine mission to the rest of humanity on behalf of liberty and democracy. Simultaneously, however, some theological negation of American exceptionalism often seems to overlook the validity of the major political institution that is constitutional democracy, to ignore intimations of the sacred in American art, philosophy, and in physical nature, the land, and wilderness. Others are content with prophetic critiques of capitalism.

For example, through incisive prophetic insights more in the tradition of Augustine than Aquinas, critiques like those of Stanley Hauerwas, Michael Baxter, and William Cavanaugh clarify much that is misguided and destructive in the political culture and the operations of American democracy, somewhat like Lactantius placed imperial culture under the judgment of Christian revelation. But do they provide much in the way of feasible ideas and a practical agenda for the hard political and legal work of step-by-step reforming of democratic practices and institutions? In answer it could be said that, like Lactantius focusing on Constantine as agent of transformation and seeking to form his conscience as the means, they too focus on the agent(s) of transformation, Christian citizens, and again like Lactantius seek to form consciences in a reforming direction.

The *Divine Institutes* recognized the need for legal and socio-economic reform. Modern Catholic social thought offers general principles for such re-

49. Digeser, 57.                          50. Garnsey, 13.

form. But the writings of John Courtney Murray (1904–1967) are exceptional in engaging many of those principles in constructive dialogue with the public life of American democracy. He has been criticized for over-assimilating Catholicism to American political culture. He grounded unreserved assent to liberal democratic institutions under the Constitution in a Catholic tradition of natural law ethics. This befits the "kingly" dimension of faith and Christianity not limited to monarchic governance. However he also had a continual orientation to the "primacy of the spiritual" as a critical principle that refused to accede to any subordinating of the spiritual to the temporal. This prophetic principle offers common ground with the Augustinian tendency yet situates the prophetic within a kingly reform.

In the context of Europe there is a phenomenon that permits a question about the kingly aspect of Catholic social thought.[51] In 2004 the European nations ranking highest in an aggregate index of social justice with four elements (poverty, labour market, family life, education) were Norway (1), Sweden (2), Denmark (3), and Finland (4). They obviously do not have a tradition of Catholic social thought. Belgium, which does, is listed at 10, tied with Great Britain. Catholic social thought also presumably would have made some difference in Austria (5), Ireland (5), and Luxembourg (6). Why not in countries with traditionally Catholic populations, such as Poland (16), Spain (17, tied with Greece), Malta (18), and Italy (19)? Poland is a special case, admittedly, because of recent emergence from the Soviet bloc. How can Catholic social thought gain a better hearing among Catholics in "Catholic countries"?

Do social democracies exemplify values and institutions taught by Catholic social thought? Are conditions for their success found or producible outside Scandinavia? Or will conditions vanish under the impact of cultural heterogeneity present in much of the rest of Europe, the United States, some nations in Latin America, and Australia, for example? Do Denmark, Norway, and Sweden exemplify a Scandinavian version of the European social model that has some universal features?[52] Are Scandinavian commitments to social

51. See an online research report from Berlinopolis, a Berlin-based think tank, translated online from "Wie gerecht ist Europa?" to "Social Justice in Europe—How Successful Are the Member States?" that ranks achievement of social justice in European Union member-countries for 2003–4, available at http://66.102.9.104/search?q=cache:mTn56Oeo4CYJ:www.berlinpolis.net/download.php%3Ffile%3 (accessed April 15, 2008).

52. See "The European Social Model," from the European Trade Union Confederation online, available at http://www.etuc.org/a/2771 (accessed April 15, 2008).

justice due in some significant way to an historic, underlying Lutheran heritage?[53] What theoretical traditions inspire and guide their social democracies? What has Scandinavia along with Ireland and Austria to teach Catholic social thought about social justice? The foregoing questions have to do with the efficacy and communication of Catholic social thought among Catholic populations. They touch on the kingly dimension insofar as they look at what actually works or does not, why, and how.

In regard to the U.S. and Europe the *Divine Institutes*, along with its clear prophetic content, can be read as a message on an essential role for a kingly, constructive strand in Christian social thought that conceives the reform of public and political institutions, neither standing pat on the validity of prophetic denunciation nor proceeding with precritical, unexamined, patriotic support for a status quo. The *Divine Institutes* conducted a searching criticism of the public heritage, values, mores, institutions, outlooks, and conduct of the emperor and classical culture in order to communicate and initiate a positive alternative for the empire, not simply to stand in prophetic distance or to teach Christian withdrawal to a sectarian enclave apart from public life, a privatized Christianity. It also sought efficacy in reform with a Christian inspiration.

## Conclusion

Benefiting from critical studies of the *Divine Institutes*, this study explored a postcritical theme, whether an affinity to social justice exists in this opus. Concluding that it does, a short further step infers that the affinity amounts to continuity between the *Divine Institutes* in late antiquity and social justice in modern Catholic social thought.

Specific threads in continuity are 1) a socio-critical analysis of the basic structure of major institutions from a perspective animated by Christian faith but incorporating knowledge from sources other than biblical revelation;

---

53. See Bernd Wegener and Stefan Liebig, "Dominant Ideologies and the Variation of Distributive Justice Norms: A Comparison of East and West Germany, and the United States," in *Social Justice and Political Change: Public Opinion in Capitalist and Post-Communist States*, ed. James R. Kluegel, David S. Mason, and Bernd Wegener (New York: de Gruyter, 1995), 239–62. The International Social Justice Project found differences in social justice between cultures imprinted by Calvinist and by Lutheran influence.

2) affirmation of the intrinsic equality in dignity of all human beings because of creation by God in the image of God; 3) a prospect on public life geared to social changes that express equity or equality in dignity; 4) attention to the lot of the poor and powerless; and 5) a focus on agency for social change.

An affinity, interpretable as continuity, between Lactantius and Catholic social thought on these points supports the fruitful interpretation of Catholic social thought advanced first by Johan Verstraeten and then developed by Judith A. Merkle.[54] They argue that Catholic social thought is actually a Catholic social tradition not reducible to fixed formulations. This exploration adds that the Catholic social tradition in the *Divine Institutes* has both prophetic and kingly elements. There are indications in U.S. and European contexts that the kingly rather than the prophetic element may be most in need of further development.

54. Johan Verstraeten, "Rethinking Catholic Social Thought as Tradition," in *Catholic Social Thought: Twilight or Renaissance?*, ed. J. S. Boswell, F. P. McHugh, and J. Verstraeten (Leuven: Leuven University Press, 2000), 59–77. Judith A. Merkle, *From the Heart of the Church: The Catholic Social Tradition* (Collegeville, Minn.: The Liturgical Press, 2004), 3–4, 16–18, 52–62.

PART IV

REFLECTIONS ON
THE THEME

# 10. The Church Fathers and Catholic Social Thought

*Reflections on the Symposium*

The topic assigned to me is to say something both of what was accomplished by the articles in this volume and of what tasks have been identified by them for future research. The volume brings to the surface a deep ambivalence about the legitimacy and extent of developing Christian social teaching today by reference to patristic texts. The manuscript seems to result in something of a "split decision." The task for the near future of a set of ongoing *quaestiones disputandae* comes directly from that ambivalence. These notes therefore proceed in two steps, beginning with a restatement of the argument for a "retrieval" of patristic insight for Christian social thought, as it seemed implied especially by the initial papers. Then some of the sources of the apparent "suspicion" about the cogency of the projects of retrieval are identified.

## The Case for "Retrieval"

The symposium began with comprehensive presentations of the thought of Paul Ricoeur (†2005), including the article by Reimund Bieringer in part I of this volume. It seems fitting then in conclusion to look back again at this acknowledged master theoretician of the narratives of memory. Especially in his later works, Paul Ricoeur wrote much on the necessity and the dangers of recollective narrative,[1] the use and misuse of memory.[2] Throughout his lifework, Ricoeur remained dedicated to his chosen role of a witness, even an advocate, for as much personal sovereignty and identity as can possibly and plausibly be acknowledged in human beings, while admitting as many limitations of human knowledge, freedom, and hope as are rendered necessary by the thought and praxis of our age. Perhaps reflecting the Calvinist sense of extrinsic justification *and* regeneration in the Holy Spirit, Ricoeur stressed programmatically, as is well known, the abiding need for a dual hermeneutic of suspicion *and* retrieval. Ricoeur admitted that, especially when striving for hope, meaning, and ethical standards, we are not "innocent" storytellers; thus, we have a need for (inevitably fallible and yet rational) strategies of self-examination as part of an *ars memoriae* that would otherwise be more easily misguided. In *Oneself as Another*, after recalling the case for understandable suspicion about personal identity and then making the case anew for the necessity of still speaking of a self, its potential for narrative development and the reemerging, ethical possibilities of the narrating and narrated self, Ricoeur returned to the thought of understandable suspicion. The eighth study of this book was dedicated to arguing for strategies of self-examination about "ethical intentions," including the self-examination of all of one's own proposals "aiming at the 'good life' with and for others, in just institutions."[3] Ricoeur pointed to Kant's categorical imperative as one example of such strategies of self-examination, asking if the maxims by which we choose a practice for ourselves were also the maxims we would want to guide others in their choices.[4]

In *Memory, History, Forgetting*, Ricoeur referred at least twice to a sentence buried deep within M. Heidegger's *Being and Time* (1927).[5] Having stressed throughout the work the many ways in which our existence is enmeshed in its history, Heidegger had noted briefly that "*remembering* is possible only on the basis of forgetting."[6] Ricoeur expressed his surprise that the positive potentiality of forgetting, suggested here in the text, had not be-

---

1. See Paul Ricoeur, *Oneself as Another* (Chicago: University of Chicago Press, 1990), particularly within the Eighth Study, 207–.

2. Paul Ricoeur, *Memory, History, Forgetting* (Chicago: University of Chicago Press, 2004), esp. part I.

3. Ricoeur, *Oneself as Another*, 172.          4. Ibid., 208–9.

5. Ibid.

6. M. Heidegger, *Sein und Zeit* (1927): "so ist die *Erinnerung* auf dem Grund des Vergessens *und nicht umgekehrt*" (§ 68 a, 339).

come more programmatic in Heidegger's *magnum opus*. Ricoeur might well have also cited at this point H.-G. Gadamer, who did much to elucidate Heidegger's insight on this point.

In ways that are largely overlooked, forgetting belongs to the relation between retaining and remembering. Forgetting means not merely loss and privation, but, as F. Nietzsche stressed, it is a necessary condition for the life of our mind. It is only by forgetting that our mind receives the possibility of a thorough-going renewal, the ability to see things anew with a fresh look, so that what was old and familiar now blends with what is newly seen into a multidimensional unity.[7]

But Ricoeur adds to these thoughts his own characteristic caution: precisely because a certain kind of forgetting is necessary for there to be genuine recollection, forgetting, too, like remembering, needs direction and self-examination; it, too, must be raised to the level of an art. Corresponding to the abuses of memory that Ricoeur saw in a merely repetitive *ars memoriae* and especially in blocked, manipulated, and abusively controlled memory, he also identified the parallel dysfunctions of forgetting, before he then said positively what would be required of a successful *ars oblivionis,* "projected as a double of *ars memoriae,* [in the sense of] a figure of happy [or flourishing] memory."[8] In asking what of patristic themes we should try to retrieve for Catholic social thought, we will need to ask as well what we should try to "forget" or, at least, set aside.

Ricoeur provides a good deal of direction for the required arts of remembering and forgetting. Already in the essays that prepared the monograph, *Memory, History, Forgetting*, Ricoeur had refined the task of a disciplined remembrance-and-forgetting by challenging Heidegger's privileging of the temporal horizon of the future. Strengthened by the "pre-Kehre" programmatic of authenticity, early Heidegger's positive interest in history had been focused on identifying never yet actualized possibilities in the midst of earlier actuality; to Heidegger's credit that also means he had identified at least *in obliquo*

---

7. H.-G. Gadamer, *Wahrheit und Methode* (Tübingen: Mohr, 1960), here according to 4th edition (1975), 13, with reference to the same source that would be recalled by Ricoeur as well as F. Nietzsche's 1874 *Unzeitgemaesse Betrachtungen* and their second section, "On the Uses and Disadvantages of History for Life."

8. Ricoeur, *Memory, History, Forgetting*, 412. With reference above all to Harald Weinrich, *Lethe. Kunst und Kritik des Vergessens* (Munich: Beck, 1997), Ricoeur also devotes a good deal of space to the misguided application of art and the artificial to memory and forgetting.

historical actualities that did not merit literal repetition. H.-G. Gadamer's observation was surely correct that Heidegger's concept of tradition had been largely a pejorative one; for two reasons, worthwhile retrieval could never be the mere repetition of the letter of historical traditions.[9] Heidegger's pejorative concept of tradition, with its sense that whatever might have been realized at some earlier stage of thought would then have been received and passed on at a far less insightful level, was inscribed into the more radical disinterest in what had been realized at all. In every realization there was necessarily an overlooking—or forgetting—of possibility; and the goal of "authentic" thought is to envision the unthought presuppositions or implications of explicit thoughts, the never yet actualized possibilities still hidden in the roots of earlier achievements. Heidegger's interest in history, driven by the pathos of authenticity, was above all an interest in shaping the future anew.

As regards the positive potential of history, Ricoeur identified in his essays on *Characterizing the Passé* a danger of this future-oriented dimension of Heideggerian hermeneutics. In these essays, written between 1996 and 1998 as part of the preparation for the monograph *Memory, History, Forgetting,* Ricoeur argued that Heidegger, in connection with the substitution of *das Gewesene* for *das Vergangene* (the "was" for the *passé*), underestimated the kind of relative independence which needs to be maintained by each of the three temporal horizons; in particular, so Ricoeur, Heidegger had underestimated the kind of independence that must be allotted to history.[10] Precisely for those with a less pejorative sense of tradition, reading history only for its potential contribution to the future can lead to revisionist histories and to a selective amnesia about the more troubled aspects of the past.

Admittedly, we can neither ignore our hopes for the future and the awareness of yet to be realized possibilities in working out what history was and where it went right or wrong, nor, conversely, can we ignore history in working out what might be the better possibilities for the future. To borrow a thought from elsewhere, we must seek the future not least from the memory of suffering; in a demand made familiar especially by J. B. Metz, hope must be "anam-

9. H.-G. Gadamer, *Philosophische Lehrjahre. Eine Rückschau* (Frankfurt: Klostermann, 1977).

10. P. Ricoeur, "La marque du passé," first in *Revue de Métaphysique et de Morale* 1(1998), together with the text of his 1996 Madrid lectures on reading past times, on memory, forgetting, and forgiveness, translated into German as *Das Rätsel der Vergangenheit. Erinnern—Vergessen—Verzeihen* (Göttingen: Wallstein, 1998).

netic." Ricoeur was acutely aware of our orientation to the future in choosing a text from the near or distant past for recollection and revision. Such a choice implies that we also have chosen a preliminary reinterpretation of that text: we have an idea of where the text could take us. We have chosen to study certain texts and not other texts for some reason: perhaps to explain, or demonstrate, or exemplify something, positive or negative, for imitation or avoidance.

But it is precisely because research of this kind always involves a self-interest in the future that Ricoeur insists that we need to develop checks upon ourselves, strategies of self-criticality, testing ourselves to see if in fact we are appropriating the text well. That in turn demands of us that we must first somehow accept the story or history for what it is and only then try to elicit its future possibilities, even if it means living with an uncomfortable memory. The success of our revision depends in part on our being more than simply revisionist, on the text's being less than fully plastic to our wishes for the future. In the earlier work, *Oneself as Another*, Ricoeur had identified in my (finally, less than cooperative) body, in other persons (with their uninvited, at times unwelcome, claims upon me), and in my conscience (bound by truths less convenient than my good intentions) three witnesses to the possibility of a genuine—because relational—self. Ricoeur's later remarks on the potential significance of the *Passé* identify what could easily be counted as a fourth witness to the possibility of a genuine self, enriched by the robust relation to that difficult "other" to which the "self" is tied: here, by the nonrevisionist relationship to difficult memory, provided that this past can be remembered without crushing the core of the self's hope for the future. This relation to that part of one's past that is remembered not for reactualization, but for what is to be set aside or gotten past, what on one level we might have preferred to forget as our past, what we still need to forget as our future, what we need to remember as the possibility to be guarded against, as that which calls for forgiveness, not emulation. As Reimund Bieringer points out in his present essay, Ricoeurian hermeneutics is meant to include critique of this kind, including self-critique. Going beyond the letter of Ricoeur, this fourth witness to the possibility of a genuine self enriched by a robust relation to the sometimes difficult memory of the self's proper past could also include listening to still canonical and classical texts that seem to have become "untimely" *(unzeitgemäß)*.

In his contribution to the volumes edited by J. Habermas, *Observations on*

*"The Spiritual Situation of the Age,"* J. B. Metz made his own the idea of "productive noncontemporaneity" that Ernst Bloch—still in the first years of his exile—had suggested and published in the 1935 work, *Die Erbschaft dieser Zeit*.[11] For both Bloch and Metz, the possibility of "productive noncontemporaneity" meant that there were nonproductive, indeed destructive modes of noncontemporaneity as well, successful and failing ways of being related at once to quite different mental and historical times. Metz speaks of a sectarian form of enthusiastic noncontemporaneity, in which the isolation from contemporary society with its developed standards of intellectual and moral virtue serves the theologian as an alleged badge of honor, but also of an accommodationalist form of regretted noncontemporaneity, in which assimilated theologians ashamed of their community's otherness seek to minimize any distinctions from the dominant cultural trends of the day. It is characteristic of productive noncontemporaneity for the theologian, with the "chronic vigour" (J. H. Newman) that liberates from servile adherence to both stagnation and modish fads, to continually bring the memory of the past into reflective conversation with the better movements of the times.

For those willing to entertain the possible retrieval of patristic writings for ethical thought, this hope for productive noncontemporaneity could be articulated well in hermeneutical terms. The question as to the possible retrieval of patristic writings for Christian social thought would need to begin by renegotiating the standard interpretative situation or average configuration, manifested in part by the statistics of the use of patristics sources in Catholic social teaching, notably the impression of the perennial sameness of patristic teaching in itself, identical to a long-since completed Catholic social teaching.[12] Recalling possibilities suggested by Ricoeur's mimetic arc, the average configuration of such a slightly tired sameness of Catholic social teaching, Catholic social thought, and patristic teaching can be replaced by the anticipation of a refiguration based on the acute need for new ethical stances in a globalized world (for example, on new issues of migration, labor, commu-

11. See J. B. Metz, "Produktive Ungleichzeitigkeit," in *Stichworte zur, Geistigen Situation der Zeit,* ed. J. Habermas (Frankfurt, 1979), 2:529–38, trans. Andrew Buchwalter as "Productive Noncontemporaneity," in *Observations on "The Spiritual Situation of the Age,"* ed. J. Habermas (Cambridge, Mass.: MIT Press, 1985), 169–77.

12. See B. Matz, "Problematic Uses of Patristic Sources in the Documents of Catholic Social Thought," *Journal of Catholic Social Thought* 4 (2007): 459–85.

nication, as well as unresolved issues of commutative and distributive justice) and the hope for not yet domesticated insights *(uneingelöste Traditionen)* prefigured in an uneven but provocative patristic literature. Motivated by a sense of suspicion regarding the adequacy of our own moral present, this anxious anticipation of the future refiguration of what was and what often remains a quite alien ("noncontemporary") text can make sense of those aspects of patristic thought which had yet to develop their dynamic (that text before the text) or are simply better "forgotten" as candidates for detailed retrieval, even while we keep seeking in patristic writings prefigurations of future societies more fully marked by justice than any ones actualized in the present or the past *(pace* Reimund Bieringer).

## The Case for "Suspicion"

If Ricoeur was cited at the conference to the effect that the text is to play with us, it became increasingly evident during the conversations that a large segment of the symposium's participants did not want to join this game at all. Presumably not the whimsical clash of *Spielverderber*, the alternatives sketched in uncommonly bold strokes in the contrast between the historical papers of Wendy Mayer and Brenda Ihssen suggested that many but not all the historians shared the scepticism with a significant minority of the ethicists. That suggests that there are two arguments here that heighten suspicion, one concerning the context "from which," the other concerning the context "into which." Taken together, these two sources of a shared skepticism that surfaced during the symposium pose a *quaestio disputanda*, the answer to which will be decisive for the shape and vitality of any project seeking to retrieve aspects of patristic writings for the enrichment of Christian social thought.

### Suspicion and the Task of Contextualizing Historical Prefigurations

The need to find the texts behind the text, identifying the older oral and written sources and the developments that led to a patristic text, their differences from that text itself and its differences from our own context is one that can never be completely satisfied; and yet that is what would be necessary (if not yet sufficient) in order to understand the text fully in its own right. Reacting to that single-mindedly instrumental recollection of the patristic material, in which the patristic writers were first united among themselves before being united with contemporary wisdom (arguably a denial of the plurality and the temporal otherness of the texts), there is a countermovement intent on stressing the particularity and incommensurability of each.[13] "If you have read one church father, you have then read just *one* church father," as the maxim might go, or better, you have then read one segment of one of his texts, the original context of which would need to be elucidated further, before the text itself, much less the "text in front of the text" with its dynamic for today's reception, could be secured. This dynamic is not unique to the conversation between patristics and ethics; a similar dynamic can be observed in the systematic consideration of biblical texts. In both cases, there likely will be an ongoing and hopefully productive tension between groups of disciplines concerned with those texts. Even without appealing to J. Derrida, it might be tempting to surrender the future potential of the text to the virtually interminable quest for its own prior contexts. The ghost of Zeno could be conjured up to suggest the impossibility of ever reaching the goal of a renewed thought, so many are the intermediate steps needed to reach an adequate starting point.

Such chasms between the past and future contexts of a patristic—or a biblical—text can be explained in part by the dynamics involved in the "The Contest of Faculties," or, better, the contest of interests, historical and systematic; for the latter set of disciplines implies the diminution of the prerogatives of the concept of time proper to historical disciplines, which necessarily seek out that past which is categorically other.[14] Heightened by the memory of an all too easy homogenization and contemporization of historical texts for systematic use, there is an increased reluctance to "forget" the infinitely receding horizons of earlier texts, even at the risk of condemning the texts to future irrelevance, forgetting instead what makes them most worth remembering. In Ricoeur's terms, memory can be "blocked" by the inability to terminate recollection. He compares this first misuse of memory with the inability to do that "work of mourning" which comes to accept the loss of the past, falling instead into a debilitating form of melancholic or morose attachment to a past with no future.[15]

---

13. See n. 12.

14. See M. Heidegger, "Der Zeitbegriff in der Geschichtswissenschaft," in *Zeitschrift für Philosophie und philosophische Kritik* (1916), 161, now in *GA* I.

15. See *Memory, History, Forgetting*, 68–80; and for the misguided use of forgetting that accompanies a type of blockage in remembering, 444–48, e.g., 446: "the working through, in which the working of re-

And yet the complete forgetfulness of such differences between a patristic text and its past or future contexts would make it impossible to recall the "merely" analogical similarity between past and future contexts of, say, the memory of the critique of usury. The search for a continuity of concern underlying the rejection of interest on loaned capital and the promotion of loaned capital within certain strictures can be plausible only if the radical shift in concrete recommendations is kept in mind. Otherwise, the "surprise" that results, when the stark differences in the concrete ethical assertions of Catholic social teaching at different times are finally identified, then would encourage the denial of any underlying continuity of principles in the Church's development of ethical stances. At the end of this symposium, it remained an open question whether the decision to "forget" some of this historical differentiation is one that could or should be exacted of historians; and yet, for them even to consider tolerating that "their" texts play themselves out among systematicians and ethicists, there must be evident in the latter's work a clearer memory of the particularities and differences that are observable in the development and retrieval of earlier texts into later contexts. There is a heightened need to "forget" earlier attempts to exaggerate the perennial shape of Catholic social teaching in order to "remember" better the continuity of its dynamic trajectory and proleptic goals. It is the plea of Kent that Lear forget his too exacting demands upon his daughters' memories in order that he might "see better."

### Suspicion and the Task of Contextualizing Contemporary Refigurations

In the discussion following the papers of participants on the topics of Catholic social teachings' audiences (a paper placed in parallel with Wendy Mayer's paper on patristic audiences) and its view of usury (in parallel with Ihssen's paper), the increasingly unsettled question developed not about the possibility, but about the desirability of a coherent, much less a unified, statement of Catholic social teaching and about whether Christian social thought was to promote or reduce the polysemy of it. Not the alleged unity of patristic prefiguration, but the opportune or inopportune character of the unity of contemporary refiguration appeared here to be the more controversial dimension of the conversation between patristics and ethics. The less thoroughgoing the unity

---

membering consists, does not occur without the work of mourning, through which we separate ourselves from our lost objects of love and hate." Stated positively, Ricoeur described the forgetting that is sought by the work of mourning as the necessary condition of the possibility of alleviating such a blockage of memory.

that is desired in the refiguration of patristic sources for Catholic social teaching, the less of a *desideratum* appears also the unity of Catholic social teaching's patristic prefiguration in itself. In the *quaestio disputanda* of whether to celebrate or to resist postmodern fragmentation and its post-Enlightenment scepticism toward moral universals or an unfolding natural law, this conversation is also not unique to the dialogue between patristics and ethics, much less to the *acta* of this symposium. It is to be found as well, for example, in the debates between second and third wave feminisms, and between liberation and postcolonial theologies. The challenge in each case seems to be not just to adjudicate, but also to interrelate and mutually enrich the claims of the universal and the particular.

This moment of suspicion should not be too quickly contrasted with Ricoeur's work, which by its attempt to reconcile critical and hermeneutical thought is admittedly more late modern than postmodern in its instincts, say, in relation to the question of universal human rights. The need to test the validity of the intentions of Catholic social teaching and Christian social thought can be admitted by all; the question is then how and to what degree. Ricoeur detailed a second form of misdirected recollection under the heading of "manipulated memory."[16] Precisely because collective memory is vital to collective identity, it is also fragile, notably when this identity is sought in models that do not adequately reflect identity a) in a continually growing development, b) in an increasing relationality to the other, or c) in the acknowledgement of one's own founding heritage of violence.[17] To choose one example: The continuity of *Nostra aetate* with ancient and medieval Christian theologies of non-Christian religions will be found less in any one set of theses put forward in the treatises of earlier centuries (here the growth in the affirmation of the other is most evident) than in the evident dissatisfaction and ongoing uneasiness of their authors' with them.[18] This moment of restlessness

16. See *Memory, History, Forgetting*, 80–86; and for the misguided use of forgetting that accompanies this type of manipulation in remembering, 448–52. The positive art of forgetting needed to overcome memory manipulated in this way is shown to include the forgetting of the obsession to define collective identity without reference to a developing relationship to once threatening others.

17. See the issues raised by John T. Noonan, *A Church that Can and Cannot Change: The Development of Catholic Moral Teaching* (Notre Dame, Ind.: University of Notre Dame Press, 2005). Noonan exemplifies the structural issues by retracing the contradictory doctrines regarding slavery, usury, and non-Christian religions and by predicting and arguing for a change in stance towards divorce.

18. See R. Schenk, "Christ, Christianity, and Non-Christian Religions: Their Relationship in the

corresponds to the hybrid character of *Nostra aetate* with its blend of inclusiv-
ist, exclusivist and pluralist thoughts.[19] As also is the case with the slavery issue
and with the interreligious context of the usury question, the reality and necessity of the development of the concrete doctrines of Catholic social teaching will
be evident only when that necessary (but not yet sufficient) condition is met,
which the late Pope John Paul II termed "the purification of memory," especially
toward the heritage of violence active in the formation of Christian identity.[20]

Such self-critical solidarity is able to overcome the temptation to what
Ricoeur identified as a third misuse of memory, memory obligated to the com-
memorative celebration and reaffirmation of the institution founded upon a
self-congratulatory narrative of its own history.[21] While Ricoeur is thinking
chiefly of overly positive portrayals of a nation's history, "obligated memory"
can just as easily include the trendy recitation of the faults and failings of ep-
ochs previous to one's "own" history, focusing on the faults of others within
the "same" generic group, as frequently in the case of criticism of one set of
Catholics by their Catholic opponents. Despite the rhetoric of "self-critique,"
such easy distantiation is in fact merely the critique of the other, the triumph-
alistic celebration of the new self distinguished from them, often little more
than a diachronic version of the prayer in Luke 18:11. The intentional "forgetting" of this contemporary, self-congratulatory misuse of obligated memory,
thinly disguised as the well-rehearsed "self-critique" of (the opponents within)

---

Thought of Robert Kilwardby," in *Christ among the Medieval Dominicans: Representations of Christ in the Texts and Images of the Order of Preachers*, ed. K. Emery Jr. and J. Wawrykow (Notre Dame, Ind.: University of Notre Dame, 1988), 344–63; Schenk, "Views of the Two Covenants in Medieval Theology," *Nova et Vetera* 4:4 (2006): 891–916.

19. See R. Schenk, "Widersprüchsfähige Vieldeutigkeit. Wahrheitsparadigmen als ein Unter-
schiedsmerkmal von Religionstheologien christlicher Provenienz," in *Ambivalenz—Ambiguität—Post-
modernität. Begrenzt Eindeutiges Denken*, Collegium Philosophicum 5, ed. R. Schenk and P. Koslowski
(Stuttgart–Bad Cannstatt: frommann-holzboog, 2004), 273–302, esp. 306.

20. See *Incarnationis Mysterium* 11 (November 1998); and the International Theological Commission, *Memory and Reconciliation: The Church and the Faults of the Past* (December 1999).

21. See *Memory, History, Forgetting*, 86–92; and for the misguided use of forgetting that accompanies this type of institutional obligation imposed violently upon remembering as a kind of celebratory
monument to chauvinistic identity, 452–56. Elaborating a qualified form of limited, i.e., amnesia-free forgetting of such a misuse of memory, Ricoeur develops in the epilogue his hope for a collective possibility
of "Difficult Forgiveness," 457–506, which he had suggested repeatedly as the goal lying just beyond but
always animating the argumentative results of the whole work. As that which in some sense can never be
obligated, at least insofar as it must be a gift, if it is to be at all, collective forgiveness is that positive mode
of forgetting which could liberate most completely from the abuses of "obligated remembering."

one's "own" tradition, allows for the development of more genuine strategies of anamnetic self-examination.

An example of the justifiable application of the hermeneutics of suspicion toward the contemporary context "into which" patristic texts could be received by Christian social thought might be taken from the widely sensed difference between the chiefly subjective concerns evident in many of the patristic texts cited as sources for Catholic social teaching and the greater concern of Christian social thought today for the more immediately social or environmental ramifications of human actions and omissions. The needs that contemporary Christian social thought primarily addresses are less the needs of the souls called to greater generosity than the needs of the human and non-human worlds that have been maltreated. Contemporary Christian social thought, sharing to this degree Ricoeur's tendency to privilege ethics over morality, is understandably suspicious of the narrowly subjective focus in many of the patristic sources of Catholic social teaching.[22] To be consistent, however, this suspicion would need to be extended to the examination of the context "into which," where Christian social thought meets a fundamental moral theology that has often shown a tendency to place excessive burdens on the subjective intentions of the individual conscience or even on the fundamental options behind its concrete intentions. A more robust hermeneutics of suspicion would need to ask of fundamental moral theology a greater concern for the ethical paradigm, the formation of conscience related to the instances of the nonsubjective "other," articulated along the lines suggested by Ricoeur, including the relation of the subject to the givens of body, other persons, history, and the environment. The test of whether apartheid is morally acceptable, for example, is not sought chiefly in the subjective intentions of its proponents. The ability to spot a characteristic weakness of patristic thought can help us to look for that same weakness in what we have inherited from it.

## Conclusions for the Near Future of Patristic-Ethical Conversation

The compatibility and, more so, the complementarity of interpretive strategies of retrieval and suspicion toward patristic texts, each with its dual use of

22. See *Oneself as Another*, especially the Seventh Study, 169–202: "The Self and the Ethical Aim."

the *artes memoriae et oblivionis*, suggest that the conversation between the history of patristic thought and the development of Christian social thought will need to remain at least for the foreseeable future one marked by the kind of dissonance expressed in the symposium and in this present volume. No one direction represented by the papers seemed superfluous or singularly conclusive, but neither did any grand, harmonious synthesis of the contraries show itself. The dialectical development of Christian social teaching, with forward motion often *in obliquo* as well as *in recto*, is mirrored by our study of the same. A sourcebook seeking to document this development will need to privilege texts that retrace the overall path forward over those that delay it with detours or retreats, but it should use the commentaries and some of the texts to sharpen the memory of the gradual and often indirect nature of its development as well as its epochal faults. It should be attentive to the eschatological difference between Christian social teaching today and the "end of history" by showing the past and present state of Christian social teaching as an ever-searching form of practical wisdom, growing in its treasury of articulated convictions and motivated by common principles, but also appropriated by many persons, in many times and places, for often disparate needs and with varying degrees of merit, guilt, and what has been called "moral luck." It should acknowledge its debt to initially alien resources that were able to be well assimilated, but it should also recall when attempts of this kind led to self-alienation and to an assimilation to what was incompatible with its genuine meaning. Aware of its own past and present fragility, it should look for those overlooked impulses among patristic writings, suggestions of a more radically genuine discipleship hidden meanwhile beneath layers of otherwise defensible domestication and institutionalization. It should show special concern for those who have been least blessed by the collective search even for just institutions. In an age tempted towards the extremes of secular and religious identities, each styled as self-sufficient, glorious and universally liberating, this admission of a sometimes halting, partial, and mendicant progress might be the greatest social teaching of all.

*Johan Leemans and Johan Verstraeten*

---

# 11. The (Im)possible Dialogue between Patristics and Catholic Social Thought

*Limits, Possibilities, and a Way Forward*

In his *First Homily on the Love of the Poor* Gregory of Nyssa exhorts his congregation to care for large groups of fugitives who had found their way into Nyssa. He vividly describes their awful fate: sleeping rough in porticoes, drinking together with animals from water springs, depending on alms for their survival. Both the phenomenon of fugitives and their awful fate are a picture that is worldwide in our cities of the twenty-first century. Equally recognisable are some of the ways by which Gregory tries to convince his congregation to open their hearts for these people as well as, by extension, to the sick and to those in need. Among these arguments are his criticism of excessive wealth and his argument that the earth belongs to all and that its treasures should be to the benefit of all and not be exploited for the benefit of the happy few. Also his idea that in the face of the poor the face of Christ is reflected continues to be relevant in our contemporary theological discourse. In reading this sermon, at times one has the impression that the sixteen hundred years between us and the sermon do not matter much and that a text like this can still be read fruitfully by contemporary readers and give them pause to think. Yet, such a presentation is highly misleading. Indeed, at the same time this sermon contains passages and features that, even in a first, superficial reading are hard to swallow for a contemporary reader and clearly make it a text from a distant past. Among these are Gregory's threat of the Last Judgment to his audience should they not show enough care to these poor.

Digging only a little bit deeper into such a text and its context widens the distance between our vantage point and that of the text to the extent that the distance becomes almost insurmountable. Indeed, a more detailed analysis of the late antique text immediately shows that one should pay careful attention to the text's original context, its literary genre, intended and unintended audiences, the underlying theological and epistemological frameworks, the influence of rhetoric and Scripture, the social context, and the self-evident truths held by a society that undergird its coherence as a society, among many further matters.[1] Thus it becomes clear that in late antiquity "the poor" were viewed in a completely different way than in our own day and that Christian discourse about them then did not serve the same purposes as it does today.[2] The "instrumentalisation" of the poor that takes place in this discourse is especially striking. The "have nots"— a volatile group—are not so much important in themselves but are at least equally as important as gatekeepers to the kingdom of God for those who have.[3] For a generation of theologians and Christians who have been affected by the idea of the preferential option for the poor such differences sit uneasily to say the least.

Against the background of these kinds of tensions between the past and the present the Leuven project on the (im)possible dialogue between patristics and Catholic social thought, to be understood as one particular type of modern Christian discourse on socio-ethical issues, finds its place. During the 2007 seminar the key question was: What is the use, if any, of patristic texts about socio-ethical issues for contemporary Christian social ethics in general and Catholic social thought in particular? To embody the dialogue between patristics and social ethics representatives of both branches of theology sat to-

1. Gregory of Nyssa, *De pauperibus amandis oratio 1*, GNO 9, ed. Adrian van Heck (Leiden: Brill, 1967), 93–108; Eng. trans. Susan Holman, *The Hungry Are Dying: Beggars and Bishops in Roman Cappadocia*, Oxford Studies in Historical Theology (Oxford: Oxford University Press, 2001), 193–99. First analysis in J. Leemans, "Les pauvres ont revêtu le visage de notre Sauveur," in *Les Pères de l'Eglise et la voix des pauvres. Actes du IIe Colloque de La Rochelle (2, 3, et 4 septembre 2005)*, ed. Pascal Delage (La Rochelle: Association histoire et culture, 2006), 75–89.

2. Richard Finn, *Almsgiving in the Later Roman Empire: Christian Promotion and Practice, 313–450*, Oxford Classical Monographs (Oxford: Oxford University Press, 2007), 18–26, 182–88.

3. Peter Brown, *Poverty and Leadership in the Later Roman Empire* (Hanover, N.H.: University Press of New England, 2002), esp. ch.1.

gether exploring the possibilities and limitations of such a venture. This seminar was a risk and a challenge, but as such also a learning process. Its aim was to create the basic condition(s) for a real dialogue between experts from two differentiated areas of specialisation: patristic theology and Catholic social thought. *A priori*, it was expected that a conversation focused on concrete topics such as contexts, the common good, and usury—while bringing to light substantial differences in approach and leading to different results and viewpoints—would be possible. The paper presentations and the ensuing interaction, however, were characterised by radically different discourses. Consequently, the intended conversation was problematic.

Reflecting on the experiences of the seminar, three fundamental questions should be raised: (1) Why is a genuine dialogue between patristic theology and Catholic social thought so difficult? (2) What could be the use and expected benefit of such a dialogue? (3) If such a dialogue is deemed useful and profitable, what ought to be done in order to make it possible in the future? In what follows tentative answers are formulated and some lines are sketched along which answers to these questions may be sought.

## What Made the Conversation Problematic?

### *There Is No Tradition on Which to Rely*

To the best of our knowledge a conversation between the subdisciplines of early Christian theology and patristics and contemporary Christian social ethics and Catholic social thought has never been attempted before. Thus, with the 2007 seminar we broke new ground and for this we inevitably paid a price. The scholars we brought together were willing to think across disciplines and entered into conversation with participants from radically different disciplines. In doing so a clear and reciprocal knowledge-deficit emerged on a very elementary level. This deficit is, however, not incidental but structural; it belongs to the inherent tradition in both disciplines not to look to one another as primary conversation partners.

From the viewpoint of patristics, this can be explained by the observation that up to now studies addressing the relevance of patristic thinking for theological challenges and projects of today are rare. Moreover, the application of modern approaches of textual interpretation—in biblical studies often indicated as contextual, hermeneutical, postcritical modes of exegesis—have only been introduced fairly recently into patristic research and in many cases do not bridge the gap between then and now but rather seek to further the understanding of the patristic text in its context. Indeed, although poststructural hermeneutical questions were intended to reestablish a connection between ancient texts and modern readers by a folding of the original context into the modern, within studies of late antique Christianity such questions have been employed rather to further lengthen the distance between text and modern reader. They explore silences and expose "otherness" in the ancient texts such that the original context is still a chief concern. Briefly, for the researcher in late antique Christianity the primary interpretative horizon always has been late antiquity and not Christianity in the present.

Conversely, within Catholic social teaching the drive to incorporate patristics has been minimal. This can be understood from the perspective of the way traditions develop throughout history. As MacIntyre has pointed out, traditions are not only confronted with epistemological crises as a consequence of confrontations with other, noncommensurable traditions, but also as a consequence of their own internal developments.[4] One of them can be the marginalization of relevant aspects of the tradition as a result of the dominance of other aspects. In the broad tradition of Catholic social thought, the influence of Thomism with its focus on natural law and its later developments in terms of a discourse on human rights has caused a situation characterized by a marginalisation of both biblical and patristic elements of the tradition. Since Vatican II a genuine attempt has been made to develop a more biblical approach in Catholic social thought. In official Catholic social teaching Pope John Paul II has made some attempts to do it, but it is more prominently the case in nonofficial social texts or in texts from bishops' conferences, which have been dependent on the work of scholars. An example par excellence of this is the USCCB text "Economic Justice for All," in which a most interesting combination of biblical and traditional arguments is put forward. But with regards to patristic thinking both official and nonofficial Catholic social thought still suffer from the

4. According to Alasdair MacIntyre, *Whose Justice, Which Rationality?* (South Bend, Ind.: Notre Dame University Press, 1988), 361–62: "[A]t any point it may happen to any tradition that by its own standards of progress it ceases to make progress, it can become sterile, there can be conflicts over rival answers to key questions which can no longer be settled rationally," and even the methods of inquiry can become so inadequate, that a systematic breakdown of inquiry becomes a real threat.

neglect of patristic arguments, though Benedict XVI's encyclical *Deus caritas est,* as well as his recent catechetical introductions on patristic authors and their relevance for today, may indicate that in that regard a hesitant opening is not excluded.[5]

### A Different Attitude toward Historical Contexts

Following from the preceding point, and despite the introductory presentations on hermeneutics, the focus of the presentations during the seminar was, to use the words of Ricoeur, much more on the "world behind the text" (context, audience, etc.) than on the world "before the text." Thus, the potential of the text as text *(écriture)* to shed a new light on particular questions as a result of the interplay between the abundance of potential meaning in the text (a meaning which escapes the limited intentions of the original authors) and the readers (individuals or communities) who are related to the text from the point of view of a particular context and or experience, was insufficiently integrated. This lack of attention to the second level of the hermeneutics of Ricoeur may, however, have consequences that will prove fruitful in the long run. It has pushed us towards the "world behind the text," and here we were indeed confronted with the necessity to elucidate the great distance between the specific context of (especially Greek) late antiquity and the contemporary context.[6] It became almost painfully clear that we were talking about two distinct worlds and it was necessary to be very cautious about all-too-easy comparisons. The general acceptance of slavery is a classic example: in general the Church Fathers took slavery for granted as a constituent element of the socio-economic fabric of society and there are very few the passages criticising slavery. The seminar made us more aware than before that any conversation between patristics and Catholic social teaching must fully acknowledge this radical contextual diversity and never succumb to the temptation of playing it down.

5. On the use of patristic material in *Deus caritas est,* see the analysis in Brian Matz, "Patristic Sources and Catholic Social Teaching, A Forgotten Dimension: A Textual, Historical, and Rhetorical Analysis of Patristic Source Citations in the Church's Social Documents," in *Annua Nuntia Lovaniensia* 63 (Leuven: Peeters, 2008), 142–52.

6. For Ricoeur see, inter alia, A. Thomasset, *Paul Ricoeur: une poétique de la morale: aux fondements d'une éthique herméneutique et narrative dans une perspective chrétienne,* Bibliotheca ephemeridum theologicarum Lovaniensium 124 (Leuven: Peeters, 1996); F. X. Amherdt, *L'herméneutique philosophique de Paul Ricoeur et son importance pour l'exégèse biblique: en débat avec le New Yale Theology School* (Paris: Éditions du Cerf, 2006), and the latter's contribution to this volume.

What is more, not only the context but also the attitude to the context is quite different between the Fathers and Catholic social thought today. The most significant feature in this regard is the fact that (Greek) patristic authors seem to have no critical attitude vis-à-vis the Roman empire and its habits (except in the case of persecution of Christians). For them the empire is a context that is given and not as such put into question. The Christian attitude today is quite different. Apart from some neoconservative revisionists, both official and nonofficial Catholic social thought as well as mainstream Protestant social ethics are more critical of the dominant political and economic powers of our era. Perhaps this is a consequence of the experience of the twentieth century as a "road littered with corpses,"[7] with two world wars, genocides, and the unbridled sacrificing of men and women for the realisation of an utopian or ideological "the lightening future," as it is reflected in the work of theologians like Johann Baptist Metz, Jürgen Moltmann, Dorothee Sölle, and David Toole. Or perhaps it is due to a growing awareness of the negative consequences from the economic prowess of international corporations and the tireless search for production of goods at the lowest possible cost of labour. In any case, the consequences of this difference between the Fathers and Catholic social thought today seems to have resulted in a distrust of the former by the latter that the former has anything meaningful to contribute to our dialogue.

## Too Much Focus on the Analysis of Cases

Although it was the intention to facilitate a genuine conversation via a focus on cases, this caused some disappointment, particularly because of the contribution of experts in Catholic social thought. Their real reference point was the contemporary debate. This was certainly the case with papers delivered by Catholic social thought experts on the topics of common good and on usury. The paper on usury, for example, strayed from its aim to explore Catholic social thought's views on usury and instead clarified usury in the light of modern economic theories. On the one hand, the paper did not make the dialogue impossible. Its reflection on Böhm-Bawerk and Irving Fisher, who explain the interest rate theory in terms of "time preference," made not only conclusions possible about specific questions of business ethics, but it also revealed deeper underlying moral questions about frugality and mastering de-

7. David Toole, *Waiting for Godot in Sarajevo* (London: SCM, 2001).

sires. These themes feature quite prominently in the theology of the Fathers. Yet, this and other Catholic social thought papers did not sufficiently connect their understanding of the contemporary debates to issues in Christian theology. Thus, although the potential for a dialogue existed, it was not sufficiently actualised. On the one hand, the seminar participants themselves could have, in spite of the papers, generated this type of discussion. On the other hand, the emphasis on cases as opposed to particular texts from the Fathers may have been at the root of the problem.

### Lack of Attention to the Underlying Theological Questions

Related to the preceding point, it is neither sufficient to look at quotations of patristic fathers in a Catholic social teaching text nor to focus on cases that might be interesting subjects for both experts in Catholic social thought and late antique Christianity. While unfortunately only implicitly revealed in the discussion, there are common, fundamental theological concerns between the Fathers and Catholic social thought. On the subject of theosis and trinitarianism, for example, a patristic way of thinking makes a difference. There is a huge difference between the Christocentric and western approach of Catholic social teaching in *Redemptor hominis* and the trinitarian anthropology in *Sollicitudo rei socialis*.[8] The two approaches are not mutually exclusive, but the trinitarian anthropology enables Catholic social teaching to articulate deeper concerns about the very nature of human relationships and community-building. Pope John Paul II refers in this perspective to "a new model of the unity of the human race which must ultimately inspire our solidarity. This supreme model of unity, which is a reflection of the intimate life of God, one God in three persons, is what we Christians mean by the word communion" (SRS, 40). In this regards the human person is not a "living image of God" as an individual or monad, but as a community-oriented being ultimately called to a kenotic love that culminates in the heroic readiness to defend the dignity of his or her neighbour, even at the cost of his or her own life (SRS, 40).

It would have been interesting (and it is a suggestion for the future) to look at what the fundamental theological categories used by patristic authors can

---

8. Johan Verstraeten, "Re-thinking Catholic Social Thought as Tradition," in *Catholic Social Thought: Twilight or Renaissance?* BETL 157, ed. J. S. Boswell, F. P. McHugh, and J. Verstraeten, (Leuven: Peeters, 2000), 68.

mean for today in the already mentioned theme of desire, the Trinity as archè-type of community, and eschatology (and the relativization of absolute property claims). Perhaps here we can learn from some attempts in the orthodox tradi-tion as well as for the project of Fribourg on patristic theology and social ethics.

In 2000 the Council of the Russian Orthodox Church published an offi-cial document entitled *Fundaments for an Orthodox Concept of Society (Osnovy sotsialnoj kontseptsi)*, the first text in which an autocephalic Orthodox Church codified its social ethic. It was influenced by conversations with some Catho-lics initiated in the 1990s by the Orthodox father Vsevolod Tchapline (De-partment of Exterior Relations of the Patriarchate of Moscow) and by a joint publication of the Institute for Europe of the Academy of Sciences of Russia and publisher Le Cerf.[9] Later on, as a result of the Seventh Russian People's World Congress, a work group published a "Code *(svod)* of moral principles and rules concerning economic life." It resonates in a second joint publication of Catholic and Orthodox authors on the ethics of the economy.[10] In these publications it is striking how much Russian Orthodox authors refer to pa-tristic sources and how much the Catholics still have to learn from them, for example, with regards to the patristic idea of the "Sacrament of the brother."[11] The University of Fribourg (Switzerland), initiated a research program on the theology of ecumenism in dialogue with Orthodox and Protestant communi-ties. One of the research topics of this project is the theological foundations of the socio-political contribution of the Russian Orthodox churches.[12]

## Why Is Such a Dialogue Necessary? What Could Be Its Contribution?

Given the huge differences between both disciplines and the apparent dif-ficulties a dialogue between them creates, it is a legitimate question whether it

9. Jean-Yves Calvez and Anatole Krassikov, eds., *Eglise et société. Un dialogue orthodoxe russe–catholique romain* (Paris: Éditions du Cerf, 1998).

10. Jean-Yves Calvez and Andrei Zoubov, eds., *Eglise et économie. Voix orthodoxes russes. Voix ortho-doxes romaines* (Paris: Éditions du Cerf, 2006).

11. See Michel Sollogoub, "Evangile et vie économique. Une réponse russe," in *Eglise et économie. Voix orthodoxes russes. Voix orthodoxes romaines*, ed. Jean-Yves Calvez and Andrei Zoubov (Paris: Éditions du Cerf, 2006), 23–25.

12. One of the leading researchers at this institute, Barbare Hallensleben is a member of the theo-logical commission of the Vatican.

is worth pursuing such an enterprise at all. If the enterprise is worth pursuing, what benefits might one expect? We think a first benefit is renewed attention to theological tradition in the development of the doctrine of the Church. With regard to the development of Catholic social teaching it can be safely said that the patristic inheritance as an integral part of that tradition has been largely neglected. This is the conclusion of Brian Matz's research into the use of patristic texts in traditional Catholic social teaching documents.[13] While the patristic influence on nonofficial Catholic social thought remains to be studied it is clear from the disappointing conclusions to his inquiry (except for the encyclical *Deus caritas est* from Benedict XVI) that there is room for a better integration of this particular part of the tradition into future Catholic social teaching documents. This is especially the case since there are several areas in which the patristic inheritance could play a vital role. One can think here especially of the theological style of the Catholic social teaching documents, which are decidedly intellectual and make for heavy reading. For their part, the patristic texts on social ethics, usually homilies, often surprise modern readers by their imaginative use of metaphors and their direct exhortations to the audience. Moreover, they introduce the reader into a compelling theological-mystagogical framework, not only communicating a message but also providing a spiritual-theological framework through which the text is understood and gets a surplus of meaning.[14] Thus they address not only the intellect but also the heart and the soul. Yet, also on a more principled level it is clear that when the Church defines its tradition as a constituent factor of its theology it is worthwhile, even necessary, to explore the richness, possibility, and usability of the parts of that tradition that are neglected.

Secondly, the dialogue offers a unique opportunity to patristic scholars. Lately, scholarly attention to socio-ethical issues has increased, as is indicated by large-scale projects at the Australian Catholic University's Centre for Early Christian Studies, the Leuven Faculty of Theology, study groups within the North American Patristic Society, and the many individual scholars who have come forward with publications on the topic. While it is perfectly legitimate to restrict one's research to the late antique context, it seems to us equally appropriate to probe whether this research into patristic texts might have an

---

13. See n. 5 and B. Matz, "Problematic Uses of Patristic Sources in the Documents of Catholic Social Thought," *Journal of Catholic Social Thought* 4 (2007): 459–85.

14. See, for example, Basil of Caesarea's *Hom.* 6 as discussed in B. Matz's article in this volume.

actual relevance for the present situation. This is especially true in our era in which both interdisciplinarity and hermeneutics are viable concepts. Scholarly enterprises can—maybe should—in principle develop along these lines. In this way, scholars of late antique Christianity would follow a similar path as scholars in biblical studies have done in recent decades with their consideration of hermeneutically oriented methods of exegesis. When partners for such an enterprise are sought, churches and church communities present themselves as obvious possibilities because, among others, they are responsible for both the development and communication of a theological discourse and the putting into practice of this discourse. The revival of the scholarly study of Christianity in late antiquity and the growing interest of a wider audience in this area provide an ideal foundation for discussion.

Thirdly, as already suggested in regard to the dialogue programs with the Russian Orthodox Church, a better knowledge of the patristic tradition would enable Catholic theologians to mediate between the specific content of Catholic social thought and the emerging social tradition in the East.

## Conclusion

Despite the fact that interesting insights were generated from a discussion on specific themes, a more fruitful approach for a next conference would be a conversation on well-chosen texts. That would allow the participants to elucidate the complexity of the hermeneutical questions, including especially the tension between, on the one hand the necessary background knowledge of author, context, and audience, and on the other hand the acknowledgment of the difficulties inherent in any attempt to articulate the potential "usefulness" of a particular text. By "usefulness" we refer to the meaning of a patristic text in view of elucidating contemporary questions of social ethics or of reconstructing normative frameworks for it. By text-oriented, complex hermeneutics it must become possible to move from a superficial "use" or transposition of an old text into the present, to a critical fusion of two different hermeneutical horizons, a fusion which will do justice both to the distinctiveness of two different worlds of meaning and to the possibility of shedding a new light on both worlds thanks to the "disclosure" generated by the confrontation between the two. In this regard, the work started at the expert seminar of 2007 has been a meaningful but problematic start of an ongoing journey of discovery.

# CONTRIBUTORS

*Pauline Allen* is professor of Early Christian Studies at the Australian Catholic University, where she directs the Centre of Early Christian Studies. She is widely published in the field of early Christianity, including spirituality, Mariology, and social ethics.

*Reimund Bieringer* is professor of New Testament at the Catholic University of Leuven. Paul's correspondence with the Corinthians, biblical theology, and biblical hermeneutics are among his research foci. Since 2008 he has been the vice dean of the Faculty of Theology.

*Susan R. Holman* is an independent scholar of early Christianity, early Christian social ethics and its relevance for contemporary theology. She is based in Cambridge, Massachusetts, and founded www.povertystudies.org, a web resource for the exchange of ideas between scholars and informed laity.

*Thomas Hughson, S.J.,* is professor of theology at Marquette University, working in the field of theological ethics.

*Brenda Llewellyn Ihssen* is visiting professor of religious studies at Pacific Lutheran University. Her research interests include usury in late antiquity and early Christianity and spirituality among communities of women in the High Middle Ages.

*Johan Leemans* is professor of early Church history and patrology at the Catholic University of Leuven. His research and publication topics include patristic sermons, early Christian martyrdom, and social ethics.

*Brian Matz* is assistant professor of historical theology at Carroll College (Montana). From 2005 to 2009 he was a researcher with the Centre for Catholic Social Thought at the Catholic University of Leuven. He has published in the field of patristic social ethics, on Gregory Nazianzen, and on the theological controversies of the ninth century.

*Wendy Mayer* is senior research fellow with the Centre for Early Christian Studies at the Australian Catholic University. She is widely published in the field of John Chrysostom studies and is senior editor for Chrysostom's texts for the SBL Press series, Writings from the Greco-Roman World.

*Helen Rhee* is assistant professor of theology at Westmont College. Her research interests include early Christian eschatology and the connection between Christian eschatology and social thought both in early Christianity and in contemporary Protestant communities.

*Richard Schenk, O.P.,* is professor of both philosophy and theology at the Dominican School of Theology and Philosophy (GTU, Berkeley, California). He is also a member of the European Academy of Science and Arts.

*Peter Van Nuffelen* is lecturer of ancient history at the University of Exeter. Graeco-Roman and late antique historiography and pagan monotheism are his most important current areas of research.

*Johan Verstraeten* is professor of moral theology and director of the Centre for Catholic Social Thought at the Catholic University of Leuven. He has published widely in the fields of Catholic moral theology and business ethics.

# BIBLIOGRAPHY

## Primary Sources

Ambrose of Milan. *Ambrosiana scritti varii publicati nel XV centenario della morte di Sant Ambrogio*. Edited by Carolus Schenkl. Milan: L. F. Cogliati, 1897.

———. *De Iacob, de Ioseph, de Patriarchis, de fuga saeculi, de interpretatione Iob et David, de apologia David, apologia David altera, de Helia et ieiunio, de Nabuthae, de Tobia*. Edited by Carolus Schenkl. CSEL 32. Vienna: F. Tempsky, 1897.

———. *Opera, Pars prima qua continentur libri: Exameron, De paradiso, De Cain et Abel, De Noe, De Abraham, De Isaac, De bono mortis*. Edited by Carolus Schenkl. CSEL 32. Part 1. Vienna: F. Tempsky, 1897.

———. *De obitu Satyri fratris laudation funebris*. Edited by Paulus B. Albers. FP 15. Bonn: Sumptibus Petri Hanstein, 1921.

———. "In Honor of His Brother Satyrus." In *Funeral Orations by Saint Gregory Nazianzen and Saint Ambrose*. Translated by John J. Sullivan and Martin R. P. McGuire. FOTC 22. Washington, D.C.: The Catholic University of America Press, 1953.

———. *De virginitate liber unus*. Edited by Egnatius Cazzaniga. CSLP. Turin: In Aedibus Io. Bapt. Paraviae et Sociorum, 1954.

———. *Letters*. Translated by Mary Melchior Beyenka. FOTC 26. Washington D.C.: The Catholic University of America Press, 1954.

———. *Opera, Pars VII: Explanatio symboli, de sacramentis, de mysteriis, de paenitentia, de excessu fratris, de obitu Valentiniani, de obitu Theodosii*. Edited by Otto Faller. CCSL 73. Turnhout: Brepols, 1955.

———. *Hexameron, Paradise, and Cain and Abel*. Translated by John J. Savage. FOTC 42. New York: Fathers of the Church, 1961.

———. "Consolation on the Death of Emperor Valentinian." In *Funeral Orations by Saint Gregory Nazianzen and Saint Ambrose*. Translated by Roy J. Deferarri. FOTC 22. Washington D.C.: The Catholic University of America Press, 1968.

———. *On Virginity*. Translated by Daniel Callam. Peregrina Translations Series 7. Toronto: Peregrina, 1980.

———. *Opera, Pars X: Epistula et Acta, Tome III: Epistularum liber decimus, Epistulae extra collectionem, Gesta concilii Aquileiensis*. Edited by Michaela Zelzer. CSEL 82. Vienna: F. Tempsky, 1982.

———. *De officiis*. Edited by Maurice Testard. CCSL 15. Turnhout: Brepols, 2000.

———. *De officiis, Volume I: Introduction, Text, and Translation*. Translated by Ivor J. Davidson. Oxford Early Christian Studies. Oxford: Oxford University Press, 2001.

Athanasius of Alexandria. *The Life of Antony and the Letter to Marcellinus*. Translated by Robert C. Gregg. CWS. New York: Paulist Press, 1980.

———. *Vie d'Antoine*. Edited by Gerhardus J. M. Bartelink. SC 400. Paris: Éditions du Cerf, 1994. Rev. 2004.

Augustine of Hippo. "Answer to the Letters of Petilian, Bishop of Cirta." In *The Writings Against the Manichaeans and Against the Donatists*. Translated by J. R. King. *NPNF* 1: 4. Edinburgh: T. & T. Clark, 1887.

———. *Confessionum libri tredecim*. Edited by Pius Knoll. CSEL 33. Vienna: F. Tempsky, 1896.

———. *De civitate Dei, Pars I: libri I–XII*. Edited by Emanuel Hoffmann. CSEL 40. Part 1. Vienna: F. Tempsky, 1899.

———. *De civitate Dei libri XXII, Vol. II: Libri XIV–XXII*. Edited by Emanuel Hoffmann. CSEL 40. Part 2. Vienna: F. Tempsky, 1899.

———. *De fide et symbolo, de fide et operibus, de agone christiano, de continentia, de bono coniugali, de sancta virginitate*. Edited by Iosephus Zycha. CSEL 41. Vienna: F. Tempsky, 1900.

———. *Scripta contra Donatistas, Pars II: Contra litteras Petiliani libri tres, Epistula ad Catholicos de secta Donatistarum, Contra Cresconium libri quattuor*. Edited by Michael Petschenig. CSEL 52. Vienna: F. Tempsky, 1909.

———. *Sancti Augustini sermones post Maurinos reperti. Probatae dumtaxat auctoritatis nunc primum disquisiti, in unum collecti et codicum fide instaurati studio et diligentia*. Edited by Germain Morin. Miscellanea Agostiniana: Testi e studi pubblicati a cura dell'ordine eremitano di S. Agostino nel XV centenario dalla morte del santo dottore 1. Rome: Tipografia Poliglotta Vaticana, 1930.

———. *Letters 1–82*. Translated by Wilfrid Parsons. FOTC 12. Washington D.C.: The Catholic University of America Press, 1951.

———. *In Iohannis Evangelium, tractatus CXXIV*. Edited by Radbodus Willems. CCSL 36. Turnhout: Brepols, 1954.

———. *De civitate Dei, libri I–X*. Edited by Bernardus Dombart and Alphonsus Kalb. CCSL 47. Turnhout: Brepols, 1955.

———. *De civitate Dei, libri XI–XXII*. Edited by Bernardus Dombart and Alphonsus Kalb. CCSL 48. Turnhout: Brepols, 1955.

———. *Enarrationes in Psalmos I–L*. Edited by D. Eligius Dekkers and Johannes Fraipont. CCSL 38. Turnhout: Brepols, 1956.

———. *Enarrationes in Psalmos LI–C*. Edited by Eligius Dekkers and Johannes Fraipont. CCSL 39. Turnhout: Brepols, 1956.

———. *Enarrationes in Psalmos CI–CL*. Edited by Eligius Dekkers and J. Fraipont. CCSL 40. Turnhout: Brepols, 1956.

———. *Sermones de Vetero Testamento, id est sermones I–L secundum ordinem Vulgatum insertis etiam novem sermonibus post Maurinos repertis*. Edited by Cyril Lambot. CCSL 41. Turnhout: Brepols, 1961.

———. *De Trinitate libri XV, Libri I–XIII*. Edited by W. J. Mountain and F. Glorie. CCSL 50. Turnhout: Brepols, 1968.

———. *Confessionum libri XIII*. Edited by Lucas Verheijen. CCSL 27. Turnhout: Brepols, 1990.

———. *Sermones II (20–50) on the Old Testament*. Translated by Edmund Hill. WSA. Part III, II. Brooklyn, N.Y.: New City Press, 1990.

———. *Confessions*. Translated by Henry Chadwick. Oxford: Oxford University Press, 1991.

———. *Sermones III (51–94) on the New Testament*. Translated by Edmund Hill. WSA. Brooklyn, N.Y.: New City Press, 1991.

———. *Tractates on the Gospel of John, 28–54*. Translated by John W. Rettig. FOTC 88. Washington D.C.: The Catholic University of America Press, 1993.

———. *The City of God Against the Pagans*. Translated by R. W. Dyson. Cambridge Texts in the History of Political Thought. Cambridge: Cambridge University Press, 1998.

———. *Expositions of the Psalms (Enarrationes in Psalmos) 33–50*. Translated by Maria Boulding. WSA 16. New York: New City Press, 2000.

———. *De bono coniugali, De sancta virginitate*. Translated by P. G. Walsh. Oxford Early Christian Texts. Oxford: Clarendon Press, 2001.

———. *Letters 1–99*. Translated by Roland Teske. WSA 2. Part 1. New York: Newman Press, 2001.

———. *On the Trinity, Books 8–15*. Translated by Stephen McKenna. Cambridge Texts in the History of Philosophy. Cambridge: Cambridge University Press, 2002.

———. *Epistulae I–LV*. Edited by Klaus D. Daur. CCSL 31. Turnhout: Brepols, 2004.

———. *Expositions of the Psalms (Enarrationes in Psalmos) 73–98*. Translated by Maria Boulding. WSA 18. New York: New City Press, 2004.

———. *Expositions of the Psalms (Enarrationes in Psalmos) 121–150*. Translated by Maria Boulding. WSA 20. New York: New City Press, 2004.

———. *Enarrationes in Psalmos 1–50, Pars 2: Enarrationes in Psalmos 34–50*. Edited by Franco Gori and Iuliana Spaccia. CSEL 103. Part 5. Vienna: Österreichischen Akademie der Wissenschaften, 2005.

———. *Enarrationes in Psalmos 51–100, Pars 5: Enarrationes in Psalmos 141–150*. Edited by Franco Gori and Iuliana Spaccia. CSEL 95. Part 5. Vienna: Österreichische Akademie der Wissenschaften, 2005.

———. *Enarrationes in Psalmos 101–150, Pars 5: Enarrationes in Psalmos 141–150*. Edited by Franco Gori and Iuliana Spaccia. CSEL 95. Part 5. Vienna: Österreichische Akademie der Wissenschaften, 2005.

Basil of Caesarea. *Homélies sur la richesse*. Edited by and translated by Yves Courtonne. Collection d'études anciennes. Paris: Firm-Didot, 1935.

―――. *Ascetical Works*. Translated by M. Monica Wagner. FOTC 9. Washington D.C.: The Catholic University of America Press, 1950.

―――. *Homilien zum Hexaemeron*. Edited by Emmanuel Amand de Mendieta. GCS 2. Berlin: Akademie Verlag, 1997.

―――. *Vita di Cipriano, Vita di Ambrogio, Vita di Agostino*. Edited by Anthony A. R. Bastiaensen. Scritti greci e latini: Vite dei santi 3. Milan: Fondazione Lorenzo Valla, 1997.

―――. *On Social Justice*. Translated by C. Paul Schroeder. Popular Patristics Series. Crestwood, N.Y.: St. Vladimir's Seminary Press, 2009.

Clement of Alexandria. *The Exhortation to the Greeks: The Rich Man's Salvation, and the fragment of an address entitled To the Newly Baptized*. Translated by G. W. Butterworth. LCL. Cambridge, Mass.: Harvard University Press, 1919.

―――. *Les Stromates: Stromata I*. Edited by Marcel Caster. SC 30. Paris: Éditions du Cerf, 1951.

―――. *Stromata: Buch VII und VIII; Excerpta ex Theodoto; Eclogae propheticae; Quis dives salvetur; Fragmente*. Edited by Otto Stählin, Ludwig Früchtel, and Ursula Treu. GCS 17. Berlin: Akademie Verlag, 1970.

―――. *Stromata: Buch I–VI*. Edited by Otto Stahlin and Ludwig Fruchtel. GCS 52. Berlin: Akademie Verlag, 1985.

―――. *Stromateis: Books One to Three*. Translated by John Ferguson. FOTC 85. Washington D.C.: The Catholic University of America Press, 1991.

Cyprian of Carthage. *Treatises*. Translated by Roy J. Deferarri. FOTC 36. Washington D.C.: The Catholic University of America Press, 1958.

―――. *Letters (1–81)*. Translated by Rose B. Donna. FOTC 51. Washington D.C.: The Catholic University of America Press, 1964.

―――. *De Lapsis and De Ecclesiae Catholicae Unitate*. Translated by Maurice Bévenot. Oxford Early Christian Texts. Oxford: Clarendon Press, 1971.

―――. *Ad Quirinum, Ad Fortunatum, De lapsis, De ecclesiae catholicae unitate*. Edited by Maurice Bévenot. CCSL 3. Part 1. Turnhout: Brepols, 1972.

―――. *The Letters of St. Cyprian of Carthage: Volume III, Letters 55–66*. Translated by G. W. Clarke. ACW 46. New York: Newman Press, 1986.

―――. *Epistularium*. Edited by G. F. Diercks. CCSL 3B. Part 3. Turnhout: Brepols, 1996.

―――. *La bienfaisance et les aumônes*. Edited by Michel Poirier. SC 440. Paris: Éditions du Cerf, 1999.

Dionysius the Areopagite. *The Complete Works*. Translated by Colm Luibheid. CWS. New York: Paulist Press, 1987.

Eusebius of Caesarea. *Eusebii Pamphili Evangelicae praeparationis Libri XV. Ad codices manuscriptos denuo collatos recensuit Anglice nunc primum reddidit notis et indicibus instruxit*. 4 vols. Translated by Edwin H. Gifford. Oxford: Typographeo Academico, 1903.

———. *La préparation évangélique, Livre I*. Edited by Jean Sirinelli. SC 206. Paris: Éditions du Cerf, 1974.

———. *Die Praeparatio Evangelica: Einleitung, die Bücher I bis X*. Edited by Édouard des Places. GCS 43. Band 2. Berlin: Akademie Verlag, 1982.

———. *Eusebius. Life of Constantine*. Translated by Averil Cameron and Stuart Hall. Oxford: Oxford University Press, 1999.

Evagrius. *Historia ecclesiastica. The Ecclesiastical History of Evagrius Scholasticus*. Translated by Michael Whitby. Liverpool: Liverpool University Press, 2000.

Gregory the Great. "The Book of Pastoral Rule and Selected Epistles." In *Leo the Great. Gregory the Great*. Translated by James Barmby. *NPNF* 2: 12. Edinburgh: T. & T. Clark, 1895.

———. *Registrum epistolarum, Tome II: Libri VIII–XIV*. Edited by Paulus Ewald. MGH. Berlin: Weidmann, 1899.

———. *Pastoral Care*. Translated by Henry Davis. ACW 11. Westminster, Md.: The Newman Press, 1950.

———. *Registrum epistularum libri I–VII*. Edited by Dag Norberg. CCSL 140. Turnhout: Brepols, 1982.

———. *Registre des lettres, Livres I et II*. Edited by Pierre Minard. SC 370. Paris: Éditions du Cerf, 1991.

———. *Règle pastorale, Tome I*. Edited by Floribert Rommel. Translated by Charles Morel. SC 381. Paris: Éditions du Cerf, 1992.

———. *Règle pastorale, Tome II*. Edited by Floribert Rommel. Translated by Charles Morel. SC 382. Paris: Éditions du Cerf, 1992.

———. *Homiliae in evangelia*. Edited by and translated by Michael Fiedrowicz. Fontes Christiani 28. Part 1. Freiburg: Herder, 1997.

———. *Homiliae in evangelia*. Edited by Raymond Étaix. CCSL 141. Turnhout: Brepols, 1999.

Gregory Nazianzen. *Discours 1–3*. SC 247. Edited by Jean Bernardi. Paris: Éditions du Cerf, 1978.

———. *Discours 32–37*. Edited by Claudio Moreschini. Translated by Paul Gallay. SC 318. Paris: Éditions du Cerf, 1985.

———. *Discours 38–41*. Edited by Claudio Moreschini. Translated by Paul Gallay. SC 358. Paris: Éditions du Cerf, 1990.

———. *Discours 6–12*. Edited by Marie-Ange Calvet-Sebasti. SC 405. Paris: Éditions du Cerf, 1995.

Gregory of Nyssa. *De vita Moysis*. Edited by Herbertus Musurillo. GNO 7. Part 1. Leiden: Brill, 1964.

———. *The Life of Moses*. Translated by A. J. Malherbe and Everett Ferguson. CWS. New York: Paulist Press, 1978.

———. *Forty Gospel Homilies*. Translated by David Hurst. Cistercian Studies Series 123. Kalamazoo, Mich.: Cistercian Publications, 1990.

Hermas. *Le pasteur*. Edited by Robert Joly. SC 53. Paris: Éditions du Cerf, 1958.

Irenaeus of Lyon. "Against Heresies." In *The Apostolic Fathers with Justin Martyr and Irenaeus*. Translated by Alexander Roberts and James Donaldson. *ANF* 1. Edinburgh: T. & T. Clark, 1867.

——. *Contre les hérésies*. Edited by Adelin Rousseau. SC 153. Paris: Éditions du Cerf, 1969.

——. *Contre les hérésies, Livre III*. Edited by Adelin Rousseau and Louis Doutreleau. SC 211. Paris: Éditions du Cerf, 1974.

——. *Contre les hérésies, Livre I*. Edited by Adelin Rousseau and Louis Doutreleau. SC 264. Paris: Éditions du Cerf, 1979.

——. *Against the Heresies, Book 1*. Translated by Dominic J. Unger and John J. Dillon. ACW 55. Mahwah, N.J.: Paulist Press, 1992.

——. *Epideixis Adversus Haereses*. Edited by Norbert Brox. Fontes Christiani 8. Part 1. Freiburg: Herder, 1993.

——. *Adversus haereses*. Edited by Norbert Brox. Fontes Christiani 8. Part 3. Freiburg: Herder, 1995.

——. *Adversus haereses*. Edited by Norbert Brox. Fontes Christiani 8. Part 5. Freiburg: Herder, 2001.

John Cassian. *The Conferences*. Translated by Boniface Ramsey. ACW 57. New York: Newman Press, 1997.

——. *Collationes XXIII*. Edited by Michael Petschenig and Rev. Gottfried Kreuz. CSEL 13. Vienna: Österreichische Akademie der Wissenschaften, 2004.

John Chrysostom. "The Homilies on the Epistle of St. Paul to the Romans." In *Saint Chrysostom: Homilies on the Acts of the Apostles and The Epistle to the Romans*. Translated by J. B. Morris and W. H. Simcox. *NPNF* 1: 11. Edinburgh: T. & T. Clark, 1877.

——. "Homilies on the Acts of the Apostles." In *John Chrysostom. Homilies on the Acts of the Apostles and the Epistle to the Romans*. Translated by H. Browne and G. B. Stevens. *NPNF* 1: 11. Edinburgh: T. & T. Clark, 1889.

——. "Homilies on the Statues, to the People of Antioch." In *John Chrysostom. On the Priesthood; Ascetic Treatises; Select Homilies and Letters; Homilies on the Statues*. Translated by W. R. W. Stephens. *NPNF* 1: 9. Edinburgh: T. & T. Clark, 1889.

——. "Two Homilies on Eutropius." In *John Chrysostom. On the Priesthood; Ascetic Treatises; Select Homilies and Letters; Homilies on the Statues*. Translated by W. R. W. Stephens. *NPNF* 1: 9. Edinburgh: T. & T. Clark, 1889.

——. *La virginité*. Edited by Herbert Musurillo. SC 125. Paris: Éditions du Cerf, 1966.

——. *On Virginity, Against Remarriage*. Translated by Sally Rieger Shore. Studies in Women and Religion 9. New York: Mellen Press, 1983.

——. *Homilies on the Gospel of Saint Matthew*. Translated by George Prevost. *NPNF* 1: 10. Grand Rapids, Mich.: Eerdmans, 1991.

——. *Sermons sur la Genèse*. Edited by Laurence Brottier. SC 433. Paris: Éditions du Cerf, 1998.

Julian the Apostate. *The Works of the Emperor Julian in Three Volumes*, vol. 3. Translated by William Cave Wright. LCL. Cambridge, Mass.: Harvard University Press, 1923.

———. *Oeuvres Complètes, tome I, 2e partie: Lettres et fragments*. Edited by Joseph Bidez. Paris: Les belles lettres, 1924.

Justin Martyr. *Opera quae feruntur omnia, Tomi I Pars I: Opera Iustini indubitata*. Edited by Johan Karl Theodor von Otto. Corpus Apologeticorum Christianorum saeculi secundi. Jena: Fischer, 1876.

———. *The First Apology; The Second Apology; Dialogue with Trypho; Exhortation to the Greeks; Discourse to the Greeks; The Monarchy or the Rule of God*. Translated by Thomas B. Falls. FOTC 6. Washington D.C.: The Catholic University of America Press, 1977.

———. *Apologiae pro Christianis*. Edited by Miroslav Marcovich. PTS 38. Berlin: de Gruyter, 1994.

———. *Apologie pour les Chrétiens*. Edited by Charles Munier. Paradosis: Études de littérature et de théologie anciennes. Fribourg, Switzerland: Éditions Universitaires, 1995.

———. *Dialogus cum Tryphone*. Edited by Miroslav Marcovich. PTS 47. Berlin: de Gruyter, 1997.

———. *The First and Second Apologies*. Translated by Leslie William Barnard. ACW 56. Mahwah, N.J.: Paulist Press, 1997.

Lactantius. *Opera omnia, Pars I: Divinae institutiones et epitome divinarum institutionum*. Edited by Samuel Brandt. CSEL 19. Prague: F. Tempsky, 1890.

———. *Institutions divines*. Edited by Pierre Monat. SC 204. Paris: Éditions du Cerf, 1973.

———. *Divine Institutes*. Translated by Anthony Bowen and Peter Garnsey. Translated Texts for Historians 40. Liverpool: Liverpool University Press, 2003.

Leo I. *Sermons, Tome IV*. Edited by René Dolle. SC 200. Paris: Éditions du Cerf, 1973.

———. *Tractatus septem et nonaginta*. Edited by Antoine Chavasse. CCSL 138 and 138A. Turnhout: Brepols, 1973.

———. *Sermons*. Translated by Jane P. Freeland and Agnes J. Conway. FOTC 93. Washington D.C.: The Catholic University of America Press, 1996.

Leo XIII. *L'Enciclica Rerum novarum: Testo autentico e redazioni preparatorie dai documenti originali*. Edited by Giovanni Antonazzi. Rome: Storia e letteratura, 1957.

Minucius Felix. *Octavius*. Translated by Rudolph Arbesmann. FOTC 10. Washington D.C.: The Catholic University of America Press, 1950.

———. *Octavius*. Edited by Michael Pellegrino. CSLP. Turin: G. B. Paravia, 1972.

———. *The Octavius*. Translated by G. W. Clarke. ACW 39. New York: Newman Press, 1974.

Possidius. *The Life of Saint Augustine*. Translated by John E. Rotelle. The Augustinian Series 1. Villanova, Pa.: The Augustinian Press, 1988.

Sulpitius Severus. "Life of St. Martin." In *The Works of Sulpitius Severus*. Translated by Alexander Roberts. NPNF 2: 11. Edinburgh: T. & T. Clark, 1894.

———. *Writings*. Translated by Bernard Peebles. FOTC 7. Washington D.C.: The Catholic University of America Press, 1949.

————. *Vie de Saint Martin, Tome I.* Edited by Jacques Fontaine. SC 133. Paris: Éditions du Cerf, 1967.

Tertullian. *Opera, Pars III.* Edited by Aemilii Kroymann. CSEL 47. Vienna: F. Tempsky, 1906.

————. *Apologeticum.* Edited by Heinrich Hoppe. CSEL 69. Vienna: F. Tempsky, 1939.

————. *Apologetical Works.* Translated by Emily Joseph Daly. FOTC 10. Washington D.C.: The Catholic University of America Press, 1950.

————. *Treatises on Marriage and Remarriage: To His Wife: An Exhortation to Chastity, Monogamy.* Translated by William P. Le Saint. ACW 13. Westminster, Md.: Newman Press, 1951.

————. *Opera, Pars I: Opera Catholica, Adversus Marcionem.* Edited by Eligius Dekkers, Janus G. P. Borleffs, and R. Willems. CCSL 1. Turnhout: Brepols, 1954.

————. *Opera, Pars II: Opera monastica.* Edited by Aloïs Gerlo. CCSL 2. Turnhout: Brepols, 1954.

————. *Treatise on the Resurrection.* Translated by Ernest Evans. London: SPCK, 1960.

————. *À son épouse.* Edited by Charles Munier. SC 273. Paris: Éditions du Cerf, 1980.

Theodoret of Cyrus. *On Divine Providence.* Translated by Thomas Halton. ACW 49. New York: Newman Press, 1988.

## Secondary Sources

Abbott, Walter M. *The Documents of Vatican II: All Sixteen Official Texts Promulgated by the Ecumenical Council 1963–1965.* Chicago: Follett, 1966.

Allen, Pauline. "Severus of Antioch and Pastoral Care." In *Prayer and Spirituality in the Early Church* 2. Edited by Pauline Allen, Wendy Mayer, and Lawrence Cross. Brisbane: Centre for Early Christian Studies, 1999.

Aubert, Roger. *Catholic Social Teaching: An Historical Perspective.* Milwaukee: Marquette University Press, 2003.

Avila, Charles. *Ownership: Early Christian Teaching.* Maryknoll, N.Y.: Orbis Books, 1983.

Avi-Yonah, M. "The Bath of the Lepers at Scythopolis." *Israel Exploration Journal* 13 (1963): 325–26.

Bagnall, Roger S. "Monks and Property: Rhetoric, Law, and Patronage in the *Apophthegmata Patrum* and the Papyri." *Greek, Roman, and Byzantine Studies* 42 (2001): 7–24.

Bainton, Roland. *Christian Attitudes Towards War and Peace.* New York: Abingdon Press, 1960.

Bakhtin, Mikhail. *The Dialogic Imagination: Four Essays.* Edited by Michael Holquist. Translated by Caryl Emerson and Michael Holquist. Austin, Tex.: University of Texas Press, 1981.

Banfi, Antonio. *Habent illi iudices suos. Studi sull' esclusivita. Della giurisdizione ecclesiastica e sulle origini del privilegium fori in diritto romano e bizantino.* Milan: Dott. A. Giuffre Editore, 2005.

Barclay, John. "Poverty in Pauline studies: a response to Steven Friesen." *JSNT* 26.3 (2004): 363–66.

Barrera, Albino. *Modern Catholic Social Documents and Political Economy*. Washington, D.C.: Georgetown University Press, 2001.

Barry, Peter. "Structuralism." In *Beginning Theory: An Introduction to Literary and Cultural Theory*. Manchester: Manchester University Press, 2002, 39–60.

Barthes, Roland. "The Death of the Author." In *Image, Music, Text: Essays Selected and Translated by Stephen Heath*. London: Fontana Press, 1977, 142–49.

Baumgartner, Ephrem. "Der Kommunismus im Urchristentum." *Zeitschrift für katholische Theologie* 33 (1909): 625–45.

Bieringer, Reimund. "The Normativity of the Future: The Authority of the Bible for Theology." *ET Bulletin: Zeitschrift für Theologie in Europa* 8 (1997): 52–67.

———. "Biblical Revelation and Exegetical Interpretation According to *Dei Verbum* 12." In *Vatican II and its Legacy*. BETL 166. Edited by Mattijs Lamberigts and Leo Kenis. Leuven: Peeters, 2002, 25–58.

———. "'Come, and You Will See' (John 1:39): Dialogical Authority and Normativity of the Future in the Fourth Gospel and in Religious Education." In *Hermeneutics and Religious Education*. BETL 180. Edited by Herman Lombaerts and Didier Pollefeyt. Leuven: Peeters, 2005, 179–201.

———. "Texts that Create a Future: The Function of Ancient Texts for Theology Today." In *Reading Patristic Social Ethics: Issues and Challenges for the Twenty-First Century*. CUA Studies in Early Christianity. Edited by Johan Leemans, Brian Matz, and Johan Verstraeten. Washington D.C.: The Catholic University of America Press, forthcoming 2011.

Bieringer, Reimund, Didier Pollefeyt, and Frederique Vandecasteele-Vanneuville. "Wrestling with Johannine Anti-Judaism: A Hermeneutical Framework for the Analysis of the Current Debate." In *Anti-Judaism and the Fourth Gospel*. Edited by Reimund Bieringer, Didier Pollefeyt, and Frederique Vandecasteele-Vanneuville. Louisville, Ky.: Westminster John Knox, 2001, 3–37.

Bieringer, Reimund, and Mary Elsbernd, with Susan M. Garthwaite, et al. *Normativity of the Future: Reading Biblical and Other Authoritative Texts in an Eschatological Perspective*. ANL 61. Leuven: Peeters, forthcoming 2009.

Bihlmeyer, Karl. *Die Apostolischen Väter*. Sammlung ausgewählter kirchen- und dogmengeschichtlicher Quellenschriften. Tübingen: Mohr, 1924.

Boersma, Hans. "Irenaeus, Derrida and Hospitality: On the Eschatological Overcoming of Violence." *Modern Theology* 19 (2003): 163–80.

Bolkestein, Hendrik. *Wohltätigkeit und Armenpflege im vorchristlichen Altertum*. Utrecht: A. Oosthoek, 1939.

Bouffartigue, Jean. "L'authenticité de la letter 84 de l'empereur Julien." *Revue de philologie* 79 (2005): 231–42.

Bourg, Florence Caffrey. *Where Two or Three Are Gathered: Christian Families as Domestic Churches*. Notre Dame, Ind.: University of Notre Dame Press, 2003.

Brabant, Christophe. "The Truth Narrated: Ricoeur on Religious Experience." In *Divinising*

*Experience: Essays in the History of Religious Experience from Origen to Ricoeur.* Studies in Philosophical Theology. Edited by Lieven Boeve and Laurence P. Hemming. Leuven: Peeters, 2004, 246–69.

Bradshaw, Paul. *The Search for the Origins of Christian Worship.* London: SPCK, 1992.

Bravo, R. Sierra, and Florentino Del Valle, eds. *Doctrina social y economica de los padres de la Iglesia: Colección general de documentos y textos.* Madrid: Biblioteca Fomento Social, 1967.

Brentano, Lujo. "Die wirtschaftlichen Lehren des christlichen Altertums." In *Sitzungsberichte der philosophische-philologischen und der historischen Klasse der königliche bayerische Akademie der Wissenschaften.* Munich, 1902, 141–93.

Briggs, Richard S. "What Does Hermeneutics Have to Do with Biblical Interpretation." *Heythrop Journal* 47 (2006): 55–74.

Brink, David O. "Eudaimonism, Love and Friendship, and Political Community." *Social Philosophy and Policy* 16 (1999): 252–89.

Brottier, Laurence. "De l'église hors de l'église au ciel anticipé sur quelques paradoxes Chrysostomiens." *Revue d'histoire et de philosophie religieuses* 76 (1996): 277–92.

Brown, Peter. *Poverty and Leadership in the Later Roman Empire.* Hanover, N.H.: University Press of New England, 2002.

Bruck, Eberhard Friedrich. *Die Kirchenväter und soziales Erbrecht. Wanderungen religiöser Ideen durch die Rechte der östlichen und westlichen Welt.* Berlin: Springer-Verlag, 1956.

Burns, Mary A. *Saint John Chrysostom's Homilies on the Statues: A Study of Their Rhetorical Qualities and Form.* Patristic Studies 22. Washington D.C.: The Catholic University of America Press, 1930.

Burns, Stuart K. "Pseudo-Macarius and the Messalians: The Use of Time for the Common Good." In *The Use and Abuse of Time in Christian History: Papers Read at the 1999 Summer Meeting and the 2000 Winter Meeting of the Ecclesiastical History Society.* Studies in Church History 37. Edited by R. N. Swanson. Suffolk: Boydell Press, 2002, 1–12.

Burt, Donald. "Friendship and Subordination in Earthly Societies." *Augustinian Studies* 22 (1991): 83–123. Reprinted and revised in *Christianity and Society: The Social World of Early Christianity.* Edited by Everett Ferguson. New York: Garland Publishing, 1999, 315–55.

Cadoux, C. John. *The Early Christian Attitude Toward War.* London: Headley Brothers, 1919.

Cady, Linell E. "Hermeneutics and Tradition: the Role of the Past in Jurisprudence and Theology." *Harvard Theological Review* 79 (1986): 439–63.

Cameron, Alan. "A Misidentified Homily of Chrysostom." *Nottingham Mediaeval Studies* 32 (1988): 34–48.

Cameron, Averil. *Christianity and the Rhetoric of Empire: The Development of Christian Discourse.* Berkeley: University of California Press, 1991.

Cameron, Averil, and J. Long, with L. Sherry. *Barbarians and Politics at the Court of Arcadius.* Berkeley: University of California Press, 1993.

Caner, Daniel. *Wandering, Begging Monks: Spiritual Authority and the Promotion of Monasticism in Late Antiquity*. Berkeley: University of California Press, 2002.

Canning, Raymond. "St. Augustine's Vocabulary of the Common Good and the Place of Love for Neighbour." *Studia Patristica* 33 (1997): 48–54.

Carrié, Jean-Michel. "*Nil habens praeter quod ipso die vestiebatur.* Comment définir le seuil de pauvreté à Rome?" In *Consuetudinis amor: fragments d'histoire romaine (II<sup>e</sup>-VI<sup>e</sup> siècles) offerts à Jean-Pierre Callu*. Edited by François Chausson and Étienne Wolff. Rome: L'Erma di Bretschneider, 2003, 71–102.

Case, Shirley Jackson. *The Social Origins of Christianity*. Chicago: University of Chicago Press, 1923.

————. *The Social Triumph of the Ancient Church*. New York: Harper and Row, 1933.

Charles, J. Daryl. "Pacifists, Patriots or Both? Second Thoughts on Early Christian Attitudes toward Soldiering and War." Unpublished paper delivered at the Annual Meeting of the Evangelical Theological Society. Philadelphia, 2005.

Chartier, Roger. "Texts, Printing, Readings." In *The New Cultural History*. Edited by Lynn Hunt. Berkeley: University of California Press, 1989.

Chastel, Etienne. *Études historiques sur l'influence de la charité durant les premiers siècles chrétiens, et considérations sur son rôle dans les sociétés modernes*. Paris: Capelle, 1853. ET: *The charity of the primitive churches: Historical studies upon the influence of Christian charity during the first centuries of our era, with some considerations touching its bearings upon modern society*. Translated by George-Auguste Matile. Philadelphia: J. B. Lippincott and Co., 1857.

Chauvot, Alain. *Procope de Gaza, Priscien de Césarée: Panégyriques de l'Empereur Anastase Ier*. Bonn: Habelt, 1986.

Christophe, Paul. *L'usage chrétien du droit de propriété dans l'Écriture et la tradition patristique*. Paris: P. Lethielleux, 1964.

Colish, Marcia L. *Ambrose's Patriarchs: Ethics for the Common Man*. Notre Dame, Ind.: University of Notre Dame Press, 2005.

Consolino, F. E. "Sante o patrone? Le aristocratiche tardoantiche e il potere della carità." *Studi Storici* 30 (1989): 969–71.

Cooper, Kate. "An(n)ianus of Celeda and the Latin readers of John Chrysostom." *Studia Patristica* 27 (1993): 249–55.

Corcoran, Gervase. "St. Augustine and the Poor." *Milltown Studies* 12 (1983): 69–76.

Coulie, Bernard. *Les richesses dans l'oeuvre de Saint Grégoire de Nazianze*. Publications de l'Institut Orientaliste de Louvain. Louvain-la-neuve: Université Catholique de Louvain, 1985.

Countryman, Louis William. *The Rich Christian in the Church of the Early Empire: Contradictions and Accomodations*. Texts and Studies in Religion. New York: Edward Mellen Press, 1980.

Crislip, Andrew T. *From monastery to hospital: Christian monasticism & the transformation of health care in late antiquity*. Ann Arbor, Mich.: Univ. of Michigan, 2005.

Cunningham, Mary B., and Pauline Allen, eds. *Preacher and Audience: Studies in Early Christian and Byzantine Homiletics.* A New History of the Sermon 1. Leiden: Brill, 1998.

Curran, Charles. *Catholic Social Teaching 1891–Present: A Historical Theological and Ethical Analysis.* Washington, D.C.: Georgetown University Press, 2002.

———. ed. *Change in Official Catholic Moral Teachings.* Readings in Moral Theology. New York: Paulist Press, 2003.

Cutrufello, Andrew. *Continental Philosophy: A Contemporary Introduction.* London: Routledge, 2005.

Dagron, Gilbert. "Les moines et la ville. Le monachisme à Constantinople jusqu'au concile de Chalcédone." *Travaux et Mémoires* 4 (1970): 229–76; esp. 246–53.

Daley, Brian. "Building a New City: The Cappadocian Fathers and the Rhetoric of Philanthropy." *JECS* 7 (1999): 431–61.

———. *Gregory of Nazianzus.* The Early Church Fathers. London: Routledge, 2006.

Daly, L. J. "Themistius' Concept of Philanthropy." *Byzantion* 45 (1975): 22–40.

Davidson, Ivor J. *Ambrose. De officiis, Volume II: Commentary.* Oxford Early Christian Studies. Oxford: Oxford University Press, 2001.

Davis, Leo D. *The First Seven Ecumenical Councils (325–787): Their History and Theology.* Theology and Life 21. Wilmington, Del.: Michael Glazier Press, 1987.

de Aldama, J. A. *Repertorium Pseudochrysostomicum.* Paris: CNRS, 1965.

de Boer, Theo. "Paul Ricoeur: Thinking the Bible." In *God in France: Eight Contemporary French Thinkers on God.* Studies in Philosophical Theology. Edited by Peter Jonkers and Ruud Welten. Leuven: Peeters, 2005, 43–67.

Deissmann, Adolf. *Das Urchristentum und die unteren Schichten,* 2nd ed. Göttingen: Vandenhoeck and Ruprecht, 1908.

Delage, Pascal-Grégoire, ed. *Les pères de l'Eglise et la voix des pauvres.* La Rochelle: Association Histoire et Culture, 2006.

de Lubac, Henri. *Medieval Exegesis.* 2 vols. Translated by Mark Sebanc and E. M. Macieroweski. Grand Rapids, Mich.: Eerdmans, 1998, 2000.

Demandt, Alexander. "Der Fürstenspiegel des Agapet." *Mediterraneo Antico* 5 (2002): 573–84.

der Hagen, Odulphus Josephus van. *De Clementis Alexandrini sententiis oeconomicis, socialibus, politicis.* Utrecht: Dekker and V. D. Vegt, 1920.

Descoeudres, Georges. "Kirche und Diakonia: Gemeinschaftsräume in den Ermitagen der Qusur el-Izeila." In *Explorations aux Qouçour el-Izeila lors des campagnes 1981, 1982, 1984, 1985, 1986, 1989 et 1990.* Edited by Philippe Bridel, et al. Mission Suisse d'archéologie copte de l'université de Genève. EK 8184. Tome III. Louvain: Peeters, 1999.

Desmond, W. D. *The Greek Praise of Poverty: Origins of Ancient Cynicism.* Notre Dame, Ind.: University of Notre Dame Press, 2006.

de Ste. Croix, G. E. M. "Early Christian Attitudes to Property and Slavery." In *Church, Soci-*

*ety and Politics: Papers Read at the Thirteenth Summer Meeting and the Fourteenth Winter Meeting of the Ecclesiastical History Society*. Studies in Church History 12. Edited by Derek Baker. Oxford: Basil Blackwell, 1975, 1–38.

———. *The Class Struggle in the Ancient Greek World*. London: Duckworth, 1981.

De Vinne, Michael J. "The Advocacy of Empty Bellies: Episcopal Representations of the Poor in the Late Empire." Ph.D. diss., Stanford University, 1995.

Dewing, H. B. *Procopius. The Anecdota or Secret History*. London: Heinemann, 1935.

Diederich, W., A. Ibarra, and T. Mormann. "Bibliography of Structuralism." *Erkenntnis* 30 (1989): 387–407.

———. "Bibliography of structuralism II (1989–1994 and Additions)." *Erkenntnis* 41 (1994): 403–18.

Domeris, William Robert. *Touching the Heart of God: The Social Construction of Poverty Among Biblical Peasants*. Library of Hebrew Bible/Old Testament Studies 466. Edinburgh: T&T Clark, 2007, 9–26.

Dorr, Donal. *Option for the Poor: A Hundred Years of Vatican Social Teaching*. Dublin: Gill and Macmillan, 1983. Rev. 1992.

Drobner, Hubertus R. *Augustinus von Hippo: Sermones ad populum*. Supplements to *VC*. Leiden: Brill, 2000.

Dulles, Avery. *Models of Revelation*. Garden City, N.Y.: Image Books, 1985.

Duncan-Jones, Richard. *The Economy of the Roman Empire*. Cambridge: Cambridge University Press, 1974.

Ehrman, Bart, ed. *The Apostolic Fathers, Volume I: I Clement, II Clement, Ignatius, Polycarp, Didache*. LCL. Cambridge, Mass.: Harvard University Press, 2003.

———. *The Apostolic Fathers, Volume II: Epistle of Barnabas, Papias and Quadratus, Epistle to Diognetus, The Shepherd of Hermas*. LCL. Cambridge, Mass.: Harvard University Press, 2003.

Elm, Susanna. *"Virgins of God": The Making of Asceticism in Early Christianity*. Oxford Classical Monographs. Oxford: Clarendon Press, 1996.

Elsbernd, Mary, and Reimund Bieringer. *When Love is not Enough: A Theo-Ethic of Justice*. Collegeville, Minn.: The Liturgical Press, 2002.

———. "Interpreting the Signs of the Times in the Light of the Gospel: Vision and Normativity of the Future." In *Scrutinizing the Signs of the Times in Light of the Gospel*. BETL 208. Edited by Johan Verstraeten. Leuven: Peeters, 2007, 41–97.

Eschmann, I. Th. "A Thomistic Glossary on the Principle of the Pre-Eminence of the Common Good." *Mediaeval Studies* 5 (1943): 123–66.

Evans, Jeanne. *Paul Ricoeur's Hermeneutics of the Imagination*. American University Studies. Series VII: Theology and Religion 143. New York: Peter Lang, 1995.

Finn, Richard. *Almsgiving in the Later Roman Empire: Christian Promotion and Practice, 313–450*. Oxford Classical Monographs. Oxford: Oxford University Press, 2006.

Foster, G. M. "Peasant society and the image of Limited Good." *American Anthropologist* 67 (1965): 293–315.

————. "A second look at Limited Good." *Anthropological Quarterly* 45 (1972): 57–64.

Fournet, J.-L. *Hellénisme dans l'Egypte du VIe siècle: la bibliothèque et l'oeuvre de Dioscore d'Aphrodité*. Cairo: Institut français, 1999.

Fox, M. M. *The Life and Times of Saint Basil the Great as Revealed in His Works*. Washington, D.C.: The Catholic University of America Press, 1939.

Freu, Christel. *Les figures du pauvre dans les sources Italiennes de l'antiquité tardive*. Études d'archéologie et d'histoire ancienne. Paris: De Boccard, 2007.

Friesen, Steven J. "Poverty in Pauline studies: beyond the so-called new consensus." *JSNT* 26.3 (2004): 323–61.

Funk, Francois-Xavier. "Über Reichtum und Handel im christlichen Altertum." *Historisch-politische Blätter* 130 (1902): 888–99.

Gadamer, Hans-Georg. *Wahrheit und Methode: Grundzüge einer philosophischen Hermeneutik*. Tübingen: Mohr-Siebeck, 1960. ET: *Truth and Method*. Translated by Joel Weinsheimer and Donald Marshall. New York: Crossroad, 1989.

Gain, Benoît. *L'église de Cappadoce au IVᵉ siècle d'après la correspondance de Basile de Césarée (330–379)*. Orientalia Christiana Analecta 225. Rome: Pontificium Institutum Orientale, 1985.

Gallay, Paul, ed. and trans. *Saint Grégoire de Nazianze. Correspondance, Tome I, Lettres I–C*. Paris: Les Belles Lettres 2003.

Garnsey, Peter. *Famine and Food Supply in the Greco-Roman World: Responses to Risk and Crisis*. Cambridge: Cambridge University Press, 1988.

————. *Ideas of Slavery from Aristotle to Augustine*. Cambridge: Cambridge University Press 1996.

————. "The originality and origins of Anonymus, *De Divitiis*." In *From Rome to Constantinople: Studies in Honour of Averil Cameron*. Late Antique History and Religion 1. Edited by Hagit Amirav and Bas ter Haar Romeny. Leuven: Peeters, 2007, 29–45.

Garsoian, Nina. "Nersês le Grand, Basile de Césarée et Eustathe de Sébaste." *Revue des études arméniennes* 17 (1983): 145–69.

Gatier, P.-L. "Villages du Proche Orient protobyzantine (4ème–7ème s.). Étude régionale." In *The Byzantine and Early Islamic Near East 2: Land Use and Settlement Patterns*. Edited by G. R. D. King and Averil Cameron. Princeton, N.J.: Darwin Press, 1994, 17–48.

Geerard, Maurits, ed. *Ab Athanasio ad Chrysostomum*. CPG 2. Turnhout: Brepols, 1974.

————. *A Cyrillo Alexandrino ad Iohannem Damascenum*. CPG 3. Turnhout: Brepols, 1979.

————. *Patres Antenicaeni*. CPG 1. Turnhout: Brepols, 1983.

Geerard, Maurits, et al. *Supplementum*. CPG. Turnhout: Brepols, 1998.

Geertz, Clifford. *Local Knowledge: Further Essays in Interpretive Anthropology*. New York: Basic Books, 1983, 1993.

————. "Thick Description: Toward an Interpretive Theory of Culture." In *The Interpretation of Cultures: Selected Essays*. London: Fontana, 1993.

Giaquinta, Carmelo J. "La función social de la propiedad según la doctrina de los Santos Padres." In *Socialismo y socialismos en America Latina*. Bogota: CELAM, 1977, 320–35.

Giet, Stanislas. "La doctrine de l'appropriation des biens chez quelques-uns des Pères." *Recherches des science religieuse* 35 (1948): 55–91.

———. "L'argumentation de quelques passages de St. Jean Chrysostome contre la propriété." In *La revelation chretienne et le droit: Colloque de philosophie du droit (24 et 25 novembre 1959).* Paris: Librairie Dalloz, 1961, 51–62.

Glare, P. G. W., ed. *Oxford Latin Dictionary.* Oxford: Clarendon Press, 1982.

Gonzales, Justo. *Faith and Wealth: A History of Early Christian Ideals on the Origin, Significance and Use of Money.* San Francisco: Harper and Row, 1990.

Gordon, Barry. "The Problem of Scarcity and the Christian Fathers: John Chrysostom and Some Contemporaries." *Studia Patristica* 22 (1989): 108–20.

———. *The Economic Problem in Biblical and Patristic Thought.* Supplements to *VC.* Texts and Studies of Early Christian Life and Language IX. Leiden: Brill, 1989.

Gould, Graham. "Basil of Caesarea and the Problem of the Wealth of Monasteries." In *The Church and Wealth: Papers Read at the 1986 Summer Meeting and the 1987 Winter Meeting of the Ecclesiastical History Society.* Edited by W. J. Shiels and Diana Wood. Oxford: Basil Blackwell, 1987, 15–24.

———. *The Desert Fathers on Monastic Community.* Oxford Early Christian Studies. Oxford: Clarendon Press, 1993.

Grant, Frederick C. *The Economic Background of the Gospels.* London: Oxford University Press, 1926.

Grant, Robert M. *Early Christianity and Society: Seven Studies.* London: Collins, 1978.

Gregory, J. R. "'Image of Limited Good', or Expectation of Reciprocity?" *Current Anthropology* 16 (1975): 73–92.

Gribomont, Jean. "Le monachisme au sein de l'eglise en Syrie et en Cappadoce." *Studia Monastica* 7 (1965): 7–24.

———. "Un aristocrate révolutionnaire, évêque et moine: s. Basile." *Augustinianum* 17 (1977): 79–191.

Grig, Lucy. "Throwing parties for the poor: poverty and splendour in the late antique church." In *Poverty in the Roman World.* Edited by Margaret Atkins and Robin Osborne. Cambridge: Cambridge University Press, 2006, 145–61.

Grodzynski, Denise. "Pauvres et indigents, vils et plebeiens. (Une étude terminologique sur le vocabulaire des petites gens dans le Code Théodosien)." In *Studia et documenta historiae et iuris.* Rome: Apollinaris, 1987, 140–218.

Gruenwald, I. "A Case Study of Scripture and Culture: Apocalypticism as Cultural Identity in Past and Present." In *Ancient and Modern Perspectives on the Bible and Culture: Essays in Honor of Hans Dieter Betz.* Edited by A. Y. Collins. Atlanta: Scholars Press, 1998, 252–80.

Gruszka, P. "Die Stellungnahme der Kirchenväter Kappadoziens zu der Gier um Gold, Silber und andere Luxuswaren im täglichen Leben der Oberschichten des 4 Jhts." *Klio* 63 (1981): 661–68.

Guijarro, Santiago. "The Family in First-Century Galilee." In *Constructing Early Christian*

*Families: Family as Social Reality and Metaphor*. Edited by Halvor Moxnes. London: Routledge, 1997, 42–64.

Guroian, Vigen. "Family and Christian Virtue: Reflections on the Ecclesial Vision of John Chrysostom." In *Ethics after Christendom: Toward an Ecclesial Christian Ethic*. Grand Rapids, Mich.: Eerdmans, 1994, 133–54.

Haarer, Fiona. *Anastasius I: Politics and Religion in the Late Roman World*. Cambridge: Francis Cairns, 2006.

Haidacher, Sebastian. "Quellen der Chrysostomus-Homilie De perfecta caritate (PG 56, 279–290)." *Zeitschrift für katholische Theologie* 19 (1895): 387–89.

Haller, W. "Die Eigentum im Glauzen und Leben der nachapostolischen Kirche." *Theologische Studien und Kritiken* 64 (1891): 478–563.

Halton, Thomas. *Theodoret of Cyrus: On Divine Providence*. ACW 49. New York: Newman, 1988.

Hamman, Adalbert Gauthier, ed. *Riches et pauvres dans l'église ancienne*. Lettres Chrétiennes 6. Paris: Grasset, 1962.

Hands, Arthur Robinson. *Charities and Social Aid in Greece and Rome*. London: Thames & Hudson, 1968.

Hankey, Wayne J. "Mind." In *Augustine Through the Ages: An Encyclopedia*. Edited by Allan D. Fitzgerald. Grand Rapids, Mich.: Eerdmans, 1999, 563–67.

Hardwick, Michael E. *Josephus as an Historical Source in Patristic Literature through Eusebius*. Brown Judaic Studies 128. Atlanta: Scholars Press, 1989.

Harmless, William. *Desert Christians: An Introduction to the Literature of Early Monasticism*. New York: Oxford University Press, 2004.

Harnack, Adolf von. *Militia Christi: die christliche Religion und der Soldatenstand in den ersten drei Jahrhunderten*. Tübingen: Mohr Siebeck, 1905. ET: *Militia Christi: The Christian Religion and the Military in the First Three Centuries*. Translated by David McInnis Gracie. Philadelphia: Fortress Press, 1981.

Harvey, Susan Ashbrook. "The Holy and the Poor: Models from Early Syriac Christianity." In *Through the Eye of a Needle: Judeo-Christian Roots of Social Welfare*. Edited by Emily A. Hanawalt and Carter Lindberg. Kirksville, Mo.: Thomas Jefferson University Press, 1994, 43–66.

———. "Praying bodies, bodies at prayer: ritual relations in early Syriac Christianity." In *Prayer and Spirituality in the Early Church 4: The Spiritual Life*. Edited by Wendy Mayer, Pauline Allen, and Lawrence Cross. Strathfield: St. Paul's Publications, 2006, 149–67.

Hauck, Friedrich. *Die Stellung des Urchristentum zu Arbeit und Geld*. Gütersloh:Bertelsmann, 1921.

Hauschild, Wolf-Dieter von. "Christentum und Eigentum: Zum Problem eines altkirchlichen 'Sozialismus.'" *Zeitschrift für Evangelische Ethik* 16 (1972): 34–49.

Helgeland, John. "Christians and the Roman Army A.D. 173–337." *Church History* 43 (1974): 149–63.

———. *Christians and the Roman Army from Marcus Aurelius to Constantine*. Berlin: de Gruyter, 1979.

———. "Time and Space: Christian and Roman." In *Religion (Vorkonstantinisches Christentum: Verhältnis zu römischem Staat und heidnischer Religion [Forts.])*. Aufstieg und Niedergang der römischen Welt. Series 2.23. Part 2. Edited by Wolfgang Haase. Berlin: de Gruyter, 1980, 724–834.

Helgeland, John, Robert J. Daly, and J. Patout Burns. *Christians and the Military: The Early Experience*. Philadelphia: Fortress Press, 1985.

Hengel, Martin. *Eigentum und Reichtum in der frühen Kirche*. Stuttgart: Calwer Verlag, 1973. ET: *Property and Riches in the Early Church*. Translated by John Bowden. Philadelphia: Fortress Press, 1974.

Herrin, Judith. "Ideals of charity, realities of welfare: the philanthropic activity of the Byzantine Church." In *Church and People in Byzantium: Society for the Promotion of Byzantine Studies.Twentieth Spring Symposium of Byzantine Studies*. Edited by Rosemary Morris. Birmingham: Centre for Byzantine, Ottoman and Modern Greek Studies, 1990, 151–64.

Herrmann, Elisabeth. *Ecclesia in Re Publica: die Entwicklung der Kirche von pseudostaatlicher zu staatlich inkorporierter Existenz*. Europaisches Forum 2. Frankfurt: Peter Lang, 1980, 205–348.

Himes, Kenneth, ed. *Modern Catholic Social Teaching: Commentaries and Interpretations*. Washington, D.C.: Georgetown University Press, 2005.

Hirschfeld, Yizhar. "Farms and Villages in Byzantine Palestine." *Dumbarton Oaks Papers* 51 (1997): 33–71.

Holman, Susan R. "Healing the Social Leper in Gregory of Nyssa's and Gregory of Nazianzus's *peri philoptochias*." *Harvard Theological Review* 92.3 (1999): 283–309.

———. "The Hungry Body: Famine, Poverty and Basil's *Hom. 8*." *JECS* 7 (1999): 337–63.

———. "The entitled poor: Human rights language in the Cappadocians." *Pro Ecclesia* 9.4 (2000): 476–88.

———. *The Hungry Are Dying: Beggars and Bishops in Roman Cappadocia*. Oxford Studies in Historical Theology. Oxford: Oxford University Press, 2001.

———. "Constructed and Consumed: The Every Day Life of the Poor in 4th C. Cappadocia." In *Social and Political Life in Late Antiquity*. Edited by W. Bowden, A. Gutteridge, and C. Machado. Leiden: Brill, 2006, 441–64.

Holmes, Augustine. *A Life Pleasing to God: The Spirituality of the Rules of St. Basil*. Cistercian Studies 189. Kalamazoo, Mich.: Cistercian, 2000.

Holtzmann, H. "Die Gütergemeinschaft der Apostelgeschichte." In *Strassburger Abhandlungen zur Philosophie: Eduard Zeller, zu seinem siebenzigsten Geburtstage*. Tübingen: Mohr, 1884, 25–60.

Holum, Kenneth. *Theodosian Empresses: Women and Imperial Dominion in Late Antiquity*. Berkeley: University of California Press, 1982.

Hornus, Jean-Michel. *Évangile et labarum: Étude sur l'attitude du christianisime primitif devant les problèmes de l'État, de la guerre et de la violence.* Nouvelle série théologique 9. Geneva: Labor et Fides, 1960.

Hünermann, Peter, and Heinrich Denzinger, eds. *Enchiridion symbolorum, definitionem et declarationum de rebus fidei et morum,* 31st ed. Bologna: Dehoniana, 2001.

Irwin, T. H. "Aristotle's Defense of Private Property." *A Companion to Aristotle's 'Politics.'* Edited by David Keyt and Fred Miller, Jr. Oxford: Blackwell, 1991, 200–25.

Jacobs, Andrew. *Remains of the Jews: The Holy Land and Christian Empire in Late Antiquity.* Divinations: Rereading Late Ancient Religion. Stanford: Stanford University Press, 2004.

Janis (Berzins), Hieroschemamonk. "Homily on the Words of St. Luke's Gospel: 'I will pull down my barns and build larger ones' and on Avarice." *Orthodox Life* 42 (1992): 10–17.

Jeanrond, Werner G. *Theological Hermeneutics: Developments and Significance.* New York: Crossroad, 1991.

Johnson, James T. *The Quest for Peace: Three Moral Traditions in Western Cultural History.* Princeton, N.J.: Princeton University Press, 1987.

Jones, Gareth Stedman. "From Historical Sociology to Theoretic History." *British Journal of Sociology* 27 (1976): 195–305.

Junker-Kenny, Maureen, and Peter Kenny, eds. *Memory, Naarrativity, Self and the Challenge to Think God: The Reception within Theology of the Recent Work of Paul Ricoeur.* Religion – Geschichte – Gesellschaft: Fundamentaltheologische Studien 17. Münster: LIT Verlag, 2004.

Kaczynski, Bernice M. "Some St. Gall Glosses on Greek Philanthropic Nomenclature." *Speculum* 58 (1983): 1008–17.

Kalsbach, A. "Diakonie." In *Reallexikon für Antike und Christentum, Lieferung* 22: *Deus internus (Forts.) – Diamant.* Edited by Theodor Klauser, et al. Stuttgart: Anton Hiersemann, 1957, 909–17.

Kalthoff, Adalbert. *Das Christus-problem: Grundlinien zu einer Sozialtheologie,* 2nd ed. Leipzig: E. Diederichs, 1903.

———. *Die Entstehung des Christentums.* Leipzig: E. Diederichs, 1904.

Kampling, Rainer. "'Have We Not Then Made a Heaven of Earth?' Rich and Poor in the Early Church." *Concilium* 22 (1986): 51–62.

Kannengiesser, Charles. *Handbook of Patristic Exegesis: The Bible in Ancient Christianity.* 2 vols. The Bible in Ancient Christianity 1. Leiden: Brill, 2004.

Karayannopoulos, Ioannes. "Basil's Social Activity." In *Basil of Caesarea: Christian, Humanist, Ascetic: A Sixteen-Hundredth Anniversary Symposium. Part One.* Edited by Paul J. Fedwick. Toronto: Pontifical Institute of Mediaeval Studies, 1981, 375–91.

Katz, Sheri. "Person." In *Augustine Through the Ages: An Encyclopedia.* Edited by Allan D. Fitzgerald. Grand Rapids, Mich.: Eerdmans, 1999, 647–50.

Kazhdan, Alexander. "Byzantium and Social Welfare." In *Through the Eye of a Needle: Judeo-Christian Roots of Social Welfare.* Edited by Emily A. Hanawalt and Carter Lindberg. Kirksville, Mo.: Thomas Jefferson University Press, 1994, 67–82.

Keck, L. "The Poor among the Saints in Jewish Christianity and Qumran." *ZNW* 57 (1966): 54–78.

Kee, Howard Clark. "Rich and Poor in the New Testament and Early Christianity." In *Through the Eye of a Needle: Judeo-Christian Roots of Social Welfare*. Edited by Emily A. Hanawalt and Carter Lindberg. Kirksville, Mo.: Thomas Jefferson University Press, 1994, 29–42.

Kelly, Thomas A. *Sancti Ambrosii Liber de consolatione Valentiniani: A Text with a Translation, Introduction and Commentary*. Patristic Studies 58. Washington D.C.: The Catholic University of America, 1940.

Kislinger, E. "Kaiser Julian und die (christlichen) Zenodochien." In *Byzantios. Festschrift für Herbert Hunger zum 70. Geburtstag*. Edited by W. Hörander, et al. Vienna: E. Beevar, 1984, 171–84.

Klein, Richard. *Die Sklaverei in der Sicht der Bischöfe Ambrosius und Augustin*. Forschungen zur antiken Sklaverei 20. Stuttgart: Steiner-Verlag, 1988.

———. *Die Haltung der kappadokischen Kirchenväter Basilius von Caesarea, Gregor von Nazianz und Gregor von Nyssa zur Sklaverei*. Forschungen zur antiken Sklaverei 32. Stuttgart: Steiner-Verlag, 1999.

Klemm, David E. *The Hermeneutical Theory of Paul Ricoeur: A Constructive Analysis*. Lewisburg, Pa.: Bucknell University Press, 1983.

Kloft, Hans. *Liberalitas principis. Herkunft und Bedeutung. Studien zur Prinzipatsideologie*. Cologne: Böhlau, 1970.

Konstan, David. "Patrons and Friends." *Classical Philology* 90 (1995): 328–42.

———. "Problems in the History of Christian Friendship." *JECS* 4 (1996): 87–113. Reprint in *Christianity and Society: The Social World of Early Christianity*. Edited by Everett Ferguson. New York: Garland Publishing, 1999, 357–83.

Krause, Jens-Uwe. "Das spätantike Städtepatronat." *Chiron* 17 (1987): 1–80.

Kristeva, Julia. *Sēmeiōtikē*. Paris: Seuil, 1969.

———. *Desire in Language: A Semiotic Approach to Literature and Art*. New York: Columbia University Press, 1980.

Kurbatov, G. L. "Klassavoja suscnost ucenija Ioanna Zlatausta." *Ezegodnik muzeja istorii i religii i ateiznoz* 2 (1958): 80–106. ET: "The Nature of Class in the Teaching of John Chrysostom." Translated by Andrius Valevicius. Available at the website of the Center for Early Christian Studies (Australian Catholic University), http://www.cecs.acu.edu.au/chrysostomresearch.htm.

LaFree, Gary. "Review Essay: Too Much Democracy or Too Much Crime? Lessons from California's Three-Strikes Law." *Law and Social Inquiry* 27 (2002): 875–902.

Laks, André, and Malcolm Schofield, eds. *Justice and Generosity: Studies in Hellenistic Social and Political Philosophy. Proceedings of the Sixth Symposium Hellenisticum*. Cambridge: Cambridge University Press, 1992.

Le Blant, Edmond. "La richesse et las christianisme a l'age des persécutions." *Revue archéologique (Series 2)* 39 (1880): 220–30.

Leemans, Johan. "'Les pauvres ont revêtu le visage de notre Sauveur.' Analyse historico-théologique du premier sermon de Grégoire de Nysse De l'amour des pauvres." In *Les pères de l'Eglise et la voix des pauvres*. Edited by Pascal-Grégoire Delage. La Rochelle: Association Histoire et Culture, 2006, 75–87.

Lepelley, Claude. "Le patronat épiscopal aux IVe et Ve siècles: continuités et ruptures avec le patronat classique." In *L'évêque dans la cité du IV au Ve siècle*. Edited by E. Rebillard and C. Sotinel. Rome: École française de Rome, 1998, 17–33.

Leppin, Hartmut. "Das Bild der kaiserlichen Frauen bei Gregor von Nyssa." In *Gregory of Nyssa: Homilies on the Beatitudes*. Edited by H. R. Drobner and A. Viciano. Leiden: Brill, 2000, 487–506 .

Leyerle, Blake. "John Chrysostom on Almsgiving and the Use of Money." *The Harvard Theological Review* 87 (1994): 29–47.

Liebeschuetz, J. H. W. G. *Barbarians and Bishops. Army, Church, and State in the Age of Arcadius and Chrysostom*. Oxford: Oxford University Press, 1990.

Lindemann, Andreas. "Die Kirche als Leib. Beobachtungen zur "demokratischen" Ekklesiologie bei Paulus." *ZTK* 92 (1995): 140–65.

Loiselle, André. "The Fathers of the Church and social inequalities." In *Attentive to the Cry of the Needy*. Ottawa: Canadian Religious Conference, 1973, 27–40.

Lunn-Rockliffe, Sophie. "A pragmatic approach to poverty and riches: Ambrosiaster's *quaestio 124*." In *Poverty in the Roman World*. Edited by Margaret Atkins and Robin Osborne. Cambridge: Cambridge University Press 2006.

MacQueen, D. J. "St. Augustine's Concept of Property Ownership." *Revue Augustiniennes* 8 (1972): 187–229.

———. "The Origins and Dynamics of Society and the State according to St. Augustine (Part 1)." *Augustinian Studies* 4 (1973): 73–101.

Malherbe, Abraham J. *Ancient Epistolary Theorists*. Society of Biblical Literature: Sources for Biblical Study 19. Atlanta: Scholars Press 1988.

Malina, B. *The New Testament World: Insights from Cultural Anthropology*. Atlanta, 1981.

Malingrey, A.-M. *Lettre d'exil*. SC 103. Paris, 1964.

Manning, C. E. "Liberalitas—The Decline and Rehabilitation of a Virtue." *Greece and Rome* 32 (1985): 73–85.

Mansbridge, Jane. "On the Contested Nature of the Public Good." In *Private Action and the Public Good*. Edited by Walter W. Powell and Elisabeth S. Clemens. New Haven: Yale University Press, 1998, 3–19.

Many, Joyce, and Carole Cox, eds. *Reader Stance and Literary Understanding: Exploring the Theories, Research, and Practice*. Norwood, N.J.: Ablex, 1992.

Markus, Robert A. *Saeculum: History and Society in the Theology of Saint Augustine*. Cambridge: Cambridge University Press, 1970. Rev. ed. 1989.

———. "De civitate dei: Pride and the Common Good." In *Collectanea Augustiniana: Augustine: "Second Founder of the Faith."* Edited by Joseph C. Schnaubelt and Frederick Van Fleteren. Frankfurt am Main: Peter Lang, 1990, 245–59.

Marrou, Henri-Irénée. "L'origine orientale des diaconies romaines." *Mélanges d'archéologie et d'histoire* 57 (1940): 95–142.

Maspero, Jean. "Sur quelques objets coptes du Musée du Caire." *Annales du Service des antiquités d'Egypte* 10 (1910): 173–74.

———. *Papyrus grecs d'époque byzantine.* Catalogue général des antiquités égyptiennes du Musée du Caire, Papyrus grecs d'époque byzantine. 4 vols. Cairo: IFAO, 1911–16.

Mause, M. *Die Darstellung des Kaisers in der lateinischen Panegyrik.* Stuttgart: Steiner, 1994.

Mayer, W. "John Chrysostom: Extraordinary Preacher, Ordinary Audience." In *Preacher and Audience: Studies in Early Christian and Byzantine Homiletics.* Edited by M. Cunningham and P. Allen. Leiden: Brill, 1998, 105–37.

———. "Constantinopolitan women in Chrysostom's circle." *VC* 53 (1999): 265–88.

———. "Female participation and the late fourth-century preacher's audience." *Augustinianum* 39 (1999): 139–47.

———. "Cathedral church or cathedral churches? The situation at Constantinople (c.360–404 AD)." *Orientalia Christiana Periodica* 66 (2000): 49–68.

———. "Who came to hear John Chrysostom preach? Recovering a late fourth-century preacher's audience." *Ephemerides Theologicae Lovanienses* 76 (2000): 73–87.

———. "Poverty and Society in the World of John Chrysostom." In *Social and Political Life in Late Antiquity.* Edited by W. Bowden, A. Gutteridge, and C. Machado. Leiden: Brill, 2006, 465–84.

———. "Poverty and generosity towards the poor in the time of John Chrysostom." In *Wealth and Poverty in Early Christianity.* Holy Cross Studies in Patristic Theology and History 1. Edited by Susan Holman. Grand Rapids, Mich.: Baker Academic, 2007, 140–58.

Mayer, Wendy, and Pauline Allen. *John Chrysostom.* The Early Church Fathers Series. New York: Routledge Press, 2000.

McCoy, Charles N. R. "The Turning Point in Political Philosophy." *The American Political Science Review* 44 (1950): 678–88.

McGuckin, John A. "The Vine and the Elm Tree: The Patristic Interpretation of Jesus' Teaching on Wealth." In *The Church and Wealth: Papers Read at the 1986 Summer Meeting and the 1987 Winter Meeting of the Ecclesiastical History Society.* Edited by W. J. Shiels and Diana Wood. Oxford: Basil Blackwell, 1987, 1–14.

McGuire, Martin R. P. *S. Ambrosii De Nabuthae: A Commentary, with an Introduction and Translation.* Patristic Studies 15. Washington D.C.: The Catholic University of America Press, 1927.

McLynn, Neil. "Gregory the Peacemaker: A Study of Oration Six." *Kyoyo-Ronso* 101 (1996): 183–216.

Meeks, Wayne A. *The First Urban Christians.* New Haven: Yale University Press, 1983.

Mendels, D. *The Media Revolution of Early Christianity: An Essay on Eusebius's Ecclesiastical History.* Grand Rapids, Mich.: Eerdmans, 1999.

Mentzou-Meimari, Konstantina. "Eparkhiaka evagé idrymata mekhri tou telous tés eikonomakhias." *Byzantina* 11 (1982): 243–308.

Miller, Patrick D., and Dennis P. McCann, eds. *In Search of the Common Good*. Theology for the Twenty-First Century. New York: T. & T. Clark, 2005.

Miller, T. S. *The Birth of the Hospital in the Byzantine Empire*. Baltimore, Md.: Johns Hopkins University Press, 1985.

Monfrin, Françoise. "Pauvreté et richesse: Le lexique latin de l'encyclique: inspiration classique ou inspiration patristique?" In *Rerum Novarum: Écriture, contenu et reception d'une encyclique: Actes du colloque international organize par l'École française de Rome et le Greco n 2 du CNRS (Rome, 18–20 avril 1991)*. Rome: École française de Rome, 1997, 133–86.

Mosheim, Johan Lorenz. *De vera natura communionis bonorum in ecclesia Hierosolymitana commentatio*. Unpublished dissertation, 1733.

Mueller, J. G. *L'Ancien Testament dans l'ecclésiologie des pères. Une lecture des Constitutions Apostoliques*. Turnhout: Brepols, 2004.

———. "The Ancient Church Order Literature: Genre or Tradition?" *JECS* 15 (2007): 337–80.

Nadon, Christopher. "From Republic to Empire: Political Revolution and the Common Good in Xenophon's *Education of Cyrus*." *American Political Science Review* 90 (1996): 361–74.

Neil, Bronwen. "On True Humility: An anonymous letter on poverty and the female ascetic." In *Prayer and Spirituality in the Early Church* 4. *The Spiritual Life*. Edited by W. Mayer, P. Allen, and L. Cross. Strathfield: St. Paul's Publishers, 2006, 233–46.

Nell-Breuning, Oswald von. *Reorganization of Social Economy: The Social Encyclical Developed and Explained*. Translated by Bernard W. Dempsey. New York: Bruce Publishing Co., 1936.

Neri, Valero. *I Marginali nell'Occidente Tardoantico. Poveri, "infames" e criminali nella nascente società cristiana*. Bari: Edipuglia, 1998.

Neyrey, J. H., and R. L. Rohrbaugh. "'He must increase, I must decrease' (John 3:30)': A cultural and social interpretation." *CBQ* 63 (2001): 464–83.

Niederer, Francis J. "Early Medieval Charity." *Church History* 21 (1952): 285–95.

Nikiprowetzky, Valentin. *Études Philoniennes*. Patrimoines Judaisme. Paris: Éditions du Cerf, 1996, esp. 243–91.

Oakes, Peter. "Constructing poverty scales for Graeco-Roman society: a response to Steven Friesen's 'Poverty in Pauline studies.'" *JSNT* 26.3 (2004): 367–71.

O'Brien, David J., and Thomas A. Shannon. *Catholic Social Thought: The Documentary Heritage*. Maryknoll, N.Y.: Orbis Books, 1992.

O'Donovan, Oliver. "Augustine's *City of God* XIX and Western Political Thought." *Dionysius* 11 (1987): 89–110.

Ogilvie, R. M. *The Library of Lactantius*. Oxford: Clarendon Press, 1978.

Osiek, Carolyn. *Rich and Poor in the* Shepherd of Hermas: *An Exegetical-Social Investigation*. The Catholic Biblical Quarterly Monograph Series 15. Washington, D.C.: The Catholic Biblical Association of America, 1983.

———. "The Feminist and the Bible: Hermeneutical Alternatives." In *Feminist Perspectives on Biblical Scholarship*. SBL Biblical Scholarship in North America. Edited by Adela Yarbro Collins. Atlanta: Scholars Press, 1985, 93–105.

Owen, Richard. "Analysis: Encyclical is Work of Two Popes." In *The Times Online* (London: Jan. 25, 2006).

Parkin, Anneliese R. "Poverty in the Early Roman Empire: Ancient and Modern Conceptions and Constructs." Ph.D. diss., Cambridge University, 2001.

Pásztori-Kupán, István. *Theodoret of Cyrus*. The Early Church Fathers. London: Routledge, 2006.

Patlagean, Evelyne. *Pauvreté économique et pauvreté sociale á Byzance 4e—7e siècles*. Civilisations et Sociétés 48. Paris: Mouton, 1977.

———. "The Poor." In *The Byzantines*. Edited by Guiglielmo Cavallo. Chicago: University of Chicago Press, 1997, 15–42.

———. "'You do him no service': An exploration of pagan almsgiving." In *Poverty in the Roman World*. Edited by Atkins and Osborne. Cambridge: Cambridge University Press, 2006, 60–82.

Paul VI. "L'homme et la révolution urbaine: Citadins et ruraux devant l'urbanisation." *La documentation Catholique* 62 (1–15 August, 1965): 1362–65.

Paul, Christophe. *Les pauvres et la pauvreté des origines au XVe siècle*. Bibliothèque d'Histoire du Christianisme 7. Paris: Desclée, 1985, esp. 21–74.

Paul, Ludwig. "Welche Reiche wird selig werden?" *ZWT* 44 (1901): 504–44.

Paverd, Frans van de. *St. John Chrysostom. The Homilies on the Statues: An Introduction*. Orientalia Christiana Analecta 239. Rome: Pontificium Institutum Studiorum Orientalium, 1991.

Peabody, Francis Greenwood. *Jesus Christ and the Social Question: An Examination of the Teaching of Jesus in it s Relation to Some of the Problems of Modern Social Life*. New York: Grosset and Dunlap, 1900.

Périn, Charles. *De la richesse dans les societés chrétiennes*. Paris: Lecoffre, 1868.

Phillips, Charles Stanley. *The New Commandment: An Inquiry into the Social Precept and Practice of the Ancient Church*. London: SPCK, 1930.

Pinches, Charles. "Friendship and Tragedy: The Fragilities of Goodness." *First Things* 3 (1990): 38–45.

Pollefeyt, Didier, and Reimund Bieringer. "The Role of the Bible in Religious Education Reconsidered: Risks and Challenges in Teaching the Bible." *International Journal of Practical Theology* 9 (2005): 117–39.

Porter, Jean. "The Common Good in Thomas Aquinas." In *In Search of the Common Good*. Edited by Dennis P. McCann and Patrick D. Miller. New York: T. & T. Clark, 2005, 94–120.

Poster, Carol, and Linda C. Mitchell, eds. *Letter-Writing Manuals and Instruction from Antiquity: Historical and Bibliographic Studies*. Studies in Rhetoric/Communication. Columbia, S.C.: The University of South Carolina Press 2007.

Potworowski, Christophe. "Origen's Hermeneutics in Light of Paul Ricoeur." In *Origeniana Quinta: Papers of the 5th International Origen Congress, Boston College, 14–18 August 1989*. BETL 105. Leuven: Peeters, 1992.

Quiroga Puertas, A. J. "Elementos hagiográficos en las 'Homilías de las estatuas' de Juan Crisóstomo." *Collectanea Christiana Orientalia* 4 (2007): 145–46.

Ramirez, Juan, and William Crano. "Deterrence and Incapacitation: An Interrupted Time-Series Analysis of California's Three-Strikes Law." *Journal of Applied Social Psychology* 33 (2006): 110–44.

Ramsey, Boniface. *Beginning to Read the Fathers*. London: Darton, Longman and Todd, 1986, esp. 182–96.

————. "Almsgiving in the Latin Church: The Late Fourth and Early Fifth Centuries." In *Acts of Piety in the Early Church*. Studies in Early Christianity 27. Edited by Everett Ferguson. New York: Garland Publishing, 1993, 226–59.

————. *Ambrose*. The Early Church Fathers. London and New York: Routledge, 1997.

Rees, B. R. *Pelagius: Life and Letters*. Woodbridge, N.Y.: The Boydell Press, 1998.

Reilly, Gerald F. *Imperium and Sacerdotium according to St. Basil the Great*. Studies in Christian Antiquity 7. Washington D.C.: The Catholic University of America Press, 1945.

Richards, I. A. *The Philosophy of Rhetoric*. New York: Oxford University Press, 1936.

Ricoeur, Paul. "Le projet d'une morale sociale." *Le Christianisme social* 74 (1966): 285–95.

————. "The Hermeneutical Function of Distanciation." *Philosophy Today* 17 (1973): 129–41.

————. "Le problème du fondement de la morale." *Sapienza* 28 (1975): 313–37.

————. *Interpretation Theory: Discourse and the Surplus of Meaning*. Forth Worth, Tex.: Texas Christian University Press, 1976.

————. *La Métaphore vive*. L'ordre philosophique. Paris: Seuil, 1975. ET: *The Rule of Metaphor: Multi-disciplinary Studies of the Creation of Meaning in Language*. Toronto: University of Toronto Press, 1977.

————. *The Rule of Metaphor: Multi-disciplinary Studies of the Creation of Meaning in Language*. Translated by Robert Czerny, Kathleen McLaughlin, and John Costello. Toronto: University of Toronto Press, 1977.

————. *Essays on Biblical Interpretation*. Philadelphia: Fortress Press, 1980.

————. "Metaphor and the Central Problem of Hermeneutics." In *Paul Ricoeur, Hermeneutics and the Human Sciences: Essays on Language, Action and Interpretation*. Edited and translated by John B. Thompson. Cambridge: Cambridge University Press, 1981.

————. "The Model of the Text: Meaningful Action Considered as a Text." In *Paul Ricoeur, Hermeneutics and the Human Sciences: Essays on Language, Action and Interpretation*. Edited and Translated by John B. Thompson. Cambridge: Cambridge University Press, 1981.

————. *Time and Narrative*. 3 vols. Translated by Kathleen Blamey. Chicago: University of Chicago Press, 1984, 1985, and 1988.

————. *From Text to Action: Essays in Hermeneutics* II. Translated by Kathleen Blamey. Evanston, Ill.: Northwestern University Press, 1991.

———. "Le statut de la *Vorstellung* dans la philosophie hégélienne de la religion (1985)." In *Lectures 3 aux frontières de la philosophie*. Paris: Seuil, 1994, 41–62.

———. *Conflict of Interpretations: Essays in Hermeneutics*. Northwestern University Studies in Phenomenology and Existential Philosophy. Evanston, Ill.: Northwestern University Press, 1996.

———. "The Canon between the Text and the Community." In *Philosophical Hermeneutics and Biblical Exegesis*. WUNT. Edited by Petr Pokorny and Jan Rosovec. Tübingen: Mohr Siebeck, 2002, 7–26.

———. *Mémoire, l'histoire, l'oubli*. L'ordre philosophique. Paris: Seuil, 2000. ET: *Memory, History, Forgetting*. Translated by Kathleen Blamey and David Pellauer. Chicago: University of Chicago Press, 2004.

Ricoeur, Paul, François Azouvi, and Marc B. De Launay. *Critique and Conviction: Conversations with François Azouvi and Marc de Launay*. Translated by Kathleen Blamey. New York: Columbia University Press, 1998.

Riddle, Donald Wayne. *The Martyrs: A Study in Social Control*. Chicago: University of Chicago Press, 1931.

Rivas Rebaque, Fernando. *Defensor pauperum. Los pobres en Basilio de Cesarea: homilias VI, VII, VIII y XIVB*. Biblioteca de Auctores Cristianos 657. Madrid: Biblioteca de Autores Cristianos, 2005.

Rohrbaugh, R. L., ed. *Using the Social Sciences in New Testament Interpretation*. Peabody, Mass., 1996.

Rosenblatt, Louise M. *The Reader, the Text, the Poem*. Carbondale, Ill.: Southern Illinois University Press, 1978.

Rougé, J. "A propos des mendiants au ive siècle." *Cahiers d'Histoire* 20 (1975): 339–46.

Rousseau, Philip. *Pachomius: The Making of a Community in Fourth-Century Egypt*. The Transformation of the Classical Heritage 6. Berkeley: University of California Press, 1985.

Rowland, R. J. "The 'Very Poor' and the Grain-Dole at Rome and Oxyrhynchus." *Zeitschrift für Papyrologie und Epigraphik* 21 (1976): 69–72.

Salamito, Jean-Marie. "*Rerum novarum*, une encyclique néo-scolastique? La question sociale ou le déclin de la communauté." In *Rerum Novarum: Écriture, contenu et reception d'une encyclique: Actes du colloque international organize par l'École française de Rome et le Greco n 2 du CNRS (Rome, 18-20 avril 1991)*. Rome: École française de Rome, 1997, 187–206.

Sandwell, I. *Religious Identity in Late Antiquity: Greeks, Jews and Christians in Antioch*. Cambridge: Cambridge University Press, 2007.

Santa Ana, Julio de. *Good News to the Poor: The Challenge of the Poor in the History of the Church*. Translated from Spanish by Helen Whittle. Geneva: World Council of Churches, 1977.

Schichor, D., and D. K. Sechrest. *Three Strikes and You're Out: Vengeance as Public Policy*. Thousand Oaks, Ca.: Sage Publications, 1996.

Schilling, Otto. *Reichtum und Eigentum in der altkirchlichen Literatur: Ein Beitrag zur sozi-alen Frage*. Freiburg in Breisgau: Herdersche Verlagshandlung, 1908.

Schneiders, Sandra M. "Feminist Ideology Criticism and Biblical Hermeneutics." *Biblical Theology Bulletin* 19 (1989): 3–10.

———. *The Revelatory Text: Interpreting the New Testament as Sacred Scripture*. San Francis-co: Harper, 1991.

Schöllgen, Georg. *Ecclesia Sordida? Zur Frage der sozialen Schichtung frühchristlicher Gemei-nden am Beispiel Karthagos zur Zeit Tertullians*. In Jahrbuch für Antike und Christen-tum. Ergänzungsbände 12. Münster: Aschendorff, 1984.

———. *Die Anfänge der Professionalisierung des Kleurs und das kirchliche Amt in der syrisch-en Didaskalie*. In Jahrbuch für Antike und Christentum. Ergänzungsbände 26. Mün-ster: Aschendorff, 1998, esp. 116–34.

Schüssler Fiorenza, Elisabeth. *In Memory of Her: A Feminist Theological Reconstruction of Christian Origins*. New York: Crossroad, 1983.

Schwer, Wolfgang. "Armenpflege." *Reallexicon für Antike und Christentum* 1 (1950): 689–98.

Sheather, Mary. "Pronouncements of the Cappadocians on Issues of Poverty and Wealth." In *Prayer and Spirituality in the Early Church* 1. Edited by Pauline Allen, Wendy Mayer, and Lawrence Cross. Brisbane, Australia: Watson Ferguson & Company, 1998, 375–92.

Sherwin, Michael. "Friends at the Table of the Lord: Friendship with God and the Transfor-mation of Patronage in the Thought of John Chrysostom." *New Blackfriars* 85 (2004): 387–98.

Shewring, Walter. *Rich and Poor in Christian Tradition: Writings of Many Centuries Chosen, Translated, and Introduced*. London: Burns, Oates and Washbourne, 1948.

Singer, Peter. "Famine, Affluence and Morality." *Philosophy and Public Affairs* 1 (1972): 229–43.

Skalitzky, R. "Annianus of Celeda, his text of Chrysostom's Homilies on Matthew." *Aevum* 45 (1971): 208–33.

Soskice, Janet. *Metaphor and Religious Language*. Oxford: Clarendon Press, 1985.

Sternberg, T. *Orientalium More Secutus. Räume und Institutionen der Caritas des 5 bis 7. Jahrhunderts in Gallien*. Jahrbuch für Antike und Christentum. Ergänzungsbände 16. Münster: Aschendorff, 1991, esp. 147–93.

Stiver, Dan R. *Theology after Ricoeur: New Directions in Hermeneutical Theology*. Louisville, Ky.: Westminster/John Knox Press, 2001.

Strubbe, J. "Armenzorg in de Grieks-Romeinse wereld." *Tijdschrift voor Geschiedenis* 107 (1994): 163–83.

Strzygowski, Josef. *Koptische Kunst*. Catalogue général des antiquités égyptiennes du Musée du Caire. Osnabrück: Zeller, 1904.

Sturrock, John. *Structuralism*. Oxford: Blackwell, 2003.

Swift, Louis J. *The Early Fathers on War and Military Service*. Message of the Fathers of the Church 19. Wilmington, Del.: Michael Glazier Press, 1983.

Tanner, Norman P. *The Councils of the Church: A Short History*. New York: Crossroad, 2002.

————, ed. *Decrees of the Ecumenical Councils.* 2 vols. Washington D.C.: Georgetown University Press, 1990.

Teja, Ramon. *Organización económica y social de Capadocia en el siglo iv. según los padres capadocios.* Acta Salmanticensia: Filosofia y letras 78. Salamanca: Universidad de Salamanca, 1974.

TeSelle, Eugene. "The Civic Vision in Augustine's *City of God*." *Thought* 62 (1987): 268–80.

Teske, Roland J. "Soul." In *Augustine Through the Ages: An Encyclopedia.* Edited by Allan D. Fitzgerald. Grand Rapids, Mich.: William B. Eerdmans, 1999, 807–12.

Thiessen, Gerd. "Wanderradikalismus: Literatur-soziologische Aspekte der Überlieferung von Worten Jesu im Urchristentum." *Zeitschrift für Theologie und Kirche* 70 (1973): 245–71.

Thomas, J. P. *Private Religious Foundations in the Byzantine Empire.* Dumbarton Oaks Studies 24. Washington, D.C.: Dumbarton Oaks, 1987.

Toal, Martin Francis. *The Sunday Sermons of the Great Fathers.* 4 vols. Chicago: Henry Regnery, 1957–63.

Tompkins, Jane B., ed. *Reader-Response Criticism: From Formalism to Post-Structuralism.* Baltimore, Md.: Johns Hopkins University Press, 1980.

Torchia, N. Joseph. "The *Commune/Proprium* Distinction in St. Augustine's Early Moral Theology." *Studia Patristica* 22 (1989): 356–63.

Troeltsch, Ernst. *Die Soziallehren der christlichen Kirchen und Gruppen, Gesammelte Schriften* 1. Tübingen: Mohr [Paul Siebeck], 1912. ET: *The Social Teaching of the Christian Churches.* Translated by Olive Wyon. London: Allen and Unwin, 1931.

————. *Augustin, die christliche Antike und das Mittelalter. Im Anschluss an die Schrift 'De civitate Dei.'* Historische Bibliotheek 36. Munich: Oldenbourg, 1915.

Tyler, Tom R., and Robert J. Boeckmann. "Three Strikes and You are Out, but Why? The Psychology of Public Support for Punishing Rule Breakers." *Law and Society Review* 31 (1997): 237–65.

Uhlhorn, Gerhard. *Die christliche Liebestätigkeit in der alten Kirche.* Stuttgart: Verlag von D. Gundert, 1882. ET: *Christian Charity in the Ancient Church.* Translated by Sophia Taylor. New York: Charles Scribner's Sons, 1883.

Urbainczyk, Theresa. *Theodoret of Cyrrhus: The Bishop and the Holy Man.* Ann Arbor: University of Michigan Press, 2002.

Van Dam, Raymond. "Governors of Cappadocia During the Fourth Century." *Medieval Prosopography* 17 (1966): 7–93.

Van Hooff, Anton J. L. "Caring for the Old: 'Quid pro quo' or 'omnia pro Deo.'" In *Fructus Centesimus: Mélanges offerts à Gerard J. M. Bartelink à l'occasion de son soixante-cinquième anniversaire.* Instrumenta Patristica 19. Edited by A. A. R. Bastiaensen, A. Hilhorst, and C. H. Kneepkens. Steenbrugge, Belgium: Abbey of St. Peter, 1989, 325–32.

Van Nuffelen, Peter. "Deux fausses lettres de Julien l'Apostat (La lettre aux Juifs, *Ep.* 51 [Wright], et la lettre à Arsacius, *Ep.* 84 [Bidez])." *VC* 56 (2002): 131–50.

————. *Un héritage de paix et de piété. Etude sur les Histoires ecclésiastiques de Socrate et de Sozomène.* Leuven: Peeters, 2004.

————. "The unstained rule of Theodosius II: A late antique panegyrical topos and moral concern." In *Imago Virtutis:* Collection des Études classiques. Edited by T. Van Houdt, et al. Leuven: Peeters, 2004, 229–56.

————. "Le plus beau vêtement pour un empereur. L'amour des pauvres et panégyrique dans l'Antiquité tardive." In *Les pères de l'Église et la voix des pauvres.* Edited by P.-G. Delage. La Rochelle: Association Histoire et culture, 2006, 163–83.

Vasey, Vincent. *The Social Ideas in the Works of St. Ambrose: A Study on De Nabuthe.* Studia Ephemeridis "Augustinianum" 17. Rome: Institutum patristicum "Augustinianum," 1982.

————. "The Social Ideas of Asterius of Amasea." *Augustinianum* 26 (1986): 413–36.

Verheijen, Luc M.J. "La charité ne cherche pas ses propres intérêts." In *Nouvelle approche de la Règle de saint Augustin II: Chemin vers la vie heureuse.* Leuven: Peeters, 1988, 220–89.

Vermeersch, Arthur. *Quaestiones de Iustitia ad usum hodiernum scholastice disputatae,* 2nd ed. Brugge: Sumptibus Beyaert, 1904, 266–79.

Verstraeten, Johan. "Re-Thinking Catholic Social Thought as Tradition." In *Catholic Social Thought: Twilight or Renaissance?* Edited by J. S. Boswell, F. P. McHugh, and J. Verstraeten. BETL 157. Leuven: Peeters, 2000, 59–77.

————. "Catholic Social Thought as Discernment." *Logos* 8 (2005): 94–111.

Veyne, Paul. *Le pain et le circque.* Paris: Seuil, 1976.

Viansino, G. "Aspetti dell'opera di Giovanni Crisostomo." *Koinonia* 25 (2001): 137–205.

Vincent, Gilbert. *La religion de Ricoeur.* La religion des philosophes. Paris: Les Éditions de l'Atelier, 2008.

Viner, J. "The Economic Doctrines of the Early Christian Fathers." In *Religious Thought and Economic Society: Four Chapters of an Unfinished Work by Jacob Viner.* Edited by J. Melitz and D. Winch. Durham, N.C.: Duke University Press, 1978, 9–18.

Vinson, Martha. *Saint Gregory of Nazianzus: Select Orations.* FOTC 107. Washington, D.C.: The Catholic University of America Press, 2004.

Vives, Josep. "Es el propriedad un robo: las ideas sobre la propriedad privada en el christianismo primitivo." *Fe y justicia.* Salamanca: Ediciones Sigu+eme, 1981, 173–213.

Voicu, S.J. "Pseudo-Giovanni Crisostomo: I confini del corpus." Jahrbuch für Antike und Christentum 39 (1996): 105–15.

————. "La volontà e il caso: La tipologia dei primi spuri di Crisostomo." In *Giovani Crisostomo: Oriente e Occidente tra IV e V secolo.* Studia Ephemeridis "Augustinianum" 93. Rome: Institut "Augustinianum," 2005.

Volpe, Giuliano. *San Giusto: Le ville, le ecclesiae.* Bari: Edipuglia, 1998.

von Ranke, Leopold. *The Theory and Practice of History.* Edited by Georg G. Iggers and Konrad von Moltke. Indianopolis: Bobbs-Merrill, 1973.

Vööbus, Arthur. *Syriac and Arabic Documents Regarding Legislation Relative to Syrian Asceticism.* Papers of the Estonian Theological Society in Exile 11. Stockholm: Etse, 1960. See the rules for monks and clergy.

Wacht, Manfred. "Wahre und falsche Armut: Bemerkungen zu Clemens Alexandrinus, Quis dives salvetur Kap 19." In *Vivarium*. Jahrbuch für Antike und Christentum 11. Münster: Aschendorff, 1984, 338–47.

Wallace-Hadrill, A. "The Social Spread of Roman Luxury: Sampling Pompeii and Herculanum." *Papers of the British School of Rome* 58 (1990): 145–92.

Walter, Gérard. *Les origines du communisme, judaiques, chrétiennes, grecques, latines*. Paris: Bibliothéque historique, 1931.

Ward, Benedicta. *The Sayings of the Desert Fathers: The Alphabetical Collection*. London: Mowbrays, 1975.

Warnke, Georgia. *Gadamer: Hermeneutics, Tradition and Reason*. Stanford: Stanford University Press, 1987.

Weinsheimer, Joel. *Gadamer's Hermeneutics: A Reading of 'Truth and Method.'* New Haven: Yale University Press, 1985.

Wheeler, Sondra Ely. *Wealth as Peril and Obligation: The New Testament on Possessions*. Grand Rapids, Mich.: Eerdmans, 1995.

Whitby, Michael. "Evagrius on Patriarchs and Emperors." *The Propaganda of Power: The Role of Panegyric in Late Antiquity*. Edited by Mary Whitby. Leiden: Brill, 1998, 321–44.

Whittaker, C. R., and Peter Garnsey. "Rural Life in the Later Roman Empire." In *Cambridge Ancient History* 13: *The Late Empire A.D. 337–425*. Edited by Averil Cameron and Peter Garnsey. Cambridge: Cambridge University Press, 1998, 277–311.

Wilder, Amos Niven. *Eschatology and Ethics in the Teaching of Jesus*. New York: Harper and Bros., 1939.

Williams, Bernard. *Ethics and the Limits of Philosophy*. London: Fontana, 1985.

Wipszycka, Ewa. "Diaconia." In *The Coptic Encylopedia* 3. Edited by Azis S. Atiya. New York: Macmillan, 1991, 895–67.

Wolin, Sheldon. *Politics and Vision: Continuity and Innovation in Western Political Thought*. Princeton, N.J.: Princeton University Press, 1960. Expanded ed. 2006, ch. 4.

Woolf, Greg. "Food, Poverty and Patronage: The Significance of the Epigraphy of the Alimentary Schemes in Early Imperial Italy." *Papers of the British School of Rome* 58 (1990): 197–228.

Xavier-Amherdt, Francois. *L'herméneutique philosophique de Paul Ricoeur et son importance pour l'exégèse biblique*. Paris: Éditions du Cerf, 2004.

Yoder, John Howard. *The Original Revolution: Essays on Christian Pacifism*. Christian Peace Shelf Series 3. Scottdale, Pa.: Herald Press, 1971.

———. *The Politics of Jesus*. Grand Rapids, Mich.: Eerdmans, 1994.

Young, Frances M. *Biblical Exegesis and the Formation of Christian Culture*. Cambridge: Cambridge University Press, 1997.

Zelzer, Michaela. "Die Briefliteratur. Kommunikation durch Briefe: Ein Gespräch mit Abwesenden." In *Neues Handbuch der Literaturwissenschaft* 4, *Spätantike mit einem Panorama der Byzantinischen Literatur*. Edited by Lodewijk J. Engels and Heinz Hofmann. Wiesbaden: AULA Verlag, 1997.

# INDEX

abuse, 138–39, 144, 156, 190; of law, 201; of memory, 211, 219n21

Adam, 36

*aequitas* (equity), 189, 193–95, 197–98, 205. *See also* equality

Agapetus, *Ekthesis*, 50–55, 58

Allen, Pauline, xiv, 187–88, 191, 196, 198–99

almsgiving, 32–33, 35, 37, 40, 59, 76–77, 82, 84, 86, 90, 92, 98, 117, 120, 123, 139, 197, 222; redemptive almsgiving, 75, 109, 121, 175, 178n46; salvific efficacy of almsgiving, 77, 81n50

Alwin, Duane, 192n28

Ambrose of Milan, 31, 37, 50, 162n1; *De officiis*, 42; *De Tobia*, 42, 129n16, 132n30, 148

Ambrosiaster, 33

Anabaptists, 64

Anastasius I, 56–57

Anianus of Celeda, 92

Anonymus, *De divitiis*, 38

Anthony the Great, 120

anthropology, 177; Trinitarian, 228

Antioch, 23, 91, 92–93, 96, 98

*apatheia* (dispassion), 118n47, 119, 123, 164

apocalyptic: critique, 84; determinism 64n2; imagery, 76; literature, 73, 78; teaching, 170n24; tradition, 65

apocrypha, 69

Apollinarius, 109

Apollonius, 132

apologists, 66

*Apostolic Constitutions*, 86, 146

Aquinas, Thomas, xvi, 106, 108–109, 113, 182n56, 192n29, 192n31, 202; Thomism, 225; Thomist, 180n52, 200

Arian(ism), 91, 93–94

Aristophanes, *Ploutos*, 165; *Ecclesiazousae*, 165n5

Aristotle, xvi, 106, 108, 110, 113, 127, 150n111, 166–67, 170; *Politics*, 111, 127n12, 152, 182n56

Arnobius, 189

Asia Minor, 89

ascetic(ism), 90, 94, 149, 153, 154. *See also* self-denial

Asterius of Amasea, 116; *The Unjust Steward*, 173

Athenagoras, 118n48

audience, xv, xvi, 30–33, 35–37, 42, 46, 57–59, 85–87, 96, 98–99, 115, 118, 145, 148, 164, 174n38, 175, 177–78, 194–95, 217, 226, 231; imaginary, 196; lay, 89; mixed, 93; primary, 196; secondary, 31, 90, 91, 94; tertiary, 91, 94. *See also* reading community

Augustine of Hippo, 31, 37–38, 40, 162n1; *City of God*, 202; *Confessions*, xii, xvi; *Ennarationes in Psalmos*, 34; *Ep. 158*, 33; *Retractationes 2.6*, 31n4; Augustinian, 200, 203

Augustus, 188n13

Aune, David E., 67n10

Ausonius, 52–53

autonomy of human thinking, 6

avarice, 36, 75, 84, 172n32, 176–77, 182, 184

Avila, Charles, 162n1

Basil of Caesarea, 33, 34n17, 39–40, 58, 108, 112–14, 116, 155–56, 169, 171n29, 183–84; *De jejunio*, 114; *Ep. 42*, 32, 120; *Ep. 150*, 32, 120; *Ep. 265*, 109; *Homilia dicta tempore famis et siccitatis*, 134n40, 138n55; *Hom. 6*, xvii, 109–111, 161, 173–79; *Hom 8*, 173n34, 174n38; *Hom. 20*, 114; *Hom 21*, 174n38; *Hom. in Ps.14*, 111, 136–37, 142, 144–45, 147–49, 158n142, 177n43; *Shorter Rules*, 174n38

Baxter, Michael, 202

Belisarius, 50

beneficence, 123; heavenly, 122; imperial, 51; social, 117; toward the needy, 150. *See also* munificence; evergetism
Biblicism, 8
Bieringer, Reimund, xiii, xiv, 191, 209, 213, 215
bishops' conference, xi, 225
Bloch, Ernst, 214
Böhm-Bawerk, Eugen, 227
Bowen, Anthony, 187n6
Brandt, Samuel, 196n40
Brown, Peter 39, 48, 50, 62n54, 163n3
business ethics, 227

Caesarea, 175
Calvinist, 210
Campaign for Human Development, 199
canon, 3–4, 8; canonico-institutional material, 86
canon law, 32
capital, 181
capital punishment, 47
capitalism, 192, 200, 202
Cappadocia (Cappadocians), 34, 37n33, 113, 174
*Captions of the Arab Canons*, 146
care: for the marginalized, xi; for the needy, 78; 96, 172n31, 222; for the poor, 47–51, 53–55, 57–60, 62–63, 69, 72n28, 75, 87, 97–98, 110n10, 157, 159, 223; for widows and orphans, 197; for the world, 184
*caritas* (charity), xv, 36, 41, 48–60, 77, 80, 123, 131, 139n58, 145, 184; as task of the church, 55; transformative impact, 62; resulting from usury, 140; as virtue, 56, 58, 63; vocabulary, 53
Carrié, Jean-Michel, 35, 38
Carthage: council of (348), 146; council of (419), 147
*Catechism of the Catholic Church*, 155
categorical imperative, 210
Catholic social teaching, xi, xii, xiv, xv, xvii, 30, 39–42, 99, 103–4, 106, 109, 121, 124, 152, 154–56, 164, 179–83, 185, 188, 190–91, 214, 217–21, 225–26, 228, 230. *See also* Christian social teaching; patristic social teaching
Catholic social teaching documents: xiin1, 42, 118, 183, 230; *Centesimus annus*, 41, 156–57; *Compendium of the Social Doctrine of the Church*, 179, 181, 191n26; *Deus caritas est* (2005), xi, 36, 42, 226; *Laborem exercens*, 181; *Mater et magistra*, 181; *Quadragesimo anno*, 180; *Providentissimus Deus*, 4n2; *Redemptor hominis*, 228;

*Rerum novarum* (1891), xi, 41, 180; *Sertum Laetitiae*, 181; *Sollicitudo rei socialis*, 228; *Ut unum sint*, 41
Catholic social thought, xi, xii, xv, xvi, xvii, 16, 103, 174, 183–91, 198–205, 209, 211, 222–25, 227–28, 230–31. *See also* Christian social thought; patristic social thought
Cavanaugh, William, 202
Chalcedon: council of (451), 23; post-Chalcedonian, 41
Christian social thought, xii, xiii, xvii, xviii, 65, 82, 204, 217, 220–21; early, 77; patristic insight for, 209, 214–15; pre-Constantine, 64. *See also* Catholic social thought; patristic social thought
Christian social teaching, 209, 221. *See also* Catholic social teaching; patristic social teaching
Christian social tradition, xvi, 123
Cicero: 198, *De officiis*, 138n55, 150n111, 152, 167, 194; *De republica*, 194; *De legibus*, 194
Claudian, 50
Cleary, Patrick, 129n16
*1 Clement*, 108, 132
*2 Clement*, 76
Clement of Alexandria, 33, 37–39, 108, 120, 155, 162n1, 172; *Paedagogus*, 130; *Quis dives salvetur*, 42, 162n1, 171, 173n34; *Stromata*, 129n16, 130–31, 132n29, 148, 171n27
clemency, 47
clergy, 146
*Codex Iustinianus*, 40, 62, 150n111
Cohen, Morris L., 124, 145
Commodianus, 140
common nature, 113
communalism, 71
communication, 214
Constantine the Great, 51, 90, 188n13, 189, 190n16, 194–99, 202
Constantinople, xv, 32n8, 51, 92–94, 96, 110
consumerism, 156
conversion, 82, 195; moral, 198
Corinth, 158
Corippus, 52–53
Countryman, L. William, 162n1
Courtonne, Yves, 174n39
credit (creditor), 124, 160
Crispus, 189
criticism: critical exegesis, 185; historical, 6–7, 15, 19, 185n2; literary, 19; narrative, 8; postcriticism (postcritical), 185–86, 191, 200, 204

critique: of capitalism, 202; Christian social critique, 202; socio-religious, 195
Cronbach, Abraham, 77
Cyprian of Carthage, *De opera et eleemosynis*, 42, 77, 83, 120n50; *On the Lapsed*, 76
Cyril of Alexandria, 41; *Paschal Homilies*, 174n38
Cyril of Jerusalem, 135; *Lecture 4*, 136n45
Cyrrhus, 23

Daley, Brian E., 115n34, 185n2
Dante, *Inferno*, 159n143
Deferrari, Roy, 120n54
democracy, 192, 200–204
Demosthenes, *Private Orations*, 134n38
DePalma Digeser, Elizabeth, 187n7, 188n13, 189n16, 195n38, 198n44
deprivation, 118
Derrida, Jacques, 216
De Ste. Croix, Geoffrey, 38, 170n24, 187–88, 190–91, 198–99
destitution, 60, 105, 163n3, 184
dialogue, xi–xiv, xvi–xvii, 28; ethical, 104
Dickens, Charles, 159n143
*Didache*, 66, 169, 174n38
*Didascalia*, 117
dignity: of the human person, 99n57, 119, 160–61, 167n14, 180, 184, 192, 194, 228; violation of dignity, 105. *See also* equality
Diocletian, 150n111, 188n13, 189, 195, 201–202
Diogenes Laertius, *Lives of the Eminent Philosophers*, 153n120
discipleship, xviii, 143, 221
divorce, 218n17
dualism: 65, 77–78, 80–81

ecclesiastical discipline, 32
economy, 192; knowledge economy, 182–83
Egypt, 93
Elsbernd, Mary, xiii
Enlightenment, 5–7, 8; post-Enlightenment, 4, 8, 13, 16, 218
Ennodius, 50, 53
environment, 220
Ephesus, council of, 23
Ephrem, 108
Epictetus, *Discourses*, 153n120
Epiphanius of Salamis, *Panarion*, 170n25, 171–72
epistle (letter), 31–32; epistolary brevity, 31n3; epistolary theory, 31n3

*Epistle of Barnabas*, 169, 174n38
*Epistula ad Diognetum*, 118n48
equality, 39, 113; created, 116n35; in dignity, 199–200, 205; political, 117; market, 127n12. *See also* aequitas
eschatology, xv, xvi, 19–20, 64–65, 67, 69, 71, 80, 83, 184, 229
Eudoxia, 89n19
Eusebius of Caesarea, 51, 108; *Ecclesiastical History*, 85, 87, 118n48, 132; *Life of Constantine*, 60
Eustratius, *In Aristotelis ethica Nicomachea vi commentaria*, 111
Eutropius, 94–95
Eutychian controversy, 23
Evagrius of Antioch, 91
Evagrius Scholasticus, 53–54, 58
*euergesia* (evergetism), 48, 53–54, 56–57; classical, 58.
exploitation: of the poor, 68n15, 199; socio-economic, 70. *See also* oppression

favouritism, 132
feminism, 218. *See also* rejectionism
Finn, Richard, 34, 86
Fischer, Irving, 227
Flavian of Antioch, 90–91
Fortin, Ernest, 180n52
fragmentation, 218
freedom, 45, 147n98, 158, 182, 184, 210. *See also* liberty
free will, 28
Freu, Christel, 163n3
Friesen, Steven, 35
forgetting, 210, 216–17; *ars oblivionis*, 211, 218n16, 221; constructive, xvii
forgiveness, 95–96, 213; collective, 219n21
future-oriented hermeneutics, 20, 23, 212–13. *See also* normativity of the future

Gadamer, Hans Georg, 5, 9–14, 16–17, 21, 29, 185n3, 211–12
Gaius, 201
Garnsey, Peter, 187n6, 188, 194, 196–97, 198, 202
*Gaudium et spes*, 180n53, 181, 191
gender roles, 105
Gennadius Scholarius II, *Tractatus de primo servitu Dei*, 110
genre (literary), 30, 33, 78, 223
Gilby, Thomas, 192n31

globalization, 183, 214

good: common good, xvi, 36, 39, 103, 105–108, 110, 112, 114, 117, 119–23, 166n12, 182, 191–93, 227; distribution, 27, 114, 119, 166, 175; limited good, 97–98; mobility, 171n26; production, 227; social good, 119; universal destination of goods, 164, 181, 199

Gordon, Barry, 163n2

Gratian, 52

greed, 50, 138, 149, 157, 159, 187, 199

Gregory the Great, 155

Gregory Nazianzen (of Nazianzus), xiii 31–32, 37, 47, 172; *Oration 14*, 59–60, 62, 115; *Oration 16*, 61n49, 134–35

Gregory of Nyssa, 38, 40, 108, 118, 136n45, 150, 153; *Contra usurarios*, 129n16, 137, 142–43, 145, 163n3; *De pauperibus amandis*, 114–15, 222–23; *Homiliae in Ecclesiastes 4*, 138; *Oratio 5*, 142n76

Gregory of Tours, *History of the Franks*, 129n16, 158n141

Grig, Lucy, 36n24

Grodzynski, Denise 35

Habermas, Jürgen, 213

Hallensleben, Barbara, 229n12

Halton, Thomas, 23

harassment, 144

Harrison, Nonna Verna, 118

Hauerwas, Stanley, 202

Hauschild, Wolf-Dieter, 171n29

health, 160, 172; healthcare, 107f6–1, 107f6–2, 119; of the poor, 28, 38

Heidegger, Martin, 10, 12–14, 20, 210–12

*Shepherd of Hermas*, 37, 75, 76n40, 78–83, 169–70

Heck, Eberhard 189n16

Hehir, Bryan 193

Hesiod, *Works and Days*, 126n7

Hightower, Lynn 159n143

historical consciousness, 5–6, 10–11, 21

Hollenbach, David, xvi, 106–7, 119, 121, 192n31, 192n32

Holman, Susan, xvi, xvii, 32, 37

Homer, *Odyssey*, 133n37

homilist, xv, 31; early Christian, 164n4

homily, 30–31, 92, 173, 229; desk-homily, 30; early Christian, xii, xiii, xiv; patristic, xv, 35; socio-ethical, xii. *See also* sermon; theological oration

hospitality, 80, 197

Hughson, Thomas, xvi, xvii

human rights, 35, 99n57, 105, 119, 122, 192, 200, 218, 225

Ihssen, Brenda, xvi, xvii, 41n53, 215, 217

*imago Dei*, 193

imitation: of God, 51, 110n10, 118n48; of Christ, 83, 114–15

inclusivity, 22, 200, 219

individualism, 188

injustice, xi, 25, 88n6, 139, 170n25, 183; as anomaly, 116n35, 167, 172n32; economic, 158; social, 64, 69, 105

Innocent I, 31

*Institutes* of civil law, 201

institutionalization, xviii, 221

integrity, 104

intention: as ethical, 210

interdisciplinarity, 231

interest (on a loan), 125, 126–29, 132–33, 135, 137, 145, 152, 158–60, 217, 227. *See also* lending; usury

investment: in God, 140–41, 143; heavenly, 157

Irenaeus, *Against Heresies*, 169–70, 174n38

Jerome, 33, 40–41, 48; *De viris illustribus*, 132n31

John XXIII, 181

John Chrysostom, 32n8, 33–34, 40, 87–89, 92–93, 108, 118, 120n50, 150, 151n113, 154–57, 162n1, 163n2, 171n29; *De Babyla contra Iulianum et gentiles*, 110n10; *De Davide et Saule*, 110n10; *De laudibus sancti Pauli apostoli*, 110n10; *In 1 Cor. hom.13*, 137n49; *In 1 Cor. hom. 21*, 97–98; *In 1 Cor. hom 43*, 138–40; *In 2 Cor Hom 3*, 140; *Homily 18*, 133; *In Eutropium*, xv, 94–96; *In Johannem hom 19*, 173n34; *In Matthaeum hom 5*, 138n55, 141–143; *In Matthaeum hom 28*, 136n46; *In Matthaeum hom 37*, 133n37; *In Matthaeum hom 56*, 143n78; *In Matthaeum hom 77*, 170n25; *In Matthaeum hom. 78*, 109, 110n10; *In Rom Hom 11*, 138n55; *In 1 Tim Hom 11*, 139n58; *In 1 Tim Hom 12*, 139n58; *Sermo 1 in Gen*, 90–91

John Damascene, 41

John Paul II, 41, 156–57, 181, 219, 225, 228

Josephus, *Bellum Judaicum*, 71

judgment: apocalyptic, 74; day of, 70–71, 178; divine, xv, 65–67, 72, 83; eschatological, 67, 72, 77. *See also* vindication

Julian, *Letter 84*, 55n33

Julius Paulus, 201
justice, xvii, 27, 36, 70, 103, 105, 114, 120–21,
   152n115, 165n7, 166–67, 184, 194, 198, 204;
   commutative, 107f6–1, 107f6–2 192, 215; contributive, 107f6–1, 107f6–2; distributive,
   107f6–1, 107f6–2, 109, 192, 215; divine, 67, 121;
   imperial, 50; eschatological, 122; for the marginalized, 193; and mercy, 117; patristic, 113; political, 106; working for, 121
justification, 210
Justin Martyr, 118n48
Justin II, 52
Justinian I, 51–52; *Novellae*, 156

Kant, Immanuel, 210
Kloft, Hans, 48

labor, 117, 169n22, 170, 176–77, 214, 227; labor-
   driven economy, xiii
Lactantius, xvii, 48, 54; *Divine Institutes*, 185–89,
   191, 194–205
laity, xi, 97
Laodicea, synod of, 147
lending: crisis, 125; exception to, 148; against interest, xvi, xvii, 41, 124–25, 129, 146, 149, 157;
   interest-free, 133, 145, 152n115; to the needy, 155;
   payday, 125; pooling, 134; system, 144
Lenski, Noel, 88n11
Leo I, 31, 120n52
Leo XIII, 4n2, 41
lepers: 34, 61, 114; needs of, xiii
Leyerle, Blake, 163n2
Libanius, 108; *Oration for the Temples*, 54–55
*liberalitas*, xv, 48–50, 52–53, 56–60
liberation, 6, 9, 184
liberty, 202. *See also* freedom
Licinius, 194
Luther(an), 204

Machiavelli, 166n12
MacIntyre, Alasdair, 225
Manichaeans (Manichaeism), 36
Maloney, Robert, 131, 133, 151
Marshall, I. Howard, 151n115
Maximus the Confessor, 41
Mayer, Wendy, xv, 33n12, 151n113, 215, 217
McCambley, Casimir, 129
McGuckin, John A., 170n24
Meislin, Bernard J., 124, 145

Melania, 120
Meletian schism, 91n27
Meletius of Antioch, 86
Meletius (Byzantine monk-physician), 112
Melito of Sardes, 118n48
memory, xvii; *ars memoriae*, 210–11, 214, 221;
   blocked, 216; manipulated, 218; narratives of,
   209–8; purification of, 219. *See also* abuse, re-
   collection, retrieval
Menander, *Dyskolos*, 167–70, 173
Mendels, Doron 85, 90
mercy, 106, 113, 117–18, 120–21, 123
Meredith, Anthony 38
Merkle, Judith A., 205
Metz, Johan Baptist, 212, 227
migration, 214
Mills, Paul, 151n115
mimetic arc, 214
Moltmann, Jürgen, 227
Monat, Pierre, 193–94, 198
Montanus (Montanism), 132
moral discourse, xvi, 45, 47
moral imagination, xiii, 175, 179
mortality, 121
mortgage, 159
Moser, Thomas, 151–52
Mueller, Joseph, 86
munificence, 48–49, 52–56, 58. *See also* benefi-
   cence; evergetism
Murray, John Courtney, 203

natural kinship, 112
necromancy, 136
Nemesius of Emesa, 112
Nero, 168n19
Nestorian controversy, 23
Newman, John Henry, 214
Nguyen Van Thuan, François-Xavier, 180n50
Nicaea, council of (325), 146
Nicene: Christianity, 94; community, 91, 93;
   Goths, 92–93; stance: 86
Nicomedia, 189
Nietzsche, Friedrich, 211n7
Nickelsburg, George W.H., 69
non-Christian religions, 218n17
noncontemporaneity, 214–15
Noonan, John T., 218n17
normativity of the future, xiv, 4, 18–19, 21–22, 28.
   *See also* future-oriented hermeneutics

normativity of the past, 6
North Africa, 189
North American Patristic Society, 230
*Nostra Aetate*, 218–19
Novatian, 94

Olympias, 89, 94
oppression, 9, 68; financial, 138n55; of the poor, 68n16, 134; socio-economic, 201; of workers, 183. *See also* exploitation
Origen, 41, 108
Osiek, Carolyn, 78, 80

paleography, 186
panegyric, 55–56, 58, 62
*panegyrici latini*, 49
Pansophius of Nicomedia, 89n19
paradox: Cynic, 88
*parousia*, 37, 66–67
Patlagean, Evelyne, 35, 163n2
patristic social teaching, 34, 85–87, 89, 92, 98–99. *See also* Catholic social teaching; Christian social teaching
patristic social thought, xii, xvi, xvii, 87. *See also* Catholic social thought; Christian social thought
patristic: socio-ethical texts, xii, 30, 33, 35, 39–40, 42, 103, 149, 189; sources, xii, 15; teaching, xvi, 214. *See also* homily; justice; social ethics
patronage, 62; episcopal, xv
Pelagians (Pelagius), 31, 33, 36, 92, 172
perennialism, 8n8
persecution: Decian, 76; Great Persecution, 189, 201
Peter of Alexandria, *On Riches*, 172
*philanthropia*, 34, 41, 56–57, 157; rhetoric of, 121; philanthropic divestment, 123
Philo of Alexandria, *De virtutibus*, 131, 148, 152
Pinian, 120
Pius XI, 180–81
Plato, 127, 130, 139, 165, 188
plight: of the poor, 28, 59, 139n58, 198; in Palestine, 72n30
Plutarch, *Moralia*, 137, 152
Pontifical Council for Justice and Peace, 179
poor, xv, 32, 50, 65, 72, 156, 193, 197, 205; concern for, 74; congregation of, 71; love for, 51, 172; instrumentalization, 223; needs, 48, 121, 172, 178, 181; neglect of, 75; option for, 223; self-identification with, 69; shallow poor, 163, 173; social obligation toward, 73; suffering of, 165n5. *See also* care; exploitation; health; oppression; plight; share; solidarity
Pontius the Deacon, *Life and Passion of Cyprian*, 120n50
*Populorum progressio*, 180n53
Posidonius, 112–13
poverty, xiv, 23–28, 33–38, 45, 50–52, 62n54, 64, 67, 70, 72, 83, 89, 95, 105, 125, 151, 155, 159–60, 163n2, 165n9, 176, 178; alleviation of, 150, 153, 172; attitude toward, 71, 88, 122n57; material, 69; spiritual, 130, 138, 142–43; voluntary, 90, 92, 162n1
Priscian of Caesarea, 56–57; *Institutio de arte grammatical*, 57
Procopius of Caesarea, *Secret History*, 50–53
Procopius of Gaza, 56–58
profit, 125, 133, 135, 146
progress: 221; belief in, 6
Promotus, 89n19
property: 37–39, 45, 113, 123, 135, 229; aquiring of, 38, 172n31, 176; common, 178–79, 199; common use of, 181; detachment from, 161, 164, 168, 169n23, 170n24, 171–77, 179, 183; private, xiii, xvii, 36, 71, 162, 164–69, 171–72, 178–83; redistribution of, 162n1, 165, 182; rights, 166, 168, 172; sufficiency of, 172n32, 179; superfluity of, 168, 171, 175, 180; use of, 170, 172. *See also* possession
providence, 23–24, 176–77, 179, 202
possession, 71, 140, 171n27; use of, 167n14. *See also* property
Pseudo-Chrysostom, *Contra theatra*, 110n10; *Eclogues*, 92; *In sanctum pascha (sermo 6)*, 110n10
Pythagoras, 130n19

Rabbula of Edessa, 34
radicalism, 64
Rawls, John, 192n27
reading community, 20, 22–23. *See also* audience
reciprocity, 98
recollection, 210–11, 213, 215, 216; misdirected, 218. *See also* memory; retrieval
reconstructionism, 9
refiguration, 214–15, 217–18
rejectionism: radical feminist, 8
renunciation, 76, 169; material, 82–84, 170n24, 171–72

resources: ethical use of, 105
responsibility: social, 74; communal, 79n46
retrieval, 209–10, 212, 215, 220. *See also* memory; recollection
revelation, 19, 78, 193–94, 202, 204
revisionism, 8–9, 212–13, 226
Rhee, Helen, xv
rhetoric, 46, 223
Ricoeur, Paul, xvii, 9–10, 9n21, 12–14, 17, 20–21, 29, 209–11, 213–16; 218–20, 226; Ricoeurian, 164, 183, 213
romantic hermeneutics, 9–10, 12, 14, 16
Russian Orthodox Church, 229, 231
Ryan, Franklin W., 126n6

salvation: 39–40, 42, 63, 65, 67, 69n17, 71–72, 130, 139n58, 158–60; of the wealthy, 36; of the usurer, 125–26, 128, 138, 143, 150, 154
Salvianus of Marseille, *De gubernatione Dei*, 61n49; *To the Church or Against Avarice*, 31, 33, 121n56
scarcity, 127, 151, 163n2
Sharples, Robert W., 112
Sheather, Mary, 157n120
Schenk, Richard, xvii
Schneiders, Sandra M., 20
selective amnesia, 212
self-denial, 142
self-emptying, 40
self-examination, 210–11, 213, 219–20
self-interest, 187
Seneca, 36, 173; *Ad Lucilium Epistulae Morales*, 153n120; *De vita beata*, 168–69; *De brevitate vitae*, 168n19, 168n20
sermon, xiii, 23–24, 27, 30, 45–47, 85–87, 90–91, 93–96, 98, 108–9, 113–16, 119, 123, 137, 147, 158, 172, 175, 222; on the poor, 59–60; late Byzantine, 110. *See also* homily
Severus of Antioch, 32–33
Shakespeare, *The Merchant of Venice*, 159n143
share: for the poor, 39; of goods, 162n1, 167, 169; of property, 166, 182
Sidonius Apollinaris, 129n16
skepticism, 215, 218
slavery, xiii, 38–39, 45, 87, 88n11, 105, 127; 193–94, 218n17, 219, 226; abolition of, 38; enslavement, 158, 190
social Catholicism, 185n1
social change, 187–88, 191, 193–94

social ethics, xiv, xv, 31, 42, 45–47, 67, 164, 166n12, 180, 229–30; patristic, 45, 128; early Christian, 65, Christian, 84, 223; diversity of, 105
social inequality, 26–27
social justice, xi, xii, 45, 68, 77, 95, 107f6–1; 107f6–2, 108–110, 117–18, 185–87, 191–93, 199–200, 204
social order, 24, 26
social problems, xvi, 165
social policies, 163n2
social unity, xvi, 165
social stratification, 166n11
societal decline, 186
socio-ethical: debates, 40; ideas, xii; issues, 32–33, 41, 46, 123, 223, 230; reflection, xii; teaching, 90; themes, xv, 30, 33, 35, 42; topics, xi
solidarity, 66, 219, 228; with the needy, 179; with the poor, 177; social, 123
Sölle, Dorothee, 227
Solon, 127n10
Sommerstein, Alan, 165n6
sovereignty, 210
Spanneut, Michel, 164n4
structuralism, 8
Stoicism (Stoics, Stoic), 33, 89, 164, 166.
Stump, Eleonore, 109
suspicion: as hermeneutic, 210, 220
*Sybilline Oracles*, 74, 75n36
Symmachus, 50, 53
Symeon Metaphrastes, 110
Syria, 23

taxes, 50–52, 54; remission of, 49, 56, 59
Tchapline, Vsevolod, 229
Theodoret of Cyrrhus, 31, 39; *De providentia, Or.6*, xiv, 23–27, 37, 170n26; *Ep. 81*, 24; *Eusebio episcopo Persicae Armeniae*, 135n44
Themistius, 49, 60n45
Theodosius I, 54–55, 86, 94
theological oration, 46
theology: of liberation, 9, 200–202, 218; of ecumenism, 229; of non-Christian religions, 218; Orthodox, 103; public, 200–202; political, 200–202; post-colonial, 218; theological unity, xvi
Tiberius, 54
tolerance, 64, 188, 201
Toole, David, 227
Torah, 68

torture, 138n55, 189, 201

tractate, 31–32. *See also* treatise

tradition, 4–5, 86, 212, 224–25, 230; appeal to, 40; attitude toward, 6; authority of, 5, 8; Christian, 104–5, 121, 164; critique of, 6; emancipation from, 5–6; Jewish, 68, 71; Orthodox, 229; patristic, 231; process of, 10, 9n21, 14, 16, 29

Trajan, 52

treatise, xii, 31, 42, 92, 218; ethical, 46. *See also* tractate

Trier, 189

trinitarianism, 228–29

Ulpian, 201

unemployed, 177

usury, xiii, xvi, xvii, 36, 41–42, 45, 61–62, 90, 109, 124, 126, 128–55, 158–58. 160, 217, 218n17, 219, 227; acceptable, 148; condemnation of, 130; as distortion of creation, 150; heavenly, 141; as legally protected, 154; as moral issue, 153; spiritual, 141

utopia(n), 18, 20, 196, 227

Valentinian II, 50

Van der Eijk, Philip J., 112

Van Nuffelen, Peter, xiv

Vatican II, council of, 225

*venationes*, 47

vindication (of God), 69–70

violence, 56, 64, 88, 218–19

Virgil, *Aeneid*, 186

virtue, 24–25, 33, 54–55, 59, 87, 139n58, 157, 168, 188, 197–98; ascetic, 117; exercise of, 89; imperial virtue, 60; personal, 99n57, 123; public, 49, 63

wealth, 23–28, 37, 42, 64, 67, 68n16, 70–71, 75, 89, 94–95, 135, 139n58, 140–41, 153–55, 163, 165n9, 168, 172, 177–79, 222; danger of, 79; deprivation of, 166; heavenly, 78, 81, 83; as God's gift, 81; imagery, 73n33; inequality of, 38–39; use of, 87–88, 91–92, 96, 163n2, 170n24

Wagner, M. Monica, 116n37, 117n45

Wallant, Edward Lewis, 159n143

Weinrich, Harald, 211n8

Williston, Samuel, 126n6

women, 146

Xenophon, *Education of Cyrus*, 166–67, 170

Yahweh, 68

Young, Frances M., 126n5, 134n41, 149n106, 196–98

*Reading Patristic Texts on Social Ethics: Issues and Challenges for Twenty-First-Century Christian Social Thought* was designed and typeset in Garamond by Kachergis Book Design of Pittsboro, North Carolina. It was printed on 60-pound House Natural Smooth and bound by Sheridan Books of Ann Arbor, Michigan.